D1559851

POETS AND POWER FROM CHAUCER TO WYATT

In the early fifteenth century, English poets responded to a changed climate of patronage, instituted by Henry IV and successor monarchs, by inventing a new tradition of public and elite poetry. Following Chaucer and others, Hoccleve and Lydgate brought to English verse a new style and subject matter to write about their king, nation, and themselves, and their innovations influenced a continuous line of poets running through and beyond Wyatt. A crucial aspect of this new tradition is its development of ideas and practices associated with the role of poet laureate. Robert J. Meyer-Lee examines the nature and significance of this tradition as it develops from the fourteenth century to Tudor times, tracing its evolution from one author to the next. This study illuminates the relationships between poets and political power and makes plain the tremendous impact this verse has had on the shape of English literary culture.

ROBERT J. MEYER-LEE is Assistant Professor of English at Goshen College, Indiana.

CAMBRIDGE STUDIES IN MEDIEVAL LITERATURE

General editor
Alastair Minnis, *Yale University*

Editorial board
Zygmunt G. Barański, *University of Cambridge*
Christopher C. Baswell, *University of California, Los Angeles*
John Burrow, *University of Bristol*
Mary Carruthers, *New York University*
Rita Copeland, *University of Pennsylvania*
Simon Gaunt, *King's College, London*
Steven Kruger, *City University of New York*
Nigel Palmer, *University of Oxford*
Winthrop Wetherbee, *Cornell University*
Jocelyn Wogan-Browne, *University of York*

This series of critical books seeks to cover the whole area of literature written in the major medieval languages – the main European vernaculars, and medieval Latin and Greek – during the period c.1100–1500. Its chief aim is to publish and stimulate fresh scholarship and criticism on medieval literature, special emphasis being placed on understanding major works of poetry, prose, and drama in relation to the contemporary culture and learning which fostered them.

POETS AND POWER
FROM CHAUCER
TO WYATT

ROBERT J. MEYER-LEE

CAMBRIDGE
UNIVERSITY PRESS

CAMBRIDGE UNIVERSITY PRESS

Cambridge, New York, Melbourne, Madrid, Cape Town, Singapore, São Paulo

Cambridge University Press
The Edinburgh Building, Cambridge CB2 8RU, UK

Published in the United States of America by
Cambridge University Press, New York

www.cambridge.org
Information on this title: www.cambridge.org/9780521863551

First published 2007

Printed in the United Kingdom at the University Press, Cambridge

A catalogue record for this publication is available from the British Library

ISBN-13 978-0-521-86355-1 hardback
ISBN-10 0-521-86355-4 hardback

For my family:
Elaine, Gabriel, Jackson, and Lucas

Contents

Acknowledgments

Individuals to whom I am indebted for reviewing drafts of portions of this book, in their various incarnations, include Seeta Chaganti, Valerie Garver, Matthew Giancarlo, Elizabeth Fowler, Kathryn Kerby-Fulton, Lezlie Knox, Traugott Lawler, Michael Leslie, Pericles Lewis, Maura Nolan, Jill Mann, Cynthia Marshall, Deborah McGrady, David Mengel, Jimmy Mixson, Annabel Patterson, Larry Scanlon, James Simpson, Ramie Targoff, and Karen Winstead (with apologies to anyone inadvertently left off this list). Lee Patterson was the original guiding beacon for the project and has since been a constant source of help and encouragement. Derek Pearsall introduced me to medieval literature, and I hope this book repays, in a small way, that marvelous initiation. Alistair Minnis and my anonymous readers for Cambridge University Press — one of whom since revealed himself as John Thompson — provided excellent feedback. Julie Bruneau supplied crucial assistance in the final pass through the typescript. The book's remaining faults no doubt lie in those places I failed to heed my many readers' advice. Linda Bree and her associates at Cambridge University Press have been wonderful to work with.

The libraries of the University of Notre Dame and Yale were essential in completing this project; I owe thanks to their canny collectors of material on late medieval English literature and culture. Thanks are also due to the libraries of Cambridge University and Trinity College, Cambridge for granting me access to Ashby's manuscripts.

I am grateful to Rhodes College for granting me a leave, Goshen College for a reduced teaching load and research funding through the Mininger Center, and the Medieval Institute at the University of Notre Dame for an appointment as visiting scholar, all of which greatly facilitated the writing of this book. And, in the place of honor, I owe more than can be said to my parents, siblings, in-laws, and, above all, to those who sacrificed most: Elaine, Gabriel, Jackson, and Lucas, to whom this book is dedicated.

Portions of this book adapt previously published work of mine:

"Laureates and Beggars in Fifteenth-Century English Poetry: The Case of George Ashby," *Speculum* 79 (2004), 688−726.

"Lydgate's Laureate Pose," in *John Lydgate: Poetry, Culture, and Lancastrian England*, ed. James Simpson and Larry Scanlon, Notre Dame: University of Notre Dame Press, 2006. © 2006 University of Notre Dame.

I thank the publishers for their permission to incorporate this material.

Notes on citations

All citations of the works of Chaucer are from *The Riverside Chaucer*, ed. Larry D. Benson, 3rd edn, Boston: Houghton Mifflin Company, 1987.

Citations of Lydgate's poetry are from the following editions:

The Minor Poems of John Lydgate, Part I: The Religious Poems, ed. H. N. MacCracken, EETS o.s. 107, London: Oxford University Press, 1911, referenced as MP I.

The Minor Poems of John Lydgate, Part II: The Secular Poems, ed. H. N. MacCracken, EETS o.s. 192, London: Oxford University Press, 1934, referenced as MP II.

Poems, ed. John Norton-Smith, Oxford: Clarendon Press, 1966.

A Critical Edition of John Lydgate's Life of Our Lady, ed. Joseph A. Lauritis, Ralph A. Klinefelter, and Vernon F. Gallagher, Pittsburgh: Duquesne University, 1961.

Siege of Thebes, ed. Axel Erdmann and Eilert Ekwall, EETS e.s. 118, 125, London: Kegan Paul, Trench and Trübner, 1911, 1930.

Troy Book, ed. Henry Bergen, EETS e.s. 97, 103, 106, 126, London: Kegan Paul, Trench and Trübner, 19061935.

The Fall of Princes, ed. Henry Bergen, EETS e.s. 121–24, London: Oxford University Press, 192327.

Citations of Hoccleve's poetry are from the following editions:

Thomas Hoccleve: The Regiment of Princes, ed. Charles R. Blyth, Kalamazoo: Medieval Institute Publications, 1999.

Thomas Hoccleve's Complaint and Dialogue, ed. J. A. Burrow, EETS o.s. 313, Oxford: Oxford University Press, 1999.

"My Compleinte" and Other Poems, ed. Roger Ellis, Exeter: University of Exeter Press, 2001, for all poems besides the *Regiment*, *Complaint*, and *Dialogue*.

All verse, except where noted, is cited by line number and, where appropriate, book or fragment. Editorial diacritics, emendation brackets, and indications of expansion are not reproduced, and I have at times modified or added punctuation.

The following abbreviations are used:

Biobib for Pearsall, Derek, *John Lydgate (1371–1449): A Bio-bibliography*, Victoria: University of Victoria, 1997.

EEBO for *Early English Books Online*, Ann Arbor: Bell & Howell Information and Learning, 1999–.

EETS o.s. for Early English Text Society, original series.

EETS e.s. for Early English Text Society, extra series.

MED for Kurath, Hans, Kuhn, Sherman M., and Lewis, R. E. (eds.), *A Middle English Dictionary*, Ann Arbor: University of Michigan Press, 1952–2001.

STC for Pollard, Alfred W., et al., *A Short-Title Catalogue of Books Printed in England, Scotland, & Ireland and of English Books Printed Abroad, 1475–1640*, 2nd edn, London: Bibliographical Society, 1976–1991.

ThomasH for Burrow, J. A., *Thomas Hoccleve*, Aldershot: Variorum, 1994.

Except where noted, translations are my own.

Introduction: Laureates and beggars

This study, most fundamentally, investigates why the idea of the poet laureate becomes so important in much of the English poetry of the fifteenth century and delineates the consequences that the development of this idea have had for the shape of English literary history. The most central figure in this investigation is John Lydgate, self-proclaimed disciple of Chaucer and monk of Bury, and the object of study may succinctly be termed Lydgatean laureate poetics. But considered from a broader perspective this study also seeks to account for fifteenth-century English poetry more comprehensively than is usual by using the notion of the laureate as a lens for tracing the trajectory and vicissitudes, over the course of more than a century, of that branch of this poetry that self-consciously presents itself as an object of high culture. From this view, this study examines what happens between the two earliest English literary encounters with that most definitive of poets laureate, Francis Petrarch: Chaucer's translation of at least one of Petrarch's sonnets in the 1380s, and the next English rendering of Petrarch's Italian in the lyrics of Sir Thomas Wyatt, some 150 years later.

The possible literary historical narratives that these two moments imply are many, but interpretations have most often fallen into one of two camps: either these moments chart the emergence of the English Renaissance, or they speak of literary continuity rather than rupture, of Wyatt recovering what Chaucer initiated rather than beginning anew with the same material. In either case, the role of Petrarch is the same: he signifies a literary sophistication whose most striking achievement is not the notion of the laureateship for which he was so much responsible but rather his rendering of a complex lyric subjectivity — one that is at odds with itself, consumed with self-definition as poet, and pervasively associated with a real (that is to say, extraliterary), historically specific person. A typical argument from the first camp contends that, because Chaucer puts Petrarch's words into the mouth of Troilus, Chaucer remains a medieval poet, albeit one in command of a repertoire of psychological representation that exceeds that of most of his contemporaries. In the *Canticus Troili* (*Troilus and Criseyde*, 1.400–20), he uses Petrarch's lyric to lend the consequences of Troilus's first sighting of Criseyde both a narrative immediacy and subjective complexity, yet the character Troilus remains, finally, within the circumference of medieval romance. In contrast, because Wyatt speaks Petrarch's words as his own, in poems such as "Whoso List to Hounte" he is able to deploy the same literary effects toward the end of rendering his apparently actual psychological responses to real experiences. With Wyatt, this argument concludes, English poetry finally becomes a true vehicle of self-expression, in the sense of a historically specific author using it to represent his own – perhaps paradigmatic, but nevertheless unique – selfhood. But from the perspective of the other camp, one might dismiss this difference in the speakers of Petrarch's lines as merely generic. Chaucer's narrative poetry by convention adapts Petrarch's lyric to the point of view of one of its characters, while Wyatt's troubadour-like lyricism just as conventionally respeaks its source material from the point of view of its current singer. In this argument, both poets make English verse an instrument for rendering a complex subjectivity, and the difference between them is more one of generic predilection (and range) than epistemic change. Wyatt, in this view, possesses no more or less of a "Renaissance" understanding of interiority than does Chaucer.

The assumptions underlying both these opposing, but nevertheless commonplace, critical narratives are questionable in a number of respects, the most relevant for present purposes being the tale that they imply about what happens – or fails to happen – *between* Chaucer and Wyatt. This tale is the familiar one of the decadence of fifteenth-century English poetry, in which the efflorescence of the Ricardians rapidly decays into stale convention, moralistic tedium, and nostalgic paeans to one's poetic ancestors. Wyatt's accomplishments from this perspective appear, though perhaps related to Chaucer's, singularly unattached to those of his most immediate vernacular predecessors, and this perception creates a sense of spontaneous genius, whether one believes these accomplishments to be England's belated second chance at a Renaissance or a return, *mutatis mutandis*, to the creative energies of an earlier golden age of English verse. The present study, like recent others of the period, rejects this depiction of fifteenth-century poetry, seeing it as an inaccurate assessment of the period's literary sophistication. Moreover, a basic premise here is that, despite the recent critical revaluation of the period, the *lasting* accomplishments of its poets — the permanent effects that they have had on the English poetic tradition — remain largely obscured. This book takes these effects as its topic, exploring what they consist of and what historical factors conditioned their appearance. An overarching aim is to show that, in the interval between Chaucer and Wyatt, one encounters not an evolutionary dead end in literary history but the place where English poets first construct the poetics and poetic ideology that make Wyatt's accomplishments possible. Or, to put this more strongly, this book argues that poets in this period make the high-culture English literary tradition in some essential respects what it remains today, and therefore the specific character of and motivations behind this period's poetry continue to shape our understanding of what, ideally, poetry can do.

To those familiar with fifteenth-century poetry, my above comments on lyric subjectivity may seem out of step with the period's most disseminated works, such as John Lydgate's mammoth *roman antique,* the *Troy Book.* Yet behind the lyric poet's rendering of subjectivity lies the more basic task of constructing a first-person poetic speaker, and the nature of this speaker is a crucial concern for fifteenth-century poets. In particular, by absorbing the possibilities and consequences for authorial self-representation of Petrarch's laureate self-fashioning (much more so than his lyricism), their innovations in this regard become among their most important — and least recognized — contributions to English literary history. Most significantly, in the course of the fifteenth century the representation of the *author* as both first-person *speaker* and authoritative, historically specific *person* becomes a normative formal feature. In earlier English verse, these three subject positions — Chaucer the man, Chaucer the poet, and Chaucer the pilgrim, to cite the most famous Middle English example — are either kept isolated or in ambiguous play with one another. In the fifteenth century, in contrast, they are frequently conflated for the most central thematic purposes.

This literary strategy develops as a multifaceted response to specific historical pressures — one that adapts, among other things, the precedent of Petrarch and the achievements of the Ricardians to create a poetic answer to, foremost among other circumstances, the significantly altered relations between power and cultural production after 1400. An aspiring court poet, in the period inaugurated by Henry of Derby's seizure of the crown from Richard II, had no choice but somehow to negotiate these relations in his verse. In the fifteenth century, unlike the fourteenth or sixteenth, the most important poets wrote, at some point in their careers, under the direct auspices of a king, queen, or prince whose claim to the throne was, without exception, contested. The first-person speakers these poets constructed were a primary means of effecting this negotiation. Almost as a side effect, this strategy turns out to have great bearing on how, to what extent, and for what purposes these poets textualize their subjectivity.

This sort of authorial self-representation I call laureate self-construction, which is just one element, albeit the most central one, of a set of poetic strategies that I term laureate poetics. Throughout the period, alongside this poetics another mode of authorial self-representation and set of related strategies appear that at first glance seem diametrically opposite. This is the pose and the poetics of the beggar poet, which are not so much categorically different as inherent aspects of laureateship in both theory and practice. Laureate and beggar both involve strategic conflation of poetic subject positions — that is, in either case the poet appears as his concrete extraliterary self. The laureate signifies a positive, mutually affirming (if, in theory, arm's-length) relation to power, while the beggar stands as an expression of the actual conditions of subjection, and consequent will to resistance, that the practice of laureate poetics inevitably involves. The laureate pose signals the poet's co-option into the project of political legitimation and at the same time his desire to reconceive that project as something non-partisan and permanently valuable for all humanity. Conversely, the beggar pose signals both the poet's recognition of his role as an instrument of power and an individualized resistance that is in part conscious and in part the inevitable surfacing of his actual, ambivalent relationship with his patron. The laureate imagines poetry to possess an autonomous authority in service to the prince but not subservient to him; the beggar reveals the utter dependence that structures actual poetic practice. The laureate pretends to possess independence while being, in extreme cases, a patent propagandist; the beggar pretends to grovel when most opposing his own desires to those of his patron. Fifteenth-century sovereigns, by demanding, in effect, that their poets be laureates, also demanded that they be beggars. In the poetry of this period — and in the verse it influenced in subsequent ones — laureate and beggar are inevitable partners.

In using laureate poetics and its mendicant other as lenses through which to view in new detail the accomplishments of fifteenth-century English verse, I necessarily leave much else out of focus. With these lenses, my emphasis falls naturally on the relations between poets and patrons (rather than between poets and other possible audiences), and my readings tend to gravitate toward metapoetic passages, especially those found in prologues and epilogues. Nonetheless, the ideas and practices associated with laureate and beggar form a powerful means for understanding, on the one hand, the complex and far-reaching relation of this period's poetry to its historical context, and, on the other, the often surprising relations among this period's poets as well as with their predecessors and successors. Indeed, the poetics of laureate and beggar are in important ways the very places where these extrinsic and intrinsic histories of English poetry intersect, and thus in this book I pursue an investigation of poetic influence that is at the same time an examination of the forces that influence poetry. In the remainder of this introduction, I locate the place of this study in the context of recent criticism, more specifically delineate the body of verse that is my object, and provide an overview of subsequent chapters.

FIFTEENTH-CENTURY POETRY AND ITS CRITICS

No longer considered merely the wasteland through which one must pass to get from the medieval genius of Chaucer to the glories of the English Renaissance, fifteenth-century poetry has greatly benefited from the critical turn toward historicism of the past two decades. A small but growing number of monographs, collections of essays, and journal articles by some of the most prominent scholars of late medieval English literature have shown that the so-called "dull" poetry of this period is, if not always (to our ears) aesthetically pleasing, as rich with complexity as the historical moment in which it was written. The New Historical tenet that history and literature intersect in their shared textuality, by now relegated to the status of a commonplace in regard to other periods, has proven unusually productive when applied to the work of the poets writing in Chaucer's immediate wake. This is a poetry directly motivated by and pervasively meditative on its moment in history, a poetry highly conscious of being both a public intervention in the social, political, and religious turmoil of its time, and the inauguration of a vernacular literary tradition. Indeed, in the past, its lack of accomplishment has often been blamed on precisely these latter two conditions — its backdrop of historical turmoil and its precarious literary historical position. The assumptions were, first, that good poetry cannot be written in an era when so many Englishmen — including, and especially, kings — were dying at each other's hands, and, second, that the overwhelming precedent of Chaucer preempted the possibility of creative originality. With the aid of more recent scholarship, however, we are now better able to see in the fifteenth-century poets' conventional gestures a compli- cated — and, in many cases, creative — response to the bloodshed that surrounded them and the achievements of Chaucer and other Ricardians. As a result, we have a more nuanced understanding of both their literature and historical moment.

Nevertheless, in the renewed critical emphasis on history one often still encounters an apology for the Chaucerian poets. Seth Lerer, for example, begins his groundbreaking *Chaucer and His Readers* by announcing, "Chaucer creates the fictional persona of the subjugated reader/imitator and, in turn, the processes by which the fifteenth century propagates a literature based on versions of that persona."[1] The badness of fifteenth- century verse ("so bad that it is virtually unreadable" [p. 4]) is the function of a multifaceted response to Chaucer's poetry, the authority of which fifteenth-century poets create for the very purpose of subjugating themselves to it. As valuable as Lerer's study is, when reading through it one retains the feeling that fifteenth-century poetry is an unpleasant rite of passage, the necessary burden of a literary tradition's first appearance of genius, which can only be shaken off with the appearance of its second genius in the form of Skelton. In comparison, for Paul Strohm, another highly influential scholar of this period, the problem is not so much Chaucer as the internal contradictions that fifteenth-century poetry reproduces in its attempt to render a unified image of Lancastrian England: "Writing in the most precarious circumstances, on the threshold of the most internecine passage in English history, Hoccleve and Lydgate produced poems which stumble constantly and even obsessively into referential difficulties they cannot afford to acknowl- edge."[2] Replacing the aesthetic criteria of traditional criticism with historical double binds, Strohm believes fifteenth-century poems stumble not because of the ineptitude of their composers but because, given the nature of the authority they reflected, they could do nothing else.

In effect, Lerer's and Strohm's depictions of the poetry of this period are more sophisticated, penetrating, and — to a degree — generous versions of the earlier critiques that wished to explain away this poetry by reference to the dominance of Chaucer or the destabilizing effects of usurpation and civil war. Inasmuch as it would be an act of willful oversight not to recognize the undoubted influence of these factors, this present study follows in these critics' footsteps. Yet what distinguishes this study's aim and procedures from theirs is its interest in the genealogical effects of these factors. This book, through its examination of a continuous poetic tradition spanning Chaucer and Wyatt, describes what fifteenth-century poets do with the precedents of the Ricardians and the deeply troubled historical moment that not only differentiates their poetry from that of their predecessors and successors but also leaves a permanent mark on the character of the English poetic tradition. "We shall not understand Spenser," David Lawton has suggestively asserted, "unless we also understand that he is at least as Lydgatean as he is Chaucerian."[3] One of the aims of this study is to discover exactly why this is true.

LYDGATEAN AND HOCCLEVEAN POETRY

In referring to fifteenth-century poetry, I mean not all verse written in the period but that composed by the poets often referred to as Chaucerians. Yet even this more refined designation is both too broad — covering poets and poems not of immediate concern — and not meaningful enough, since the fact of Chaucer's influence tells us little about the actual character of the poetry. Another frequent label, "court poetry," says more about this character but is somewhat misleading. Few of the authors examined in subsequent chapters are courtiers and, while all possess some actual or desired relation to the English court, much of their verse they direct at a wider audience — in some cases, even wider than that of the aristocracy. To be as specific as possible, the poetry I examine is that English verse that contains implicit and often explicit claims to cultural ascendancy and that is written by an individual whose social identity is at least partially invested in the idea of being a poet in some relation to the English court. It is, in other words, that high-culture, proto-professional verse of which the few examples we find in English before the fifteenth century contrast starkly with the hundreds of thousands of lines we encounter in the several decades following Chaucer's death.

This poetry largely occurs in three distinct modes, which may be designated courtly, Lydgatean, and Hocclevean. The courtly mode (and again the root word "court" is not entirely accurate) in its best instances consists of a mixture of stoic philosophy and *fin' amor*. Its paradigmatic English precedent is *Troilus and Criseyde*, and fifteenth-century examples include the *Kingis Quair* of James I, Lydgate's *Temple of Glas*, and the lyrics of Charles d'Orléans.[4] The Lydgatean mode, as its label suggests, consists of that amalgam of secular, classicizing

convention, pious moralism, and monastic encyclopedism that characterizes Lydgate's most ambitious works and that is imitated by his
successors. Its most important fourteenth-century vernacular precedent
is what Anne Middleton has described as Ricardian "public poetry,"
but, as we will see, it is both more encompassing and qualitatively
different from this precedent.[5] It is the primary vessel of laureate poetics.
The Hocclevean mode imbricates many features of Lydgateanism with
those other features for which the poetry of Lydgate's contemporary
Thomas Hoccleve is best known: autobiographical passages deployed
with nuance and irony, and ambivalent meditations on the relationship
between poet and actual or imagined patron. Its sources include
Ricardian, goliardic, and contemporary French poetry, although, like its
Lydgatean counterpart, it differs from its sources in substantial ways.
It is the primary vessel of mendicant poetics.

   In naming the latter two of these modes after particular poets, I do
not mean to imply that they are exclusive to them. Both Hoccleve's
and Lydgate's oeuvres, in fact, include verse in each of the three modes.
Moreover, as I suggest above, Lydgateanism and Hoccleveanism are
not mutually exclusive options but rather form a dialectical pair.
Nevertheless, in the predominant characters of these two poets' works, we
encounter distinct (if interdependent) responses to Ricardian precedent
and fifteenth-century historical pressures. The poets' respective productions, not least because of their overlapping sets of royal patrons, become
mutually implicated alternative models for how one may situate high-
culture vernacular poetry in Lancastrian and early Tudor England.

   Admittedly, however, to speak of Hoccleve and Lydgate as alternatives
is a little misleading. By far the most dominant poet of the fifteenth
century is Lydgate. His manuscripts — unlike, for example, Chaucer's —
were widely disseminated in his lifetime; he was patronized by a broad
spectrum of society, from royalty to gentry; and he was imitated and
praised by name by a number of contemporary and successor poets, even
into the seventeenth century. Although he left behind several instances of
courtly poetry, the basic character of the bulk of his immense output is, in
respect to English verse, quite novel. In sum, in this period the breadth
and duration of Lydgate's influence is unmatched. For this reason, to
understand fifteenth-century poetry is in many ways (if not, of course, in
entirety) to understand how Lydgateanism arose from the possibilities
opened up by the Ricardians. Most of this study I have therefore devoted
to an investigation of the nature, significance, and evolution of Lydgatean
laureate poetics. But by the same token, to understand Lydgateanism

is also to discover why the less visible Hoccleveanism remains its persistent alter ego. In Hoccleveanism we encounter the primary expression for the tensions and paradoxes endemic to fifteenth-century proto-professional poetry – the flaws in its poetic ideology on which Lydgate expends great effort to conceal and to which his successors inevitably at times fall prey. The courtly mode, in comparison, is not as entangled in these particular problems. Although always present as an option, it does not distinguish the poetry of this period to the same degree. For this reason, the often sophisticated courtly productions of the fifteenth century – most prominently, that of Charles d'Orléans – enter my argument only as momentary points of contrast.

The characteristic features of Lydgatean poetry include, but are not limited to, an elevation of the vernacular by means of aureate diction and ornate rhetorical style to a status equivalent to Latin; generic affiliations with such monastic productions as encyclopedia, chronicle, saint's life, homily, and devotional lyric; an explicit embrace of politics; relentless moralism and traditionalism; and recurrent thematization of its own patronage. A central feature, as I have indicated, is the authorial pose as laureate. This pose draws from Ricardian and other precedents an intentional confusion of author-figure with first-person speaker, such that the "I" of a poem possesses a thematically active link to an individualized poet. Like the Ricardian "I," the Lydgatean "I" can be the sign of an individual subjectivity, the marker of an elusive controlling consciousness, or a personification of the moral perspective of the common man. But the Lydgatean "I" is also characteristically bound to a historically specific, extraliterary person who carries moral, spiritual, and cultural authority – a flesh-and-blood person who is simultaneously a personification of authority, a figure both as idealized and as historically concrete as the sovereign whom he addresses. The laureate pose – to define it in the most political terms – designates the person of the sovereign displaced from the realm of power into the realm of letters. Like the timeless and time-bound two bodies of the king, the pose points both to an abstract authorial role and to the historically specific occupant of that role. With this pose in place, all the other features of Lydgateanism receive the legitimating authority to which they also then contribute. What finally validates the presumption behind aureate diction, for example, is a person-centered authority signaled in the text by laureate self-representation. Because of this authority, and toward the end of maintaining and extending it, English may be raised to the status of Latin, chronicle to epic poem, and propaganda to cultural capital.

This study follows Lydgate in naming this authorial pose the poet laureate. Lydgate's use of this term, though always only indirectly applied to himself, marks the beginning of a practice of English laureate self-representation that pervades the fifteenth century, reaches an evolutionary endpoint in Skelton, and reappears in modified form in Spenser, Jonson, and Milton — that is, in those early modern poets whom Richard Helgerson has described as "self-crowned laureates."[6] While the self-representational strategies of these later poets have, as Helgerson shows, much to do with their specific place within the "literary system" of their day, their understandings of the idea of the laureate do not fundamentally differ from Lydgate's. The multifaceted, mutually constitutive relationship between poet and sovereign that, for example, Louis Montrose has described in respect to Spenser and Queen Elizabeth has, as we will see, its earlier English instance in the relationship between Lydgate and Henry V.[7] Lerer speaks of his *Chaucer and His Readers* as "a gesture toward a prehistory of the laureate self-fashioning described by Helgerson" (5), and this description also aptly applies to the present study. But Lerer goes on to insist that "fifteenth-century poetics is the projection rather than enactment of laureate performance — a self-fashioning not of professional or amateur, but of the patronized and the subservient" (5). I argue instead that Lydgate's practice is indeed a laureate performance, the very first such successful performance in English. Rather than being a projection, Lydgate's poetry uses such a projection (onto Chaucer) in order to underwrite its own practice. Further, while Lydgate is indeed patronized and subservient, I argue that such subjection has always been, at least since Petrarch, an integral part of the notion and practice of the laureateship.[8] And it is precisely this subjection that is responsible for the Hocclevean beggar's inevitable surfacing as the laureate's counterpart.

I look briefly at the tensions within the *trecento* notion of the laureate in my first chapter. In subsequent chapters, I examine how these tensions affect the shape of English poetry in the period between Chaucer and Wyatt. Throughout, I emphasize the role of political power as the most prominent motivator of laureate poetics and prolific contributor to the contradictions within its practice. In fifteenth-century England, the ascendance of a high-culture vernacular tradition, with the poet laureate as a central conceit, cannot be separated from the ascendance of a series of kings with questionable claims to the throne: for the poets of this period, laureate self-construction finds its not-so-secret sharer in dynastic legitimation. In Chapter 1, I outline the differences between Ricardian and Lancastrian poetics in respect to the key feature of authorial self-representation, and, in Chapter 2, I turn to Lydgate, the Lancastrian poet *par excellence*, and describe the development of his laureate poetics over the course of his career — the ways in which it is produced by and seeks to alter his historical circumstances. Hoccleve is the topic of Chapter 3, where I examine how his slightly earlier response to the same set of historical factors and poetic problems differs from Lydgate's. This response — and especially his pose as beggar poet — represents both a unique literary achievement and the pronounced debut of what would become the inevitable companion to Lydgateanism. In Chapter 4, I analyze the practice of, or responses to, Lydgateanism (and, in one case, Hoccleveanism) of poets who wrote in the period spanning the 1440s (the last decade of Lydgate's life) to Caxton's appearance in England in the 1470s. In the work of these minor poets, we witness how a major poet is constituted: these authors' adaptations of, or reactions to, Lydgate's laureate poetics help us to understand how Lydgateanism was perpetuated and its ideology understood. In Chapter 5, I turn to three poets writing at the beginning of the sixteenth century who, to varying degrees, still understand themselves as working within the Lydgatean tradition: Stephen Hawes, Alexander Barclay, and John Skelton. I investigate how each of these authors negotiates this heritage in a historical context that suddenly possesses a laureateship as an actual political office, and how their relative failures at this negotiation make evident the Hocclevean alternative that always lurks within laureate poetics. In an epilogue, I turn to England's first Renaissance courtly maker, the apparently un-Lydgatean poet, Sir Thomas Wyatt, and argue that a full understanding of Wyatt's poetry requires an acknowledgment of its dialectical dependence on the normative tradition against which it seeks to distinguish itself. I end with the suggestion that, if Lydgateanism has had a hand in shaping Wyatt's verse, then its influence must be even more strongly felt in the long line of the English poetic tradition — extending at least as far as to Wordsworth — that desperately wishes the laureateship to be something that it cannot possibly become.

PART I

Backgrounds

CHAPTER I

Laureate poetics

Believing poetry to convey the most essential truths and yet being asked to use it to legitimate the blunt use of power in the highest places, the fifteenth-century English poet developed a laureate poetics, a set of practices aimed at resolving this conundrum. This book tells the story of the rise and subsequent influence of this poetics as well as its doppelganger, the poetics of begging. The burden of this first chapter is to offer defenses for some of the assumptions underlying this story and, in the process, to introduce terms, concepts, and argumentative frameworks that will recur throughout the study.

Although the post of poet laureate as we know it was not established until John Dryden's appointment in 1668, much earlier the ideas and practices associated with the laureateship exerted influence on the course of English poetry. Making their way northward from *trecento* Italy, these ideas and practices affected each of the vernacular traditions they encountered, reaching England in the late fourteenth century in the work of Chaucer. The very marked impact that they subsequently had on English verse was, however, by no means inevitable. Indeed, their initial explicit appearance in the prologue to the *Clerk's Tale* (1390s?) was hardly auspicious. In their brief debut, Chaucer, characteristically, subjects their authority to scrutiny and doubt, even while invoking it.[1] Yet, in the years following his death in 1400, the very poets who proclaimed themselves his disciples — and, in particular, John Lydgate — took up laureate ideas and practices with gusto, retroactively fashioning Chaucer into England's first poet laureate and implicitly installing themselves as his successors.[2] The reasons for this embrace of what Chaucer himself held suspect are many, but prominent on the list are the changed political climate following Henry Bolingbroke's seizure of the throne from Richard II in 1399 and the concomitant changes in the relations between princes and poets, poets and audiences, and audiences and the English language. In England at the beginning of the fifteenth century, the concept of the laureateship was simultaneously politically and poetically propitious, and, to the extent that it remains part of the English poetic tradition, one is justified in suspecting that it continues to be doubly effective in this regard.

This is not to say, however, that the notion of the laureateship and its associated practices are straightforwardly or merely political. In fact, the *trecento* version of this notion was in many ways construed in contradistinction to the realm of political power. Ideally, the territory governed by the laureate should adjoin but be independent of this realm, and the poet should serve the public through a cultural excellence that has bearing on but is not reducible to political expedience. Yet, the delicate balance in this relationship with power is virtually impossible to maintain even in theory, and *trecento* discussions of the role of the poet tend to fall off the beam to one side or the other — to, that is, conceptions of the poet as divinely inspired *vates* or as materially self-interested servant of a prince. In the first section of this chapter, I examine, in the work of Petrarch and Boccaccio, key formulations of the ideal uses to which poetry should be put and the conditions under which a poet should write. As idealizations of poetic practice, these formulations demarcate a late medieval laureate ideology, one which provokes Chaucer's skepticism but, for his successors, becomes the conceptual ground on which they develop their initial strains of laureate poetics. In this chapter's second section, I briefly review the changes in the climate of literary patronage between the Ricardian and Lancastrian courts that most encourage the adoption of this ideology and, in turn, facilitate the development of this poetics. Then, in the third and longest section, I make the case for the novelty of this poetics in respect to earlier English poetry by focusing on changes in authorial self-representation. This new mode of self-representation, I conclude, develops as one of the key poetic practices actuating the laureate ideology made suddenly so attractive with the accession of the Lancastrians.

LAUREATE IDEOLOGY

Not surprisingly, the poet Chaucer names when he introduces the notion of poet laureate into English verse is Petrarch, the most famous laureate in the Middle Ages and beyond. Among the many places one might look in Petrarch's corpus for meditations on the nature and purpose of the laureateship, perhaps the most self-evident is the address he gave at his laureation in Rome in 1341. This oration, as one would expect, he devotes to a celebration (mostly a self-celebration) of the poet's gifts, a trumpeting of his value to civilization, and a mystification of his relation to power. Even so, one also witnesses a conceptual pendulum swing between poles of sacred and profane — between, that is, conceptions of the laureate as *vates* and as self-interested servant. The burden of the address — which Petrarch frames as a commentary on Virgil's lines, "Sed me Parnasi deserta per ardua dulcis/raptat amor" — is to define the nature of the desire for poetic excellence (*amor*) and the proper reward for achieving such excellence (attaining *deserta Parnasi*).[3] On the one hand, Petrarch claims that the laureate's inspiration has divine origin ("nothing can be accomplished unless a certain inner and divinely given energy is infused in the poet's spirit" [p. 301]) and that his desire for excellence and consequent rewards are therefore accoutrements of his own particular person vis-à-vis his creator. The laureate, in this view, is a self-determining artist who answers only to past models of excellence and the stewardship of his God-given ability, and who seeks nothing but the permanence of his name. On the other hand, in the very historical event of Petrarch's own laureation, as in the one he imagines for Virgil, the laureate obtains his crown, not from God, but from an emperor. The laureate is always *someone's* laureate, and, to the degree that the possessive pronoun indicates real possession rather than mere association, the theoretical self-determination of the laureate falls away to reveal his subjection.

Even if he wished to conceal the political significance of his laureation, Petrarch could hardly do so with Roman senator Orso dell'Anguillara and Robert of Anjou, king of Naples and Sicily, standing by waiting to bestow the crown. He thus instead attempts to harmonize the political and poetic by inverting — or at least balancing — their relationship: he depicts rulers and governments supporting poets laureate, rather than vice versa. Early on, for example, he mentions in passing that the great poets of antiquity flourished "especially when Caesar Augustus held imperial sway" (p. 303), emphasizing the poetic fecundity coterminous with Augustus's political domination, instead of the emperor's control of his poets. A little later, he again takes up this task of inversion — this time much more extensively and suggestively — when he enumerates the three-part "disposition of the spirit" that drove him to seek an actual laureation (rather than provide himself, as Dante did, with a figurative one): "first, the honor of the Republic; second, the charm of personal glory; and third, the stimulation of other men to a like endeavor" (p. 304). Initially, the privileged position he bestows on "the honor of the Republic" seems to indicate that the interests of this republic have priority over whatever personal interests a laureateship might serve. Yet, when he addresses each of these factors in turn, he does so in such a way as to fold the first and third into the second.

In his comments on the honor of the republic, he mentions nothing about that republic per se but rather immediately makes comparisons with ancient Rome and Athens, recollecting "so many and such great poets" who "have received the laurel crown they had deserved" (p. 304). The glory of the republic becomes the reflected glory of Petrarch himself, who as a new Virgil may begin to make late medieval Rome a simulacrum of her own past: "I am moved also by the hope that, if God wills, I may renew in the now aged Republic a beauteous custom of its flourishing youth" (p. 304). Here God, not senator or king, wills the laureation; the republic does not so much create a poet for its own purposes as a divinely created poet restores that republic to its former glory. Indeed, Petrarch underscores the largely inessential nature of the republic's actual interests by devoting much of his discussion of this first point to the fact that he was also invited to Paris to receive this honor. Although these conflicting invitations presented him with a difficult decision, he tells us that he finally chose Rome because of his "reverence for those ancient poets of excellent genius who flourished in this very city" (p. 305). The "honor of the Republic," as it turns out, is a mere reflex of Petrarch's self-identification as a new Virgil.

With the hurdle of his laureation's political dimensions thus overleaped, Petrarch moves quickly through the next two motivating factors. About the "charm of personal glory" he says nothing specific at this point, other than to argue, with Cicero and Ovid as his authorities, that despite the "contempt of glory" many philosophers express, "few or none can be found who really condemn it" (p. 305). And in regard to the third factor, "the stimulation of other men," he simply recasts his personal quest for glory into an example for those gifted men who remain hindered by "modesty and humility": "Boldly, therefore, perhaps, but ... with no unworthy intention, since others are holding back I am venturing to offer myself as guide for this toilsome and dangerous path" (p. 306). In the same way that the glory of the republic becomes a reflection of his personal glory, the stimulation of others becomes an iterative confirmation of his trailblazing greatness. Although at first he seems to sandwich his individual glory between the self-sacrificing requirements of state service and pedagogical necessity, by the midpoint of his oration he has turned this impression inside out and restored himself — and thereby his self-determination — to the place of honor.

Appropriately, then, Petrarch devotes most of the remainder of the oration to a more expansive consideration of the "charm of personal glory." This he divides between two subtopics: the reward that the laureate seeks and the significance of the laurel crown. For Petrarch, the reward corresponding to "personal glory" is, quite simply, "the immortality of one's name" (p. 307), i.e., the elevation of one's historical specificity into the timeless realm of fame and the concomitant elevation of one's work into the realm of universal truth. Turning then to the laurel crown, he details the properties of the laurel and their attendant symbolism, punctuating his discussion with analogies between poets and "Caesars." For example, he concludes that, "since both Caesars and poets move toward the same goal, though by different paths, it is fitting that one and the same reward be prepared for both, namely, a wreath from a fragrant tree, symbolizing the fragrance of good fame and of glory" (p. 309). Throughout, poets are not subjects of Caesars but equivalents of them within their specific domain of authority, their "different path." This altogether self-inflating commentary, the longest passage dedicated to a single topic in the oration, is also Petrarch's final one, after which he turns to Orso dell'Anguillara to receive his wreath. Retrospectively, one perceives that he has carefully structured the entire address to ensure that this concluding moment appears not as a submission to political power but as a public recognition of his at least equal standing — the acknowledgment by a figure of power of a parallel figure of friendly but untethered poetic authority.

This final interpretive frame notwithstanding, however, Petrarch cannot in fact fully realize this alignment of the relationship between poet and prince — even within the conceptual boundaries of his address. At the very moment when he lays claim to the most traditional and transcendental poetic prize, the immortality of his name, he abruptly switches his focus from poet to patron: "This immortality is itself twofold," he observes, "for it includes both the immortality of the poet's own name and the immortality of the names of *those whom he celebrates*" (p. 307, emphasis added). These objects of poetic celebration must be, preeminently, Caesars, those other possessors of the laurel, most famously and pertinently Virgil's Augustus. Petrarch goes on to issue a warning regarding those "mighty men and warriors" who have "passed into oblivion" because they were not memorialized by "capable authors," and then he bluntly observes, "Certain illustrious men, foreseeing such a possibility, have kept [*habuere*] poets with them and held them in high honor, so that there might be someone who would hand down their praises to posterity" (p. 308). Such a kept poet, despite whatever honor he achieves, is obviously far from the divinely inspired, self-determining figure who claims *equal* status with Caesars. He is rather more like the Anglo-Saxon *scop* Widsith, who, in the poem titled from his name, makes bold claims for his poetic prowess even while he coins verses for any man who possesses power and treasure.[4] The kept laureate, in short, is a paid servant, and, although Petrarch never explicitly mentions financial reward in his oration, the specter of the economic exchange that underwrites the relationship between "illustrious men" and those who write their praises is not absent from his speech. It briefly but suggestively appears in the cryptic statement that forms the crucial bridge between this passage on the servant-poet and the following one on the properties of the laurel crown that the poet supposedly shares with emperors: "Other rewards, also, come to poets; but passing over [*pretermissis*] these I come to the laurel crown" (p. 309). In this "passing over," Petrarch traverses the immense distance between the ideas of poet as paid propagandist and as self-determining *vates*. After this traversal, the propagandist has no further role in his oration, except obliquely at the end in the conventional humility he assumes before senator and king.

One may fairly wonder why the propagandist appears at all in this speech — why Petrarch, in an address so much devoted to the elevation and mystification of the poet's authority, feels compelled to include such a stark, if brief, account of the poet's subjection to power. Of the many possible explanations, the simplest points to a consciousness on Petrarch's part of the need to advertise the *practical* usefulness of a poet laureate. He surely was aware that his laureateship — as his series of princely patrons and ecclesiastical livings would later attest — would not be an *economically* autonomous post, whatever the status of its notional authority.[5] Hence, after creating the impression that the glory he wishes to bring the republic is in fact that of his own poetic achievement, he must, in a sense, backpedal. He must remind his noble auditors that one of the most useful functions of poets laureate is their memorialization of the glory of those whom they serve — a task that the laureate performs for economic favors, the most essential of the "other rewards" that he tactfully declines to mention. In his idealization of classical Rome, Petrarch represents Virgil and Augustus as equals, the paradigms, respectively, of poetic and political authority and together the model of happy interchange between the two. By figuring himself as a new Virgil, he implicitly claims a status analogous to that of his contemporary princes. But this claim could not, in his actual career, be much more than notionally realized. Although Petrarch managed at times to achieve a semblance of autonomy by the sheer multiplication of sources of support, he could never rid himself of the exigencies of his dependence, and this situation is precisely what his circumspect rhetoric of "passing over" both elides and predicts.

Among the more infamous of these exigencies were Petrarch's relationships with despots, about which he received stern criticism from Boccaccio, his friend and fellow proto-humanist. Yet Boccaccio, although an enthusiastic defender of literary discourse, was far from naïve in regard to the relationship between poets and power. For example, in his *Trattatello in laude di Dante*, he insists, following Petrarch, that "poetry is theology" and that "theology is nothing other than a poetry of God."[6] The poet, in other words, possesses a divinely bestowed gift for expressing ultimate truths in the form of poetic fictions. In this role, he is a Christian *vates*, a fiction-making prophet whom God calls upon to fill a crucial function in the sublunary world, and who answers, finally, to no merely temporal authority. But just prior to these grand proclamations, Boccaccio supplies a related but very different account of the poet and poetry – namely, the story of the origins of poetic *utility*.[7]

He first describes the rise of kings, those extraordinary individuals who "make themselves masters of the uneducated multitudes of their districts" (p. 493). Kings maintain their domination both by sheer might – resisting "whatever adverse things might come along with physical force" (p. 493) – and by the implied threat conveyed by spectacular displays of power, as when they appear "before the people with both slaves and ornaments, things unheard of among men before this time" (p. 493). Slaves serve the practical function of being a physical extension of the king's strength and the conceptual function of signifying the principle of subjection. Similarly, ornaments are both physical evidence of the king's economic might and subjective generators of the aura that conveys his innate superiority, which in turn justifies his domination. Over time, Boccaccio relates, kings began to require more potent aura-generating machinery, and, turning to a more profound source of mystery, they "began to stoke up religious sentiment and to use the resultant faith to frighten their subjects, and to secure by oaths the obedience of those that they would not have been able to constrain by force" (p. 494). It is at this point that poets first enter the story:

These things they could not accomplish satisfactorily without the collaboration of poets, who in order to amplify their own fame, to please the princes, to delight the princes' subjects, and to urge virtuous behaviour upon everyone ... employed various and masterly fictions ... thereby causing to be believed that which the princes wished to be believed. Both for the new gods and for the men who imagined themselves to be descended from gods, the poets employed that same style that the first people had reserved for the true God alone, and for his praise. From this the feats of brave men came to be compared with those of gods; and this originated the practice of singing the battles and other notable doings of men in sublime verse, mixing them in with those of the gods. Such was, and still is, the office and business of every poet. (p. 494)

In this account, poets are not only prince-pleasers and self-celebrants but also hired disseminators of a prince's ideology, "causing to be believed that which the princes wished to be believed." Somewhat surprisingly, given his later hieratic claims, Boccaccio does not seem to register much discomfort with this knowledge. Perhaps, for him, although it is still "the office and business of every poet" to trumpet the "notable doings of men in sublime verse," there are men who in fact deserve this memorialization. In any event, he leaves the door open for poetry to evolve back into its ideal state, to become once again the perfect vehicle for praising "the true God alone," as only in this respect may it legitimately be theology in the Christian era. Yet such a development is hardly predicated by the assumptions of Boccaccio's story. The problem lies with the apparent stability of the medium: while the *aims* of poets may differ categorically, poetry itself remains constant. Hence, if poets use the "same style" to praise false as well as true gods and unworthy as well as worthy men, how may they authenticate their evolution of poetry into a conduit of truth from, say, a cultural weapon of a tyrant? The ends of poetry may distinguish the true poet from the propagandist, but these ends are neither formally nor stylistically marked.

Boccaccio does not explicitly address this problem in the *Trattatello*. Instead, following his account of the rise of the poet as propagandist, he abruptly changes topics and takes up the aforementioned argument for poetry's fundamentally theological nature. In effect, he conjoins without comment two related but apparently diametrically opposed accounts of the nature of poetry and the poet. For Boccaccio, these arguments are able to coexist because of a basic assumption that none of his contemporary readers would have questioned, which is that their theology fundamentally differs from, say, Virgil's. To the extent that pagan religion is mere human construction, it is not an autonomous source of truth but instead an instrument for controlling some aspect of the fallen human world – a tool, for example, for creating and maintaining social order. In comparison, Christianity, while also encouraging of social order, is true regardless of the uses to which it is put. The apparent contradiction between Boccaccio's accounts of the nature of poetry and the poet thus evaporates under the assumption that, while Virgil and Dante are both theologians, they are of categorically different sorts: Virgil represents the culmination of a line of poets who versify a false theology for political purposes, whereas Dante versifies Christian truth for its own sake (at his best; Boccaccio does not hesitate to criticize Dante for his moments of factionalism). In the difference between pagan and Christian poet lies, for Boccaccio, the difference between subjection before a king and self-determination in the work of God.

In practice, however, the latter difference is not always easy to discern, as Boccaccio's development of these ideas in Chapter 4 of Book 14 of *Genealogia deorum gentilium* (1350–75) suggests.[8] His definition here of the characteristics of the true poet may be revealingly tested against Petrarch's poetic practices and circumstances. First, Boccaccio maintains that the true poet must be poor: "For, with ... poverty as our leader, we by choice attain to liberty and peace of mind, and thereby to honorable ease" (p. 29). The "liberty" or self-determination of a poet, in other words, is inversely proportional to his wealth. But at what point does a poet's wealth *preclude* him from being a *true* poet? Does material comfort, such as that enjoyed by Petrarch, axiomatically presume a vitiated poetry? Second, the true poet "never seeks a habitation in the towering palaces of kings or the easy abodes of the luxurious," but rather "visits caves on the steep mountainside, or shady groves, or argent springs, where are retreats of the studious" (p. 24). Petrarch's fondness for depicting himself as a solitary may be understood in this light. Yet, his actual habits aside, how is one to reconcile this requirement with the very public, politicized ceremony of his laureation? Third, the true poet's reward should not be material but rather ethereal, his payment being the immortality of his name: "if the privilege of long life is not granted a man in any other way, poetry, at any rate, through fame vouchsafes to her followers the lasting benefit of survival" (p. 26). But the poet laureate, as Petrarch insists, makes permanent not just his own name, but those of his economic and/or political sponsors, i.e., those who occupy the very palaces and reward him in the very manner that he is to avoid. Apparently, for Boccaccio — in his greatest and perhaps *the* greatest *trecento* defense of poetry — the definition of a true poet excludes Petrarch, the paradigmatic poet laureate from the late Middle Ages on up to the present. Laureate ideology, in its initial late medieval formulations, proves itself both an attractive and inadequate account of laureate practice. A few decades later and far away in England, Chaucer, in his political context, could afford to invoke this ideology, imply his recognition of its inadequacy, and put it aside. In contrast, his fifteenth-century successors had no such luxury.

RICARDIAN TO LANCASTRIAN

If the literary bookends of this study are, as I indicated in my introduction, Chaucer and Wyatt, the political bookends are the deposition of Richard II and the divorce of Henry VIII. These events had both immediate and far-reaching effects on English literature. Henry's divorce signaled the beginning of the English Reformation and the consequent end of the poet-cleric's domination of English verse. Thenceforth, Lydgateanism proper persists only in subterranean channels and displaced formations. The fall of Richard (the more crucial event, obviously, for the time span covered by this book) enabled the rise of the Lancastrian dynasty, which throughout its duration was haunted by this original sin of usurpation. The regimes of each of the Lancastrian kings, in an attempt to contain the personal and public ramifications of this usurpation, pursued various and sophisticated strategies of legitimation. In recent years, the procedures and outcomes of these strategies have become familiar to students of fifteenth-century literature. Over the last two decades or so, several studies have demonstrated how the Lancastrians' activities of legitimation sometimes took very subtle, indirect, and even self-contradictory cultural forms.[9] Among these forms is high-culture vernacular verse; almost immediately after Henry's IV's seizure of the throne, this verse displays a newly urgent concern with its relationship to power. English poetry becomes suddenly more calculated in its political import, and its understanding of its *own* legitimacy becomes more explicitly implicated (if often ambivalently) in the dynastic dimensions of its motives and themes.

Under Richard II, the appreciation of certain types of literary objects was a cultic preoccupation of the powerful. It was more than a mark of their prestige — it was a sign of their inherent difference from the non-powerful, an externalization of their personhood aimed at making them appear categorically different from their subjects. Today, we refer to this function of literary objects as the production of distinction, which is, more generally, an effect of cultural capital. According to Pierre Bourdieu, cultural capital, to operate as such, must to some extent be *misrecognized* (i.e., the utilitarian value of a cultural object must be more or less invisibly embedded within its aesthetic value).[10] Strictly considered, such misrecognition on the part of Richard, his nobles, and their subjects is open to some doubt; misrecognition per se probably only became possible after the establishment of a Kantian disinterested aesthetic. Before the eighteenth century, and certainly in the Middle Ages, no great contradiction was seen between the utilitarian and the aesthetic. Nonetheless, for a number of reasons, a disinclination to have the instrumentality of a literary object be *entirely* transparent does mark the Ricardian period, which is evident in the poets' adoption of strategies of indirection, obscurity, and displacement. The ambiguous depiction of Richard as God of Love that many detect in the prologue to Chaucer's *Legend of Good Women* exemplifies these strategies. This prologue is neither politically innocent nor a political statement (at least, not a straightforward one). Rather, it participates — as does, in a different way, Gower's *Confessio Amantis* — in the desire of the court to view images of itself, even somewhat negative images, both for the pleasure of the self-gaze and for the production of distinction. Indeed, the very debate over how much Richard himself encouraged literary production suggests that the political utility of literary objects was not for him an obvious given. One supposes instead that, for Richard, literary texts held value not so much in their specific utility as in their general aura — a supposition that seems confirmed by Richard's comparison of himself, in his perhaps self-authored epitaph, to Homer.[11]

In contrast, beginning with dynastic patriarch John of Gaunt, the Lancastrians displayed a full appreciation for the political utility of *belles lettres*. As Paul Strohm puts it, speaking more generally about any sort of text, the Lancastrians possessed a "keen and precocious awareness of the value of textualization, of the sense in which a written account placed in the right kind of circulation can generate its own kind of historical truth."[12] In particular, after 1400, the Lancastrians, in need of legitimation from sources with any claim to an authority *independent* of theirs, demanded a poetry that both in itself possessed cultural capital and could also serve as political weapon.[13] This need for legitimation and the inclination to satisfy it through cultural intervention is what most distinguishes the Lancastrian court's literary habits from those of its predecessor, and, in turn, these literary predilections are what most influence the development of post-Ricardian high-culture vernacular verse. It would be reductive, however, to attribute the development of this verse solely to this factor. As recent scholarship has documented, a number of other factors also played key roles, including, but not limited to: the growing desire on the part of the established temporal and spiritual powers to reclaim the vernacular from the Lollards; the shift away from French and toward English as the literary and administrative language of choice; an expanding and more diverse audience for the poetry traditionally associated with court or cloister and hence a newly emergent demand for secular and devotional verse with pretensions of high culture; and the slow seepage into England of humanistic ideas about poetry and poets. Nonetheless, despite the indisputable bearing of each of these factors, the Lancastrian court remains a signal component of each: it was the alignment of the Lancastrians with the Church against Lollardy that produced such vituperative poetic polemics as Hoccleve's *Remonstrance against Oldcastle* and Lydgate's *A Defence of Holy Church*; it was the Lancastrians' (and in particular Henry V's) policy, motivated in part by the renewed war with France, to elevate the status of English over that of French; it was the royal patronage of such poets as Lydgate that made their works a desirable commodity among the growing reading public; and it was the Lancastrians' (and in particular Duke Humphrey's) understanding of the political utility of humanism that was responsible for its encouragement in England.[14]

One may fairly conclude, then, that, in comparison with the diffuse (if still significant) impact of Ricardian politics on Ricardian poetry, the specific interests of the Lancastrian court had a much more penetrating influence on the poets it patronized or otherwise encouraged. And the most vested interest of this court was to legitimize itself. In this climate, poems written under the auspices of the court frequently possessed some element of propagandistic intent, although this intent did not preclude other, even contradictory ones, and was rarely realized unproblematically. (Indeed, sometimes, as in much of Hoccleve's work, a Lancastrian poem fails to be propagandistic rather spectacularly.) To make this assertion, however, is not to claim its novelty. Even if one considers only verse in the English vernacular, one encounters a depiction of a similar relationship between poets and princes as far back as in the (perhaps) seventh-century *Widsith* — that is, as far back as records of this verse extend. What *was* new to English verse in the fifteenth century (if not to verse in other languages) was the *trecento* laureate ideology that, through whatever conduit, was seized upon by Lydgate and others as well suited to the Lancastrian clime.[15] This ideology served as a conceptual bridge between politics and poetics — between, that is, the imperatives of the Lancastrian court and the features of poetic practice. It cued specific changes in this practice, even while it created the backdrop upon which these changes signaled to readers (and thereby helped to constitute) a specific politico-cultural role for the poet. In the next section, I examine one such change: the fifteenth-century poet's self-representation as an empirical, historically specific *auctor*.

THE REAL POET

Let us return once again to the comparison between Chaucer's and Wyatt's encounters with Petrarch with which I began this book. Regardless of whether the interiority represented in Wyatt's adaptations is more "modern" than the one in Chaucer's, Wyatt appears to foreground much more than Chaucer does the idea of his own empirical person. Against this claim, however, one might object that Wyatt's strategy of authorial self-representation was available to Chaucer, as evident in such lyrics as *Lenvoy de Chaucer a Scogan*, and was thus simply an option he usually declined. But then the character of Chaucer's habitual decisions in this regard becomes significant. Moreover, when he does include gestures toward his empirical person, they are not nearly as unambiguous or thematically central as those of his successors. Yet, one might further object that the difference between the poets lies, as I suggested in the introduction, not so much in the nature of their authorial poses as in the genres in which they wrote most of their work. Chaucer's narratives, with their multiple characters and points of view, encourage a distancing of the narrator's "I" from the person of the poet, whereas the lyrics of Wyatt encourage the opposite. The difference between them reflects not so much literary historical change as it does simple generic affiliation. This objection is more far-reaching than the first, and to some extent its point is undeniable. Nonetheless, a poet's generic affiliation and the set of literary features comprising genres are themselves, of course, historically conditioned. Specifically, in respect to the relationship between first-person speaker and empirical author, it is important to remember that, at the advent of the Ricardian period, English narrative and lyric were, normatively speaking, the converse of what they are now. Narratives often presumed a conflation between speaker and author, while the voice of lyric was typically that of a type of man or woman, a voice functionally − and, in most cases, in fact − anonymous. In this conventional context, Chaucer's predilection for narratives that do invoke his person, but in a highly ambiguous manner, contrasts sharply with Wyatt's decision to write in a lyric mode that depends upon a confusion of speaker and specific poet. Chaucer, that is, chooses to distance voices that were conventionally conflated, while Wyatt chooses to merge voices that were conventionally kept apart.[16]

In his narrative works and most famously in the *Canterbury Tales*, Chaucer plays with the distance between his empirical person and textual alter ego, but he does so within a generic expectation that minimizes that difference. At the outset of the *Tales*, for example, his alter ego assumes the pose of pseudo-historian. After the lofty opening sentence (which, as is well known, derives from the *Historia destructionis Troiae* of Guido delle Colonne), this alter ego turns to the putative facts of the event: the names of the neighborhood and pub in which he has met his fellow pilgrims, the number of these, and the destination of their pilgrimage. These facts are understood by the reader as facts per se to the extent that the "I" speaking them is understood as a real person, and there is no more powerful or straightforward way of creating this latter impression than by associating this "I" with the real person who must have written the poem. In suggesting this association, Chaucer mimics for rather different purposes the "auctorial" strategy of medieval historians in all linguistic traditions, from Bede through Froissart.[17] In English prior to Chaucer, this strategy was deployed in verse histories and was responsible for an early and persistent strain of vernacular authorial self-definition. Laȝamon, for example, begins his late twelfth- or early thirteenth-century *Brut* by declaring, "An preost wes on leoden, Laȝamon wes ihoten." Similarly, some 100 years later, Robert Mannyng begins his *Chronicle* by informing the "Lordynges þat be now here" that "alle þe story of Inglande/als Robert Mannyng wryten it fand/& on Inglysch has it shewed[.]"[18] For these poets − as for their Latin and French models − the veracity of the history they report receives its authenticating analogy in the empirical fact of the author-speaker. Textual truth finds its corroboration in biographical facticity. Thus, when Chaucer assumes his ironized version of this pose a few decades after Mannyng completes his *Chronicle* (1338), he does so within a horizon of expectation that associates historical narratives with an empirical author-speaker.

In contrast, the "I" of the English lyric before the second half of the fourteenth century typically (if not uniformly) designates the opposite of such an author-speaker. This is Leo Spitzer's "poetic I," a pronoun that, according to him, does not point to a historically specific individual but is rather a "representative of mankind."[19] Although Spitzer grossly overstates the applicability of this convention, his formulation does fairly describe a generic norm that most, if not all, writers of early Middle English lyrics seem to have accepted. Deployed by friars, monks, and *scops*, the "I" of most pre-Ricardian lyrics is the common property of a community of singers and listeners. More often than not an element of poems both in theme and in actual practice homiletic,[20] this "I," like that of public prayer, has for its very purpose its occupation by any particular subscriber. By design, it obscures the differences among individual subjectivities, and this convention also dominates secular lyric, as it was often the case that the same (usually clerical) author wrote in both modes. Consider, for example, the thirteenth-century *Foweles in þe Frith*, which records a subjective response to a landscape every bit as profound (albeit radically more laconic) as that of a romantic nature poem:

> Foweles in þe frith,
> Þe fisses in þe flod,
> And i mon waxe wod.
> Mulch sorw I walke with
> for beste of bon and blod.[21]

Here the interiority designated by the "I" becomes available to the reader through its complex and uncertain relation with the exterior world in which it walks — just as in, say, *Tintern Abbey*. In Wordsworth's poem, however, the "I" can only designate the specific individual who is responsible for the *Lines Written a Few Miles above Tintern Abbey, on Revisiting the Banks of the Wye During a Tour, July 13, 1798.*[22] The composer of *Foweles in þe Frith*, in comparison, has left no record of his or her specificity, and therefore possesses no necessary association with the poem's "I" more than that of any of its readers.

Similarly, even when we know the name of a poet, as in the lyrics attributed to Richard Rolle (d. 1349), we typically still encounter a lyric ego emptied of particularity. In Rolle's case this is all the more striking,

given the preoccupation with himself that he so consistently displays
elsewhere. Consider, for example, his *A Song of Mercy*:

> Mercy es maste in my mynde, for mercy es þat I mast prayse.
> Mercy es curtayse and kynde; fra al mischeves he mai me rayse.
> Allas, sa lang I have bene blynd, and walked will alwayse.
> Mercy walde I fayne fynd, to lede me in my last dayse.
> Mercy, lede me at þe last, when owt of þis world sal wende;
> To þe cryand I trayst fast, þat þou save me fra þe fende.[23]

Alongside the relentless repetition of the poem's topic, in these lines
resides an equally insistent indication of the speaker's presence. With at
least one first-person pronoun in each line, the topic seems not so much
mercy per se as the speaker's meditation on and experience of it. Yet to
name this speaker Richard Rolle would subvert the very *raison d'être*
of the poem. These verses, as an instance of devotional pedagogy,
are to be voiced by any devout Christian as his or her own. The first-
person pronouns are insubstantial indices, markers of the places
where the reader enters into and takes over the voice of the poem.[24]
In the English short poem, a generic lyric ego along these lines,
especially in devotional contexts but in secular ones as well, remains
the predominant lyric convention up through Chaucer's time — and
even, to some extent, beyond. Chaucer's "I," in many of his short
poems, does not significantly stray from this convention, and an
alternative norm becomes fully established only with the fifteenth-century
Chaucerians.

The generic nature of this lyric ego should not, of course, be mistaken
for an actual epistemology. Most students of medieval discursive
conventions have at this point moved beyond the Burckhardtian view
that this lyric ego indicates the poet's *unawareness* of the possibility of
an irreducibly individual interiority. Indeed, this ego's generic nature —
in addition to what it practically achieves homiletically — frequently
signals the poet's grappling with this very awareness, his or her striving
toward the disclosure of a *homo interior* that is individuated but
undifferentiated, "the discovery within oneself of human nature made
in the image of God — an *imago Dei* that is the same for all human
beings."[25] The opponent in this struggle is the initially pessimistic
postulate that one's interiority is not reducible to an essential divine
sameness but is instead the particularizing cloak of sin — a condition
of fallen humanity that limits an individual's knowledge of anything
besides the phantoms of his or her own desires. Turned upside down,

however, this postulate becomes an optimistic and proto-humanistic assertion of the principle of individual sovereignty in a fallen world — and, as such an assertion, potentially a threat to the normative, group-based notion of individual identity that underwrites conservative ideologies of social order. This postulate in some form or another, with its attendant thematic and narrative possibilities, attracted more than a few medieval poets, including those of late fourteenth-century England. Nevertheless, the aim of most of these poets was not so much to assert this postulate as to contain, displace, repress, or — most creatively — transcend its implications.

Pre-Ricardian poetry does not take many risks in this regard. Narrative verse, as I have mentioned, frequently features an individuated first-person speaker, but, since the role played by the auctorial conflation of speaker and empirical author is typically so narrow, it may perform its task of textual authentication without significant disturbance to any epistemological assumptions or thematic aims. Present almost exclusively only in prologues and epilogues, this conflation, having invested the "I" with the authority of the empirical, is elsewhere inert, acting as a kind of enabling but dead metaphor within the impersonal "I" that speaks the body of the text. The interiority of Robert Mannyng, for example, has no real role in his *Chronicle*; once his person credentializes the work's historical veracity, it becomes the mere repository from which the facts of history are drawn. In comparison, in lyric verse, since the topic is so often the interior state of the speaker, any suggestion of identification between speaker and historically specific author may radically alter the poem, transforming its paradigmatic or purely grammatical "I" into an index of the irreducibly unique. For this reason, most early Middle English short poems are anonymous by design. And, for the same reason, prior to the Ricardian period the English tradition lacks a single instance of a compound text — that is, a text like Dante's *Vita nuova*, which combines first-person narrative and lyric. By fusing auctorial self-advertisement with the interiority of lyric, such a text potentially represents the poet as a living "autonomous human *auctor*."[26] In English one encounters nothing along these lines until the capacious generic experiments of Chaucer, Langland, and Gower. Prior to this — although one might wish to pause for a moment over *The Owl and the Nightingale*, in which a Nicholas of Guildford, possibly the author, is mentioned within the world of the fiction — first-person speakers remain divided into the two camps of named but largely impersonal narrators and unnamed markers of generic interiority.[27]

THE RICARDIAN "I"

George Kane observed several years ago that Spitzer's categorical distinction between the poetic "I" and the empirical author does not adequately account for the Ricardians' use of the first person. "The speaking person in their works," he argued, referring to Chaucer and Langland, "is both more and less than the poet; in him creator and thing created simultaneously merge and are distinguished ..."[28] Kane's primary concern in this essay was to exhort literary critics to sift through the referential complexities of the Ricardian "I" and not to commit the "autobiographical fallacy" by confusing "creator" with "thing created." But he also implied, through his insistence that this confusion (in the etymological sense of the word) was itself an essential feature of this "I," that what differentiated the Ricardian "I" from its vernacular precedents was its *constituent*, if unstable, historical specificity. In the work of Chaucer, Langland, and Gower, this specificity creeps into the poetic "I," not altogether usurping its generic representationality but creating a thematically rich tension with it. In much Ricardian poetry, the first-person speaker is at once (or at different times) the representation of a particular poet in all his subjective complexity *and* a conventional figure for a type of individual – and it is this give and take between particular and general that (among many other things) distinguishes this poetry from that which precedes it. Unlike the chronicler's "I," the Ricardian "I" rarely devolves into mere impersonal narrative device; and, unlike the lyric "I," it often cannot be divorced from the idea of a specific individual.

This newly persistent specificity has multifarious thematic functions, one of the most important being the staging of its own subsumption – that is, the designation of a particular individual in order to emphasize, finally, his paradigmatic status, his representation of the plight of any Christian in the world of late fourteenth-century England.[29] At the end of the *Canterbury Tales*, for example, it is possible to understand Chaucer the person, Chaucer the poet, and Chaucer the pilgrim as one and the same figure: the person retracts the work of the poet and by doing so becomes a generic penitent and pilgrim on the road to the New Jerusalem.[30] Langland's Will in *Piers Plowman* and Gower's Amans in the *Confessio Amantis* have similar status. Although these personae differ in countless ways, in each case the author-figure's historical specificity at some point evaporates into a representation of a general human condition. While these poets indeed grapple with the importance increasingly being attached to the unique individual, their considerations of this notion display a marked ambivalence and even at times appear to reaffirm the communitarian ethos in which individual distinctiveness is mere accident to the homogeneity of human substance.[31]

Yet, even when prompted by the most conservative of motives, any recognition of an author's unique individuality can remain potentially unsettling. There is always the chance of an imperfect subsumption – the possibility that, once invoked, the notion of the unique individual, as embodied by the figure of the poet, will leave behind a residue of significance that cannot be entirely assimilated by a traditionalist ethos. (And, indeed, it is perhaps the Ricardian poets' alertness to this residue that helps give their works their open-ended quality.) This risk is especially evident in those moments in which the poet names himself, for it is then that the empirical person of the author vividly enters the poetic fiction and most threatens to usurp permanently a formerly typological "I." Chaucer, Langland, and Gower negotiate this risk in different ways, but in each case (albeit to different degrees) the poet, after drawing on the energy of the normative threat, seeks to redirect the significance of his self-naming through formal and thematic strategies of deflection and obfuscation.

In Chaucer's work, the most fraught moment of self-naming may well be that juncture in the *Canterbury Tales* that turns out not to be such a moment. Following the conclusion of the *Prioress's Tale*, the Host, in an attempt to dispel the group's somber mood, jocularly turns to the narrator and asks, "What man artow?" In the fiction of the *Tales*, this is, of course, an exceedingly apt question, since the social identity of the tale-teller is so often important to the tale he or she supplies, and, indeed, the narrator is the only pilgrim whose social identity we do not know. If Chaucer were to answer the Host's question and supply this identity (e.g., "I am Chaucer, clerk of the kinges works"), he would bring his empirical person fully into the poem. But Chaucer introduces this possiblity only to sidestep it. He leaves his alter ego staring at the ground and lets the loquacious Host answer his own question:

> He in the waast is shape as wel as I;
> This were a popet in an arm t'enbrace
> For any womman, smal and fair of face.
> He semeth elvyssh by his contenaunce,
> For unto no wight dooth he daliaunce. (7.700–4)

By referring to himself indirectly as a "popet" and "elvyssh," Chaucer has left us with an indelible impression of a mischievous but wise personality.

Yet he nowhere indicates that this personality must be necessarily attached to Geoffrey Chaucer, esquire. Indeed, this self-portrait is remarkable for the extent to which it *avoids* any index of social identity, any historically localized detail that would bind the specific person of Chaucer to the "I" of the poem. It individualizes the speaker, but it does not invoke his historical specificity.[32]

Chaucer's actual moments of self-naming, of which there are only two, in the end pose less of a normative threat than this non-moment does, as both have their force significantly dampened through inter-textual irony. In the *House of Fame*, the Eagle, near the beginning of its explanation of how all sounds find their way to Fame's dwelling, addresses the first-person speaker as "Geffrey" (729). In a poem that has much to say about poetic authority, such an act of self-naming has the potential to elevate the authority of the individualized poet. Yet not only does the Eagle use the relatively underdetermined given name (and that just once), but also this act of naming is more a gesture toward other texts than toward the empirical world. On the one hand, it is a nod to the *dits amoureux* of Chaucer's French contemporaries, in which, in such texts as Machaut's *Voir dit*, a complex identification of protagonist and poet is mined for rich thematic ends. And, on the other hand, given that the source for Chaucer's Eagle is Canto 9 of the *Purgatorio*, it is a comment on Dante's striking (and singular) self-naming via Beatrice in Canto 30. As many have argued, Chaucer's poem, in part, is a parody of the *Comedia* — and, indeed, nothing could be more parodic of Beatrice's extensive and technical theological expositions than the lecture on sound that follows the Eagle's naming of the poet. Considered in its intertextual context, Chaucer's act of self-naming appears as a gentle mockery of the presumption of that very act.[33]

The poet's other act of self-naming occurs in the Man of Law's introduction, when the Man of Law compares unfavorably his own tale-telling abilities to those of "Chaucer" and speaks about the poet and his works as if the poet himself were not present (2.46–76). As in the *House of Fame*, poetic authority and its potential residence in a particular, living author are once again at issue. Yet, as in the earlier poem, this passage does not so much assert this authority as offer a critique of its presumption. After listing some of Chaucer's works, the Man of Law goes on to condemn those poets who write "Of thilke wikke ensample of Canacee" (2.78), i.e., those poets like Gower in the *Confessio Amantis*. In this intertextual context, as in that of the *House of Fame*, the Man of Law's utterance of Chaucer's surname contains an element of parody.

In this case, it parodies the twice-uttered "Gower" at the conclusion of the *Confessio* — a parody that takes on added bite if, as has often been suggested, the Man of Law is himself a stand-in for Gower.[34] Chaucer, reading Gower's self-naming as presumptuously auctorial, temporarily absents his alter ego from his fiction to enable a Gower-figure to attach Chaucer's surname to a selective celebration of Chaucer's work — and then has the same figure critique Gower's work without mentioning Gower's name. The lesson of this naming/not-naming game, despite the unhappy way I have described it, is plain: while it is entirely permissible to name another individual living poet, as Chaucer names "moral Gower" at the end of *Troilus and Criseyde* (5.1856), *self*-naming actuates a presumption that must be checked through ridicule.

For the most part, the thematic range of Chaucer's acts of self-naming extends no further than this intertextual critique; indeed, other than for this, these acts probably functioned principally as jokes that his coterie audience would heartily appreciate.[35] In comparison, Gower and Langland, although they may also have been writing (at least most immediately) for a coterie, indicate in their works a much broader intended audience.[36] The most daring of these two, in respect to the potential import of his self-naming, is Langland, given his poem's public nature, its capaciousness and originality, and the centrality of its narrator. If one were fully to identify this poem's narrator/protagonist Will with its empirical author, then *Piers Plowman* would become less a tale of a paradigmatic Christian's search for *dowel, dobet,* and *dobest* and more a crypto-autobiographical account of the struggles of one, unique such Christian. Accordingly, the first-person speaker of *Piers Plowman* would become more an authority from whom we might learn and less one with whom we might identify.

Anne Middleton, in her magisterial essay on Langland's signatures, describes the function of Langland's coded acts of self-naming as "narratively pivotal events that render biographical and poetic self-awareness synonymous."[37] Langland's signatures form an essential device for achieving the project of the poem, which is at once a cry in the wilderness and the story of the crier. But Middleton also believes Langland intended to stop well short of depicting this crier as, most essentially, a unique individual. Although his coded self-naming encourages "the reader's sense that the author's social, vocal, and even physical presence is also somehow 'in' the text, that the words on the page represent a person as well as his product," this person always remains the sign of a "paradigmatic and exemplary form of . . . life."[38] As Middleton has observed elsewhere, *Piers Plowman* is a "lyric history," in which Langland imbricates a particularized narratorial "I" with the generic "I" of lyric. Langland's aim, though, is not to infuse the particular with the authority of the generic (which, as Thomas Stillinger argues, is Dante's aim in the *Vita nuova*), but rather to bestow upon the particular the intrinsically exemplary status of the generic. In spatial terms, Langland's strategy is a movement outward rather than inward. If one mistakes the direction of this movement — if, that is, one sees in Langland's signatures a restriction of the poem's "I" to its author — one reduces the narrator to merely a kind of "instructor *in propria persona*."[39] Correspondingly, Langland's lyric history threatens to devolve into a didactic treatise with illustrative narratives. For these and other reasons, Langland, unlike Chaucer and Gower, never names himself in a straightforward manner. His given name "Will" is always also (and perhaps more so) a personification, and his surname is buried in the famous anagram, "I haue lyued in londe ... my name is longe wille."[40] This strategy of obfuscation, as it turns out, was too successful, as many of Langland's contemporaries believed the empirical author to be a fellow named Piers Plowman.[41] Langland's poem — having been constructed, more so than those of the other Ricardians, around the subjective experience of a singular individual — remains in the end the most enigmatic as to what its narratorial "I" signifies.

In comparison, Gower's "I," in some instances, possesses a much more definite semantic field. In particular, Gower's late work *In Praise of Peace* can be fairly said to foreshadow much of what was soon to become normative in high-culture English verse. In this poem, an authoritative first-person speaker addresses a king in an explicitly political, advisory context; he names both himself and his addressee; and he manages to be at once obsequious and critical. Urging the recently rebellious Henry of Derby to follow the ways of peace, this speaker begins with a panegyric to the now "worthi noble kyng, Henry the ferthe" and in his conclusion states, "I, Gower, which am al thi liege man,/This lettre unto thin excellence y sende."[42] The pose he assumes here is similar to the one he assumes in the Latin *Vox clamantis*, in which he represents himself, via the convention of the academic preface, as a living *auctor*.[43] In the English poem, however, he depicts a near symbiotic relationship between the new English king and an authoritative poet supplying him political wisdom in the native language of the realm, and this depiction moves the poet's auctorial pose nearer to that of the laureate. In short, this poem comes closer than any other to being an English precursor to the laureate performances that Lydgate and his followers would soon make ubiquitous.

As an illustration of the nature of this poem's influence – and as an indication of that influence's limits – we may consider the poem Lydgate composed for the coronation of Henry IV's grandson. At times, the resemblance between this work and *In Praise of Peace* is quite marked:

> Prynce excellent, be feythful, truwe and stable;
> Dreed God, do lawe, chastyce extorcyoun,
> Be liberal, of courage vnmutable,
> Cherisshe þe Chirche with hoole affeccyoun,
> Loue þy lyeges of eyþer regyoun,
> Preferre þe pees, eschuwe werre and debate,
> And God shal sende frome þe heven adovne
> Grace and good hure to þy royal estate.[44]

In this passage, as in Gower's poem, we encounter an authoritative, historically specific poet counseling his king to pursue peace in a political climate of factional strife. Although not strictly a source, *In Praise of Peace* was likely a model for Lydgate's poetics not only in this effort but elsewhere as well. (David Lawton, for example, has suggested Gower's poem to be behind the peace position Lydgate promulgates in the *Siege of Thebes*.)[45] And yet, even if one grants that Gower's influence on Lydgate may be as profound as hard evidence for it is scant, the ground of the poets' similarity remains at the same time the ground of their difference. In particular, while in *In Praise of Peace* Gower does employ his own person as a personification of moral authority (so that the "Gower" of the poem becomes an embodiment of the moral demands placed on the prince), he only minimally connects the idea of this person with the empirical, historically specific John Gower. As we will shortly see, Lydgate, in such works as the *Siege of Thebes*, is fond of providing at the *outset* a number of details pertaining both to his extraliterary existence and the circumstances of composition – details which have the effect of placing his empirical person on center stage. Gower's poem, in comparison, moves quickly from its opening panegyric to its primary task of advising the king, and this lack of extrinsic detail at the outset lends its first-person voice a generic, if authoritative, quality. When the speaker finally does identify himself near the end of the poem, his name strikes the reader as the signature of an exemplary citizen, a loyal and devout composer of a political epistle. In effect, the name "Gower" is ultimately not as crucial as the label "liege man" that follows it: the voice of this poem, to apply Middleton's argument about Ricardian public poetry more generally, is that of the concerned subject, a "common voice" serving the "common good." It is not so much the voice of a specific individual as it is a "rhetorical embodiment of [his] audience's best and most actively responsible selves."[46]

If Gower was an amateur poet with ambivalent laureate pretensions, Lydgate was, in comparison, a proto-professional poet who for all practical purposes was an acting laureate. In the next chapter, I examine Lydgate's laureateship in some detail. At this point, to help illuminate Lydgate's differences from the Ricardians in respect to his strategies of self-representation, I offer a single example of his poetic practice. In the prologue to the *Siege of Thebes*, which he stages as a continuation of the *Canterbury Tales*, Lydgate inhabits Chaucer's writing more intimately than anywhere else in his oeuvre. Depicting himself as encountering the pilgrims in Canterbury, he supplies a self-description after the fashion of the *General Prologue* — not, that is, a self-portrait along the lines of the inscrutable *popet* passage, but the efficient identification of the author-narrator-pilgrim's social station and character that is pointedly missing from the *Tales*: e.g., he appears "In a Cope of blak and not of grene,/On a palfrey slender, long, and lene,/with rusty brydel mad nat for the sale" (pro. 73–75). Here Lydgate identifies himself unambiguously as a Benedictine "blak" monk who, in accord with his vow of poverty, possesses an appropriately ragged appearance. When the Host subsequently greets this figure, he interrogates him with much more specific and revealing questions than Chaucer's Host's "What man artow":

> daun Pers,
> Daun Domynyk/Dan Godfrey/or Clement,
> ȝe be welcom/newly into kent,
> Though ȝoure bridel/haue neiþer boos ne belle;
> Besechinge ȝou/þat ȝe wil me telle
> First ȝoure name/and of what contre
> With-oute more shorte-ly that ȝe be,
> That loke so pale/al deuoyde of blood,
> Vpon ȝoure hede/a wonder thred-bar hood,
> Wel araied/for to ride late. (82–91)

As in Chaucer's *popet passage*, this indirect self-portrait emphasizes physical description, but here the point is to reinforce the already tendered image of poverty appropriate to Lydgate's social station — an image that, as has been frequently noted, stands as Lydgate's self-conscious differentiation of his actual, personal practice of monasticism from that of the *General Prologue's* worldly but fictional monk.[47] And, quite unlike the parallel *Canterbury Tales* passage, Lydgate places special emphasis on the author-narrator-pilgrim's name – on the specific signifier that would decisively conflate all three subject positions with the identity of the poet's extraliterary person. Finally, in stark contrast with Chaucer's reticent *popet*, Lydgate's alter ego does not hesitate to respond to the host's question:

> I answerde, "my name was Lydgate,
> Monk of Bery/ny3 fyfty 3ere of age,
> Come to this toune/to do my pilgrimage,
> As I haue hight/I haue therof no shame." (92–95)

In these lines the speaker efficiently provides his surname, his social identity, the town of his Abbey, his age, and a polite insistence on the propriety of his being away from the cloister. This blunt self-identification has often received comment, but for the most part critics dismiss it as evidence of Lydgate's poetic incompetence. In his clumsy attempt to imitate a Chaucerian persona, Lydgate, according to these critics, confuses fact with fiction and thereby dramatically dilutes the aesthetic power of the latter.[48]

Such charges of incompetence are frequently leveled against fifteenth-century poets in general and Lydgate in particular. But if we defer these charges and search first for a thematic purpose behind Lydgate's revisions of Ricardian precedents, we must then ask why Lydgate, if he simply meant to imitate Chaucer, would, in a manner so unlike his master, identify his narrator not only as pilgrim and poet but also as "man" – the empirical, historically specific monk of Bury. A full answer to this question lies ahead; at this point, I suggest only that he does indeed confuse fact with fiction, but this confusion is both necessary and strategic. By the time he began work on the *Siege*, he had, through such efforts as the *Troy Book*, established himself as the de facto poet laureate of the Lancastrian regime. The politically fraught *Siege*, as it apparently had no patron and includes no mention of a source, rests all its claims to authority – and it possesses some considerable ones – on the living *auctor* it introduces in its prologue. Lydgate enters this text, therefore, to bestow upon it the authority that he possesses outside it. The agon with Chaucer that he stages through his imitation of the *Canterbury Tales* – as well as through his accompanying eulogy of his master – aims not so much at a depiction of himself as authentic disciple as it does at a transformation of Chaucer into a flesh-and-blood laureate, one who retroactively defines the role that Lydgate implicitly claims to occupy. Like Gower at the end of the *Confessio*, like Langland in C-5, and like Chaucer in his so-called *Retraction*, Lydgate in the prologue of the *Siege* is both fictional character and empirical individual. Unlike the alter egos of the other poets, however, Lydgate's author-figure enters his fiction as his extraliterary, historically specific self from its inception, thereby fusing the extrinsic authority of that self with the literary authority of his poetic forebear and investing his text with both. Once Lydgate has established this authority, he disperses the fiction, underscoring throughout most of the narrative proper the *reality* and *specificity* of his narratorial voice. After the prologue, the narrator is no fictional pilgrim, no everyman figure of doubt and longing, but a "real" poet: a historically specific mouthpiece of moral authority who turns the matter of Thebes into a laureate performance, a high-culture vehicle for his own relentlessly didactic commentary.

This abandonment of narratorial fiction and concomitant shrinkage of a poem's imaginative space, so uncharacteristic of the Ricardian poets, become habitual with Lydgate and the poets who follow him. Such is the aesthetic cost of their thoroughgoing conflation of first-person speaker and named, historically specific author. This cost is predictable, as one would not expect a traditionalist — and especially a manifestly pious monk like Lydgate — to deploy a literary device possessing a potential threat to subjective homogeneity without first emptying that device of its fiction and hence much of its capacity to represent interiority. A standard criticism of fifteenth-century poetry — that it is lifeless — is in this limited sense justified; a constriction of the interior space of the first-person speaker is the only good-faith means Lydgatean poets have for implementing their characteristic strategy of making their empirical persons central to their poems. Shorter works as well as long narratives, such as Lydgate's *Life of Our Lady* and *Troy Book*, tend to modulate into epideictic or homiletic modes in which the first-person speaker becomes at least as important as what that speaker says; but these poems unfold not so much that speaker's interiority as the construction of his authority. Nevertheless, although this authority is directed outward toward political, religious, and moral questions, such externalization stops short of fully depersonalizing the speaker, as it would in a straightforward didactic treatise or history. The aim, rather, is first to idealize the speaker's authority by embedding it in an already-idealized ideology and next to circle back to the empirical person of the poet, who is then understood as the historically specific embodiment of this ideology. This movement, although it may sometimes be imaginatively poor, may also be formally rich, making use of whatever generic features are most favorable to it in any given context. For example, in the *Troy Book* Lydgate combines the pose of the monastic historian, the self-aggrandizing idiom of the epideictic lyric, and the moral authority of homiletic verse to forge a self-representation at once specific and universal, real and ideal.

But more important than the formal constitution of this self-representation is the literary historical trajectory that it evidences. One wishes to know, that is, why Lydgate adopted this self-representation in the first place — what his precise motivations were, and what consequences these have both for his work and the entire high-culture vernacular tradition. The most decisive of these motivations, as I have suggested, may be found in Lydgate's political context. Through the auspices of *trecento* laureate ideology, Lancastrian politics inspires the set of formal innovations and thematic preoccupations that I have called laureate poetics. In particular, for Lydgate and his followers, the idea of a Lancastrian laureateship stands behind their innovative strategies of self-representation. This idea requires the deployment of a poet's person as an embodiment of authority at once historically specific and transhistorically ideal. Such an embodiment serves both political and literary interests by being their very site of intersection. And yet, just as in the laureate meditations of Petrarch and Boccaccio, the residual tension within this intersection inevitably discloses the laureate's secret sharer, the beggar, creating a compound figure who puts one foot on Parnassus and stretches the other behind a knee bent in supplication, his eyes looking up at the heavens while he holds his hand out in anticipation of payment. As we will see in the remainder of this book, this compound figure haunts Lydgatean laureate poetics in all its variations across the century.

In the context of the rather unsettled dynastic situation within which laureate and beggar traded places on center stage of high-culture English poetry, the literary efforts of the poets who played these roles — although they could and, indeed, *had* to proceed to some degree toward their own independent ends — were thus profoundly subject to political interests. For this very reason, however, it is all the more important to remember that most of these poets — and especially Lydgate, the most influential one — played these roles in good faith. Lydgate fully believed in the nobility of the poetic endeavor, and for him the fact that this endeavor pursued the prince's interests did not contradict but was rather evidence for this nobility. This good faith is what, in the end, always infuses some amount of pathos into laureate poetics. Poets like Lydgate were believers in a world of cynics and advocates for stability in an age of conflict, and they tied their heartfelt claims for the truth of poetry to a dynasty doomed to disappear at the end of a bloody civil war.

PART II

The first Lancastrian poets

Although the only place in which Chaucer explicitly mentions the notion of the poet laureate is in the prologue of the *Clerk's Tale*, ideas associated with this notion hover in the background in many of his other works, and no more so than in that text singularly devoted to poetry and poets, the *House of Fame*. Not coincidentally, this work also contains the sole moment in Chaucer's oeuvre in which the poet unambiguously textualizes not just his person but also his extraliterary social identity. This occurs in Book 2 through the voice of the Eagle, who is explaining to "Geffrey" that Jupiter has granted him a visit to the House of Fame because, among other reasons, he works too hard to hear "tydynges/Of Loves folk" (644–45) in a more ordinary fashion:

> For when thy labour doon al ys,
> And hast mad alle thy rekenynges,
> In stede of reste and newe thynges
> Thou goost hom to thy hous anoon,
> And, also doomb as any stoon,
> Thou sittest at another book
> Tyl fully daswed ys thy look[.] (652–68)

The extraliterary valence in this passage hinges on one word, "rekenynges." Because of this word, we understand more generic ones such as "labour" and "another book" to refer to Chaucer's duties as comptroller of the wool custom, for which he was required to keep records *manu sua propria*.[1] Self-references of this nature, as we will see, are one of the constitutive devices of laureate poetics. Yet, for Chaucer, this rather cryptic allusion to extraliterary identity, although no doubt recognized by the likely coterie audience of the poem (it survives in just three manuscripts), was obviously not intended to evoke powerfully an image of Chaucer as civil servant. It is in fact quickly overwhelmed by the more dominant (and, in the tradition of Guillaume de Machaut,

45

conventional) image of the speaker as a bookish clerk/poet, sitting in front of volume after volume "[t]yl fully daswed."

Three or so decades later, Thomas Hoccleve, another poet with a "day job" as civil servant — and, moreover, self-proclaimed disciple of Chaucer — would be dramatically and repeatedly less circumspect about his extraliterary identity. Consider, for example, the well-known moment in the *Regiment of Princes* when Hoccleve's first-person alter ego receives from his interlocutor a very specific question, which he immediately answers accordingly:

> "Sauf first, or thow any ferther proceede,
> O thyng of thee wite wolde I, my sone:
> Wher dwellist thow?" "Fadir, withouten dreede,
> In the office of the Privee Seel I wone
> And wryte — there is my custume and wone
> Unto the Seel, and have twenti yeer
> And foure come Estren, and that is neer." (799–805)

Here the first-person speaker says explicitly where he works ("the office of the Privee Seel"), indicates what he does there ("wryte"), and gives precisely how long he has held this job (twenty-four years come next Easter). And, once encouraged, he goes on to fill stanza after stanza with such detail, describing the travails of his professional life for some 232 additional lines (digressing only to lament the fate of poverty-stricken veterans of the French wars, to whom he compares himself). He ends, finally, with an apology to his interlocutor — and, implicitly, to the reader — for what he realizes to be the unusual nature of this self-regarding discourse: "I am right sikir it hath been an helle/Yow for to herkne me thus jangle and clappe" (1,034–35).

Passages such as this, in which Hoccleve strides forth like no English poet before him, have made his poetry in recent years the object of a booming critical industry. Furnivall's "weak, sensitive, look-on-the-worst side kind of man" has struck a chord with a generation of critics who have been taught to be suspicious of such vivid illusions of authorial personality — and are hence fascinated by them.[2] Investigators newly attentive to the vicissitudes of literary subjectivity have sought to explain how an ostensibly regressive early fifteenth-century English culture may be reconciled with the extravagances of a poet whose self-observation finds no peer "until at least Donne, or perhaps even Wordsworth and the high Romantics."[3] Initially, much of this renewed attention was concerned with articulating precisely what is and is not unusual about Hoccleve's self-observation, a task led by John Burrow in a series of illuminating articles. More recently, scholars have sought to locate the poet's achievements in the confluence of literary precedent and the pressures of his historical moment, paying special attention to how his experiences in the nascent Westminster bureaucracy in newly Lancastrian England bear on what seems so unprecedented in his verse. In most of this work, the anomaly of Hoccleve's achievement is taken as more or less self-evident; the apparent fact that his verse is so *unlike* that of the other major early Lancastrian poet, his contemporary John Lydgate, is the point of departure.

And yet, apologetic, self-regarding discourse is also an important aspect of Lydgate's poetic practice. Although appearing in somewhat different form and not quite to the same degree, this discourse nonetheless possesses enough similarity with Hoccleve's (and corresponding difference from that of their shared poetic precursors) that it begs a common framework of explanation. These two poets' lives and careers overlap in so many ways; among other things, Lydgate was only about four years younger than Hoccleve, and they wrote similar poems for the same Lancastrian princes. The differences in their poetic practices are, as we will see, to a large extent conditioned departures from the same basic orientation toward the production of verse. The features of this orientation, moreover, are more straightforwardly visible in Lydgate's poetry, for the simple fact that Lydgate was more successful at meeting their requirements (if success is measured by circulation and influence). Indeed, the ways in which Hoccleve fails to meet some of these requirements are great contributors, I argue, to the anomalous nature of his verse. For this reason — and because the larger aim of this book is to investigate the impact, over the *longue durée*, of this common initial orientation of the first Lancastrians — I begin this section with Lydgate rather than Hoccleve. I choose this order despite the fact that Hoccleve's major poetic productions predate most of Lydgate's and, accordingly, it is Hoccleve, rather than Lydgate, who first versifies such famous Lancastrian tropes as "Father Chaucer." Yet, because Hoccleve's poetic career may be understood in important ways as a historically conditioned — and to an extent willed — failure to be the kind of poet that Lydgate would later successfully become, Lydgate stands as the more quintessentially Lancastrian poet. In the light of the model Lydgate later establishes, important features of Hoccleve's poetry retrospectively emerge as inherent aspects of Lancastrian verse that Lydgate's poetry, in being more successful, seeks more strenuously to hide.

CHAPTER 2

John Lydgate: the invention of the English laureate

> One is persuaded that his morality is official and impersonal — a
> system of life which it was his duty to support — and it is perhaps a
> half understanding of this that has made so many generations believe
> that he was the first poet laureate, the first salaried moralist among
> the poets. (W. B. Yeats[1])

In his seminal *Self-Crowned Laureates*, Richard Helgerson singles out
this remark of Yeats's about Spenser to illustrate the modern antipathy
toward laureate poetics. In the anachronistic assumption that Spenser
was England's first poet laureate, Yeats detects an alignment with power
that to many seems deeply embedded within the Elizabethan poet's
authorial ideology. Yet, from a wider perspective, this anachronism
is simply a misplaced point of origin. The first "salaried moralist among
the poets" — if one counts a royal annuity as a salary — did not postdate
Spenser but predated him by nearly 200 years, arriving in the form of
John Lydgate, monk of Bury St. Edmunds, 1371–1449. Chaucer and
Hoccleve received annuities earlier, but these were *prima facie* for their
work as civil servants rather than as poets. Gower wore a Lancastrian
collar but does not seem to have been on the king's payroll other than for
his annual grant of two pipes of wine, and no known evidence relates the
collar or grant to his literary activity. In comparison, because the work
Lydgate performed for the Crown consisted solely of his verse (as far as
we know), it seems fair to assume that his annuity — for which he had
to wait until 1439 — was a belated recognition of his long service as poet
to Lancastrian kings and princes.[2] In this poetic service, Lydgate expressed
a morality that was indeed both "official" and (from a modern
perspective) "impersonal," and Spenser, who would have had at his
disposal the mid-sixteenth-century prints of the *Troy Book* and *Fall of
Princes*,[3] perhaps there discovered a precedent for the authorial ideology
that Yeats found so off-putting. Although the laureateship in its present

49

form did not appear until the second half of the seventeenth century, the epithet "Laureate Lydgate" — the title of a chapter in Derek Pearsall's authoritative monograph on the poet — is no anachronism.

In this chapter, I argue that Lydgate not only produced the kind of work one expects from a laureate, but he also brought into English a laureate poetics that serves as the ground of laureate performance — now as well as then. In pursuing this argument, I investigate the nature of this poetics as it develops through the course of his career. After reviewing the extrinsic elements of Lydgate's laureateship, I examine some aspects and sources of the poetic practice that comes to define this laureateship intrinsically, focusing on his productive combination of devotional epideixis and literary relationships with Chaucer and Christine de Pizan. I then discuss how, in the watershed event of the *Troy Book*, he invents an English laureateship by aligning this practice with that of the monastic historian and putting the resulting poetics into a reflexive relationship with power. After tracing his continuing construction of this laureateship through a few other works, I conclude by exploring how its inherent internal tensions appear in his verse, especially in his obsessive deployment of the humility topos. Lydgate's laureate poetics, as we will see, sustains a remarkable career, one in which he produces some 145,000 lines of verse largely under the patronage of the most powerful men and women in England.[4] Yet, this poetics also confronts the poet who practices it with the contradiction that lies at its heart. That Lydgate proves so adept at obscuring this contradiction testifies neither to his inadequacies nor to his sycophancy but, rather, to his persistent idealism. This idealism and ability to suppress that which ought to deflate it is, in turn, what makes him so important to later laureate dreamers like Spenser.

THE ELEMENTS OF LYDGATE'S LAUREATESHIP

A number of extrinsic aspects of Lydgate's poetic practice coincide to situate him effectively as England's first — albeit unofficial — poet laureate. At the forefront stands his royal patronage. Lydgate wrote officially commissioned poetry for both the fifth and sixth Henries as well as for Lancastrian princes (and at times virtual rulers) John, duke of Bedford, and Humphrey, duke of Gloucester. Around this royal core, the circle of his patrons extends broadly through the ranks of the aristocracy and Church hierarchy, including such notables as Henry V's queen, Katherine of Valois; Richard Beauchamp, earl of Warwick, his wife, Isabella Despenser, and his eldest daughter, Lady Margaret Talbot;

Anne, countess of Stafford, and her daughter, Anne, wife of Edmund Mortimer, earl of March; Thomas Montague, earl of Salisbury; William de la Pole, earl (later duke) of Suffolk; the powerful abbots Curteys of Bury St. Edmunds and Whethamstede of St. Albans; and the dean of Windsor (later bishop of Exeter), Edmund Lacy. At its outer limits, this circle reached, on the one hand, the marginal gentry, such as Lady Sibille Boys of Holm Hale, and, on the other, the London civic authorities and commercial establishment.[5]

Prior English poets, of course, had royal patrons, Gower being the closest predecessor both in time and in how he represents such patronage in his verse. Yet, the precise nature of Gower's patronage still eludes us, and this fact suggests by way of contrast the unprecedented status of Lydgate's: no other English poet was patronized so consistently by the dominant political figures of his day nor by so broad a spectrum of society, and, most likely, these two facts are closely related. Seth Lerer speculates that the scope of Lydgate's patronage represents his active search for new patrons following the death of Henry V. But it seems more likely — given Lydgate's tremendous output, the sheer variety of his patrons, and the travel restrictions on monks — that it was his patrons who sought him.[6] Lydgate's royal patronage made his texts desirable cultural commodities for those nobles who sought the aura of royalty, as well as for those gentry who wished to emulate courtly behavior. Because he was the first poet to be so closely identified with royal power, he was also the first *living* author writing in English whose name became, as it were, a name brand. Although an appreciation for poetry had long been a marker of aristocratic lineage, in the fifteenth-century this marker possessed more prestige — and therefore more efficacy — if it carried the name "Lydgate."[7] In a more theorized vein, one might say that the political capital Lancastrian kings and princes hoped to gain through their commissions redounded upon the poet in the form of cultural capital, which in turn was highly desired by various levels of fifteenth-century English society. Countless examples of the sociocultural deployment of Lydgate's verse illustrate its value in this regard. Among them are Sir John Paston's use of the *Temple of Glas* for the wooing of his future wife; the status-conscious design of the Rushall Psalter, which to a significant degree is organized around Lydgate's texts or those texts of Chaucer's that seem most Lydgatean; a codex celebrating the Percy family built around a copy of the *Troy Book* and the *Siege of Thebes*; and the widespread appearance of the monk's most didactic works (such as *Stans puer ad mensam*) in low-budget anthologies of "utilitarian" texts aimed at the growing market of literate gentry, merchants, and professionals.[8] One might counter this claim by noting that Chaucer's name also accrued immense cultural capital in the fifteenth century and that Lydgate's name-value may therefore be a "coattail" effect. But the postmortem investment in Chaucer — of which we will shortly see examples — was part of the very politico-cultural project in which Lydgate was a central agent. Indeed, as Lerer and others have argued, Lydgate, along with his friend and scribe John Shirley and contemporary poet Hoccleve, was among those most responsible for giving Chaucer's name this sort of currency.

Lydgate's brand value, moreover, crossed factional as well as estate and class boundaries. The bitter conflicts between Humphrey and Bedford and, later, Humphrey and Suffolk did not in either case prevent both sides from turning to Lydgate for the most politically sensitive verse, such as his pieces celebrating the politically fraught marriage between Humphrey and Jacqueline of Hainault (which Bedford vehemently opposed) and that between Margaret of Anjou and Henry VI (which Suffolk engineered following the decline of Humphrey's influence).[9] Both the cultural prestige of Lydgate's poetry and its political efficacy were, it seems, perceived as non-partisan, the poet and his work embodying a laureate authority that was theoretically independent of the specific political or sociocultural uses to which it was put. This perception was in turn both self-fulfilling and dizzyingly self-perpetuating: the more Lydgate's work appeared to hold freestanding cultural value, the more the poet was patronized by a diverse spectrum of society for diverse kinds of poems, causing his poetry to appear even more free from partisan control, thus further increasing its cultural value.

Given the poetic productivity that would seem to accompany such a reciprocal cycle of value bestowal and accrual, one expects to be impressed by both the variety of his poems and the number of their surviving manuscripts, and in both cases one is not disappointed. Lydgate's oeuvre includes epic-sized devotional works, such as the *Life of Our Lady*; works of religious education, such as *An Exposition of the Pater Noster*; relatively straightforward saints' lives, such as the *Legend of St. George*; courtly exercises in *fin' amor*, such as *A Gentlewoman's Lament*; philosophically more complex courtly productions such as the *Temple of Glas*; monumental histories, such as the *Troy Book*, and encyclopedic ones, such as the *Fall of Princes*; short satirical pieces, such as *Ryght as a Rammes Horne*; longer moral fables such as the *Churl and the Bird*; the scripts for mummings for various organizations and occasions; brief amplifications of proverbs, such as *Mesure is Tresour*; purely didactic and mundane works such as *A Tretise for Lauandres*;[10] and, finally, many instances of precisely the kind of occasional, political verse one expects from a laureate, such as *Ballade to King Henry VI upon His Coronation*. Tellingly, what is not found within this ponderous oeuvre is a single instance of a poem akin to Chaucer's *House of Fame* — that is, an exploratory and reflective work aimed at a coterie audience. (Despite its self-conscious emulation of aspects of the *House of Fame*, the *Temple of Glas* is quite different from its precursor.) Lydgate's poetry, notwithstanding its diversity of genre and matter, is — again as one would expect from a laureate — uniformly public and authoritative in nature.

The numbers of Lydgate's surviving manuscripts are staggering. Pearsall lists some 180 different manuscripts containing one or more of the poet's major works; in addition, a sizable number survive containing fragments of the larger works or anthologies of the shorter ones.[11] Many of these circulated during the poet's lifetime, and, from similar features among some of them, A. I. Doyle and M. B. Parkes have suggested that Lydgate had control of his exemplars and perhaps even oversaw the production of his texts.[12] His close relationship with the proto-publisher Shirley has been well documented, although the nature of that relationship remains somewhat obscure.[13] Shirley doubtlessly played a key role in the constitution of Lydgate's laureate practice through the dissemination of poems he explicitly associated with the monk; yet, equally doubtlessly, Lydgate provided the cultural capital that attracted readers to Shirley's manuscripts. Whatever the precise nature of their relationship, the manuscripts spawned by their collaboration became a model for the rest of the century, during which period poems identified as authored by Lydgate, as well as those by his self-proclaimed precursor Chaucer, served as the organizing principle for many an anthology.[14] And, with the advent of commercial printing, this model was not eclipsed but obtained new life; for example, as Pearsall observes, "one of Wynkyn de Worde's most profitable publishing ventures was his *Proverbs of Lydgate*," which the printer cobbled together from envoys to the *Fall of Princes* and other poems.[15] The similarity of this commercial venture to a modern "greatest hits" compilation assembled long after a recording artist's death suggests just how entrenched Lydgate's cultural value had become.

If this wide dissemination represents a laureate's cultural dominance and not merely a hack's popularity, one would expect to find the stamp of Lydgate's influence in the work of contemporary and subsequent poets.

Here again, as I show in subsequent chapters, one is not disappointed. At this point I make only two observations. First, almost every fifteenth-century English and Scottish poet whose name we know (as well as much of the anonymous poetry) exhibits Lydgate's direct influence. Second, two of the earliest instances of this influence appear in the form of personalized acknowledgments of Lydgate's poetic authority that, as I argue in Chapter 4, have no real precedent in prior English verse. For the monk of Bury to wield an influence both so pervasive and personal suggests that, in respect to the cultural capital of fifteenth-century vernacular poetry, Lydgate was the gold standard.

Nonetheless, what remains conspicuously missing from this list of the extrinsic elements of Lydgate's laureateship is an actual, institutionalized office as poet laureate. For this reason, these extrinsic elements were in practice held together by those intrinsic features of his verse that reflexively construct their composer as laureate. Lydgate's laureateship, without official recognition, is most fundamentally perpetuated through the idea of such a post as conveyed in his poetry. In each laureate performance this idea must be present, for it is this idea that both legitimates the continued investment in his work and ensures its politico-cultural efficacy.

BEFORE THE LAURELS: CHAUCER, CHRISTINE DE PIZAN, AND THE PRAISING MONK

Lydgate's laureate poetics, properly speaking, only comes into being with the first effort that we know without doubt to be the product of Lancastrian patronage: the *Troy Book*, which he began in 1412. Yet in (perhaps) earlier works of a much smaller scale, one may witness several characteristic literary strategies that lay the ground for this poetics. One such strategy is Lydgate's literary historical personalization of his sources, which is strikingly evident in, for example, the opening to *A Balade in Commendation of Our Lady*.[16] In this lofty panegyric to the Virgin, we wait three stanzas for the commendation proper to begin, during which we encounter the poet talking about himself and, in the process, supplying a telling allusion:

> A thowsand storiis kowede I mo reherse
> Off olde poets touchyng this matere:
> How that Cupide the hertis gan to perse
> Off his seruauntis, settyng tham affer.

Lo here the fin of th'errour and the weere,
Lo here of loue the guerdoun and greuaunce
That euyr with woo his seruaunts doth avaunce. (1–7)

In foregrounding a speaker who could rehearse, but does not (here, at least), a "thowsand storiis" of "Cupide" from the "olde poets," these opening lines establish much: the thematic importance of the first-person speaker, that speaker's poetic knowledge and authority, the fact that he is rejecting secular erotic verse, and – through the allusion of the last three lines to the *Troilus and Criseyde* narrator's concluding Christian disgust with his pagan narrative – a complex interpoetic relationship that seeks to depict Lydgate as a spiritually correct successor to his lay predecessor. Lydgate in fact earlier alludes to these lines of *Troilus* in his *Complaynt of a Lovere's Lyfe*, a reworking of the *Book of the Duchess* in which his version of the Black Knight uses Chaucer's anaphora to lament the fate of love-struck men.[17] The implication of what is thus a double allusion is that Lydgate, as he has demonstrated in the *Complaynt*, could, if he wished, supply yet another effort in the vein of Chaucer's courtly work, but he has already attained a level of spiritual insight that Chaucer reaches only at the end of *Troilus*.

The point of this stanza is not that Lydgate is advertising his actual rejection of a prior career as a poet of secular, amorous verse. (Indeed, we are not even certain when either poem was written, although an earlier date has traditionally been assumed for the *Complaynt*, if only by analogy with the chronology of Chaucer's oeuvre.) The point is rather that Lydgate is making a claim, vis-à-vis his poetic relationship with Chaucer, that he, specifically, is qualified to produce a more exalted form of poetry. In the following stanza, he makes this claim almost explicit:

Wherefore I wil now pleynly my stile redresse,
Of on to speke, at nede that will not faile.
Allas, for dool I ne can nor may expresse
Hir passand pris, and that is no mervaile.
O wynd of grace, now blowe into my saile,
O auriat lycour of Clyo, for to wryte
Mi penne enspire of that I wold endyte. (8–14)

By punningly affirming that he will his "stile redresse," he is saying, on the one hand, simply that he will redirect his "penne" from the "thowsand" rejected "storiis" (of, for example, unfaithful women like Criseyde) to the Virgin, who, rather than advancing her servants "with woo," "will not faile" "at nede." On the other hand – and more

significantly — he is saying that he will make the *style* of his writing more
suitable to this divine rather than erotic object of praise.[18] In particular, he
will write in the ostentatiously lofty style he names here and elsewhere
"auriat" — a semantically rich term which was one of his many
contributions to the English language. Next, by insisting that he "ne can
nor may expresse" the "passand pris" of his object, he is — given the
119-line panegyric that follows — calling attention to his qualification, as
wielder of aureate language, for doing just this. Revealingly, it is "Clyo,"
the muse of history, on whom he calls for aid. This invocation may at first
seem both generically and (given the anti-pagan allusion of the previous
stanza) thematically inappropriate, until we realize that its function is
self-referential. It is a reminder that the speaker is a monastic writer who,
given the histories and chronicles for which monasteries were famous,
would be identified with this muse more than any other. This invocation
thus associates him with the high-style secular poetic tradition that, in
respect to English poetry, Chaucer represents, and, at the same time,
serves as a marker of his own personalization of that tradition.[19]

Related to this strategy of personalization is the specificity of
the poem's first-person pronoun, such that it may only be occupied
by a unique authorial speaker.[20] Although this is a characteristic feature of
the *dit*, in devotional works the "I" is much more commonly generic and
hence occupiable by any reader who wishes to use the poem in his or her
devotions. The most pertinent example of such a work is Chaucer's *An
ABC*, a translation of a prayer to the Virgin in Deguileville's *La pelerinage
de la vie humaine*. Lydgate knew both the original and the translation
quite well, and the latter has been said to have influenced his
Commendation.[21] The first-person pronoun in Chaucer's poem is that
of a public prayer; it belongs to the poet but also, by design, to any of the
poem's reciters. If Lydgate had left off the first three stanzas of his
Commendation, this poem — much of the rest of which comes from the
Anticlaudianus of Alan of Lille — would have been no exception; or, to
put this point another way, with his strategically placed metapoetic
exordium, he has made the poem's "I" unoccupiable by design.[22]

A third aspect of Lydgate's poetic practice exemplified by this poem
is its deployment of epideictic address, which is in one sense its
most obvious and predictable feature, the fourth stanza beginning,
"O sterne of sternys with thi stremys clere" (22). The epideictic mode
(i.e., verse that possesses the aim of praise or blame) was a natural avenue
of expression for someone in Lydgate's position. This mode, as Curtius
has documented, pervaded the Latin poetry of the clerisy, and

Lydgate's reading as well as his writing of verse would have been guided by the theory, current in the late Middle Ages through Averroes's paraphrase of Aristotle's *Poetics*, that held poetic discourse to be fundamentally epideictic.[23] Yet, in another sense, epideixis becomes for Lydgate his special and most powerful formal strategy in what eventually constitutes his laureate poetics. With this mode he produces a circuit of relays among poet, addressee, and poem, thereby elevating the status of each.

In its encomiastic register, an epideictic poem expresses the ideality of its praised object through some effect of heightening. Whether through style, rhetoric, or matter, the poem must in some way supply a verbal analogue for the extraordinary nature of that which it praises — it must, as Joel Fineman has said, "add something to merely mimetic description."[24] Further, epideictic heightening is essentializing as well as additive — it stands for what is most true about its object even while adding something that is not phenomenally present.[25] By design this heightening raises the praised object above the sphere of the ordinary, and yet its stylistic grandeur and hyperboles are not intended as fictions. They are, rather, an attempt to hypostatize the object's transcendental quality. In short, the great claim of the epideictic poet is that he or she brings into being a verbal double of the ideal nature of that which he or she praises. In the extreme, this claim goes beyond the analogical and insists that poetry may manifest ideality per se. Epideictic poetry may become, as Fineman puts it, "a self-example of what it speaks about ... an identification guaranteed by a specific kind of idealizing speech: a speech of Cratylitic actuality in which sign and referent forcefully correspond." In epideictic poetry, "knowledge of the ideal *is* the ideal," and this situation "produces a discourse whose referential truth is tautologically or autologically confirmed because such language *is* the things of which it speaks."[26] The most authentic poem of praise, according to this understanding, evolves from super-mimesis into pure being; it no longer only represents that which it praises, but becomes an instance of the same ideal nature that makes that very object praiseworthy.

This understanding of poetic praise would have been quite familiar to Lydgate. When he writes, in his verse commentary on Psalm 88, the "Fynal intent of euery creature/Shulde resounne to Goddys hih preysing,"[27] he articulates what amounts to the same theory, through the theological commonplace that a human being becomes most fundamentally God-like when praising God. To the extent that poetry has been singled out — since at least the time of the Psalmist and perhaps from its very beginnings — as the privileged medium of praise, it becomes the place *par excellence* where a human being may reveal the divinity of his or her soul. Surely not coincidentally, Lydgate's most accomplished verse, as has long been recognized, is most often a species of praise.[28] Moreover, because of the close relation between the epideictic and the didactic ("The most important innovation in epideictic theory after Aristotle," writes O. B. Hardison, "was the idea that praise and blame should be didactic")[29] — one may fairly say that praise is the single most pervasive aim of Lydgate's poetry. For him, the celebration of an ideal is always implied by a didactic exhortation toward that ideal. And if we include, as variants of these exhortations, laments for, and condemnations of, a departure from an ideal (i.e., complaints and satire), we account for most of Lydgate's hugely varied oeuvre. Even his long historical poems, as many have observed, are less filled with story-telling than with pious or patriotic celebration and moralistic exhortation.[30]

What is more, for Lydgate, poetry — and aureate poetry in partic- ular — is itself a worthy object of praise, and the terms in which he expresses this worthiness shed light on the crucial role that epideixis plays in his poetics. On the one hand, poetry translates the ideal into the human sphere by a process of illumination. As he puts it in the paean to poets and writing that opens Book 4 of the *Fall of Princes* (to glance ahead in his career), "God sette writyng & lettres in sentence,/Ageyn the dulnesse of our infirmyte,/This world tenlumyne be crafft of elloquence" (4.29–31).[31] For Lydgate, the "crafft of elloquence" is a mode of illuminating bestowed by God on writers so that they may make manifest eternal truths not otherwise available in our state of "infirmyte." On the other hand, this illumination not only describes what poetry provides but also, as the following passage from the *Life of Our Lady* illustrates, describes the process of its own inspiration:

> Now, fayre sterre, O sterre of sterres all —
> Whose light to see angelleȝ delyte —
> So late the golde dewe of thy grace fall
> Into my breste like skales, fayre and white,
> Me to enspyre of that I wolde endyte —
> With thylke bame sent downe by myracle
> Whan the hooly goost the made his habitacle —
> And the licour of thy grace shede
> Into my penne, tenlumyne this dite,

Throrough thy supporte þat I may procede
Sumwaht to saye in laude ande preys of the. (50–60)

Here, both poet and poem receive divine inspiration through the illuminating power of the "fayre sterre" in a manner analogous to the way that the Virgin is impregnated by the "hooly goost"; so illuminated, the poet "may procede" to reflect back that very divine light, in the "laude and preys" that will illuminate his readers. In short, for Lydgate, poetry both divinely illuminates and is divinely illuminated. And by figuring the Virgin's illumination as the falling of "golde dewe," he all but names his aureate style as his poetry's corresponding illumination. He thereby conceives of this style as both instrument for illuminating and manifestation of his poetry's illuminated state — the "licour of [the Virgin's] grace" of this passage being one and the same as the "auriat lycour of Clyo" that he invokes at the beginning of the *Commendation*. Crucially, he supplements this description of this double illumination by supplying a reflexive *instance* of it: the lofty, ornate rendering of this very passage. Through its own aureation, this passage radiates the divine inspiration for which it asks, and in this way it exemplifies what Fineman terms the autological quality of epideictic representation: in pointing toward something else, it is always also pointing back at itself.[32]

When combined with Lydgate's literary historical personalization of his sources and the specificity of the poet's "I," this autological dynamic takes in the historically specific person of the poet as well as the poem. Not only does an equivalence obtain between the praised object and the praising medium, but also the praising subject must likewise be elevated; to be adequate to the poetry that is in turn adequate to the ideal nature of that which it describes, this subject becomes symmetrically idealized. When a poem's first-person speaker is occupiable, as is typical of devotional poetry, this idealization serves as an instrument for the formation of a spiritual community. The poet, as well as his or her readers, in the moment of experiencing the poem, are all joined in communion with God. In contrast, a first-person pronoun specifically denoted as the author's, as in much of Lydgate's work, restricts this elevation to the historically unique poet, relegating to the reader the role of vicarious author rather than participant subject.

Lydgate himself theorizes this particularized version of self-elevating epideixis in the paean to poets and writing in the *Fall of Princes*. After providing a long list of the persons and things that writing has monumentalized (e.g., "Writyng is cause that herto is remembrid/Lyf of prophetis & patriarches olde" [4.43—44]), he adds, "Wryting of old, with lettres aureate,/Labour of poetis doth hili magnefie," and provides as an example of such writing that of "Petrak, in Rome laureat" (4.106—8). His claim is that a writer, in transforming "with lettres aureate" the fleeting into the permanent, at the same time memorializes his specific person. Hence, the idealization of Petrarch as laureate is a direct consequence of the latter having, e.g., "in his Affrik comendid Scipioun" (4.114).[33] Lydgate, with his own "lettres aureate," seeks both to textualize an ideal and in the process to "magnefie" his own "[l]abour." We should not, however, understand this aim as merely self-serving; for Lydgate, there was, no doubt, great spiritual value in this ontological identification of praising subject, praised object, and medium of praise. Since in this sort of epideixis the gulfs collapse between speaker and spoken — between word and thing — his aureate poetry, in theory, does not merely utter truth but is the very form truth takes in a fallen world.

To return to the *Commendation*, we may now understand the nature of Lydgate's lament, in the third stanza, to be "vnworthi . . . to loue such on [i.e., the Virgin]" and his request for the aid of "hir grace" to enable his "laude and presying" (15—20). He is here at once asking for and demonstrating the same sort of illumination as in the *Life of Our Lady*, in which he makes present "the licour of [the Virgin's] grace" through his "laude ande preys." He is asserting that, once so illuminated, he will no longer be "vnworthi," and, not coincidentally, he begins his praise proper in the following stanza with that most characteristic of epideictic tropes, an image of stellar superabundance that is virtually identical to the one that dominates the prologue of the *Life of Our Lady*: "O sterne of sternys with thi stremys clere."[34] The remainder of the poem consists of a series of traditional metaphorical apostrophes and amplifications, e.g., "O closid gardeyn" (36), "O tresti turtyl" (78), and "O precyous perle" (127). With these images, the reader receives an overabundance of supplementary description, which, as a conscious exaltation of poetic language, becomes itself a manifestation of that which it describes. Yet, lest the reader, after 16 stanzas of such rhetoric, forget the thrust of the first three and that, in this instance, the exaltation of the medium not only exalts the praised object but also a historically specific praising subject, in the final stanza the poet, quite intrusively, reappears. "Why nere I connyng the forto discrive?" (137) he interjects in the stanza's central line, and once more we are confronted with a first-person pronoun that we, as readers, cannot occupy. This line awkwardly refers back to — which is to say, is a strategically placed signpost of — the poet who in the second stanza laments that he "ne can nor may expresse" the Virgin's "passand pris." And at the same time, it lays claim to the very "connyng" that it denies. Inspired with the "auriat lycour of Clyo," this poet has in fact nearly completed his description of the Virgin, and, just as he earlier conveyed his mastery of the poetry of "Cupide," he now implicitly claims mastery of epideictic devotional verse. Leveraging the long-established convention of the humility topos, Lydgate characteristically points the epideictic finger back at himself by claiming that he has not (successfully) pointed at all.[35]

One may justifiably wonder why Lydgate, as a monk, would have been inclined to indulge in such poetic self-aggrandizement. The first three stanzas, after all, are plainly inessential to the poem's devotional function, and the remainder, *sans* the line in the final stanza, reads well enough without them. Surely from a monk — whose most basic selfhood ought to be a homogeneous *imago dei* — we should expect the specificity of his "I" to be emptied into a universalized, Spitzerian lyric ego.[36] Of course, Lydgate was to some extent encouraged to depart from this requirement by the precedent of the Ricardians, as his experiments with the English *dit* indicate. But his eclipse of even his English predecessors in this regard requires a fuller explanation.

Lydgate did in fact have a model for this sort of self-aggrandizement, but one not where most might look. Following the Lancastrian revolution, on the threshold of his laureate career, he took a cue in this regard not from Chaucer, the so-called father of English poetry, but from Christine de Pizan, in her day one of the reigning literary authorities in France. As discussed in Chapter 1, with the ascendancy of the Lancastrians, the court's understanding of the value of poetry shifted markedly. Formerly considered primarily cultural capital, poetry was valued by Lancastrians as a political instrument that nonetheless retained cultural prestige. In adjusting to this climate, a vernacular poet seeking royal patronage would have been alert to the ramifications of any attempt of the new king to secure the services of another vernacular poet. Hence, when very soon after his seizure of the crown — as early as 1400 — Henry IV tried to persuade Christine de Pizan to come to England, even going so far as to keep her son Jean de Castel virtually hostage, an aspiring poet might very well have sought to discover what it was that so attracted the king to Christine's writing.

Among the works of Christine that Henry saw was her *Epistre Othea*.[37] Framed as a pedagogical letter from Othea, a goddess of Wisdom whom Christine apparently invents, to Hector of Troy, whom the French royal family considered their ancestor, this didactic, authoritative, and encyclopedic work consists of 100 verse texts given in the voice of Othea and, for each, a sometimes extensive accompanying prose gloss and spiritualized allegory given in the voice of the author. Although the scope of its matter and the sheer complexity of its form suggest that Christine intended the work to serve a variety of purposes, there is no doubt that one of these was to be a *Fürstenspiegel*, as indicated by the pedagogical frame and introductory rubric ("Ci commence l'epistre Othea la deesse, que elle envoya a Hector de Troye quant il estoit en l'aage de quinze ans" ["Here begins the letter of Othea, the goddess, which she sent to Hector of Troy when he was 15 years old"]).[38] As such, the work aims to supply, in the form of a systematic reconciliation of classical and Christian thought, the basis for the formation of a wise and virtuous prince (although she certainly also had her own 15-year-old son in mind as an audience). Further, like all mirrors for princes, this one serves the additional purpose of making the noble reader to whom it is dedicated appear to possess the qualities that it transmits and therefore be truly both noble and qualified to rule, and making the author who voices the dedication appear to possess the innate worthiness and authority needed to bestow such advice on a prince. That these sorts of texts were in great demand by the late medieval nobility is well attested by the exceptional popularity of the paradigm of the genre, the *Secreta secretorum*. This work pretends to be a letter of Aristotle to Alexander the Great, and, from its earliest extant versions in Arabic, made its way into Latin and then into most of the European vernaculars, including a version begun by Lydgate late in life and finished after his death by Benedict Burgh.[39] The *Epistre* also was quite popular — albeit on a smaller scale — surviving in some 45 manuscripts and even receiving a translation in Lancastrian England by Stephen Scrope (c.1440).[40]

Henry IV not only read at least one version of the *Epistre* dedication, but he was also the object of it. As J. C. Laidlaw has shown, the unnamed king in the dedication of the version in London, BL Harley 219, long thought to be Charles VI of France, is instead Henry, and the manuscript therefore one of those Christine reports sending to him to persuade him to allow her son to return.[41] In addition, Henry perhaps saw an earlier version of the work sent by Christine to her son via John Montague, earl of Salisbury, who had brought Jean to England in 1398 as a companion for his son (likely Thomas, one of Lydgate's future patrons). When Montague was killed in 1400 in his attempt to restore Richard II to the throne, Henry inherited his manuscripts, and perhaps this is what spurred him to invite

Christine to England. But, regardless of whether he was already familiar with the *Epistre*, upon reading her dedication in the Harley copy he no doubt quickly saw its propagandistic value. Having just deposed a legitimate monarch and facing numerous armed challenges to his claim, he must have been pleased at having in his possession an authoritative *Fürstenspiegel* by an eminent foreign poet (and friend of a former enemy) that begins by addressing him as "Prince excellent de haute renommee" ("Excellent prince of high renown") (1) and later refers to him as "Roy noble et haut chivaler conquerour" ("Noble and high king, conqueror knight") (5). Assuming the role of a contemporary Aristotle, Christine figures Henry as Alexander, and in this way makes him appear a kingly conqueror rather than an upstart usurper. Although Henry could put down rebellions by force, he knew he could not achieve legitimacy in this manner, and hence he rather urgently sought the cultural aura provided by the kind of works he discovered Christine capable of producing.[42]

Hence, although it is rather easily overlooked, Christine's 54-line verse dedication represents a historically crucial instance of epideictic address. It is among the key literary texts that together inspired the large-scale Lancastrian intervention into high culture, which in turn led to Lydgate's domination of fifteenth-century poetry. Significantly, in this dedication, the central figure is Christine herself. After an initial eight lines of obsequious praise — which, compared to the versions she made for French nobles, are notable for their brevity and restraint — the dedication becomes more or less entirely self-referential: she provides first her given name ("Ffemme ignorant, suy nomee Cristine" ["Uneducated woman, I am named Christine"] [12]); and next, by way of touting the intellectual authority of her father, her surname ("Meistre Thomas de Pizan autrement/De Boulloigne fu dit et surnommee" ["Master Tommaso de Pizan he was, otherwise called and named De Boulogne"] [18–19]); and then proceeds to explain and defend the work that follows.[43] Quite plainly not at all "ignorant," in this passage Christine, by her self-naming and recording of her paternity, closely associates her empirical person with her literary authority. This association, as a number of critics have observed, is characteristic of her work as a whole and — even in the context of the very author-conscious literature of late medieval France — in many ways unprecedented.[44] Although in this instance the structure of epideictic address encourages this association, in all cases the most basic motivating factor is, for Christine, not genre but gender. Throughout her career, she creates authority for herself through a confrontation with the long history of male authors, insisting that her sex allows her to perceive what they have not. In conveying this authority, she repeatedly asserts (sometimes directly, sometimes less so) the fact that her "I" is not the traditional impersonal poetic or scholarly "I" — which was always indeed a male "I" — but is instead the "I" of Christine, a particularized "Ffemme ignorant."

This agenda was doubtlessly lost on Henry IV, who would have been too much absorbed by the political ramifications of her texts to notice their ubiquitous polemic against antifeminism. What must have struck him about the *Epistre* dedication was its prominent representation of its author as a living, historically specific, authoritative poet, and, concomitantly, the manner in which this representation, through the structure of epideictic address, constructed *him* as a historically specific and legitimate living king. This is the great magic of epideixis: as long as poet and king may be understood to have fundamentally *different* and therefore independent bases of authority — and, as a female poet from Italy residing in France, this was obviously the case with Christine vis-à-vis Henry — they may participate in a cycle of reciprocal elevation.[45] A poet transmutes his or her eminence into princely magnificence, and, conversely, the aura of the prince whom the poet addresses becomes a sign of the poet's intellectual and moral authority. In short, inasmuch as the poet's eminence is not already patently the product of royal projection, poet and prince may mutually legitimize each other. Henry IV's illegitimate seizure of the throne served as a powerful motivating force for such literary strategies. With many in England either still believing Richard II to be alive or backing a better claimant to the throne, the royalty of Henry's person specifically — rather than his kingship more generally — desperately required legitimation.

Henry, however, was unable to procure the services of Christine. Not long after receiving her manuscripts, he allowed her son to return, after which she had no more contact with the king, whom she, like most observers in France, thought to be mere usurper (a few years later she refers to him as "la dure pestilence" ["the cruel pestilence"] of Fortune who had "sattribua la couronne" ["stolen the crown"]).[46] Nonetheless, the lesson of Henry's interest in her work was not lost on the new generation of English poets seeking his patronage. As we will see in the next chapter, Hoccleve seems to have begun at least the public phase of his poetic career as an explicit attempt to become Christine's English (and male) substitute. Lydgate also had some sort of early acquaintance with Christine's work and specifically with the *Epistre Othea*, his most explicit (if not most significant) debt appearing in the *Troy Book*'s account of Hector's death, when he departs from his source to draw on the *Epistre*'s moralizing explanation of the fall of this prince.[47]

Although we do not know precisely when Lydgate first saw the *Epistre*, we do know that by the first decade of the fifteenth century (that is, quite early in his career) he had some form of contact with a member of the family that had possession of the manuscript – namely, heir apparent Henry of Monmouth. (A letter survives, probably written sometime between 1406 and 1408, from the Prince of Wales to the abbot of Bury St. Edmunds requesting that Lydgate be allowed to remain at Gloucester College, Oxford, to pursue his studies.)[48] At about the time that Henry IV received his dedicated copy of the *Epistre*, the Prince of Wales turned 15.[49] It is not unreasonable to suppose that the king would pass on this authoritative education for a 15-year-old Hector, prince of Troy, to his own ambitious son, prince of Troynovaunt. And if this is the case, it is likely that the prince in turn showed the manuscript to the monk and aspiring poet whom he had met at Oxford – and for whom, as it turned out, he had great plans.

THE FIRST ENGLISH LAUREATE

In retrospect, one sees that Prince Hal found in the monk of Bury precisely what his father was hoping but failed to get from Christine. With some irony, however, the prince, in commissioning the *Troy Book* from Lydgate, was seeking to intervene in high culture to legitimate himself not just in the eyes of the public but also in those of the king. After having virtually ruled the country in his sick father's stead during 1410–11, he had been summarily dismissed by the latter in November 1411. Then, at the end of September 1412, he had entered London with a large group of supporters and held his famous tête-à-tête with his father, during which he supposedly offered the king a dagger so that he might kill him. Although they reconciled, the prince's position was still shaky, as he had no role in government or in affairs overseas. No doubt fully aware that his father's health was tenuous, the prince turned to rebuilding his aura, restoring his image as military hero and epitome of English chivalric culture. As Lydgate tells us in the prologue of the *Troy Book*, the prince commissioned the poet on 31 October 1412 to render into English verse what was considered to be the most authoritative version of the most important narrative of ancient history, the *Historia destructionis Troiae* of Guido delle Colonne.[50]

One may plausibly suppose that the prince, then 26 and a military as well as political veteran, remembered the teenaged Hector of the *Epistre Othea* from his own teen years and wished to have at his disposal an epic account of Hector's later heroism. It may be objected, of course, that the central importance of the matter of Troy to late medieval culture in general and England in particular would have been by itself enough to motivate the prince's commission. Yet, the series of invocations with which Lydgate opens the *Troy Book* encodes a more specific royal interest. Initially, with its opening words "O Myghty Mars," this passage works the same way as does the one from the *Life of Our Lady* examined above, only in this case it is Mars rather than Mary who is the object of epideictic address, who emanates the illuminating "sterne light," directs Lydgate's "stile," and fills his "penne" with "aureat lycour" (pro. 1, 29–31). But then, from this address to him who "hast of manhod the magnificence," Lydgate abruptly turns to seek aid instead from a number of *feminine* sources, beginning with, rather remarkably, "Othea, goddesse of prudence," who serves as an intercessor, a means to "make[n] Clyo for to ben [his] muse" (pro. 37–40). In turn it is one of the latter's "sustren," Calliope, whom he finally asks "tenlumyne ... þis wirk" (pro. 41, 59). Clio, as muse of history, is, as I have already mentioned, a signpost for Lydgate's person, which is especially marked in this case, given the genre of this work and, more particularly, the historiographical musings that follow in the prologue. (Notably, he claims Clio in these lines as specifically *his* muse.) Mars, as "myghty lorde" and "souereyn and patrown" of "cheualry" (pro. 4, 7), is a more or less transparent marker for the rather martial prince. Othea thus appears as the medium that relates these two, and the outcome of this relationship is Calliope, who, as the muse of epic, stands for the work that follows. To put these relationships formulaically, Mars joined with Clio by means of Othea produces Calliope, which amounts to saying that the Prince of Wales brought together with Lydgate by means of the *Epistre Othea* produces the *Troy Book*.

Invocations to Mars, Clio, and Calliope are, of course, appropriate in this context and hence do not by themselves imply anything special, but the presence of Othea, which cannot so easily be explained, disrupts the conventionality and flags the more specific meaning of this series of names. In these very opening lines, Lydgate puts into operation an epideictic circuit involving the prince, himself, the style and matter of the poem, and the authority of both the antique poetic tradition and an eminent contemporary vernacular poet; and he acknowledges his source for this strategy and signals its nature to his patron by tipping his hat to Christine's authoritative divine self-projection, if not to Christine herself. With this circuit established, he then recounts the circumstances of the prince's commissioning. At the beginning and end of this well-known passage (pro. 69–120) stands its author, who initially asserts the purity of his motives ("For God I take hy3ly to wyttenesse . . ." [pro. 69]) and who concludes by announcing his intention to begin the "emprise" (pro. 119) that the prince has commissioned. Between these poles the passage is all about the prince, and one of the functions of this intervening matter is to reinforce the associations of the introductory invocations. If we were earlier in doubt about the prince's association with Mars, these lines make that plain through their repeated concern with the prince's martial "manhood" (pro. 85, 93). The mediating role of the *Epistre Othea*, as well, is perhaps reprised in the reference to the "Ioye" that the Prince has found reading the matter "of antiquite" (pro. 79–80). The more primary aim of this passage, however, is to document the prince's twofold rationale for the project and indicate the relations between his royal person and that rationale. First, the prince (according to Lydgate) understands the Troy story to be filled with examples of exemplary aristocratic martial behavior – the "worthynes" of "verray kny3thod" and the "prowesse of olde chiualrie" (pro. 75–78). Readers of the *Troy Book* should, as the prince himself does with his "bokys of antiquite," pursue "vertu" by "example" of the ideal knights the work depicts (pro. 80–82). Second, England ought to have this "noble story" available in its own "tonge"; if England is to realize its imperial destiny, then it may no longer be culturally and linguistically dependent on "latyn" and, especially, "frensche" (pro. 112–15; "y-writen as wel in oure langage" [114] means both "written also in our language" and "written as skillfully in our language").[51] In relation to these two aims, on the one hand the prince represents a living ideal knight – as indicated by the 21-line panegyric sandwiched between the accounts of the aims (pro. 84–104). On the other hand, as the individual "To whom schal longe by successioun/For to gouerne Brutys Albyoun" (pro. 103), he is an embodiment of the nation that is laying claim to its share of the "trouthe" of the Troy story. With this double valence, the person of the prince hypostatizes the stated *raison d'être* of the *Troy Book*: he is at once a living instance of its exempla and a personification of its political claims. Hence, when Lydgate says he will "write it for his sake," and, in conclusion, will begin "[i]n his worship for a memorial" (pro. 110, 120), he is quite concisely describing the essence of (at least what the prince wants from) the project: an authoritative and moralistic historical narrative that is also a memorial to a living prince, his massively amplified encomium.[52]

In the lines that immediately follow, Lydgate supplies an exceedingly ornate, 26-line astronomical dating of the moment at which he is beginning his translation. Although jarring in its sudden appearance, this passage or something akin to it, in the context of the dialectic governing the epideictic aims of this prologue, is precisely what we should expect. Through his elevated diction and lavish rhetoric, Lydgate casts a historically transcendent aura upon the moment at which he sets out on his great work, thereby quasi-sacralizing a spot in time in the same manner that, for example, Guido does for the moment in which the Greeks set out for Troy: "Whan þat þe soote stormis of Aprille,/Vn-to þe rote ful lawe gan distille ...." (1.3907–8, which Lydgate copies from Chaucer via their common source in Guido). The lofty style that Guido uses to describe this event conveys the elevation to atemporal permanence of a discrete point in time, the apotheosis of history into myth. When Lydgate deploys the same loftiness to describe the moment at which he begins the *Troy Book*, he seeks to give his own work and his role as its composer this aspect of permanence, to elevate both poem and poet into the realm of the mythological and ideal. Along with being a "memorial" to Henry, the poem, this dating passage suggests, will be a memorial to itself, the passage functioning to this end as an inaugurating auto-panegyric, raising the poem and poet to the same status as its patron.

The *Troy Book* thus has two idealized agents at its center: the prince who commissions it, who exemplifies its ideals, and who will presumably recover in the future what it describes as lost in the past; and the translator who fulfills the commission and thereby effects the first stage of recovery. Tellingly, it is to the second of these agents that the last two-thirds of the prologue is devoted. In this space, Lydgate describes the ideal practice the *poet* ought to exemplify – namely, the conveying of "trouthe" – and, as he makes clear, in this context "trouthe" means historical veracity. Without "writyng" that records "[w]ith-oute feynynge" and "[w]ith-oute fauour," no models of "grete prowes" would remain, and we would be "begyled/Of necligence thoruӡ forӡetilnesse" (pro. 154–83). If, in contrast, the past is rendered truthfully, the "lack or prys" apportioned by "clerkis" will be authoritative directives for the behavior of future "conquerouris" (pro. 174–88).

This formulation of literary truth, although it largely derives from Guido's concerns in his prologue, conveniently conforms to the tradition of monastic history writing.[53] Lydgate, having earlier hinted at this tradition with the figure of Clio, here ushers it into the foreground, and he does so because a social identity as monastic historian proves, for two principal reasons, crucial to his purposes. First, this tradition possesses a (putatively) autonomous authority vis-à-vis whatever political regime happens to be current. A monastic historian owes his allegiance first to the Church, then to his order, and then to the tradition in which he writes — the very continuity of which takes codicological form in the many continuations of, for example, Higden's *Polychronicon*.[54] Any allegiance a historian may feel toward his sovereign is — in theory, at least — a distant fourth, and precisely because of this distance, a historian may effectively operate as legitimizer of a specific political regime. As long as readers believe that a historian does indeed distribute "lak or prys" only as "men disserue" (pro. 187) and not according to political interest, then that historian's praise of a sovereign carries the authoritative weight of both Church and history. Second, monastic history writing supplies a wholly traditional precedent for Lydgate's making his own person central to his authorizing strategies. This genre of writing, as I observed in Chapter 1, uses the biographical element of the academic preface as an analogue for the veracity of the history it reports. The factuality of this history receives confirmation via the self-evident factuality of a named, historically specific author. What Matthew Paris, for example, claims about the past seems true at least partially because he textualizes signposts that locate *him* outside the text in a particular time and place.[55]

By assuming the pose of monastic historian, Lydgate thus takes up a natural and convincing authorial persona that possesses a parallel function to Christine's in her dedication of the *Epistre*. Christine, as a historically specific author, possesses patently different authority than that of the English court, and this enables her fulsome praises to appear to authenticate the king as such. Praise from Lydgate as monastic historian operates in the same fashion: as a monk of the powerful abbey of Bury St. Edmunds, writing in a tradition initiated by Bede and persisting in an unbroken line through William of Malmesbury, Matthew Paris, Higden, and Lydgate's own contemporary, Thomas Walsingham, he bestows praise from the standpoint of an independent authority that goes back as far as the English royalty itself.[56] It is hence hardly a coincidence that Lydgate's first explicit mention of his social identity appears to occur in the *Troy Book*; in this historical encomium, he presents his Benedictine

status to credentialize his participation in the genre, to distinguish his
authority from his patron's, and as an excuse to call attention to himself.

In short, Lydgate's social identity provides a reflexive and mutually
reinforcing counterpart to the figure of the prince. Possessing an entirely
distinct basis of authority, Lydgate's monastic historical veracity finds a
not-so-secret sharer in the prince's dynastic authenticity. Or, to put this
point another way, if the cultural authority of the *Troy Book* finds its
ultimate confirmation in its royal commissioning, the historical truth the
poem claims to recover conversely underwrites the political authority of
the prince. Hardly the naïve propagandist he is sometimes taken to be,
Lydgate records his full cognizance of the mutuality of this corroboration.
After stating once again the maxim of objective history writing —
"Clerkis wil write, and excepte noon,/The playne trouthe whan a man is
goon" (pro. 193–94) — he (unlike Guido) goes on to argue for the
political utility of this supposedly politically neutral writing. Sounding
much like Boccaccio in the *Trattatello*, Lydgate states that the "writing
trewe" of historical poets ought to be "cherisched" and "hounoured
gretly" by "lordes," because it is precisely this writing that advertises
those lords' "manhood and prowes,/Her kny3thood eke and her
worthynes" (pro. 195–200) — i.e., that establishes the intrinsic merit
which legitimates their status as lords. Importantly, clerks have not simply
"enacted" the "renoun" of lords (and here the verb "enact" means to
record in a chronicle),[57] but they have also "gilte" it (pro. 198–99). "To
gild," as its more common denotation suggests, means for Lydgate to put
into aureate language or, more generally, to heighten panegyrically. He
therefore insists that historical poetry, just like its devotional counterpart,
should not simply record the "worthynes" of the object it describes,
but should also imitate that worthiness in the loftiness of its style.
It should not merely rehearse "al þe trouthe/With-oute fraude"
(pro. 203–4) about "her manhood and prowes" but *manifest* martial
glory in an act of stylistic prowess.

This notion raises potential problems of crossed purposes and generic
conflict, which have in fact been present from the beginning of the
prologue. These may be expressed collectively as the question of how one
may create in a single text both factual history and encomium without the
history becoming mere flattery and the encomium patently disingenuous.
Such problems arise not because Lydgate is a poor thinker but because the
potential advantages of his conflation of historian and panegyrist
outweigh its liabilities. As suggested by the immediately subsequent
passage, with this conflation Lydgate reaches toward a sociopolitical

identity as poet that would enable the implicit claims of the dating passage to be realized. In this passage, he seeks to establish the poet as possessing a literary authority akin to the prince's political one so that the poet may serve the prince without being a servant of the prince:

> For elles certeyn [without writing] the grete worthynesse
> Of her [i.e., lords'] dedis hadde ben in veyn;
> For-dirked age elles wolde haue slayn
> By lenthe of ʒeris þe noble worthi fame
> Of conquerours, and pleynly of her name
> For-dymmed eke the lettris aureat,
> And diffaced the palme laureat,
> Whiche þat þei wan by knyʒthod in her dayes,
> Whos fretyng rust newe and newe assayes
> For to eclipse the honour and the glorie
> Of hiʒe prowes, which clerkis in memorie
> Han trewly set thoruʒ diligent labour,
> And enlumyned with many corious flour
> Of rethorik, to make us comprehende
> The trouthe of al, as it was kende[.] (206–20)

There is a seamless transition here from the epideictic object's "grete worthynesse" to the "enlumyned" nature of the epideictic poet's language, a transition accomplished by the double duty performed by the couplet "aureat"/"laureat." This couplet refers backward syntactically and figuratively to the praised object's "worthynesse," and in the same gesture refers forward – via the standard Lydgatean connotations of *aureat* – to the "many corious flour/Of rethorik" of "clerkis." Just as we saw in Petrarch's laureation address, the implied claim is that poets, as conquerors of time, deserve as much fame – and, hence, as much autonomy – as the "conquerours" whose "worthi fame" they "[h]an trewly set."

Lydgate at this point has laid the groundwork for his later explicit designation of this claim as that of a poet laureate, the rhyme pair "aureat"/"laureat" – one of his favorites, as Seth Lerer has shown – more or less revealing his hand.[58] In writing a poem in the "worschip for a memorial" of the man who, perhaps more than any previous English prince, conflated his individuality with his nation, Lydgate hints here at the homologous conflation of his own individuality with his literary authority.[59] In the climate of patronage that existed in 1412, the epideictic formula had to include the prince's historically specific individuality, as well as his abstract, generalized worthiness. The most effective reflexive

construction of the prince's royal aura would therefore be performed by a
historically specific, but generically authoritative, poet laureate. Like the
prince, this poet must possess an authority tied to his empirical person
and at the same time be an individual putatively without internal conflict.
Idealized, flawlessly unified, and transparently devoted to orthodox
values, this poetic individuality, like the prince's political one, would
represent a selfhood essentially without an interior.

   Lydgate devotes much of the remainder of the prologue to
a measurement of the literary past according to the historian's ruler,
running through a catalogue of Troy story *auctores* from Homer to the
very source for this passage, "Guydo" (pro. 360), and holding each up
to the standard of "cronyculeris" (pro. 246). But what he does not
locate among these is a precedent for the somewhat different
literary authority that he is claiming – not merely that of the historian,
but that of a living, English laureate. Such a precedent is crucially needed,
since, in early fifteenth-century England, literary decorum, especially
when addressing a prince, did not allow a living author directly to claim
an authority equivalent to his patron's. This claim instead had to be made
through a proxy, a past *auctor* whose intellectual and cultural authority is
self-evident and whose ancestor-like relationship to the present author is
apparent. In Lydgate's case, the most suitable such *auctor* would be one
who wrote vernacular poetry in the high style and who, moreover, had
only recently died, so that he could be both eulogized and imagined as a
living, empirical person rather than as merely an authoritative name. The
obvious candidate for such an *auctor* was, of course, Chaucer, the father
of Lydgate's and Henry's common friend Thomas Chaucer and the man
who left behind his own Trojan tale, *Troilus and Criseyde*.

   In the prologue of the *Troy Book*, Lydgate, needing to distinguish
Chaucer from long-dead Latin and Greek *auctores* (or perhaps
simply finding it inappropriate to mention him in this context),
only alludes to his predecessor through the latter's own famously elusive
auctor, "Lollius" (pro. 309). In Book 2, he finds a better opportunity;
confronting the moment at which he must supply an epideictic
description of Criseyde, he demurs, insisting that his "maister Chaucer
dide his dilligence/To discryve þe gret excellence/Of hir bewte, and þat so
maisterly" (2.4679–81). He then goes on to eulogize his "maister" in
Criseyde's place, praising him for rendering into English precisely the
kind of poetry that he associates with himself, i.e., "gold dewe-dropis of
rethorik so fine" (2.4699). By singling out Chaucer's "rethorik" for
praise, Lydgate (perhaps following Hoccleve) cannily creates a verbal basis

for the inheritability of the retroactively bestowed role of "poete of Breteyne" (2.4697). Since rhetoric may be manifestly imitated, his almost exclusive emphasis on this aspect of Chaucer's verse ensures that his own deployment of "gold dewe-dropis of rethorik" exudes the same authority as that which he attributes to "Noble Galfride" (2.4697).[60] Moreover, by praising Chaucer in lofty language for his skill at, in particular, rendering lofty praise, he sets up an epideictic equivalency between himself and his predecessor. In this way, Lydgate retroactively carves out a precedent for his laureate pretensions. And, in next going on to do just what he has insisted he cannot and supply a long, aureate description of Criseyde (3.4736–61), he adds the final touch to his implied claim to be Chaucer's revisionary successor: because, as a monkish poet, he cannot "þe trouthe leue/Of Troye boke" (3.4687–88), he rewrites Chaucer's poetry in his own image.

This relationship with Chaucer and the claims it entails become most explicit in Book 3, when Lydgate reaches that notoriously fraught moment of Criseyde's abandonment of Troilus. This passage, beginning as a simple reference to Chaucer's much more detailed account of the event, develops into a quite intricate eulogy of his poetic master. Here, as in Book 2, Lydgate's Chaucer, having "gilte" (3.4237) the English language, exemplifies Lydgatean poetics. But, in this case, Chaucer's achievement qualifies him for the "laurer of oure englishe tonge" (3.4246), and Lydgate insists that Chaucer is to England what the paradigmatic poet laureate "Petrak Fraunceis" is to "Ytaille" (3.4251). In turn, he conveys the nature of his own relationship with this English laureate by means of the key term "magnifie," which appears here both in respect to what Chaucer does to the English language ("þoruȝ his poetrie/Gan oure tonge firste to magnifie" [3.4241–42]) and in respect to what Lydgate does to Chaucer ("I wil neuer fyne/So as I can, hym to magnifie/In my writynge pleinly til I dye" [3.4260–62]). In this context, the verb means at once "to adorn," "to make famous," "to praise," and "to make great or powerful"; by asserting that he will "magnifie" his predecessor through his writing in the same way that Chaucer has magnified English, Lydgate thereby constructs a pronounced epideictic equivalency, which in this instance all but explicitly names himself as heir to the "laurer."[61] At this point, he has completed his retroactive reconfiguration of his predecessor into an English poet laureate, and, since Chaucer is dead and the seat vacated, he has opened up a space for himself in the present for precisely this role.

Lydgate waits to name himself, however, until near the end of the *Troy Book*. Having finished the narrative, he records in verse the date of the poem's completion. This he gives in respect to both the birth of Christ and the reign of his patron, now Henry V and recent conqueror of France, and this latter dating naturally leads into another panegyric for Henry, a rather longer and more aureate one than that of the prologue. After digressing pointedly into a call for peace (with Henry as emperor over both realms, of course), this panegyric concludes, conventionally, in a prayer for its object of praise. But in the immediately following lines Lydgate, as by now should be expected, turns back to himself, briefly recounting the poem's commissioning, and this time naming himself and explicitly providing his social identity:

> Thus shal I ay—ther is no more to seye—
> Day & nygt for his [i.e, Henry's] expleit y-preye
> Of feythful herte & of hool entent,
> That whylom gaf me in commaundement,
> Nat yore a-go, in his faderes tyme,
> The sege of Troye on my maner to ryme,
> Moste for his sake, to speke in special.
> Al-thoug that I be boistous and rual,
> He gaf me charge this story to translate,
> Rude of konnynge, called Iohn Lydgate,
> Monke of Burie be professioun[.] (5.3459—69)

In this passage, what may at first seem a throwaway tag, "Moste for his sake," stands for the tripartite epideictic structure of the entire project. It binds together in a circuit of mutual elevation the poem, "The sege of Troye"; the patron for whose "sake" Lydgate began in his "maner to ryme"; and, finally, the specific poet doing this rhyming, "called Iohn Lydgate,/Monk of Burie be professioun." It may be objected that the latter figure appears here as more depreciated than elevated, and, indeed, following this full disclosure of Lydgate's extraliterary person, we encounter an involved insistence on his inadequacy as both monk and versifier, which continues for nearly 50 lines, culminating in a conventional plea for "correccioun" (5.3516) and a final eulogy for his "maister Chaucer" (5.3521). Yet, in initiating this self-abnegation by naming himself in his own, authorial voice and providing, as well, his specific extraliterary social identity, he has done here what his "maister" never does — and, indeed, what very few poets writing in English have done before him. Further, this final depiction of Chaucer figures his predecessor not so much, as in the prior eulogies, as a proxy for his own poetic authority but as an ideal reader, one who "liste nat poinche nor gruche at euery blot ... but seide alweie þe best" (5.3522–24). The elaborately amplified humility topos separating his self-naming from his naming of Chaucer thus serves as a signpost of what is in fact a moment of self-aggrandizement. The implication is that Chaucer has given ground to his successor, and now that the disciple has gone beyond his master he may respectfully declare for his dead precursor that there "Was neuer noon to þis day alyue ... Þat worþi was his ynkhorn for to holde" (5.3528–30).

The anxiety of influence operative this passage is unmistakable, and one function of these lines is to redirect and thereby vent this anxiety. But, from a larger perspective, this passage ushers Lydgate's laureateship into being. More than any other gesture, an act of self-identification in the context of political and poetic epideixis brings together and embodies in Lydgate's empirical person the instrumental aims of his royal patronage and the ethereal claims of the high-culture literary tradition. With this compound embodiment, an English laureateship is invented. The poet laureate — at once a notional and an embodied site of intersection between politics and culture — need not possess an actual, institutionalized title. In fact, as we will see in Chapter 5, such institutionalization spells the demise of the laureateship in its most potent form, since once it possesses concrete sociopolitical existence, the mystification it relies upon for its authority becomes much more difficult to maintain. Lydgate — as is evident, for example, in the elaborate dating of the *Troy Book* — effects this mystification by elevating the occasionality of his works from the time bound to the timeless, from something by definition historically contingent to something standing above history.[62] In the process of this elevation, the specificity of the occasion is not evaporated but rather idealized: the reasons for a poem's composition, the time at which it was begun, and the person writing it are all in the same moment both contingencies and ideals. Once these ideal contingencies are recognized by readers as such — that is, once readers acknowledge the relationship between the historically specific and the permanently authoritative — the poet who has textualized himself in this manner becomes a practicing poet laureate. Nonetheless, if this recognition is not embedded in an institution, it must, to be maintained, be constantly reproduced. Hence, it is no surprise that, scattered across the remainder of Lydgate's career, we encounter, in a wide variety of works, strategies of laureate construction similar to those that we have seen him deploy in the *Troy Book*.

Some of Lydgate's later exercises in laureate construction border on the absurd. In *The Title and Pedigree of Henry VI*, his account of the poem's commissioning and his elaborate specification of the date of composition together amount to nearly half the poem's length.[63] In this bluntly political poem, Lydgate translates, from the French of Laurence Calot (the duke of Bedford's French secretary), genealogical verses patently designed to legitimate Henry VI's dual monarchy. As he tells us in the prologue, he rendered these verses into English in 1426 for Richard Beauchamp, "My lord of Warrewyk," as well as for his commander, "My lord of Bedford, of Fraunce þe regent" (15, 47). Yet, by supplementing these 182 lines of genealogy with a 74-line self-referential prologue and a 73-line equally self-regarding epilogue (37 lines of which he dedicates to designating "þe very true date/Of this labour" [287–88]), he attempts to turn the work into something more significant than a mere translation of propagandistic verses. In particular, he attempts to exalt the historical contingencies surrounding the dual monarchy into the realm of the ideal and in this way make them appear divinely ordained, and he does this by putting this monarchy into a reflexive relationship with the authority of his notional laureateship. The overabundance of attention he gives to the poem's commissioning and composition thus serves to reaffirm (and thereby reconstruct) this laureateship both prior and subsequent to the genealogical verses he wishes to be understood as a laureate performance rather than as a transparent manipulation of history. Indeed, the sheer disproportion of this supplementary material may strike some readers as protesting too much and suggest the ideological stress that Lancastrian imperialism placed on the dynasty's fabrication of its legitimacy. Perhaps it is not an overestimation of the poet's craft to credit him with intending this effect as a formal expression of his doubts about what he was required to defend.[64]

Even more formally curious is the effect Lydgate's laureate construction has on some of his expository religious poems. Ostensibly, such poems are meant to be purely instructive and used by the lower clergy for "the transmission to the laity in an effective manner of the basic tenets of the Christian code."[65] Such instruction is rendered into verse as a mnemotechnic, and, accordingly, the language of this verse ought to be simple and straightforward, the *sentence* uncluttered, and the authorial persona, if there is one, authoritative but anonymous (and therefore reusable by any member of the clergy). For example, in *Keep Well Christ's Commandments* in the Vernon MS,[66] an unnamed but plainly sacerdotal speaker begins by admonishing, "I Warne vche leod that liueth in londe/. . . ./To kepe wel Cristes Comaundement" (1—8). He then treats each of the commandments in turn, e.g., "Stele thou nougt thi neigebors thing" (57). Lydgate, in contrast, in *An Exposition of the Pater Noster* — a poem dealing with an equally fundamental element of lay piety — begins in an entirely different register:

> Atwyxe dred and tremblying reuerence
> Astoned I am
>
> . . .
>
> My wit but feble, my memorye dulled for old,
> To medele of thyng solemply be-gonne
>
> . . .
>
> My torche is queynt, his brihtnesse doth nat procede,
> Wherfore I sholde pleynly me Excuse,
> Neer that good hope doth my brydel leede
> Toward Pernaso, to fynde there som muse[.] (1—16)[67]

A member of the laity may justifiably wonder why he or she should care that this putatively sacerdotal speaker is "[a]twyxe dred and tremblying" and, more puzzling, what "Pernaso" has to do with the Lord's Prayer. But when one places these lines in the context of Lydgate's career, one notices that within their carefully constructed modesty topos lies a coded assertion of the speaker's special status; one understands that his claims of poetic inadequacy are belied by the aid he expects to receive from "som muse" on "Pernaso." In short, one suspects that the poem possesses a purpose other than that of devotional pedagogy.

In the subsequent exposition, this suspicion seems confirmed, since, even at its most didactic moments, the poem deploys an aureate language that is hardly conducive to pedagogy, much less to memorization. For example:

> This woord Pater shewith in substaunce
> His myght ys moost grettest of excellence
> Of hevene and erthe hath al the ordenaunce
> Callyd welle of grace, myrour of sapience,
> Wich to his children, of ffadirly providence,
> Hath yeue a fraunchise aboue fraunchises alle,
> That we may boldly with devout reuerence
> Ageyn al myschef to hym for helpe calle. (95—102)

One receives the impression from such lines that the point is not so much to communicate an understanding of the "woord Pater" as it is to exude a sense of high-culture vernacular verbal mastery.[68] Improving a reader's understanding of the Lord's Prayer is less important than prompting that reader's acknowledgment of the speaker's authority over vernacular theological discourse. As if to reiterate that the latter is the real function of the poem, at the conclusion of this commentary Lydgate adds a personalized epilogue – which in itself, like the similar prologue, is inappropriate to the genre. In the event one has failed to notice the relationship between the poem's hyperbolically lofty style and the authority claimed by the speaker, Lydgate laments, "The aureat lycour was in my study dreye,/Of Calliope and al hir favour spent," and insists that he has produced "No thyng elumyned with gold, asour, nor red" (315–17). Predictably deploying conventional self-deprecation in order to elevate himself, his poem, and his characteristic style, he has wrought not so much a work of religious instruction as another laureate performance in the sphere of public devotion, one that builds on the earlier devotional works he had completed for Henry V, but in this case, perhaps, aimed at a broader audience.

In the *Fall of Princes*, the greatest work of his later career, Lydgate similarly foregrounds his authorial person, and yet this massive effort initially strikes one as a different sort of performance than that of, say, the *Troy Book*. An encyclopedic account of the inevitable fall of the great throughout history, it seems more purely cultural and scholarly in nature. Written not for a king but for that bookish Lancastrian prince, Humphrey of Gloucester, it, unlike the *Troy Book*, does not ostentatiously declare its political utility in its opening lines. Rather, in its prologue, following that of Boccaccio's translator Laurent de Premierfait, Lydgate reflects on the nature of translation and on the work before him, and then provides a list of other eminent *auctores* of "tragedies," including "Senek in Rome," "Tullius, cheeff welle off eloquence," and "Franceis Petrak" (1.253–57). Among these, the most preeminent is his "maistir Chaucer," who not only wrote "fresh comedies" but also "ful pitous tragedies" (1.246–48), and for his English predecessor he supplies an annotated bibliography occupying some 84 lines (1.274–357). He then concludes the prologue by observing how in "old tyme" poets were favored by "kyngis, pryncis in euery regioun" (1.359–60) and how in his day there remains at least one such poet-friendly prince, the "Duc off Gloucestre[,]" whose "corage neuer doth appalle/To studie in bookis off antiquite" (1.393–96), and who has therefore commanded that Lydgate should "This book translate, hym to do pleasunce/To shewe the chaung off the worldli variaunce" (1.433–34). Overall, the impression one receives is that Lydgate is a writer's writer, a learned poet self-consciously working in a long tradition, acknowledging his debts and sources, and showing his appreciation for a patron who understands the value of intellectual pursuit.

At the time of Humphrey's commission (sometime after May 1431), however, the nine-year-old Henry VI was in France and the duke was regent of England. Having regained most of the popularity he had forfeited upon his abandonment of Jacqueline of Hainault, Gloucester was soon (in November) to make his move against his archenemy, Cardinal Beaufort, in an (ultimately unsuccessful) attempt to consolidate his power and become — as long as his brother Bedford remained in France — the de facto ruler of the country.[69] The timing of his commission thus appears politically propitious, a suspicion that seems confirmed when we recall that, as a rule, Humphrey's interventions into high culture, and most famously his patronage of such Italian humanists as Pier Candido Decembrio and Tito Livio Frulovisi, were always at least partially motivated by their political utility. As Roberto Weiss puts this point, speaking of the duke's commissioning of Frulovisi's *Vita Henrici Quinti*, "In all but name it was a pamphlet to glorify Gloucester in his loyalty to his dead brother's cause, and an attempt on behalf of Gloucester's policy to inspire enthusiasm for a war that was turning inevitably to defeat."[70] Frulovisi's subsequent *Humfroidos* represents an even bolder attempt to turn the cultural capital of Italian humanism into sheer political self-aggrandizement.[71]

In the context of the duke's ambitions as regent and his utilitarian interest in high culture, the politics of the *Fall of Princes* prologue appears more plainly. The overall structure of the prologue — which moves from eminent classical and foreign writers, to Chaucer, to Humphrey, and finally to Lydgate — rests on the epideictic circuitry that we have seen more obviously deployed in the *Troy Book*.[72] Tellingly, when Lydgate turns to the topic of his patron, what he first emphasizes is the precise nature of the duke's political status:

> Eek in this land, I dar afferme a thyng:
> There is a prynce ful myhti off puissaunce,
> A kyngis sone and vncle to the kyng
> Henry the Sexte, which is now in Fraunce,
> And is lieftenant, and hath the gouernaunce
> Off our Breteyne .... (1.372–77)

The poet draws attention here to Humphrey's close familial proximity to the crown and the fact that he is "in this land" while "Henry the Sexte ... is now in Fraunce," and, therefore, as "lieftenant," he, not Henry, "hath the gouernaunce" of the country. He next goes on to praise the duke for keeping the "Pes and quiete" in the realm (a rather disingenuous compliment, considering his feud with Beaufort); for having been "proued a goode knyght"; and for being "expert in language" (1.380–88). Finally, he goes out of his way to allude to Humphrey's successful – and brutal – suppression of a recent Lollard uprising, declaring that "in this land no Lollard dar abide" (1.403) and characterizing the duke as a divinely chosen defender of the Church.[73] In these lines, Humphrey becomes an idealized embodiment of the second estate's service to the first; better than a (child) king, he is God's "owyn knyht" (1.408). The movement in the following stanzas – through a reference to Humphrey's "Reedyng off bookis" (1.415) to an account of his commissioning of the poet who, predictably, laments his own lack of "sugred aureat licour" (1.461) – then completes the epideictic circuit by bringing the person of the author to the foreground. By the end of the prologue, Lydgate, vis-à-vis his eulogistic relationships with Gloucester, Chaucer, and other poetic predecessors, has figured himself as both heir of a long tradition of high-culture poetry and idealized embodiment of the first estate's service to the second – both the poetic successor of Chaucer and an essential agent in the defense of the realm. The prologue of the *Fall of Princes* therefore turns out to be just as much a laureate performance as that of the *Troy Book*, albeit one adjusted to the political realities of Henry VI's minority. Humphrey, seeking to consolidate a king-like power, could not have wished for anything more from the longtime Lancastrian laureate.

In fact, in some ways, the more indirect manner in which the *Fall of Princes* articulates its politics and the less obviously imperial nature of its source text make it Lydgate's purest instance of a laureate performance. If, as laureate ideology posits, poetry is to be a truly autonomous enterprise, the laureate must serve his state not as propagandist but as prophet – he must, as David Lawton has said of Lydgatean poetics more generally, "tell the truth, particularly to the great."[74] Throughout his career, and especially in his moments of laureate construction, Lydgate no doubt believed he was doing just this. As conscious as he was of the mutually aggrandizing and legitimating relationship between Lancastrian politics and laureate poetics, the conviction of his orthodox sentiments suggests that he believed that this poetics was doing the work of God. In the case of the *Fall of Princes*, he was given the opportunity to tell the most powerful man in the country the basic truth, repeated over the course of some 36,000 lines, that he, like all powerful men before him, was doomed to fall (as the duke indeed did) — even while assisting in the perpetuation and extension of Humphrey's power.[75] Not coincidentally, in this work more than any other, Lydgate found opportunities to reflect on the permanence and value of poetry; the *Fall of Princes* relentlessly asserts that, at the final tally, princes are defeated and empires destroyed, but the poetry — and thereby the poet — that records this fall remains. As Lydgate states in Book 4, "Writyng caused poetis to recure/A name eternal, the laurer whan thei wan,/In adamaunt graue perpetuelli tendure" (4.64–66). Like Petrarch in his laureation address, Lydgate insists that the laureate's reward is the translation of his historical specificity into the realm of fame outside time — and no work stakes his claim to this reward more patently (and extensively) than this one that contains this very meditation on it. If Lydgate invents an English laureateship with the *Troy Book*, with the *Fall of Princes* he supplies its most perfect performance. Despite the many subsequent attempts to follow the monk's lead in this respect, the laureate performance of the *Fall* would never quite be matched — at least until well into the next century, with Spenser's *Faerie Queene*.

"AL-THOUG THAT I BE BOISTOUS AND RUAL": LYDGATE'S HUMILITY, SUBJECTION, AND RESISTANCE

Before ending this chapter I must return to a topic that I have admittedly explained away too easily — the humility topos, which appears everywhere in Lydgate's work and especially at those moments in which he is positioning himself as an English poet laureate. Gestures of humility are for Lydgate no empty convention but serve a variety of essential functions, only one of which I have mentioned thus far — namely, by conveying precisely the opposite of what they literally communicate, they are a means of tactful self-aggrandizement. This function cannot be overemphasized, and not only because so many readers have simply taken Lydgate's self-abnegation at his word, and agreed that yes, he certainly is a dim star in the sunlight of Chaucer, and, indeed, the "defaute ys in Lydegate." But even more important is that this inverted self-aggrandizement, given the notional nature of his laureateship, forms this laureateship's very fiber. Without official status as laureate, Lydgate must reinstall himself in that office with each poem, and one of his most powerful rhetorical strategies for doing so is to proclaim ostentatiously his unsuitability for it. Lydgate's laureateship, produced and perpetuated by the manner in which he puts it into verse, receives its being by being denied.

Two other functions of the humility topos, however, have at least equal bearing on the nature and practice of this laureateship. First, as Lawton has argued, this topos allows fifteenth-century poets to utter sometimes-unwelcome truths to those in power. In respect to Lydgate specifically, some scholars contend — *pace* those that emphasize his propagandistic efforts — that the monk voices a veiled but consistent critique of militaristic royal policy, even within such monuments to royal power as the *Troy Book*.[76] According to this view, since voicing criticism *in propria persona* — even coded criticism — can be dangerous, Lydgate's self-abnegation helps to dampen the force of the possible affront to his patrons. One may fairly wonder why Lydgate even risks such an affront, but in fact he has no choice: such a risk is entailed by the very mutual legitimation that both he and his patrons seek. Lydgate, as I have argued, is only able to be an effective agent of legitimation because, in his identity as a monastic writer, he in theory possesses an authority independent of that of his patrons. In order to maintain this identity and therefore also his efficacy as a legitimizing agent, he must, so to speak, stay in character. He must take positions and voice concerns consistent with this identity, drawing on a set of interests distinct from — and therefore at times in conflict with — those of his patrons. Like all dialectical relationships, this one contains a paradox, which is that in order to be an effective propagandist Lydgate must also be a stern critic.[77] Faced with this necessity, at the end of the *Troy Book* he couches the declaration of his name, social identity, and the fact that the reigning king himself gave him "charge this story to translate" in an equally pronounced insistence that, as recipient of this charge, he is unworthy, "boistous and rual." He must, to be the monkish laureate Henry V wants him to be, utter unpleasant truths (e.g., of the horrors and fruitlessness of royal militarism), but he is wary enough to deliver these truths with a large dose of self-deprecation.

The other important function of the humility topos possesses a much less intentional nature, operating like a nervous tic that relieves the pressure created by basic tensions within laureate poetics. These tensions, as I argued in respect to Petrarch and Boccaccio, pertain to both theory and practice: in theory, the poet laureate is somehow at once self-determining analogue of the prince and also servant monumentalizer or mystifier for that prince; in practice, his intent to speak the truth is severely circumscribed by his economic and political dependence on those to whom he speaks. In respect to these tensions, the humility topos functions as an acknowledgment of the profound asymmetry between patron and poet — signaling the vast gulf between them in social status, wealth, and power. It is, simply put, the appropriate manner in which to address one's superiors, and, as such, it is a bald admission of inferiority. While this admission does serve, in turn, as a *via negativa* toward self-aggrandizement, it does so only at the cost of exposing the notional basis of laureate authority and hence that authority's ultimate subjection to the more concrete political and economic power of the prince.

These two functions of the humility topos — its acknowledgment of the laureate's subjection and its dampening of the laureate's at least partially oppositional stance toward his patron — more or less encompass what Louis Montrose, writing about Spenser, terms the "resistance" inhering within laureate self-representation. This resistance derives from the friction between Spenser's "exalted self-representation as an Author and his subjection to the authority of an other [i.e., Queen Elizabeth], the contradiction between a specific authorial ideology — that of 'the Laureate' — and the social conditions of literary production."[78] On the one hand, a mutually legitimating relationship between poet and patron is the engine that drives the laureate poetics of Spenser, Lydgate, or any other "self-crowned" laureate; on the other, such a relationship is, both in theory and practice, irreducibly ambivalent. In the case of the monk of Bury, the full nature of this relationship is most apparent in those moments that are at once his most self-aggrandizing and self-denigrating. Importantly, for Lydgate, as I have observed, a significant portion of this ambivalence derives not just from his underlying condition of subjection but also from his persistent belief in the civilizing power of high-culture literature — a belief that, as the awkwardness of poems such as *The Title and Pedigree* suggest, he found difficult to maintain as a practicing laureate in Lancastrian England. Lydgate's self-aggrandizing self-denigration serves as his humble claim that the transcendent good of poetry — in his terms, its illuminated nature and illuminating power — has a particular incarnation in his own work. For poetry to realize this ideal, he believes, following Boccaccio and Petrarch, that it must be grounded upon the authority of a laureate. His many moments of self-aggrandizing self-denigration are good-faith attempts at constructing this authority vis-à-vis the morally uncertain political authority of the Lancastrians — its necessary sponsoring counterpart.

One final example of such a moment may serve as a conclusion to this chapter, as it recapitulates many of the facets of Lydgatean laureate poetics. In the prologue to his rendition of *Isopes Fabules*,[79] Lydgate, as in the prologue to the *Troy Book*, offers a brief defense of poetry. In this instance he focuses, appropriately, on fabular writing, the "bestis" and "fyssh" of which "fables rude" he compares to a dish of mere pewter that nonetheless contains "[r]yall dentees" (15–20). The basic thrust of these particular lines, which echo that of their source (the *Fables* of Marie de France), is conventional and appears in English in Chaucer and elsewhere; Lydgate's additions, characteristically, consist of rhetorical amplification and ornament. In the context of the immediately preceding lines, however, this defense obtains new significance, as we must take into account a rather radical departure from Marie — namely, Lydgate's transformation of their *auctor* Aesop from a slave into a poet laureate:[80]

> Vnto purpos þe poete laureate
> Callyd Isopus dyd hym occupy
> Whylom in Rome to plese þe senate,
> Fonde out fables, þat men myght hem apply
> To Sondry matyrs, yche man for hys party,
> Aftyr þeyr lust, to conclude in substaunce,
> Dyuerse moralytees set out to þeyr plesaunce. (8–14)

For Lydgate, fables do not simply have moral utility but possess this utility within the specific context of governance. The fabulist, correspondingly, is not a slave but a master of the literary arts: he is not commanded to perform literary service for the state but chooses for himself this endeavor (he "dyd hym occupy . . . to plese þe senate"); like Petrarch's self-ideal, he is a servant only to the good of the republic. Lydgate, as in his eulogies of Chaucer in the *Troy Book* and elsewhere, has retroactively reconfigured an authoritative literary predecessor into an ideal possessor of the role he imagines himself to occupy. And he does this, moreover, in order to underwrite what Edward Wheatley has shown to be a highly politicized rendering of the subsequent fables. As in the prologue of the *Troy Book*, he legitimizes his political repositioning of a well-known antique text by constructing a notion of the author as political agent parallel to the prince (or, in this case, to a senator) and implying that he himself has obtained this authorial position.

A crucial element of this strategy is the tactfully self-denigrating presentation of his own historically specific person. This presentation follows his depiction of Aesop as laureate, after two intervening stanzas

that put forth his aforementioned defense of fabular writing (now understood as defending a particular species of laureate performance):

> For whyche I cast to folow þys poete
> And hys fables in Englyssh to translate,
> And, þough I haue no rethoryk swete,
> Haue me excusyd: I was born in Lydgate;
> Of Tullius gardeyn I passyd nat þe gate,
> And cause, why: I had no lycence
> There to gadyr floures of elloquence. (29—35)

In following "þys poete" whom he has just elevated to the status
of laureate, he implicitly claims the same rank: what Aesop was
then to the Roman senate, Lydgate is now to Lancastrian England.
Having projected his laureate poetics backward upon antiquity, he makes
his particular politico-literary practice appear as a present-day incarnation
of that of imperial Rome. As expected, he couches this claim in self-
denigration, constructing his notional role as laureate under the sign of its
denial. (Indeed, these lines' close echo of the self-aspersions of Chaucer's
Franklin [5.719—27] suggests both their disingenuousness and an
association between Aesop and Chaucer as, respectively, ancient and
contemporary precedents for Lydgate.) Although Marie also names
herself in the verse, Lydgate has tellingly relocated this moment of
authorial self-identification from her epilogue, with the effect that the
authoritative voice that narrates the subsequent fables is understood to
belong to his specific empirical person, "born in Lydgate." He has also
entirely eliminated Marie's rationale for her self-naming (and, in fact,
Marie herself), which she gives as, "Put cel estre que clerc plusur/
Prendreient sur eus mun labur" ("It may be that many clerks will claim
my work as their own") (5—6).[81] Marie — as Christine de Pizan does later
to a much greater extent — brings her empirical person into the text
because of the traditional literary hostility to her sex. To prevent the
clerisy from erasing the fact of her authorship, she explicitly equates
herself with her *auctor*, whose role she gives as simply another translator — in his case, from Greek into Latin. Lydgate, in rewriting this
passage, not only removes Marie from the chain of authorship (as she
feared), but he also replaces her self-elevation with his laureate self-
construction, casting away her feminist resistance to the clerisy and
putting in its place an exclusively masculine laureate paternity.

As I have said, he accomplishes this self-aggrandizing body switching
by ostentatiously denying himself membership in such a paternity.

But what of the other two functions of the humility topos? In regard to its blunting of the edge of unwelcome truth-telling, Lydgate's self-abnegation helps to enable his consistent adaptation of the fables and their morals to largely sociopolitical themes. Within this arena, more often than not, he voices a stern critique of a government tending toward tyranny.[82] Wheatley finds this sentiment, in view of the poet's efforts as propagandist, so remarkable that he is tentatively willing to credit questionable manuscript evidence and date *Isopes Fabules* to the first decade of the fifteenth century, before the *Troy Book* or any other of Lydgate's datable poems. In fact, this evidence does not hold up to scrutiny, and, given the development of Lydgate's laureate poetics traced in this chapter, it seems more likely that this laureate-centered prologue (if not necessarily all the individual fables) was a relatively late composition. The work may be fairly compared to the *Siege of Thebes* (completed just before or after the death of Henry V), as in the prologues of both Lydgate appears as himself, is apparently confident of his proto-laureate status, and is working without a patron. In addition, both works possess an overall monitory nature, directed to the powerful but critical of their ambitions and abuses. As in the *Siege*, Lydgate takes on the role of political conscience, and in this respect the third function of the humility topos becomes evident. Unlike the Aesop he imagines, who autono-mously bestows moral wisdom upon Roman senators, Lydgate possesses a literary authority deeply (if not always obviously) complicit with the very powers he is criticizing. Thus, not surprisingly, his self-denigration greatly amplifies Marie's in her prologue, extending across the two stanzas following the one in which he presents himself. Although he claims, following his depiction of Aesop's motives, that he supplies his collection of fables for the "plesaunce" of those "þat shall it rede," he tellingly belabors this point, begging his intended audience to take his "compilacion ... at gree" and repeating his insistence that this "compilacion" is only for "theym to plese" (38–42). He attributes any translation errors to his "ignoraunce" (43), and this excuse, in the face of his overt manipulation of his source, serves as a preemptive apology for any possible affront his interpretations of the tales may cause. With this apology he emphasizes again his subjection, in which, "[l]owly of hert & feyþfull obeysaunce," he submits his interpretations "to þeyr correcioun," conventionally ascribing to his intended audience "more clere inspeccion/ In matyrs, þat touche poetry" than himself (45–48). Once again, Lydgate's laureate poetic practice ineluctably – if briefly – reveals the sociopolitical conditions that both enable and vitiate it.

This last aspect of Lydgate's practice surfaces in some form in the work of all contemporary and subsequent poets who occupy a similar position vis-à-vis royal power. In extreme cases, if the fifteenth-century English proto-laureate is forced — or chooses — to recognize his inherent subjection explicitly, his notional laureateship may suddenly collapse, and in turn his self-regard may become less a method of self-authorization and more so the petitionary strategy of an abject subject kneeling before his lord. Lydgate, as an eminent member of an ancient religious order and a representative of a wealthy and powerful abbey, is to a large degree able to finesse the tensions in laureate poetics, since to some extent he is economically and socially independent of his patrons. In contrast, Lydgate's contemporary Hoccleve, as we will see in the next chapter, has no such advantage, and the consequences of this fact are both profoundly debilitating and oddly inspiring.

CHAPTER 3

Thomas Hoccleve: beggar laureate

In this chapter, as I indicated at the opening of Part II of this book, I take as my point of departure the consensus that Hoccleve's work differs in fundamental ways from Lydgate's; I argue that these differences can only be fully understood by keeping the poetry and poetic careers of both authors in view. I contend, further, that a full discernment of not just the nature of Hoccleve's achievements but also his place in the trajectory of the English literary tradition requires a consideration of laureate poetics, to the development of which he contributed, and that came to dominate this tradition in his own lifetime. In particular, in regard to Hoccleve's textualization of his identity as privy seal clerk, I insist on the structural similarity of this strategy to Lydgate's appearance in his verse as "monk of Bury": in both cases the author textualizes his historically specific existence and links his identity as poet to the social identity he possesses in the empirical world. Hoccleve, motivated by the same historical conditions and influenced by the same circulation of ideas as Lydgate, was the first candidate for the proto-laureateship that the latter achieved. That Hoccleve ultimately failed to maintain this status, however, points us to the differences that lie alongside the similarities between his and Lydgate's poetic strategies. Although Hoccleve was largely responding to the same climate of patronage, in his position vis-à-vis his patrons he was neither able nor content to develop a coherent laureate poetics. Instead, by foregrounding what we have seen to be the cross-purposes inherent in laureate theory and practice (which he, in his still relatively novel sociocultural position as poet and civil servant, could not obscure even if he wished), he invented a complex, conflicted literary selfhood that to us seems quite apart from the late medieval norm.

In this chapter, therefore, I aim to show that many of Hoccleve's most characteristic achievements result from his ingenious response to the circumstances that frustate his laureate potential. In particular, his failure brings to the surface the subjection inherent in both the idea and practice of the role, and his remarkably creative use of this subjection allows us to view plainly the great dialectical alternative to Lydgateanism: the beggar, who in all his subjection displays both a vexed interiority and a resistance to power. Although this alternative is, as we have seen, at some level necessarily present in Lydgate's work, it is there rechanneled rather than leveraged, suppressed rather than indulged. In contrast, by foregrounding this subjection, Hoccleve relinquishes the official, quasi-transcendental authority of the laureate and puts into its place a fragmented selfhood of frustrated and stubbornly persistent desire. To attain this conclusion, I first make the case for construing Hoccleve's poetic career as that of a failed laureate by outlining the similarities and differences between the extrinsic aspects of his career and Lydgate's. I then work chronologically through a selection of Hoccleve's major poems, showing how a Hocclevean mendicant poetics develops as the product of the thwarted laureate desire and crafty textual maneuverings of a professional letter writer and belated Ricardian ironist.

LAUREATE HOCCLEVE?

Comparisons between Hoccleve and Lydgate occur less frequently than one might expect, given that they were virtually exact contemporaries.[1] When they do occur, their purpose tends to be evaluative – to criticize one poet in order to praise the other.[2] But, if one puts aside such intentions, a direct comparison of the two poets suggests that they share much more than is usually acknowledged. Like Lydgate, Hoccleve was a cleric (albeit one in minor orders) and, at least on the surface, politically conservative and religiously orthodox. In the *Regiment of Princes*, by far his longest (at 5463 lines) and most widely disseminated poem (with 44 surviving manuscripts), he shows himself capable of the same relentless moral, social, and religious didacticism as pervades Lydgate's work.[3] Both poets make extensive use of the humility topos. Both claim Chaucer as their primary mentor and establish him as the origin of the nascent English poetic tradition. And, as M. C. Seymour has pointed out, the most public efforts of their respective careers run in parallel. Hoccleve's *Regiment of Princes*, completed around 1411 for the Prince of Wales, is matched by Lydgate's *Troy Book*, begun for the prince in 1412. Hoccleve's 1415 *Remonstrance against Oldcastle* – essentially (if not always comfortably) an anti-Lollard polemic indirectly addressed to Henry V via an appeal to his rebellious former comrade-in-arms – is matched by

Lydgate's 1413–14 *A Defence of Holy Church*, also addressed to the young king and concerned with the same matter. And, by the early 1420s, both poets were writing poems for Henry's brother Humphrey, duke of Gloucester: Hoccleve, the multipart poem known as the *Series*, and Lydgate, *On Gloucester's Approaching Marriage*.[4]

These parallels are hardly coincidental. Back in London following his distinguished military leadership in Wales, Prince Henry, in the last years of his father's reign, asserted himself politically. To this end he enlisted the aid of these two different vernacular poets with whom he had had some contact, commissioning the *Troy Book* directly and having at least indirect responsibility for the production of the *Regiment of Princes*.[5] Both of these works possess the aim (if not the *sole* aim) of depicting the prince as worthy of and prepared for the kingship. After his accession, when in the first years of his reign he sought to increase the scale of his opposition to Lollardy, Henry turned (either directly, or through a climate of encouragement) to the same two poets to create public, English exhortations for him to do just that. Finally, both poets found in the last years of Henry's reign a new patron in Humphrey, whose political ascendancy, as *custos Angliae* while his brother was in France, was most likely the motivation behind his famous investments in cultural capital.[6]

These parallels are so suggestive that many have read the course of Hoccleve's career retrospectively against the less ambiguous model that Lydgate – as proto-laureate author of such works as *The Title and Pedigree of Henry VI* – consolidated for the most part in the years after Hoccleve's death.[7] No record survives, however, that explicitly indicates that Hoccleve possessed such a role. The evidence usually cited – besides the *Regiment*'s wide dissemination – is that, for the most part, Hoccleve wrote his politically oriented poems soon after his completion of the *Regiment*, and that among these are examples of the sort of occasional pieces one expects from an officially sanctioned poet. In addition, the rather sudden cessation of these supposed political commissions – all but one of which may be dated during or before 1416 – has been taken as evidence both of the veracity of the mental illness he later reports experiencing about this time and of the officially recognized position that he subsequently lost due to this illness, leaving an empty seat that Lydgate more than willingly filled.[8] Yet, unlike Lydgate (as in, for example, *The Title and Pedigree*), Hoccleve never furnishes the details of a specific commissioning, leading some to presume that these poems represent speculations rather than certain commissions.[9] And, in regard to the evidence of his career-ending mental illness, even if we allow its circular reasoning, problems remain. If Hoccleve were replaced by Lydgate at this juncture, one would expect to see a shift in official patronage. Yet we have no incontrovertible evidence of Lydgate receiving royal commissions in the period immediately following Hoccleve's illness; he was still at work on the *Troy Book*, which he completed in December, 1420.[10] Moreover, the purest example of a royal panegyric in Hoccleve's corpus – his *Balade on King Henry V* – is a celebration of Henry's return to England following the Treaty of Troyes and hence must have been written after May 1421, well after Hoccleve's so-called laureate period.[11] A not unreasonable conclusion, then, is that the sudden cessation of his stream of politically oriented poems, rather than representing the loss of a proto-laureate post, indicates instead simply a lapse of interest in vernacular poetry on Henry's part.

Amidst these doubts, however, stands one piece of external evidence that suggests that Hoccleve, like Lydgate, did in fact possess some sort of informally recognized role in the Lancastrian project of dynastic legitimation: his inclusion in the series of author portraits in London, BL Add. MS 42131, the Psalter-Hours made for John, duke of Bedford, c.1414–16. This manuscript, as Sylvia Wright has shown, represents a fairly transparent attempt to triangulate cultural, spiritual, and political authority to underwrite the legitimacy and interests of the Lancastrian regime.[12] Not surprisingly, Gower, an early and widely disseminated Lancastrian apologist, is the vernacular author who figures most prominently, with 10 separate portraits. These form, Wright argues, an integral part of the manuscript's thematic design, which makes use of Gower's "moral authority" as a "unifying motif" (p. 197). In places, the effect of this design is crassly political, as in the juxtaposition of a Gower portrait alongside psalm 141 with one of Richard II alongside psalm 142 so that "[a]t the most elementary level Gower represents good and Richard evil" (p. 195). Significantly, the only two identifiable living vernacular authors who appear are Lydgate, with two portraits, and Hoccleve, with one and possibly two others.[13] The evidence of this portrait, when considered alongside the wide and strategic dissemination of the *Regiment*[14] and the nature and timing of his subsequent political verse, thus does make it likely that Hoccleve's role as poet was functionally that of a quasi-laureate – which is to say that he participated in the same officially encouraged, if not always sponsored, project of Lancastrian intervention into vernacular high culture to which Lydgate owed so much of his career. But, ultimately, neither Hoccleve's literary inclinations nor — what is more important — his position in respect to this court was well suited to this project.

Lydgate, as a monk, in theory stood outside the Lancastrian regime and could draw on the moral, religious, and intellectual authority deriving from his social status and from the long tradition of monastic writing. Hoccleve, as privy seal clerk, had no such advantage. Not only was he located fully *within* the administrative structure of the regime, but he was also positioned near the bottom of it, lower in the civil servant hierarchy than Chaucer was, and without the latter's family connections. He was, therefore, entirely dependent on the Lancastrians for his livelihood, and, significantly, this livelihood formed the very basis of his social identity. As a petty civil servant in the early fifteenth century, he had no pre-established place in the ideology of estates: he was neither gentle, nor (actively) clerical, nor a laborer. Even in respect to the much more complex actual class structure of London, he was not easily placed. Instead, as Hoccleve himself vividly explains in his *Male regle*, his social status derives primarily from the fact that he received a royal income:

> Wher was a gretter maister eek than Y,
> Or bet aqweyntid at Westmynstre Yate,
> Among the tauerneres namely
> And cookes, whan I cam eerly or late?
> I pynchid nat at hem in myn acate,
> But paied hem as þat they axe wolde,
> Wherfore I was the welcomer algate
> And for a verray gentilman yholde
> . . .
> Othir than maistir callid was I neuere
> Among this meynee, in myn audience
> Methoughte I was ymaad a man for euere[.] (177–203)

His ironically bestowed title of "maister" and status as "gentilman" depended not upon anything inherent in his position, but upon the fact that he "paied" the tavern keepers, cooks, and (as described in elided lines) boatmen "as þat they axe wolde." Rather than possessing a fixed social identity, such as Lydgate's, that presupposes moral authority, Hoccleve occupied an ambiguous position bankrolled by his Lancastrian employers. This position, as it was manifestly founded on money, was not only vacant of intrinsic authority but also could only be maintained by continually spending the very income that produced it.[15]

Hoccleve was acutely aware of the contingency of this money-propped social identity and the profound dependence upon his employers that it entailed — an awareness made all the more unsettling by the fact that the payment of his annuity was routinely months late, on occasion suspended, and, given the Lancastrians' constant state of fiscal crisis, always in jeopardy of being diminished or ceased. Consequently, Hoccleve is not able to textualize his social identity without also referring to his financial anxiety and, specifically, to his worry over the payment of his annuity. For example, in the famous passage from the *Regiment* describing his labor at the privy seal, despite its preponderance of detail regarding the strenuous physical and mental demands of scribal work ("We stowpe and stare upon the sheepes skyn,/And keepe moot our song and wordes yn" [1014–15]), his ultimate concern is not with the work itself but the payment he should receive:

> In th'eschequeer, he [i.e., Henry IV] of his special grace
> Hath to me grauntid an annuitee
> Of twenti mark whyle I have lyves space.
> Mighte I ay payd been of that duetee,
> It sholde stonde wel ynow with me;
> But paiement is hard to gete adayes,
> And that me putte in many foule affrayes. (820–26)

The density of detail here pertaining to his actual socioeconomic existence is astounding. In three lines he provides us with the fact of his annuity, the office from which it is paid ("th'eschequeer"), and its precise amount ("twenti mark"); and each of these details is corroborated by the historical record.[16] In his position as a privy seal clerk who received an uncertain royal income, Hoccleve — as these stanzas suggest — was compelled to become quite literally a beggar poet. No matter what other functions his public verse might have served, it almost always also served as a petition for a "paiement" that "is hard to gete."

To the extent that Hoccleve and Lydgate faced the same patronage demands, their poetry possesses a similar set of motivations, problems to resolve, and methods to resolve them. Yet to the extent that Hoccleve's social, economic, and political position vis-à-vis his patrons differed from Lydgate's, the relative emphases he gives to various motivations and the manner in which he negotiates some key problems are radically dissimilar. Several important features of Lydgate's poetry are comparatively infrequent in Hoccleve's, such as strategic use of aureation, a tendency to monumentalize patronage, and meditations on poetry and the role of the poet. These features, as described in the previous chapter, may be understood as signs of successful adaptation to the demands of Lancastrian patronage. Conversely, the most remarkable feature of

Hoccleve's poetry — his extensive self-observation — may be understood as a wonderful failure to succeed in the new climate. Because of extrinsic factors, Hoccleve must, unlike Lydgate, address *a priori* the deficiencies in laureate poetics — the most debilitating of which being that the laureate's claims to self-sufficiency are belied by his dependency on his patron. The manner in which Hoccleve negotiates this and other problems brings to the foreground what is in fact always latent in this poetics, even in Lydgate's virtuoso performances of it: the unfulfilled desire of the poet who would be laureate. This desire makes visible the otherwise occluded interiority of the poetic speaker, and it refuses full complicity with the will of the patron (who, after all, is responsible for the poet's frustration). In viewing Hoccleve's accomplishments retro-spectively against the backdrop of Lydgate's, one perceives that a poet laureate is always, to different degrees, verging on becoming a beggar — and that, in Hoccleve's case, the eclipse of his proto-laureateship by the imperatives of mendicancy makes possible profound avenues of literary expression.

HOCCLEVE AND CHRISTINE: THE "EPISTRE DE CUPIDE"

Henry IV's attempt to bring Christine de Pizan to his court shortly after his seizure of the crown must have served, as I mentioned in Chapter 2, as an indication to contemporary English poets of the kind of work that the new king was interested in patronizing. For Lydgate, the dedication of Christine's *Epistre Othea* became a crucial source for the epideictic strategies he later deployed to great success in such works as the *Troy Book*. In comparison, Hoccleve seems to have understood the poetic opportunity Christine represented more straightforwardly. In 1402, with Christine having spurned the king's invitation, Chaucer having recently died, and Gower in his seventies, an opportunity arose for Hoccleve to make his mark as a court poet. Once Christine's son was back in France (no later than early that year) and therefore all chances of securing her presence lost, Hoccleve wasted no time in positioning himself, quite literally, as her replacement, rendering in May of that year her *Epistre au dieu d'Amours* into English rhyme royal stanzas.

In one sense, Hoccleve's decision to rework this poem of Christine's rather than another (assuming he had a choice of texts) was quite propitious. This poem assumes the form of a letter written from the God of Love to "toutes femmes generaument" ("all of womankind"),

who have inundated him with complaints regarding "des oultrages tres
griefs . . . Que chacun jour des desloyaulx reçoivent,/Qui les blamant,
diffament, et deçoivent" ("the very grievous wrongs . . . Endured each day
from those disloyal men/Who blame and shame, defame and deceive
them").[17] Cupid takes the women's side, and the poem as a whole serves
as a wide-ranging critique of the antifeminist basis of the culture of *fin'
amor*. By taking to task Jean de Meun in particular, the poem achieved
notoriety and, through the ensuing *Querelle de la Rose*, Christine achieved
literary stature.[18] Hoccleve thus chose to translate what was at that time
likely Christine's best-known poem, hoping, we may suppose, to build a
career as court poet on the model of Chaucer, whose reworking of
contemporary French poetry marked the first phase of his career. Taking
as his source a work of a fashionable continental author and freely
adapting this material to his own idiom and purposes much as Chaucer
did, Hoccleve insinuates his succession to his master's place. This
insinuation becomes almost explicit when he alludes to Chaucer's
"legende of martirs" (316) — i.e., the *Legend of Good Women* — soon after
his attack on the "Romance of the Rose" (283). Hoccleve, using Chaucer
as his proxy much as Lydgate does, here suggests that, if Chaucer's *Legend*
opposes the *Roman* in the same way that Christine's *Epistre* does, by
rendering Christine's poem into Chaucerian stanzas he inherits the
prestige of both poets.

Yet, in another sense, this poem was not at all the most suitable vehicle
for achieving success in the Lancastrian court. While it does bestow
prestige upon Hoccleve, this prestige ultimately lacks the morally
authoritative character of Christine's and instead possesses that of the
subtle, ironizing, poetic craftsman. This latter character is evident in the
very allusion to the "Romance of the Rose"; given the title's
Anglicization, this allusion suggests not so much the French antitext of
Chaucer's *Legend* but rather Chaucer's own translation of the *Roman*,
which Cupid himself cites in the prologue to the *Legend* as one of the
principal pieces of evidence *against* the poet.[19] This complex intertextual
reference positions Hoccleve's English *auctor* as both protagonist and
antagonist, and consequently his deployment of Chaucer's prestige evokes
not so much the proper moral stance toward women as it does virtuosity
with allusive and self-referential literary discourse. Further, Hoccleve's
audience no doubt knew his trendy source text, and thus what he was
advertising in his rendition — given its rather significant reorganization,
condensation, and additions — was not just his skill as translator but also
his wit as a poetic provocateur.[20]

This wit has at base a structural irony that would not have been lost on Hoccleve's readers. In her poem, Christine's moral authority resides, as it does throughout her career, in her sex; as a woman, her voicing of the complaints of womankind seems to transcend mere literary convention and be as authentic as the empirical fact of her womanhood. By voicing these complaints in this case through the figure of the God of Love, she emphasizes both this fact, through the mismatch between her sex and Cupid's, and her intervention in the tradition of *fin' amor*, through her impersonation of the very emblem of that tradition. Simply put, she trumps literary convention with reality, and her trump card is her empirical person. In contrast, Hoccleve's audience would have understood the poet to be impersonating a woman impersonating a male god.[21] As a widely read cleric in minor orders, Hoccleve was an unlikely figure to voice complaints against the "wrong wrytyng" of "clerkes" (218–19), and hence such statements would have been perceived as possessing, at the very least, suspect sincerity. Indeed, if one credits Hoccleve's later report, some contemporary readers thought the entire poem to be a tongue-in-cheek exercise in antifeminism – an opinion that survives to this day in the poem's critical response.[22]

Yet both this interpretation and its opposite (which understands Hoccleve as more or less sincere) are ultimately only rungs on the ladder to the poem's full purpose, which is to convey precisely this ambiguity of motive. Hoccleve, in fact, goes out of his way to emphasize the impossibility of knowing true intentions, adding to Christine's complaint about men's deceptions the observation,

> Ful hard it is to knowe a mannes herte,
> For outward may no man the truthe deeme,
> Whan word out of his mowth may ther noon sterte,
> But it sholde any wight by reson qweeme.
> So is it seid of herte, it wolde seeme. (36–40)

Speaking here generally but also about the very work he is writing, Hoccleve insists that there is a virtually impassable gulf between what one says – the "word out of his mowth" – and one's intentions, the "mannes herte." This sentiment, as well as the self-reflexivity of its articulation, demonstrates not so much Hoccleve's allegiance to Christine's project as his mastery of that characteristic feature of Chaucer's poetry, its self-conscious and thematically functional ambiguity. In seeking to occupy both Christine's and Chaucer's shoes, Hoccleve renders a poem of the former into the ironizing mode of the latter. In the process, he barters the moral authority of his source for an advertisement of his skills as a crafty usurper of an established text.

Such craftiness was not at all what Henry IV — as a usurper of a different sort — desired in his court poets.[23] He needed a poet of authentic speech, one who stood on a platform of irrefutably legitimate authority, and who, from this position, could refract this legitimacy back onto his kingship. Instead, with the *Epistre de Cupide* he encountered a poem that not only shows its composer to be merely one his own privy seal clerks — by way of its form, which is that of a patent letter[24] — but one that also tends to put into question sources of authority as quickly as it harnesses them. For Hoccleve, these sources include not only literary but also political authority, and in this regard one moment early in the poem would likely have been so unsettling to the king that we may only surmise that Hoccleve believed that Henry would never read through the entire work. After supplying as an example of a deceptive man the one who "ouerthrowe" "the citee/Of Troie," the poet observes more generally, "Betrayen men nat remes grete and kynges?" (80–85). His source contains a similar line ("Ne traÿst on et royaumes et roys? [542]), but Christine places it much later in the work, thereby softening, through the preceding contextualization, whatever impact it would have had on her French readers. Hoccleve's decision to move this line forward is remarkably pointed. In 1402, many in England — including no small portion of the aristocracy — believed that the man who currently held the throne had indeed betrayed this particular great realm and its true king. Hoccleve's comment, while ostensibly referring to examples from the mists of ancient history, could not but have had acute resonance in the present.[25] Daringly, if briefly, he here widens the scope of the poem's interrogation of authority to indict the authority of the reader whom he most desires to have. If by doing this he proves himself worthy to wear the mantle of Chaucer — who, in the *Legend*, similarly tiptoes around the authority of Richard II — he at the same time proves himself poorly adapted to the Lancastrian climate of patronage. Whether his choice of this text of Christine's was the result of calculation or chance, with the *Epistre de Cupide* Hoccleve shows himself to be, at the opening of his poetic career, not (yet) the first of the Lancastrian poets but the last of the Ricardians.

THE BEGGAR LAUREATE: THE "MALE REGLE"

Even if Hoccleve had seen Christine's *Epistre Othea* at the same time as her *Epistre au dieu d'Amours*, one may suppose it doubtful that he would have chosen the former over the latter as his initial foray into writing for a court audience. As a privy seal clerk, he would have thought himself an unlikely candidate to voice the encyclopedic learning and pedagogical agenda of the rather un-Chaucerian *Othea*. In contrast, as a disciple of Chaucer, he would have been naturally drawn to the ironic potential of the *Epistre au dieu d'Amours*. Perhaps too he was simply more comfortable with the latter's more distinctly epistolary form. Although this vocational self-reference was a happy accident of his source text, it no doubt helped to stimulate the development of his autobiographical style. Nonetheless, as premonitory and accomplished as the *Epistre de Cupide* is in some respects, it stands in relative isolation from the rest of his corpus. Given the substantially different direction of his subsequent work — and especially that of his *magnum opus*, the *Regiment* — one may fairly suppose that he soon recognized that an ironic poetic tour de force was not the best vehicle for attracting royal attention.

In his next significant poetic effort, the pivotal *Male regle*, he displays a developing awareness of Lancastrian literary predilections. He retains irony, but he also attempts to create a platform for a public, morally authoritative voice. In addition, he dramatically broadens the scope of vocational self-reference, so that it includes not merely the form of the poem but much of the thematic and narrative content. Together, these strategies lay the foundation for the poetics that he would later put to much grander and more visible use in his *Regiment*. This later work, as a full-length English *Fürstenspiegel*, represents Hoccleve's bid to be a Lancastrian laureate. In contrast, the 448-line *Male regle* (written in late 1405 or early 1406) is most fundamentally a begging poem, a petition to the then treasurer Thomas Neville, Lord Furnivall, for Hoccleve's belated annuity. The occasion of the poem is hence neither a royal commission nor even an attempt to win such, but a personal financial hardship caused by royal policy. (Council and Parliament had, because of the disastrous state of Henry's finances, suspended payment of annuities for 12 months.)[26] This motivation would seem to preclude the project of developing an authoritative public voice, but in fact for Hoccleve it was an inspiration: in this poem, he seeks to turn precisely this imperative of personal financial need into the ground for such a voice. Begging, because it never masks another desire, is an inherently authentic practice. And in Hoccleve's case, because he depicts himself as one of the kingdom's casualties, begging carries the moral authority of the victimized. Since this authority is a consequence, ultimately, of the king's failure to run a healthy kingdom, it is patently distinct from the king's authority. Thus, with the role of beggar, Hoccleve discovers a means to transcend the confines of his employee status and to speak authentically from an authoritative position distinguishable from that of those to whom he owes his livelihood and social identity. Somewhat paradoxically, then, his abject depiction of himself *in propria persona* petitioning for money is what enables him to personify an independent moral authority. By bringing his historically specific person into the text in the role of beggar, he conflates the historically specific and the generically authoritative in the same fashion and toward similar ends as does Lydgate with his laureate pose.[27]

The paradox in the relation between begging and moral authority is, however, not so easily overcome. Once self-interest is introduced, it becomes difficult to transcend; all truths that a poem purports to convey are suspicious as potential ruses of instrumental motivation. While begging is inherently true, the language a beggar uses is greatly prone to falsehood: although begging does not mask another desire, the beggar is the wearer of masks *par excellence*. For mendicancy to serve as a platform for moral authority, discrete acts of begging must accord with the logic of this authority, rather than to invoke this authority as guise of self-interest. In the *Male regle*, Hoccleve pursues this accord by suggesting the poem's instrumental nature throughout but deferring its full revelation until the end, in which position it may strike the reader as the culmination of the poem's logic rather than its inaugurating purpose. Appearing explicitly only at the conclusion, the act of begging may, in theory, stand as an exemplification of the truth the poem reveals, rather than the motivation behind the truth claims it uses to persuade.

Hoccleve effects this deferral through a play of genre. He begins the poem with (what we later learn to be) his financial need turned inward and generalized, voicing a mock penitential address to the god Health about his comprehensive failure to lead a wholesome life.[28] From the poem's heading, which in Hoccleve's own hand reads "Cy ensuyt la male regle de T. Hoccleue," we learn from the start that the speaker is to be associated with the historically specific author.[29] But in the initial stanza, the instrumental purpose behind this association (that is, the necessary identification of the petitioner) is only figuratively present. Hoccleve loads his opening prayer with the language of material wealth (e.g., in the first three lines, "precious tresor," "prosperitee," "excellent richesse") and even names "worldly welthe" (6) explicitly, before finally revealing the actual addressee to be the more general personification "helthe" (8). In the following stanzas, Hoccleve confesses health to be specifically what he has lost, and it thereby comes to stand for a spiritual as well as mental and physical ideal. Correspondingly, the imagery of material wealth, for the time being, recedes a little more into the background. Hoccleve's language and reasoning at this point manifestly draw on the conventions of the penitential lyric — so much so, in fact, that some later *compilator* found it easy to cannibalize the poem to produce an apparently sincere instance of the genre, carefully selecting and revising lines to ensure that the newly created lyric speaker is not particularized but rather represents a Christian everyman (replacing, for example, "Hoccleue" at line 351 with "ther fore").[30] The subject of these lines is thus indeed a subject of lack, but a lack that reaches beyond what we later learn to be its specific cause and toward the more general condition of the penitent. Although patently a parody, these stanzas nonetheless create the sheen of intimate sincerity radiated by the genre they imitate. Our guard, so to speak, is lowered, and we are invited to believe what the speaker tells us.

With this accomplished, Hoccleve is in position to make the conventional but still dramatic turn from self-loathing to public moralism. He effects this by confessing the particular source of his troubles — the dissolute wasting of money — and then using his experiences in this regard as the ground from which he may redirect his moral focus outward. In particular, after several stanzas in which he confesses his tavern experiences, he makes the observation quoted above regarding the relation between the money in his pocket and his socially inflated status of "maistir." This observation triggers a long moralizing digression:

> So tikelid me þat nyce reuerence
> Þat it me made larger of despense
> Than þat I thoghte han been. O flaterie,
> The guyse of thy traiterous diligence
> Is, folk to mescheef haasten and to hie. (204–8)

Having been "larger of despense" than he intended, Hoccleve presumably no longer had the ready cash to purchase the "nyce reuerence" of the boatmen. In retrospect, he realizes his social inflation to be a mere trick of language motivated by greed. He records this insight, however, not (only) for the sake of self-reformation but as a platform on which to preach a sermon decrying the debilitating social and political effects of "flaterie." Rather than quickly returning to his confession, he pursues this topic for 80 lines, and, because of this passage's sheer length (almost one-fifth of the poem's total lines) and position in the poem, this digression confronts us as not a disgression at all, but the work's thematic centerpiece.

The voice of this passage differs strikingly from that of the preceding stanzas. It resembles the voice of Ricardian "public poetry" – the voice of an individual who speaks not from the position of his own particularity but as the moral mouthpiece of the community:[31]

> Albeit þat my yeeres be but yonge,
> Yit haue I seen in folk of hy degree,
> How þat the venym of faueles tonge
> Hath mortified hir prosperitee
> And broght hem in so sharp aduersitee
> Þat it hir lyf hath also throwe adoun.
> And yit ther can no man in this contree
> Vnnethe eschue this confusioun. (209–16)

The long complaint against "faueles tonge" that begins with this stanza is an entirely serious, carefully worded, and even somewhat daring excursion into public moralizing. The "folk of hy degree" here is a circumlocution for Richard II, whose notorious penchant for keeping a court of flatterers ultimately resulted – according to the logic of these lines – in his life being "throwe adoun." This displacement of the agent of his death from Henry Bolingbroke to Richard's own *misreule* is a pointed rehearsal of Lancastrian propaganda, and as such shows Hoccleve to be newly attuned to Lancastrian poetic predilections. But in the last two lines, Hoccleve also hints that *favel* is still alive and well in the realm. And, by the end of the sermon, his animus reaches a veritable peak of generality, depicting a categorical struggle between *favel* and *trouthe:*

> Men setten nat by trouthe nowadayes.
> Men loue it nat. Men wole it nat cherice.
> And yit is trouthe best at all assayes.
> When þat fals fauel, soustenour of vice,
> Nat wite shal how hire to cheuyce,
> Ful boldely shal trouthe hir heed vp bere.
> Lordes, lest fauel yow fro wele tryce,
> No lenger souffre hir nestlen in your ere. (281–88)

At this point, the poem has traveled far from its earlier whimsical account of the dissolute life of a privy seal clerk and seems now to be a homiletic screed on greed-induced flattery and the trials of living in a fallen world in which *favel* nestles in the ears of humanity.

Nonetheless, as suggested by the pecuniary resonance present even in this stanza (in such words as "cherice," "cheuyce," and "wele"), more personal and specific motivations remain subtly active within this voice of public moralism. For what authorizes Hoccleve's pronouncements on flattery is not — as it would be for Lydgate — anything essential about his social identity, but the fact of his extensive experience with *favel* and especially this experience's bearing on his financial straits. Not surprisingly, then, after his peroration, he abruptly returns to his personal situation and specifically to his scanty "purs of coyn":

> Be as be may, no more of this as now,
> But to my misreule wole I refeere,
> Wheras I was at ese weel ynow,
> Or excesse vnto me leef was and deere,
> And, or I kneew his ernestful maneere,
> My purs of coyn had resonable wone:
> But now therin can ther but scant appeere.
> Excesse hath ny exyled hem echone. (289–96)

"Yes, flattery is destroying truth throughout the world," Hoccleve seems to say here, "but now let's return to my spending habits, and in particular to my sadly empty wallet": in this poem, the voice of moral authority is enabled by and thus must return to a voice of personal need. The poet's pronouncements on the sociopolitical illness of flattery are underwritten by the fact of his suffering from this illness. This suffering, in turn, is authenticated by his confession of flattery-induced free-spending. Through the first three-quarters of the poem, confession (or its close counterpart, personal complaint) has served as the platform for public exhortation, and through this play of genre the first-person voice of the poem has taken on moral authority even while retaining a strict association with the historically specific person of the author.

In order for these genres to play their roles, their individual voices must — at least provisionally — be kept distinct, and the consequent tension between them (as evident in the poem's abrupt transitions and changes in tone) creates for the reader an expectation of their reconciliation. This tension comes fully in view late in the poem, when Hoccleve, following a few additional stanzas of personal complaint and confession, depicts these generic voices in dialogue:

> Despenses large enhaunce a mannes loos
> Whil they endure, and whan they be forbore
> His name is deed. Men keepe hir mowthes cloos,
> As nat a peny had he spent tofore.
> My thank is qweynt, my purs his stuf hath lore,
> And my carkeis repleet with heuynesse.

Bewaar, Hoccleue, I rede thee therfore,
And to a mene reule thow thee dresse. (345–52)

In the first four lines of this stanza, the voice of moral authority
reappears, once again decrying the corrosive social effects of money. In
the next two lines, the voice of personal complaint responds by offering
itself as an example of what the first voice warns against, and, in the
concluding two lines, the first voice seeks to ameliorate the second,
advising it to follow a "mene reule" rather than *misreule*. The poem,
presumably, will continue until this amelioration is realized – until, that
is, the wisdom of the impersonal Goweresque voice finds a home within
the voice of personal failure. At this point, in theory, the poem's multiple
voices will be united, thereby exemplifying a morally reformed and
psychologically reintegrated individual. And yet, as we have seen, what
motivates the personal voice is not merely Hoccleve's wasteful
expenditures but, ultimately, the continuing scantiness of his "purs of
coyn." Since Hoccleve has already lost the "stuf" of his "purs," he needs
money in addition to moral reform. Indeed, considered logically, this
need *predicates* such reform, as it first brings about the confession that in
turn serves as the basis for the ameliorative voice.

Money, therefore, is both what Hoccleve decries in this poem and, as it
turns out, the poem's principle of resolution. This rather untenable
situation becomes explicit a few stanzas later; in the interval, the voice of
moral authority continues for another 40 lines to admonish the voice of
personal complaint (e.g., "Thy rentes annuel, as thow wel woost,/To
scarse been greet costes to susteene" [361–62]). The very duration of this
passage signifies the difficulty of the proposed reconciliation, as the latter
voice continues to resist the former. Then, in a stunning acknowledgment
of the eccentricity of this dramatized self-admonishment, Hoccleve enters
his poem in what seems a third voice:

Ey, what is me, þat to myself thus longe
Clappid haue I? I trowe þat I raue.
A, nay, my poore purs and peynes stronge
Han artid me speke as I spoken haue.
Whoso him shapith mercy for to craue
His lesson moot recorde in sundry wyse,
And whil my breeth may in my body waue,
To recorde it vnnethe I may souffyse. (393–400)

In the first half of this stanza, this new voice momentarily waves
away the morally authoritative one, accusing it of having merely

"[c]lappid" and ascribing its appearance – and, implicitly, the entire poem – to his "poore purs and peynes stronge." Ostensibly, the personal penitential voice then returns in the last half of the stanza and interprets the new voice as asserting that a penitent's plea for absolution must be made "in sundry wyse" – for example, through the generic play of this very poem. This interpretation seems confirmed by the following two stanzas, in which Hoccleve reprises his opening address to health and completes his prayer by asking for "a drope of [health's] largesse" (415).

This second address to health, however, rather than functioning as a neatly symmetrical conclusion to the poem, instead sets up a quite different prayer – one densely detailed, extradiegetic, and baldly pragmatic:

> Lo, lat my lord the Fourneval, I preye,
> My noble lord þat now is tresoreer,
> From thyn hynesse haue a tokne or tweye
> To paie me þat due is for this yeer
> Of my yeerly x li. in th'eschequeer,
> Nat but for Michel terme þat was last.
> I dar nat speke a word of ferne yeer,
> So is my spirit symple and sore agast. (417–24)

Hoccleve here versifies the title, name, and office of Henry IV's treasurer, the precise amount of the annuity due him, the missed date of its payment ("Michel terme þat was last"), and even a reference to the prior year's suspension of annuities (those of "ferne yeer"), the loss of which he humbly but somewhat presumptuously accepts. (In addition, lest the reader mistake the precise historical reference, in his own late copy of the poem he notes, "Annus ille fuit annus restrictionis annuitatum" ["That year was the year of the restriction of annuities."]) With the poem almost completed, Hoccleve has finally revealed its *raison d'être*: having suffered through a year without his principal source of income and having yet to receive the first payment of the following year, he is petitioning the king's treasurer for the overdue payment. In retrospect, we now understand that the third voice, which ascribed the generic play of the poem to his "poore purs and peynes stronge," is not a new voice after all, but rather the penitential voice throwing off its disguise. When the petition to health for "largesse" becomes a petition to Lord Furnivall for the poet's "yeerly x li.," the penitential voice that "shapith mercy for to craue" reveals itself to be that which it has in fact been since the beginning: a petitionary voice craving money.

Ideally, this petitionary voice should not subvert the one of impersonal moral authority but rather disclose the principle by which the personal and public may converge. The point of having Furnivall take the place of health and the poet's annuity take the place of health's "largesse" should be not to reduce health to financial solvency but to make financial solvency stand for a state of economic, social, political, and even spiritual health more generally. Indeed, as the political context Hoccleve alludes to in the petitionary stanza suggests, in pleading for money he speaks not just for himself but also for the king.[32] At the time indicated, annuities were one of Henry IV's larger headaches, as he had reconfirmed most of those granted by Richard and, in his desperate need to cement alliances, had also granted many new ones. Having promised at his accession to live off his own revenue, he was roundly criticized by the Commons for having overburdened royal coffers with such a large annual expenditure; at the same time, he was taken to task for being constantly behind in payments, as many of the recipients of annuities were themselves MPs. Hoccleve, in asking the treasurer of the realm for more money, thus puts himself in a position analogous to the king's. He represents himself both as victim of the king's policies and as the king's diminished twin, and this coincident distance from and similarity to the royal person serves his poetic purposes much as we saw Lydgate's monastic identity to serve his. In theory, his act of begging not only concludes the earlier generic play by showing how the voices of personal complaint and impersonal moralism may be reconciled, but it also makes a provisional case for the poet as actor in the Lancastrian public arena.

The question remains, however, whether the act of begging, even granting its bearing on the circumstances of the Crown, can ever transcend self-interest — that is, whether this poem, instead of opening out into the public arena, dissolves public interest into the pecuniary imperatives of the poet's desire. At stake in this question is the viability of Hoccleve's survival as poet in the climate of Lancastrian patronage, and, even at this preliminary juncture in his public career, he leaves the reader with reasons to doubt his success. In the next two stanzas, the poet meditates on the social effects of money one final time, but in this instance he does not so much decry these effects as face up to them; correspondingly, he does not so much transcend his self-interest as apologize for it:

> I kepte nat to be seen inportune
> In my pursuyte. I am therto ful looth.

> And yit þat gyse ryf is, and commune
> Among the peple now, withouten ooth.
> As the shamelees crauour wole, it gooth,
>   . . .
> Neede hath no lawe, as þat the clerkes trete,
> And thus to craue artith me my neede,
> And right wole eek þat I me entremete,
> For þat I axe is due, as God me speede. (425–40)

The essential purpose of these stanzas is to justify the poem that has
led up to them and, in particular, that poem's progressive modulation
from confession to public moralism to petition. Integral to this
justification is a defense of the "shamelees crauour," an apology for the
petitioner who uses language in whatever way necessary to obtain what he
or she wants.[33] Flattery, of course, is the most typical such use of
language, and hence the poet's earlier condemnations of, for example,
silver-tongued boatmen now seem to be vacated in favor of their defense.
Although the multiple voices in this poem protect Hoccleve from
appearing at this point merely self-contradictory, the generic gymnastics
he has performed do not, in the end, appear to establish a firm ground for
quasi-laureate authority. Instead, at the conclusion of the poem he
insinuates that all authority is ultimately in service to the "[n]eede [that]
hath no lawe." In the final analysis, *his* personal need, his desire for
payment, stands first. It therefore registers a partial but persistent
resistance to both complicity with and subjection to the royal will –
which in this case desires his payment to be suppressed.

Even though the *Male regle* was composed well before his laureate
period, it thus illustrates how Hoccleve aims to establish a voice of moral
authority but cannot achieve this without recourse to a subjected
petitionary position that both underwrites and, to some degree,
necessarily undercuts this authority. In the *Male regle*, public, moral
discourse is always also instrumental, as well as vice versa. By the same
token, the stance of the quasi-laureate is analytically distinct from, but
nevertheless mutually productive of, that of the beggar. The fragmentation of the poem's voice (and the impression of interiority that this
fragmentation produces) owes something, as Burrow has shown, to
Hoccleve's French contemporaries.[34] But its primary source is Hoccleve's
desire to speak authoritatively from an entrapment within the personal
and specific imposed on him by socioeconomic circumstances. If
Hoccleve does find an avenue to success as a Lancastrian poet in this
poem, it lies in the possibility that this entrapment, although it

necessarily foregrounds the instrumentality of his verse, does not preclude that instrumentality from being itself a worthy poetic theme. In this sense, the *Male regle* testifies to Hoccleve's belief that a poem that voices a desire for payment may also be a serious public meditation on the political, social, moral, and spiritual ramifications of money. To the extent that this belief possesses an ameliorative aim, Hoccleve shares with Lydgate an understanding of the civilizing power of poetry. And yet, the desire for payment – the desire of the shameless craver – cannot, perhaps, be so tidily deployed. Once let loose, this desire threatens to consume all discourse, and with the tensions attending this threat Hoccleve invents a poetry of the self that is Lydgateanism's hidden other.

POET TO A PRINCE: THE ''REGIMENT OF PRINCES''

In the final years of Henry IV's reign, when Hoccleve began composing a *speculum principis* for the Prince of Wales, he had in hand a ready strategy with which to accomplish this task. According to Pearsall, he completed this work just months before the prince commissioned Lydgate's *Troy Book*, while the heir apparent was still in control of the government (i.e., between November 1410 and November 1411).[35] As in the case of the *Troy Book*, the inaugurating aim (if not the final effect) of the *Regiment* is to be a monumental contribution to vernacular high culture that at the same time serves the political interests of the prince, both in general and specifically in respect to his fraught relationship with his father. In comparison with Lydgate's epic history, however, the *Regiment* much more directly voices the prince's political program and depicts his readiness for the crown, and yet it does not explicitly present itself as commissioned. These two aspects are most likely related: a putatively unsolicited, unpaid work of a concerned citizen may embed the prince's agenda in the commonplaces of traditional advice literature with less risk of appearing to be pure propaganda, pure flattery, or both.

Hoccleve, though, was an unlikely candidate for such a work for two principal reasons. First, as mere clerk of the privy seal, who had to this point achieved little recognition as poet, he was, so to speak, no English Aristotle (the supposed author of that most paradigmatic *Fürstenspiegel*, the *Secreta Secretorum*). Although Lydgate's career was also in its early stages when the prince commissioned the *Troy Book*, the genre of that work was well suited to the monk's institutional identity. In comparison, one expects the composer of a *Fürstenspiegel* already to hold some sort of authority in the matter of advising princes, which Hoccleve plainly did not (at least in any traditional sense).[36] Second, as an employee of the Lancastrian regime, any authority he did possess would seem to derive from royal power and hence not position him propitiously as adviser, much less legitimizer, of the individual holding that power. The most authentic advice — and the most effective legitimation — is voiced by one who apparently has no personal interest in giving that advice, other than his concern for the common good. In the *Regiment*, Hoccleve is in a sense publicly offering advice to his master, and thus this advice necessarily carries the suspicion of being either directed by that master, shaped by the servant's interest in his own promotion, or, at the very least, shorn of any content that the master would not want to hear (and therefore hardly very useful). Of course, properly speaking, Hoccleve worked not for the prince but for his father, and since the prince had a somewhat antagonistic relationship with the king, one might under-stand Hoccleve as — at least administratively — the prince's political opponent. But these distinctions are exceedingly fine. Indeed, the poet's most immediate master at this time — John Prophet, keeper of the privy seal — was a member of the king's council, from the leadership of which the prince directed the government in the king's name. Hoccleve possessed, therefore, neither an appropriate institu-tional affiliation nor the intellectual credentials best suited for an author of a *Fürstenspiegel*. Consequently, he would seem to face a near insurmountable problem of legitimacy at the outset of the project. His opportunity to become, as such an author, the first English laureate threatens to dissolve at the point of its offering.

Yet, having already confronted a similar problem of legitimacy in the *Male regle*, Hoccleve was prepared to answer this challenge. In the *Regiment*'s famously long prologue (occupying 2016 of the work's 5463 lines), he supplies a pseudo-autobiographical dialogue with an Old Man that addresses directly his motivations behind and qualifications for writing such a text. As in the *Male regle*, he uses autobiography to generate experiential authority, and, again as in the earlier poem, this authority ultimately rests in his financial insufficiency. He is, once more, a beggar who uses both the empirical authenticity of his condition and the distance from royal power it implies to underwrite the truth of the statements he makes about a wide range of social, political, and religious issues. In contrast with the *Male regle*, however, in this instance he cannot defer the full revelation of mendicancy until the work's conclusion. While the mock penitential opening of the earlier poem does not require any authorization beyond appropriate generic gestures, the much grander and more scholarly *Regiment*, following the convention of the academic preface, must begin with some form of statement of the author's qualifications. Hoccleve's prologue serves this purpose. By taking the form of an extended dialogue, it enables many of the pronouncements of the following advice text to appear grounded in the poet's real experience. Most important, it places the reality of the poet's financial hardship at the center of a range of problems the very existence of which predicates the need for such a text to be addressed to the current de facto ruler of the realm. Begging, in this context, is not only an authentic practice but also, more plainly than in the *Male regle*, an ameliorative one — if Hoccleve may perform a service for the prince while improving his own condition, then, by analogy, the prince may best serve his own interests by improving the conditions of the realm.

This argument about the *Regiment* has been developed by others and hence need not be recapitulated in full here.[37] Instead, to illustrate the operation of the work's mendicant poetics and to evaluate the feasibility of this poetics as a platform for quasi-laureate authority, I examine just a few of the poem's more crucial moments, beginning with the opening stanzas. Hoccleve here turns to the Boethian tradition to bring into focus the anxiety of an individualized speaker. As in the *Male regle*, we begin with a meditative, troubled first-person speaker, "[m]usynge upon the restlees bysynesse" (1), whom we know to be Thomas Hoccleve in particular because, in this case, he happens to drop the name and place of his residence ("At Chestres In, right fast be the Stronde" [5]). In contrast with the earlier poem, however, what troubles this speaker is not so much his own *misreule* as the apparent misgovernance of human existence, "this troubly world" (2). He voices, that is, a generalized Boethian lament over the vicissitudes of fortune, and this continues for the next few stanzas. Only if one has been a careful reader of the *Male regle* would one notice the preponderance of language in this passage suggestive of material wealth (or the lack thereof): e.g., his "poore goost" so "vexed" that "of angwissh and pyne/No rycher man was nowhere in no coost" (9–11); the "welthe unseur of every creature" that he in his "mynde... gan revolve" (15–16); and the "poore estat" where Fortune "pighte hir pavyloun" (29). But, by the sixth stanza, the import of this language rises to the surface, and a meditation apparently on the general condition of humankind gives way to a specific complaint about the empirical Hoccleve's unpredictable annuity: "And thus unsikir of my smal lyflode,/Thoght leide on me ful many an hevy lode" (41–42). Hoccleve's sense of insecurity in respect to his "smal lyflode," more so than a general unease in respect to the unpredictability of "Fortunes strook" (23), is responsible for his *thoght* or obsessive anxiety. As in the *Male regle*, a personal pecuniary problem becomes the generative source for, and primary example of, a broad range of more public issues.

Just how fundamental the personal and pecuniary are in this poem becomes plain when Hoccleve reveals more precisely the cause of his anxiety and subsequently the true motivation behind the text we are reading. Yet, because these revelations seem to arise naturally within the dialogue with the Old Man, the corrosive effect of the self-interest they signal is deflected. The uncertainty of the poet's annuity appears at first as an etiology of the poet's emotional condition and not merely as the instrumental motivation of the poem. As the Old Man summarizes for us, Hoccleve can scarcely obtain his current "annuitee" since "it is so streit" (glossed by Blyth as "restricted"), and he worries further that it will be "restreyned" when he retires and is "from court absent" (1780–84). The solution to this problem, the Old Man suggests, is to find a "lordshipe" who will "availle" him for all his "long service and ... travaille" (1791–92), and, a few stanzas later, after Hoccleve has rather disingenuously lamented his ignorance of such a "lordshipe," the Old Man suggests turning to the prince:

> Now syn thow me toldist
> My lord, the Prince, is good lord thee to,
> No maistrie is it for thee if thow woldist
> To be releeved. Woost thow what to do?
> Wryte to him a goodly tale or two,
> On which he may desporten him by nyght,
> And his free grace shal upon thee lyght. (1898–1904)

As the Old Man makes clear, the project of writing for the prince – at this point, merely "a goodly tale or two" – is, most fundamentally, a means for obtaining his "free grace" in regard to the poet's annuity. Through the voice of his interlocutor, Hoccleve thus baldly confesses the instrumental nature of the text we are reading. And with this confession – and its relation to the many social, political, and religious topics the two have discussed – he has laid the foundation for an authority that, precisely *because* it derives from his pecuniary need and dependence on the prince, qualifies him as his advisor.

After making this confession, however, Hoccleve shortly appears to deploy a very different authorizing strategy, one more similar to Lydgate's. The latter's laureate poetics, as we have seen, involves his establishing his person as both a vessel of moral authority and a cultural reflection of the political authority embodied in the Lancastrian prince. To achieve this, he peppers epideictic discourse with self-reference to create a mutually affirming set of relays among object, subject, and medium of poetic praise: epideictic idealization pulses through each node in the circuit, producing a divinely sanctioned prince, a laureate poet, and an aureate utterance of truth. Hoccleve, at the pivotal point in the *Regiment* — when the rambling, dialogical prologue gives way to a scholarly advice text — deploys a similar strategy by opening that advice text with a highly formal address to the prince:

> Hy noble and mighty Prince excellent,
> My lord the Prince, o my lord gracious,
> I, humble servant and obedient
> Unto your estat hy and glorious,
> Of which I am ful tendre and ful gelous,
> Me recommande unto your worthynesse,
> With herte enteer and spirit of meeknesse[.] (2017–23)

In this address, Hoccleve constructs a mutually constituting relationship between the prince's "worthynesse," that of the text that follows, and that of the text's "obedient" poet, whose conventional gestures of humility enable the presumption of such an equation. As Larry Scanlon has cogently observed, "the very ornateness of these introductory lines" indicates that "direct address does not simply locate [the prince's] *persona* but constitutes it as well. Hoccleve is not simply addressing a prince all of whose attributes are immediately available outside the text, but a prince whom he makes high, noble, and excellent by so addressing."[38] Since this bestowal of ideality necessarily redounds upon the bestower and his bestowing medium, Hoccleve elevates his own status and that of his poem at the same time as he textualizes the prince's. This reflexive aggrandizement continues in the following stanza, in which the poet requests permission to serve as the prince's poetic advisor:

> Right humbley axyng of yow the licence
> That with my penne I may to yow declare
> (So as that can my wittes innocence)
> Myn inward wil that thristith the welfare
> Of your persone, and elles be I bare

> Of blisse whan that the colde strook of deeth
> My lyf hath qweynt and me byreft my breeth. (2024–30)

Despite his continued insistence on his subjection, Hoccleve here speaks much more about himself than about his addressee, and, moreover, about himself as authoritative poet, one who declares his "inward wil" with a "penne." Indeed, in these two stanzas Hoccleve uses some form of the first person thirteen times, compared to just five instances of the second.[39] Although his authority is underwritten here by the fictional presence of the prince, that presence is in turn produced by an epideictic address the style and form of which carries an authority in some ways inherent in its structure and in other ways inseparable from the poet who can compose it.

If Hoccleve had possessed Lydgate's poetic inclinations or, what is more significant, his social identity, he probably would have amplified the same epideictic matter across several more stanzas. He might even have indulged, as Lydgate does in the *Troy Book*, in a self-aggrandizing meditation on the nature of the genre in which he is writing. What he does instead in the next stanza reflects the difference in his social location and consequently the very different strategy of self-authorization to which he is obliged to return:

> Thogh that my lyflode and possessioun
> Be scant, I ryche am of benevolence;
> To you therof can I be no nygoun.
> Good have I noon by which your excellence
> May plesid be, and for myn inpotence
> Stoppith the way to do as I were holde,
> I wryte as he that your good lyf fayn wolde. (2031–37)

Here, in a gesture of both authenticity and self-interest, Hoccleve turns back to the matter of his prologue. As the Old Man recommended, he reveals to the prince the substance of his anxiety and the primary motivating circumstance behind the present writing — that his "lyflode and possessioun" are "scant" — and in this way confirms the prologue's claims to empirical veracity. At the same time, he suggests that his financial insufficiency is precisely what enables him to produce the putatively disinterested advice text that follows. The paucity of his "possessioun" begets the wealth of his "benevolence"; since he has no "[g]ood" to win the prince's favor, he offers instead a text that furthers the prince's "good lyf."

Despite this suggestion, however, this return to the matter of the prologue immediately following the epideictic opening of the advice text ensures that a functionally enabling self-interest lies just beneath the surface of its apparently disinterested advice. And at one point late in the work, this self-interest again becomes bluntly explicit. Having just finished illustrating the evils of prodigality through his tale of John of Canace and his empty box, he goes on to confess his own wasteful spending habits, and then uses the occasion to ask for his belated annuity payment:

> My yeerly guerdoun, myn annuitee,
> That was me grauntid for my long labour,
> Is al behynde — I may nat payed be;
> Which causith me to lyven in langour.
> O, liberal Prince, ensample of honour,
> Unto your grace lyke it to promoote
> My poore estat, and to my wo beeth boote. (4383–89)

Explicitly here, but implicitly throughout the advice text, Hoccleve begs from the same "liberal Prince" that he is advising.[40] By acknowledging this potential conflict of interest, he seeks to use it as a sign of his truthfulness. Nevertheless, as in the *Male regle*, the sheer persistence of the poem's mendicancy ultimately raises the question of whether in fact begging may serve as the ground of moral authority, or whether in the end it discloses that authority to be a money-making ruse. This question has been explored by a number of critics, often in the form of a consideration of the unity between the autobiographical prologue and the advice text. Most have rendered a judgment in favor of unity — concluding that, as I have been suggesting, mendicancy and counsel are mutually affirming. Others, noting such aspects of the work as its pervasive obsession with the evils of flattery and avarice, suspect that Hoccleve's self-interest cannot be so easily reconciled with the prince's. Rather than understanding Hoccleve's begging to be a personal matter rhetorically transformed into a means of serving the public, these critics tend to see the poet as funneling the interest of the public into the well of his financial desire.[41]

Both groups of critics, I believe, have it right. Hoccleve no doubt *designed* his begging in the *Regiment* to serve an authorizing function, but in practice, just as in the *Male regle*, he left uncertain whether mendicant poetics can truly serve as the basis for a quasi-laureate authority. What keeps this possibility provisional is, among other things, the fact that if the material aim of his begging were to be realized, the begging would cease to have a legitimate purpose and hence any authority it possesses would vanish. If, in other words, Hoccleve were to receive prompt payment of his annuity, then as a poet he would disappear once again into the undistinguished category of low-level civil servant, no longer possessing an active experiential basis on which to found an authority located in his own person and not deriving from the prince's. The looming problem in Hoccleve's strategy is that the authority of his begging is conditional and not — like Lydgate's social identity as monk — absolute. To circumvent this problem, he must imply that if his request were fulfilled, then he would become *more* of a laureate rather than less of one — that his lack of money, rather then enabling (as it, in fact, does) his voice of moral authority, is an obstacle to such a voice. With a plenitude of money, his socioeconomic dependence on the prince would vanish, and he could then fully occupy the position of self-determining laureate. In this logic, his desire for money becomes one and the same as his desire for a laureateship, his anxiety over his income a sign of his thwarted longing for a poetic crown, and the *Regiment* a vitiated instance of the kind of poetic performance the prince may expect to receive if he makes permanent and plenteous the poet's "yeerly guerdoun."

As we saw in respect to Lydgate's self-authorizing maneuvers in the *Troy Book*, however, English vernacular poetry in the early fifteenth century possessed neither the precedent nor the protocol for such direct laureate self-fashioning. Hence, Hoccleve, preempting Lydgate in this regard, turns to the obvious proxy, pointing to Chaucer as the analogue of the prince in the realm of high culture that he himself would be if he were not constrained to plead for money. The resulting well-known nods to his poetic predecessor appear at four key points in the *Regiment*: directly following the moment in the prologue in which Hoccleve names himself on consecutive lines; at the end of the prologue, immediately after he finally commits himself to writing the advice text; paired with the epideictic address to Prince Henry that opens the advice text proper; and near the end of the penultimate section of the advice text, subtitled *De consilio habendo in omnibus factis*, in which Chaucer — along with his famous portrait — appears as the vernacular poetic counselor *par excellence*. The strategy of each of these moments is to praise his predecessor reflexively as a possessor of the status that he holds out as the ideal for himself.[42]

Here I consider just the first and by far briefest mention of Chaucer, which occurs when Hoccleve, immediately after twice revealing his surname during a discussion of the best way to approach the prince, has the Old Man declare, "Sone, I have herd or this men speke of thee;/Thow were aqweyntid with Chaucer, pardee" (1866—67). The suddenness of this response conveys both the eminence of Hoccleve's predecessor and, at the same time, a presumption of Hoccleve's own stature as poet in the public eye — as one who, through his close association with his master, would be a topic of conversation. After a one-line paean to Chaucer, in the next stanza Hoccleve seizes the opportunity (again through the voice of the Old Man) to suggest that his own particular accomplishments and abilities especially qualify him as the prince's vernacular writer:

> "Althogh thow seye that thow in Latyn
> Ne in Frensshe neither canst but smal endyte,
> In Englissh tonge canstow wel afyn."
> "Fadir, thereof can I eek but a lyte."
> "Yee, straw! Let be! Thy penne take and wryte
> As thow canst, and thy sorowe torne shal
> Into gladnesse — I doute it nat at al." (1870—76)

We know from Hoccleve's *Formulary* that the poet's humble disparagement of his Latin and French is disingenuous. The humility topos operates here in its typical fashion — to lay claim to what it denies — and in this instance the distinction the poet makes among languages further underscores his implicit claim to expertise in English: "If, in my role as clerk of the privy seal, I have mastered Latin and French," Hoccleve implies, "then surely I am qualified as a writer of English." Speaking for the poet, the Old Man insists that in the "Englissh tonge" Hoccleve can write "wel afyn" (glossed by Blyth as "perfectly") and that he should therefore take up his "penne" and "wryte" for the prince.

Nonetheless, as the next stanza indicates, for Hoccleve even such inverted and indirect self-aggrandizement must be matched with an unmistakable reminder of the underlying instrumentality of the effort. For the topic of this entire passage, despite its brief memorialization of Chaucer, has been how to *use* the prince as a means of securing his payment:

> "Syn thow maist nat be payed in th'eschequer,
> Unto my lord the Prince make instance
> That thy patente into the hanaper
> May chaunged be." "Fadir, by your souffrance,
> It may not so by cause of th'ordenance:
> Longe aftir this shal no graunt chargeable
> Out passe — fadir myn, this is no fable." (1877—83)

Hoccleve has his Old Man suggest that his annuity be paid out of the more reliable hanaper (the department of chancery that received fees for the sealing of documents) rather than the exchequer, and then depicts himself as rejecting this suggestion, referring to Henry Beaufort's decision in 1403 to stop all annuities payable by this department — a decision that the prince, while in control of the council, confirmed.[43] These lines, as they *precede* the Old Man's recommendation that Hoccleve write a "goodly tale or two" for the prince, represent the first proposal for what he should write. Instead of the high-culture advice text that actually follows, the Old Man would have the poet pen a simple administrative petition: "Unto my lord the Prince make instance/That thy patente into the hanaper/May chaunged be." In this sense, the advice text only comes into being because the prince has, through his conservative fiscal policy, preemptively rejected such a petition. The advice text — and, indeed, the poem as a whole — is therefore from this standpoint simply the poet's replacement petition, greatly amplified. By the same token, the remarkable density of historically specific detail in this stanza does not — as does Lydgate's self-description as the "monk of Bury" — contribute to the poet's self-aggrandizement, but rather emphasizes his entrapment in the personal and material. Lydgate always follows his eulogies of Chaucer with some sort of coded assertion of his inheritance of his predecessor's (retroactively bestowed) laureateship. In contrast, Hoccleve associates this brief nod to his master — as he does with his three longer ones — with an indication of the pecuniary obstacle that supposedly blocks the path of his poetic career. As in the *Male regle*, we begin to suspect that in the *Regiment* Hoccleve's desire always comes first: the prince — his royal addressee, employer, and would-be literary patron — would reduce the financial burden of annuities, but Hoccleve, the groveling subject, would have his pay.

THE SELFHOOD OF THE FAILED LAUREATE: THE "SERIES"

Given the persistent return of the personal in Hoccleve's mendicant poetics, his career as quasi-official Lancastrian poet would likely have collapsed on its own. The mental illness he reports experiencing during or before 1416 thus largely brought on the inevitable. But in compensation, this illness turned out to be a profound source of poetic inspiration, as his recovery from it lies behind the *Series*, his single most remarkable achievement. This multipart, generically variegated poem consists of five linked texts: the *Complaint*, in which the author reveals his past mental illness and laments that, despite his recovery, his former acquaintances still shun him; the *Dialogue*, which dramatizes a conversation between the

author and a friend regarding, among other things, the *Complaint*; an
English rendering of the tale *Jereslaus's Wife* from the *Gesta Romanorum*
and that tale's moralization; a verse translation of the penitential treatise
Learn to Die and the abrupt termination of this in favor of the brief prose
of the *Joys of Heaven*; and another *Gesta Romanorum* tale, *Jonathas and
Fellicula*, and its moralization.[44] The pervasive self-referential and
metapoetic gestures in this work — which, according to Burrow, is "far
and away the most reflexive of all medieval English writings" — have been
much commented upon and are typically explained as imitative of his
mental illness and/or his recovery.[45] Equally well noted are the poem's
unprecedented development of the psychological terrain of its speaker
and its insistence on irreducibility of the psychological in the face of more
conventional explanatory categories.[46]

Both of these aspects of the poem are well illustrated by perhaps its
best-known passage, the moment in the *Complaint* in which Hoccleve
examines his own reflection for any signs of abnormality (155–61).
In this depiction of himself "allone" in his "chambre," staring at
his reflection in a "mirour" in the hope of amending it if it were
not "right," he supplies a specular analogue of the very poem he is
writing: because of the social isolation that persists following his illness,
he must confirm himself recovered through solitary, self-reflective
writing, through which he attempts to construe in the "chambre" of his
own versified thoughts the logic of his renewed health. But what he
discovers is not the means to his desired end, his reinsertion into social
"communynge" (217), but instead the radical isolation of individual
subjectivity. Realizing that "men in [regard to] hire owne cas" are
"blynde alday" (170), he understands that an individual cannot
transcend his own subjectivity and view himself from the standpoint
of others. Self-reflection, whether scopic or poetic, may provide insight,
but in this case that insight amounts only to the discovery of his
entrapment within his own psyche.

Nonetheless, although we must not underestimate the role that
mental illness plays in precipitating this epistemology, when the
Complaint gives way to the *Dialogue* it becomes apparent that this
epistemology derives from other factors as well. In the opening of the
poem's second section, we depart from Hoccleve's psychological interior
to hear with him a knock on his "chambre dore" and the voice of a
"good freend/of fern agoon" who calls out, "'How, Hoccleue, art thow
heere?//Opne thy dore'" (2–8). In this diegetic and thematic context,
this request for him to "[o]pne [his] dore" appears as an invitation to

leave psychological enclosure behind and reestablish social communion. The poet's surname stands for his public identity, and the question of whether or not that particular identity is "heere" surfaces as the fundamental question of the entire work. Simply put, the *Dialogue* stands against the *Complaint* as the social to the psychological, and therefore thematic development arises from generic conflict. Hoccleve's attempt to restore *communynge* becomes, at least initially, the problem of what to do with the *Complaint*, which now transmogrifies from a self-reflective meditation to a recently written text that the poet intends to circulate as an advertisement of his recovery. As a preview of its public circulation, Hoccleve reads the *Complaint* to his friend, and the latter's negative response ("Reherce thow it nat/ne it awake;//Keepe al þat cloos/ for thyn honoures sake" [27–28]) leads us to understand the other factors that lie behind the work as a whole. Inasmuch as the friend represents the potential for restoration of social relationships – and, in particular, the reestablishment of a public readership – the friend's insistence that the psychological landscape depicted in the *Complaint* is best kept "cloos" stands for the more general response to Hoccleve's autobiographical writings. For a poet who at the time would have been best known as the author of the *Regiment* and its strikingly disproportionate autobiographical prologue, the friend's response figures the official reaction to the manner in which he sought, in that work, to underwrite his authority. If in the *Regiment* he attempts to use personal and instrumental discourse to establish its public and moral counterpart, in the *Series* we learn that this bid to be England's first poet laureate failed – a fact which, despite the *Regiment's* wide circulation, appears confirmed by Hoccleve's exceptionally muted reception in the rest of the century and beyond.[47] What brings the *Series* and its poetics of selfhood about, therefore, is not just a desire for social reintegration following an episode of madness but also a longing for public restoration following a failure as Lancastrian poet.

That the friend indeed stands for the official response to his poetry becomes more apparent several stanzas later in the *Dialogue*, when the debate travels beyond the matter of the *Complaint* and takes up the question of what texts Hoccleve ought to be writing more generally and for what reasons. After defending the value of his *Complaint* and pursuing a lengthy digression condemning coin clippers, Hoccleve, so to speak, rests his case.[48] In reply, the friend, rather than affirming or further questioning his choice, instead asks him if he had thought to write anything else: "'Whan thy compleynte/was to thende ybroght,//Cam it aght in thy purpos/and thy thoght//Aght elles therwith/to han madd than that?'" (200–1). This non-response and blunt change in topic represent, respectively, the silent disapproval of Hoccleve's autobiographical efforts and the desire of his audience for some other sort of writing. Hoccleve, in the face of this silence and desire, relinquishes his case for the *Complaint* without further comment. He answers that, indeed, he had "purposid to translate" "a small tretice//Which Lerne for to Die/callid is[,]" so that he may "clense" his "bodyes gilt" as well as that of "[m]any anothir wight" (205–19). After this revelation, discussion of the *Complaint* is left behind. In this brief exchange, Hoccleve dramatizes the rejection of his characteristic mode of writing for one more acceptable to his readership. In the place of a poetry of personal desire, he offers a penitential treatise aimed at redeeming his own and others' souls.

This replacement, as it turns out, represents only the first step in his self-recuperation as public poet. At the conclusion of a long and very digressive debate, in which Hoccleve's interlocutor claims that his work on such texts was precisely what brought on his illness, the friend, who seems to be losing this argument, once again abruptly changes topics. He recalls that Hoccleve had mentioned "a book" that he owed to "my lord/þat now is lieutenant,//My lord of Gloucestre" (531–33), and wonders whether this debt is the real motivation behind the poet's proposed translation of *Learn to Die*. At first, Hoccleve's readily affirmative answer ("'Yee sikir, freend, ful treewe is your deemynge'" [540]) and his sudden desire to choose some other text for the purpose ("'But of sum othir thyng fayn trete I wolde//My noble lordes herte/with/ to glade'"[547–48]) may seem strangely to cancel much of what he has just asserted. Now he has decided to pursue the translation not (solely) as a salve for his and his readers' souls but also as payment of a patronage "dette" (532). And, despite his elaborate defense of *Learn to Die* as his next (and last) writing project, he would just as soon "trete" of "sum othir thyng." This odd self-cancellation, however, dramatizes exactly the recuperation that he seeks. His original motive for writing *Learn to Die* (as well as, to some extent, the interiorized nature of the treatise) remains, for someone in his situation, too personal. In recalling his debt to the duke, he dramatizes the replacement of this motive with one unquestionably in line with his heretofore quasi-laureate status: the commission of a Lancastrian prince. With the reestablishment of (actual or hoped for) royal patronage, he need no longer be concerned with the intrinsic merits of his project but instead only with whether it will "glade" the "herte" of his patron.

From the stanzas that follow we may initially receive the impression that he has indeed recovered a position as high-culture versifier of Lancastrian interests. These stanzas, containing as they do a rather long (63-line) panegyric of Humphrey, could be the opening to a second edition of the *Regiment*'s advice text, and, as such, retroactively transform what has preceded into an autobiographical prologue parallel to that of the first edition:

> Next our lord lige/our kyng victorioius,
> In al this wyde world/lord is ther noon
> Vnto me so good ne so gracious,
> And haath been swich/yeeres ful many oon.
> God yilde it him/as sad as any stoon
> His herte set is/and nat change can
> Fro me, his humble seruant & and man. (554–60)

In these lines Hoccleve emphasizes the duke's close proximity to the king, just as Lydgate does in his address to Humphrey in the *Fall of Princes*. In addition, as in the address to Prince Henry in the *Regiment*, we encounter a poet more concerned with himself – the "humble seruant" to whom Humphrey "haath been" and presumably will again be "so gracious" – than with the prince whom he is praising. Yet, what follows this panegyric is neither an advice text nor anything similar, but instead a return to the debate about what text Hoccleve ought to be writing. With a jarring shift in tone and style, the encomium of Humphrey ceases abruptly, and Hoccleve asks, "'Now good freend/shoue at the cart, I yow preye.//What thyng may I make vnto his plesance?'" (617–18). The joke here is that the speaker, as the author of an extensive, well-known *Fürstenspiegel*, plainly knows what sort of "thyng" would be appropriate to "make" for Humphrey. And, lest we miss this joke, the friend, after briefly illustrating the importance of careful decision making, remarks, "'This [exemplum] may been vnto thee/in thy *makyngel*/A good *mirour*'" (645–46, emphasis added). In theory, Hoccleve ought to be supplying *Humphrey* a "good mirour" full of exempla such as the one the friend has just given. To further this point, Hoccleve provides a gloss indicating that this entire passage derives from Geoffrey of Vinsauf's *Poetria nova*.[49] By calling attention to this prestigious source, he makes plain that he is fully in command as poet. In the midst of this pretense of being ignorant of what to do next, he signals his complete awareness of what he ought to be doing.

Even more pointedly, a few stanzas earlier, near the beginning of the panegyric, he admits that he considered translating nothing less than

Vegetius's *De re militari*, a text that would, as the veritable bible of medieval military practice, advertise its patron as both learned and martial. Humphrey, as one would expect, was quite familiar with Vegetius, and even donated a Latin copy of the work to Oxford.[50] If Hoccleve had translated this work, he would have returned full circle to his initial strategy for gaining the attention of the Lancastrians by presenting himself once again as a male, English version of Christine de Pizan – except this time choosing a more propitious text: Christine's *Le livre des faits d'armes et de chevalerie* (about 1404), which draws on Vegetius, and which was widely popular in both France and England.[51] But Hoccleve represents himself rejecting Vegetius because, as he obsequiously reasons, the duke has already reached perfection as a knight: "But I see his knyghthode so encrece//þat no thyng my labour sholde edifie" (563–64). A little later, he suggests that to "cronicle" Humphrey's own martial "actes/were a good deede" (603), since "It is a greet auauntage/A man before him/to haue a mirour,/Therin to see the path vnto honour" (609). And yet, this suggestion, even more so than the first, turns out to be a mere reflex of flattery. We begin to suspect that not only this uncertainty over what to write for Humphrey but also this entire excursion into the matter of royal patronage is performed tongue in cheek. And, a little further on, this passage indeed reveals itself to be an extended joke, and a somewhat bitter one at that, for the friend, after much waffling, changes subjects once again and turns to Hoccleve's supposed history of antifeminist writing, for which he must now do penance. The ensuing debate eventually revolves around the *Epistre de Cupide*. Even if Hoccleve was in actuality writing the *Series* for Humphrey (which, considering what comes next, is doubtful), the potential prestige and authority that commission might bestow he abandons at this point in favor of a return to the primal scene of his baffled career. Rather than dramatizing the recovery of his former quasi-laureate status, the *Series*, with this recursive gesture, portrays the inevitability of his failure.[52]

The choice of text that he finally settles on provides a considerably more pungent indication of the ultimate direction of the work. Still in the *Dialogue*, he feigns surprise at the friend's suggestion that he write a profeminist text, quite reasonably asking, "'what lust or pleisir//Shal my lord haue in þat?/Noon/thynkith me'" (701–2). The friend responds,

> "Yes Thomas, yis/his lust and his desir
> Is/as it wel sit/to his hy degree,

For his desport/& mirthe in honestee
With ladyes/to haue daliance;
And this book/wole he shewen hem parchance." (703–7)

Although when Hoccleve wrote these lines (most likely, according to
Burrow, in 1420)[53] Humphrey's notorious "daliance" with Jacqueline of
Hainault and Eleanor Cobham was still to come, their taste and tone are
nonetheless questionable, especially in juxtaposition with the preceding
panegyric much more suited to the duke's "hy degree." There is
calculated disrespect here, albeit subtly and jocularly expressed. In
comparison, when Hoccleve finally provides the "book" that will
"shewen" the duke "desport" and "mirthe," this disrespect becomes
bluntly evident. As Patterson observes,

> The tale of *Jereslaus's Wife*, written for Humphrey, records, among other things,
> the political and sexual misbehavior of the emperor's brother while "steward" of
> the empire in his brother's absence. Since Duke Humphrey was at this very time
> serving as the king's lieutenant in England while Henry was in France [as
> Hoccleve himself notes in the *Dialogue*, line 533], Hoccleve's narrative has an
> obvious and stunningly tactless political relevance.[54]

Instead of a *Fürstenspiegel*, Vegetius, or chronicle of the duke's
accomplishments, what the duke receives with *Jereslaus's Wife* is an
insulting caricature, an image of him not as ideal regent but as sordid
steward. The *Series*, therefore, far from being (or even soliciting) a
recuperation of Lancastrian patronage, is instead an ironic comment
upon – if not, indeed, a mockery of – the entire system of such
patronage and the laureate performances it demands. What in
Hoccleve's earlier works emerged as the insistence of his unfulfilled
desire to priority over (and therefore resistance to) the will of his patron,
in the *Series* surfaces as the latent hostility of one too long refused his
wishes. The remainder of the work confirms this impression, as it
continues in the same vein, supplying *Learn to Die* despite the previous
decision to forego it and offering another *Gesta Romanorum* tale even
more remorselessly tactless in respect to the noble personage to whom it
is (eventually) dedicated.[55] Instead of signaling, through a developmental
progression of genre, a release from psychological enclosure and a
restoration of a quasi-official laureateship, the *Series* represents quite the
opposite: it depicts the collapse of the very notion of laureate
performance into a starkly acrid (if at the same time humorously
endearing) performance of a virtuoso, if socially enforced, poetics of
selfhood.

At the center of this poetics, in this work and elsewhere, is the poet's self-representation as beggar. Like Lydgate's monastic laureate, the beggar is politically useful to the extent that his authority can never be fully aligned with royal power. But, in contrast with Lydgate's persona, the beggar's misalignment, at bottom, bespeaks a fundamental antagonism. Simply stated, it is the prince's fault that Hoccleve is a beggar, and thus in his very acts of praising and petitioning this beggar laureate is also blaming. This blame appears in various guises throughout Hoccleve's oeuvre and especially as allusive reminders of the Lancastrians' illegitimacy (as in the *Epistre de Cupide*) or coded critiques of royal policy (as in the *Regiment*). Hoccleve's mental illness, from this standpoint, only widens the scope of this inherent antagonism. Because this illness has the effect of increasing the distance between poet and potential patrons, the endemic self-obsession and sugarcoated hostility of his mendicant poetics become, in the *Series*, his main point rather than a means to a potential end. Accordingly, the thwarted poetic and vocational desires of a historically concrete individual, rather than serving as the ground for some other purpose, take center stage — and this, as it turns out, is the work's remarkable achievement. If, as Joel Fineman argues in respect to Shakespeare's sonnets, literary subjectivity is an effect of ironic epideictic lyric,[56] then, by the same token, literary interiority is an effect of an ironic version of that more extensive species of encomium, a laureate performance.

We do not encounter in English verse a representation of interiority of near the same depth as Hoccleve's until well into the next century, in the work of Sir Thomas Wyatt — who, for somewhat different reasons, possessed a similarly ambivalent relationship with royal power. From this perspective, Hoccleve's poetry is a brilliant failure, a precocious immersion into selfhood's tangle of public and private that was to have little apparent influence on the course of English verse. As we will see, Hoccleve would go unacknowledged even by George Ashby, the sole fifteenth-century poet who demonstrates close acquaintance with his work. Nonetheless, throughout the history of laureate performances from Hoccleve's day onward, a Hocclevean beggar always lurks under the skin of the poet's authoritative pose — and, indeed, at times inevitably reveals himself. In respect to the prince for whom he is writing, the poet is always to some degree a beggar. To the extent that he can appear otherwise, he may fashion himself as laureate; conversely, to the extent that his mendicancy envelops his verse, he may succeed at writing his selfhood.

PART III

From Lancaster to early Tudor

In 1614, an obscure poet named Thomas Freeman published a diptych of epigram collections in which biting satirical and moralistic pieces alternate with increasingly more frequent, and apparently heartfelt, paeans to other poets. The subjects of the latter include many of his most illustrious contemporaries: Daniel, Donne, Heywood, Nash, Shakespeare, and Spenser. But they also reach back to the misty beginnings of the English poetic tradition in a eulogy to its founding triumvirate:

> Pitty ô pitty, death had power
> Ouer Chaucer, Lidgate, Gower:
> They that equal'd all the Sages
> Of these, their owne, of former Ages[.][1]

Important to Freeman is nothing specific about the poems of Chaucer, Lydgate, or Gower, but rather the idea of an embodied origin of vernacular poetic authority. This origin is locatable in history and generative of successors, and at the same time transcends history as the point of entry of the timeless wisdom of "all the Sages." It is, in other words, the notionally absolute intellectual and moral basis on which a tradition may be built. Most likely, Freeman was not aware that, of the three authors making up the conventional formula, Lydgate provides the most direct precedent for this self-authorizing strategy. Freeman no doubt understood himself as inspired by classical precedent, and his immediate vernacular model was Ben Jonson. Yet, in opening his collection with a series of seven epideictic addresses to the politically powerful (from King James down to Freeman's immediate patron, Lord Windsor), identifying his first-person speaker with his historically specific person, and locating moral authority in the latter by means of reflexive praise, he reproduces the basics of Lydgate's laureate poetics.

The year 1614 may seem late for such an earnest deployment of this formula, as it is often claimed that eulogies of the English triumvirate were commonplace already in the first half of the fifteenth century. In fact, before 1500 the formula is quite rare. I know of only two authors who render it in verse as such: Osbern Bokenham and George Ashby. It becomes a cliché only with its repeated instances in the poems of Hawes and Skelton in the early sixteenth century and, in Scotland, in the work of William Dunbar and Gavin Douglas. In comparison, in the 1420s, James I of Scotland can end his *Kingis Quair* – a poem quite obviously influenced by Lydgate – by recommending it only to "Gowere and Chaucere ... Superlatiue as poetis laureate/In moralitee and eloquence ornate."[2] Here James apes the Lydgatean envoy virtually to the letter, but without including Lydgate among the poets from whom he seeks authorization. This absence has been explained by the fact that Lydgate was still alive.[3] But it seems more likely – given that Bokenham shows no reluctance to name Lydgate in the 1440s and even emphasizes the fact that the poet still lives – that James does not name Lydgate simply because he is not trying to *be* Lydgate. As the rest of the poem makes plain, he seeks not so much to align himself with Lydgatean poetics as to use Lydgate's language, imagery, and conceits for rather different purposes. (The same might be said, albeit in respect to a less marked degree of Lydgatean influence, about that more prolific princely maker of courtly verse, Charles d'Orléans.)

This is not to say that we should be surprised by the later elevation of Lydgate to the founding group of English *auctores*. Such a widely disseminated poet was a highly visible model of success, and naming him was an obvious way both to imitate one of his strategies (i.e., his naming of Chaucer) and to lay claim to his authority. Yet, as we saw in Chapter 2, Lydgate's wide dissemination itself should not be taken for granted. It was the product of a particular set of historical circumstances, most prominent among them the need to legitimize the various agenda of the Lancastrian dynasty. As these circumstances changed, poets would have sought authority through the name of Lydgate only to the extent that it maintained its currency – that is, only inasmuch as it became understood as a constituent part of a poetic tradition, which, through its seeming timelessness, may be adapted to myriad situations and purposes. In this regard, the obvious difference between James Stewart and Freeman is that, even though James possessed a much more extensive knowledge of Lydgate's poetry, he wrote the *Kingis Quair* at a point when Lydgate was still inventing the tradition into which he would later be stellified.

Between James and Freeman occurred the gradual process of canonization, through which a poet of a particular time and place becomes a marker of timeless literary authority, and, as such, a historically empty (and thereby adaptable) instrument in the toolbox of literary convention. And, though there are myriad ways in which this process may be realized, before the era of print a crucial one is conscious imitation. A poet may be understood as canonical if he possesses non-canonical shadows; major authors appear as such in the light of minor disciples. To understand, then, how Lydgate emerges from the fifteenth century as one of the founding fathers of English poetry, one must understand why and how the most overlooked group of poets in English literary history, the mid-fifteenth-century Lydgateans, take up a poetic practice in which they understand themselves – and come to be understood – as such disciples. In turn, one may then understand why the next generation of poets, the first early Tudors, continue to monumentalize Lydgate even while their inclination and ability to imitate him, for various reasons, begins to wane. Finally, in this period we may also witness how Hoccleveanism remains Lydgateanism's persistent alter ego, even while Hoccleve himself would go almost completely unrecognized.

Space prohibits me from covering all the poets who somehow engage with the Lydgatean tradition in the period covered by the following two chapters. English poets who make little or no appearance, but who nonetheless left behind varied and revealing encounters with this tradition, include John Audelay, John Capgrave, John Metham, John Hardyng, and Bokenham. More conspicuously missing are those authors typically referred to as Scottish Chaucerians, i.e., Robert Henryson, Douglas, and, especially, Dunbar. The work of these poets forms an important branch of Lydgateanism, and among their poems are some of the finest examples of verse written in this tradition. But, because my focus in this book is on poets who conceive of their careers in some relation (whether desired or actual) to the English court, I leave to a different project a consideration of how Lydgateanism is practiced by Scottish poets in their particular social, cultural, and political contexts.

CHAPTER 4

Lydgateanism

In this chapter, I argue that mid-century Lydgatean poets are not opportunistic, mindless imitators, but rather discover in Lydgate's laureate poetics a powerful strategy with which (or against which) to position themselves in respect to their particular historical circumstances. Moreover, in reproducing (or critiquing) this poetics, they necessarily reproduce its dynamic of self-laureation vis-à-vis a laureate original. In other words, Lydgate's canonicity arises as reflex of his own canonization of Chaucer. To imitate Lydgate praising Chaucer means to praise Lydgate, and therefore the mid-century Lydgateans not only serve as the conduit through which Lydgate becomes part of the English poetic tradition, but they also do so in such a manner as to make Lydgate's role in that tradition reflect rather closely his own poetic ideology. From this perspective, Lydgate becomes the inevitable third member of the founding triumvirate because he, more than any other fifteenth-century poet, establishes as part of the native tradition the poetics that a celebration of this triumvirate both signifies and puts into operation.

In the pages that follow, I first examine a short poem each for two poets who address Lydgate directly during his lifetime: Benedict Burgh and William de la Pole, duke of Suffolk (or someone possessing a similar social status). These rather remarkable little poems illustrate how Lydgateanism may be constituted either positively or negatively – that is, either by obsequious emulation (Burgh) or by condescending critique (Suffolk). As a more comprehensive case study, I then devote a long section to George Ashby, whose surviving poems date to a decade or so after Lydgate's death amidst the political chaos of the Wars of the Roses, and whose work exhibits with particular clarity the inevitable copresence of the Hocclevean beggar within the Lydgatean laureate. I conclude with a brief look at how the emergence of commercial printing in the 1470s effectively terminates one avenue of Lydgateanism, even while reifying the tradition in a newly potent manner. Spanning a period of some 50 years, this chapter seeks to document the maneuverings of poets who confront a literary scene dominated by a living or lately expired master, and to chart the rise and retrenchment of the tradition this master brings about. At the start of this period, Burgh makes personal obeisance to a still-living Lydgate. At its end, Caxton helps to disassociate Lydgateanism from a necessary association with any particular poet, making it the free-floating authoritative poetics that a secular epigrammist like Thomas Freeman, over 100 years later, may seize upon and deploy as self-evidently empowering.

THE DISCIPLE WHO MAKES A MASTER: BENEDICT BURGH

Sometime before Lydgate's death in 1449, two short poems appeared that not only have Lydgate as their principal addressee but also take him as their principal topic. The first of these, Burgh's *Letter to John Lydgate*, is an encomiastic verse epistle requesting appointment as a poetic apprentice, and as such represents the first poem in English wholly devoted to one poet's celebration of his more illustrious, living contemporary.[1] In contrast, the second, *A Reproof to Lydgate*, which has been attributed to the duke of Suffolk, represents the first explicit versified critique of a fellow vernacular poet.[2] Though opposed in their evaluation of Lydgate, both of these poems contain the quite novel assumption that the living author whom they address plays a role amounting to that of a poet laureate, and is hence an apt target for the sycophancy and abuse that such a position of authority attracts.

Of the two, Burgh's *Letter* has the greater historical importance (if lesser aesthetic success), as it provides the earliest evidence of a patronage nexus that, in retrospect, proved crucial to the constitution of the Lydgatean tradition. Burgh was born c.1413, lived through the tumults of the middle of the century, and died in 1483, having had a "prosperous although inconspicuous career in the Church," the highlight of which was the "rich prebend" bestowed on him "by the hand of Edward the Fourth direct."[3] In the years 1433–40, Burgh was vicar of Maldon in Essex. Bylegh Abbey at Little Maldon, from where Burgh dates the *Letter*, was not far from Hatfield Broadoak, where Lydgate had been prior and where he still resided perhaps as late as November 1433.[4] Sometime during his vicarship, Burgh composed a rhyme royal translation of the *Disticha Catonis* for the young William (later viscount) Bourchier, son of Henry (later earl of Essex) and Isabel (the sister of Richard, duke of York).[5] Henry's mother, Anne, countess of Stafford, was the patron of Lydgate's

An Invocation to Seynte Anne, and Henry's half-sister Ann, lady March, the patron of Lydgate's *The Legend of Seynt Margarete.*[6] In 1440, Henry's father William, count of Eu, and his brother John were admitted to the fraternity of the abbey of Bury.[7] Given these relationships and the timing of Burgh's Maldon living, we may suppose that Burgh composed his *Letter* to his eminent neighbor poet as an attempt to gain entré into the world of the latter's local patronage connections. Probably written soon after Burgh's arrival in Maldon in 1433, the *Letter* no doubt flattered Lydgate and led to his recommendation of Burgh to the Bourchier family and thence to the commissioning of the *Disticha Catonis.*[8]

Considered as poem rather than as historical document, the *Letter* stands as a virtually paradigmatic articulation of the principles and practices of inheritance upon which Lydgatean authority rests and by which it is perpetuated. This poem, in its aureately rendered humility and hyperbolic praise of its addressee, mimics rather precisely (if, unintentionally, parodically) the style, authorial pose, and subsumptive strategies of Lydgate's own epideictic obeisance to his poetic precursors. As in Lydgate's practice, praise of another in the *Letter* is above all a means of self-aggrandizement; revealingly, half of the piece's eight rhyme royal stanzas are not so much about Lydgate as about the speaker and his poem. Burgh plainly recognizes in Lydgate's groveling before Chaucer and others thinly veiled claims for the inheritance of his predecessors' authority, and by imitating this subjection, Burgh seeks to extend the poetic lineage through Lydgate to himself.

This subsumptive strategy is apparent from the start. Burgh devotes the poem's first two stanzas to an elaborate "I never dwelled with the muses" topos, which together manage to form an extended compliment to the addressee while actually being all about the speaker:

> Nat dremyd I in ye mownt of pernaso,
> ne dranke I nevar at pegases welle,
> the pale pirus saw I never also,
> ne wist I never where ye muses dwelle,
> ne of goldyn Tagus can I no thynge telle,
> And to wete my lippis I cowde not atteyne
> In citero or elicon sustres tweyne. (1–7)

For English poetry, the *locus classicus* of this topos is Chaucer's Franklin's prologue, where the self-effacing "burel man" insists, "I sleep nevere on the Mount of Pernaso" (5.716–28). But Burgh imitates not Chaucer but Lydgate, the Ricardian poet's disciple and Burgh's master, who rehearses the Franklin's rhetorical exercise several times in his corpus, placing it in his own voice and, typically, amplifying it greatly. Consider, for example, the passage that begins with the second stanza of the prologue to Book 3 of the *Fall of Princes*:

> I meene as thus: I haue no fressh licour
> Out off the conduitis off Calliope,
> Nor thoruh Clio in rethorik no flour
> In my labour for to refresshe me,
> Nor off the sustren, in noumbre thries thre,
> Which with Cithera on Pernaso duell, —
> Thei neuer me gaff drynk onys off ther well! (3.8–14)

Lydgate here means exactly the opposite of what he says. In the very act of writing these lofty verses, which are original to him, he is indeed, figuratively speaking, dwelling on Parnassus and drinking from the well of the "sustren" nine. With the signal phrase "I meene as thus," he interrupts the opening conceit of his source, which figures writing as a pilgrimage. His "I" thus usurps that of the previous stanza, which belongs to his *auctor* "Iohn Bochas," and in the subsequent 12 stanzas of his own matter, he consolidates this usurpation by dwelling on his own alleged inadequacy. In this way he lays an implicit claim to the very auctorial status from which he explicitly demurs. Burgh — who may well have had this very passage in mind[9] — similarly insists on his unfamiliarity with "Pernaso" and his lack of refreshment from the well of the sister muses. He understands Lydgate's denials to be a means of elevating himself to the status of his *auctor*, and, by attributing to Lydgate that which the elder poet denies for himself, he lays claim to an inheritance that may now pass to him through the monk of Bury.

As in Lydgate's poetry, in the *Letter* the operative mode of this succession is epideixis. In the poem's third stanza, Burgh foregrounds the idea of poetic lineage by versifying a list of eminent *auctores* from Homer through Virgil, Statius, and others, culminating in "lauriate bocase" (21). This list serves the double function of rolling out a figurative red carpet for the grand entrance of the name of the addressee and further demonstrating Burgh's own knowledge of poetic history and thus his qualifications as Lydgate's ephebe. He spends the next two stanzas setting the stage for his naming of Lydgate, offering a series of elaborate, linked eulogistic conceits. He praises the senior poet for having "gadred" the "flowris" of past *auctores*, and, "thowghe they be go," he asserts, "the wordis be not dede," since "thes and mo be in this londe legeble" in "th'enlumynyd boke" (23–26). This "boke" turns out to be not merely a volume of Lydgate's poetry, but, as Burgh puts it in an extravagant and even impious metaphor, the person of Lydgate himself: "ye be the same; ye be the goldyn bible" (28). Trusting someday to behold "this blisfull booke wt ye goldyn clasppes seven," in which he will learn his "a.b.c.," he imagines it to be his "paradyse" and "heven" (29–32). Finally, evoking the spiritual ecstasy of a disciple, he names his master in a rhetorical question filled with bewildered admiration: "so god my sowle save — a benedicite! —/Maister Lidgate, what man be ye?" (34–35). This couplet forms the hyperbolic climax of Burgh's praise and is at the same time the ultimate proof of his own worthiness. Using the very language and conceits of his master, he has written the answer to his own putatively unanswerable question. What man is Lydgate? None other than the master made visible as such through his disciple's poetic emulation. Like all such deployments of epideictic address, the praising subject elevates himself and his poem along with his elevation of the praised object.

Indeed, in the next stanza, Burgh outdoes even Lydgate in the boldness of his self-elevation. Ostensibly merely stating formally the proposed relationship between the two poets, Burgh in fact claims much more:

> Now, god my maister, preserve yow longe on lyve,
> that yet I may be yowr prentice or I dye;
> then sholde myne herte at ye porte of blise aryve.
> Ye be the flowre and tresure of poise,
> the garland of Ive and lawre of victorye.
> By my trowghte, & I myght ben a emperowr,
> for yowr konynge I shulde yowr heres honor. (36–42)

In these lines, Burgh claims to wish to be a "prentice" to the English poet currently wearing "the garland of Ive and lawre of victorye," thereby explicitly representing himself as a disciple of a living English laureate. And then he goes further: he imagines himself as the "emperowr" who honors Lydgate's "heres." In a remarkable inversion of the hierarchy between master and disciple, Burgh figuratively places himself in the position of the sovereign who bestows the laurel. No longer merely an apprentice, he becomes, at least, his master's notional equal, and in this way firmly stakes a claim to the mantle of the tradition that Lydgate has inaugurated. It should come, then, as no surprise that, after this climactic moment, Burgh devotes the final two stanzas of the poem — a quarter of its entirety — to an elaborate rendering of the date and location (but not, alas, the year) of the moment of its composition. Outdoing Lydgate once again — this time in respect to the senior poet's periphrastic self-datings in such works as *The Title and Pedigree of Henry VI* — in the closing stanzas Burgh celebrates the moment of his own installation as Lydgate's heir.

As the example of Freeman's epigram suggests, this type of poem becomes commonplace in the early modern period. The *Letter*, however — written by an ambitious churchman to a poet-monk almost 200 years earlier — survives as a precocious expression of a newly entrenched laureate sensibility. In this poem, Lydgate is not only to Burgh the most famous and successful living vernacular poet, but he also provides the archetype of laureate practice to be imitated and thereby claimed as one's own.

THE CRITIC WHO MAKES A MASTER: THE DUKE OF SUFFOLK

Relative to what we know about Burgh's celebrations of Lydgate, we know much less about the circumstances surrounding the verse critique known as *A Reproof to Lydgate*, the unique copy of which appears in that deluxe manuscript of Chaucerian verse (Oxford, Bodleian Library MS Fairfax 16). If this 84-line lyric does allude, as has been plausibly argued, to antifeminist moments in the *Fall of Princes*, then a date between the completion of that work in 1438 and the death of Lydgate in 1449 is likely. Hence, Johannes Jansen, the most recent editor of the poem, dates it in the "fifth decade of the fifteenth century."[10] The attribution to Suffolk was first argued by Henry MacCracken in 1911 and remains, admittedly, speculative.[11] Suffolk married Alice Chaucer, the poet's granddaughter, in 1430. He was appointed steward of Henry VI's household in 1433, at which point he began his notorious ascendancy in English politics. From 1432 to 1436 he was responsible for England's most eminent prisoner of war, the poet and prince Charles d'Orléans, and he later visited Charles at Blois in 1444. By the 1440s, if not earlier, Lydgate was well known to the duke. Since Lydgate directed his *Virtues of the Mass* to the "Countesse de Suthefolchia," Alice Chaucer served as his patron subsequent to her marriage to Suffolk.[12] (Indeed, the countess may have been the one who introduced Lydgate to the duke, as she certainly knew the poet prior to receiving *Virtues*: Thomas Montacute, earl of Salisbury, the countess's husband before Suffolk, had commissioned Lydgate's *Pilgrimage of the Life of Man*, of which she herself owned a copy, and before that Lydgate had written *On the Departing of Thomas Chaucer* for her father.)[13] Suffolk also owned "the best MS. ([London, BL MS] Arundel 119) of the [*Siege of*] *Thebes*" and had "supported Lydgate's application, in 1441, for the renewal of his grant from the crown."[14] At the very least, the *Reproof*'s first-person speaker's assumption of an aristocratic superiority in respect to Lydgate is unmistakable. Thus, even apart from the inconclusive manuscript evidence offered by MacCracken, Suffolk's familiarity with the poet and known literary interests make him a good, if in no way definitive, candidate for the poem's author.

The *Reproof* begins conventionally with a courtly vow of service to a "white and rede" flower (454; 7), which, from the French *marguerite* for the English daisy, is often taken to designate Margaret of Anjou. Yet the poem's sudden swerve in its third stanza from amorous pledge to poetic eulogy (and, later, critique) would be better explained if one takes the object of amorous attraction as Suffolk's wife:

> So wolde god that my symple connyng
> Ware sufficiaunt this goodly flour to prayse,
> For as to me ys non so ryche a thyng
> That able were this flour to countirpayse.
> O noble Chaucer — passyd ben thy dayse —
> Off poetrye ynaymd worthyest,
> And of makyng in alle othir days the best. (462–8; 15–21)

Pretending to be unable to find words sufficient to praise his lady, the speaker instead eulogizes the "worthyest" poet — perhaps his lady's own grandfather — who could best render an appropriate panegyric. In this way he establishes an epideictic circuit, in which the idealized praised object, the "goodly flour," demands an equally idealized praiser, "noble Chaucer," as well as an idealized medium of praise, the latter's "poetrye" and "makyng." Accordingly, the speaker also seems to imply the eminence of his own place as poetic maker, as it is he and his poem that praise both lady and predecessor poet. But he then turns abruptly to the third party, whom he and perhaps also his wife recognize as Chaucer's successor:

> And to the, monke of bury, now speke I —
> For thy connyng ys syche, and eke thy grace,
> After Chaucer to occupye his place —
> Besechyng the, my penne enlumyne
> This flour to prayse, os I before haue ment. (473–77; 26–30)

Since Chaucer is dead, the speaker requests aid from Lydgate's well-documented reserves of aureate panegyric — from, that is, the most eminent living resource of idealized praise poetry. Like Burgh, the speaker explicitly recognizes the principle of poetic inheritance, and, also like the

obsequious churchman, he makes his flattering request of the living
laureate — in this case, to "enlumyne" his "penne" — in the form of an
unmistakable imitation.

As it turns out, however, the *Reproof* poet's design is quite different
from that of a clerkly disciple. As MacCracken recognizes, there is
a note of mockery in his imitation,[15] and from this point through the
entire second half of the poem the speaker develops an increasingly
hostile critique of Lydgate's antifeminism, culminating in his bitingly
ad hominem reproach, "A, fye, for schame, O thou envyous man!....
Thy corupt speche enfectyth alle the air!" (511–15; 64–68). Yet, the
apparent venom of these lines should not be taken entirely at face value.
Rather, this accusation, given the overall spirit of the poem, should be
read as a baron's urbane, half-serious reproach of one of his over-serious
subjects. Such a tone is manifestly signaled in the final stanza, in which
the speaker instructs Lydgate to be "not to hasty, com not in presence"
and to "Lat thyn attournay sew and speke for the" (526–27; 79–80). The
possible joke here is that Lydgate did in fact have an attorney well known
to Suffolk: John Baret, treasurer of the abbey of St. Edmunds, who is
named as Lydgate's corecipient in the petition to renew the poet's
annuity — a petition backed by a note from Suffolk's protégé,
Adam Moleyns, and endorsed by Suffolk himself.[16] If the poem's
author is indeed the duke, this cryptic, insider allusion — with its implied
threat against Lydgate's annual £7 13s. 4d. — puts teeth into the speaker's
subsequent demand for poetic "recompence" (529; 82) for Lydgate's
literary crimes against women. But, regardless of the authorship question,
with this demand the poet of the *Reproof,* despite his apparent earlier
insertion of himself into the line of eminent vernacular poets, depicts
himself not as laureate but as the socially and economically superior —
and potentially hostile — *patron* of laureates.

It is surely no accident that the recompense that the speaker demands
recalls the poetic penance that Chaucer is compelled to perform for the
God of Love in the prologue to the *Legend of Good Women.* Not only does
Suffolk (or whoever his seigneurial equivalent may be) fit comfortably
into the role of the lordly God of Love (originally designed, most likely,
for Richard II), but also the discursive opponents drawn with ironic
ambiguity in Chaucer's poem are the same ones laid out starkly here: viz.,
clerkly antifeminism versus courtly *fin' amor.* "Yit God defende," the
speaker exclaims (sounding in this case much like the Wife of Bath), "that
every thing were trew/That clerkes wrtye" (506–507; 59–60): the battle
lines have been set between two modes of literary discourse, one

represented by the daisy worship that initiates both this poem and Chaucer's *Legend*, the other by the allusions to the *Fall of Princes*. The speaker's concern in this lyric is thus not merely to put Lydgate back in his place, but to oppose the type of verse of which Lydgate is a master and, correspondingly, to reaffirm the type that has traditionally served as an important class marker. The poem, that is, enacts an aristocratic resistance to a nascent literary norm as embodied by the living poet who, at that point, had been writing for princes and kings for decades. As I have mentioned, there is no precedent in English verse for this sort of poem: this fact suggests, along with the fact that someone like Suffolk even felt the need to compose such a work (no matter how playful its hostility may be), how much Lydgateanism was perceived as a threat to those with a vested interest in other sorts of verse. Like Burgh's *Letter*, the *Reproof* makes visible — and thereby helps to constitute — the newly dominant tradition of Lydgateanism. But in this case this bolstering comes about through a relation of opposition, through the identification of an authoritative but erroneous poetics with the "monke of bury."

THE LAST LANCASTRIAN LAUREATE: GEORGE ASHBY

Dying in late 1449, Lydgate was spared the events of the suc-ceeding months, during which time his sponsors, the duke of Suffolk and Adam Moleyns, were both murdered, and Jack Cade led his eponymous, nearly successful rebellion. More generally, the aged poet — who over the last quarter-century of his life had already witnessed the decline of the Lancastrian court into bitter, dysfunctional factionalism, the loss of much of England's French territories, and, closest to home, the arrest and mysterious death of Humphrey of Gloucester at Bury St. Edmunds (1447) — did not have to endure the precipitous further descent of Lancastrian fortunes in the following decade. A few years after Lydgate's death, Henry VI collapsed mentally and physically, and by 1461 he was disinherited and dethroned. As if in ironic eulogy to the poet who so dominated the first half of the century, history seems to have confirmed the truth of his most monumental laureate performance, the *Fall of Princes*, by adding real-life chapters to it that recorded the fall of the very dynasty that underwrote that performance.

During the prolonged, final collapse of this dynasty — after Henry's dethronement but before his death a decade later — the last Lancastrian laureate, George Ashby, composed the three poems that we know to be his: *A Prisoner's Reflections*, a 350-line meditation in the prison consolation genre established for the Middle Ages by Boethius; the *Active Policy of a Prince*, a 918-line *Fürstenspiegel* written for Prince Edward, son of Henry VI and Margaret of Anjou; and the *Dicta & opiniones diversorum philosophorum*, an incomplete, 1263-line compilation of *sententiae* translated from a Latin source (the same compilation that Anthony Woodville later translated from a French intermediary and that was published by Caxton after 1473).[17] The latter two works were composed, like Hoccleve's *Regiment of Princes* and Lydgate's *Troy Book*, for a Lancastrian prince and heir apparent, and yet they survive only in a manuscript so humble (Cambridge University Library MS Mm.IV.42) that one would like to congratulate its original collector for deciding it fit for preservation. The contrast between this manuscript and the lavish presentation copies that survive for the *Regiment* and *Troy Book* could not be more striking and supplies a material manifestation of just how much Lancastrian laureate poetics mirrored the dynasty's political prospects. This is not to say, however, that Ashby's poems themselves are merely poor, disenfranchised imitations of those of his forebears. Indeed, contrary to what the paucity of critical work on him might suggest, Ashby possesses a significant place in English literary history. He is the sole poet whose work displays a direct debt to both Lydgate and Hoccleve.[18] Because he wrote, as those predecessors did, for Lancastrian royalty, we may approach his poetry as a sort of laboratory for analyzing the persistence of, and relations between, the different responses to this task that characterize the earlier poets' work. Most important, because he was the Lancastrians' final poet, his verse baldly exhibits the tensions inherent in the politico-literary experiment that, under the circumstances, was stressed to the breaking point. In this section I examine closely Ashby's poetry against the backdrop of his historical circumstances. I argue that each of his poems, which I believe he made public at about the same time, represents a strategic and often clever deployment of high-culture verse for starkly political motives. As such, they are manifestly efforts at perpetuating Lydgatean laureate poetics. Yet, they also unmistakably express the self-interested, abject desire characteristic of Hoccleve – and it is this jarring combination of laureate and beggar that makes Ashby's poetry special.

The prisoner in the Fleet

The battle of Towton, fought all through Palm Sunday 1461 in bitter cold and driving snow, ended finally in gruesome pursuit of the routed Lancastrians, who were cut down, as one chronicler puts it, "like so many sheep for the slaughter."[19] In York awaiting news of the battle, Henry VI, Queen Margaret, and their son Edward fled the city immediately upon hearing of the catastrophic loss, guessing correctly that the new Yorkist king, Edward of March, would hurry there the next day to take down the head of his father, placed on the city wall after Wakefield. Among those in the royal retinue likely left to fend for himself was Ashby, one of Margaret's signet clerks. He eluded capture through the summer months but by September was taken and imprisoned in the Fleet, where he remained for almost two years or more.

Ashby's career rode the rise and fall of the Lancastrian dynasty. Born sometime in the 1380s, he died an old man in 1475.[20] From about 1423 he worked in some administrative capacity for Humphrey of Gloucester. In 1437, he accompanied the energetic and talented Thomas Bekynton (a k a Beckington), then Humphrey's chancellor, to the court of Henry VI. At this juncture, the king, having ended his minority, was reestablishing the long dormant office of the king's secretary, and Bekynton was summoned to fill this role; Ashby accompanied him as one of his clerks. Shortly after Queen Margaret's arrival in England in 1446, Ashby also became a clerk of her signet. In this employ he remained until the ouster of the Lancastrians in 1460, not long thereafter finding himself in the Fleet. Although in this predicament he suffered the fate of many other minor Lancastrians netted at Towton and its aftermath, what distinguishes him is that our primary source for this information is the poem, known as *A Prisoner's Reflections*, that he wrote about himself while incarcerated. This poem, preserved only in Cambridge, Trinity College, MS R.3.19, names its author, tells of his background and current condition, and recommends for its reader a stoic attitude toward the whims of fortune. In a brief space, that is, Ashby makes himself out to be the Boethius of the Wars of the Roses.[21]

Ashby was not, of course, the first author writing in English to model a literary work on the *Consolation of Philosophy*. Earlier English (or Scottish) instances of this genre include Thomas Usk's *Testament of Love*, the *Kingis Quair* of James I, and, in somewhat different modes, the English lyrics of Charles d'Orléans, and Chaucer's *Knight's Tale*.[22] All these works were completed in the late fourteenth or early fifteenth century, and, except for the *Knight's Tale*, all share with the *Consolation* a structure in which an apparently autobiographical element serves as the platform on which a philosophical meditation is presented within a more or less prominent fictional framework. Although we cannot be certain that Ashby knew any of these texts other than the *Consolation*, it remains noteworthy that his adaptation of this genre differs in two basic respects from its precedents. In Ashby's poem, the autobiographical element occupies proportionally more space and is significantly more detailed, and an obvious structuring fiction is completely lacking – such as Boethius's dialogue with Lady Philosophy, or Usk's with Lady Love, or the love stories of James I, Charles d'Orléans, and the *Knight's Tale*. This departure from the norm – in essence, the apparent removal of the fictional and its replacement with a stronger autobiographical element – was no accident of ineptitude but rather Ashby's strategic transformation of the genre to suit his specific purposes.

As it exists in its unique manuscript copy, the poem has three clearly demarcated sections: a 119-line "Prohemium unius Prisonarii" containing the autobiographical matter, a 189-line philosophical sermon entitled "Ad sustinendum pacienciam in aduersis," and a 35-line "Lenuoy."[23] The opening of the *prohemium* seems at first to be a conventional seasonal topos, but on closer examination one sees how it deploys in miniature the strategy of the entire poem:

> At the ende of Somer, when wynter began,
> And trees, herbes, and flowres dyd fade –
> Blosteryng and blowyng the gret wyndes than
> Threw doune the frutes with whyche they were lade,
> Levyng theym sone bare/of that whyche they hade –
> Afore myghelmas, that tyme of season,
> I was commyttyd, geynst ryght and reason,
> In to a pryson, whos name the Flete hight,
> By a gret commaundment of a lord,
> To whom .I. must obey for hys gret myght,
> Though .I. cannat therto sadly acord,
> Yet .I. must hyt for a lesson record,
> Ther'yn abydyng without help singler,
> Sauf of god and hys blessyd modyr ther. (1–14)

The first five lines of this opening evoke a progressively active force of decline and decay. Simply beginning in the first line, this force is felt passively in the fading of "trees, herbes, and flowres" in the second, more actively in the "Blosteryng" and "blowyng" winds in the third, and, in lines four and five, is revealed to be that which throws down the fruits of trees, stripping them bare. The scene has been set for an incident appropriate to its natural imagery, and the first word of line seven, "I," acts as a fulcrum between scene and narrative. This "I," as both deferred subject of the sentence and index of the speaker's subjectivity, turns what

comes before into pathetic fallacy, the speaker's sense of his powerlessness
before political misfortune, as reflected by the ineluctable processes of
nature. In line eight, the specificity of the ensuing narrative, in contrast
with the generality of the scene of decline, rather suddenly surfaces in the
apparently superfluous but pointed naming of the place of imprisonment.
In the next two lines, the "gret commaundment of a lord" and "hys gret
myght" echo the "gret wyndes" of the third line, making the narrative/
scene relationship virtually allegorical. The violence of the wind the
reader now understands to be the abusive power of the "lord," i.e.,
the recently crowned Edward IV (whom no loyal Lancastrian would refer
to as king); the fading tree, the Lancastrian dynasty; and the throwing
down of fruits, the disinheritance of the Lancastrian line. In short,
the natural has become the political. Yet, what follows is not political
complaint but a return to the inward state of the speaker, as evoked by a
series of first-person statements. The syntactic redundancy of these lines
calls attention to the interior travails of the "I" who must obey but
cannot reconcile himself to the injustice of his plight, and who must in
addition transform his experience into a "lesson" to "record." The pair of
stanzas then concludes by depicting this isolated individual turning
toward that which transcends both nature and politics, "god and hys
blessyd modyr ther."[24]

In just a few lines, Ashby has thus linked the decline of the natural
world with the decline of the political world and located their
intersection in his internal struggle to regain a sense of cosmic order.
At the center of this strategy is the poet himself, and from this point on
historically specific detail pertaining to him accumulates quickly. Indeed,
in the rapidity with which he supplies such detail, Ashby even outdoes
his most immediate model, the opening stanzas of Hoccleve's
Complaint:

> Aftir þat heruest inned had his sheeues,
> And þat the broun sesoun of Mighelmesse
> Was come/and gan/the trees robbe of hir leeues
> Þat greene had been/and in lusty fresshnesse,
> And hem into colour/of yelownesse
> Had died/and doun throwen vndir foote,
> Þat chaunge sank/into myn herte roote. (1–7)

The imagery, syntax, and diction of Ashby's stanzas are so similar to
Hoccleve's that it seems likely — especially given the existence of other
echoes of the *Complaint* — that Ashby had Hoccleve's poem in mind as

he wrote.[25] It is therefore noteworthy that, while Hoccleve waits until line 18 to use the nominative first-person pronoun ("Sighynge sore/as I in my bed lay"), Ashby uses it four times by line 12; and, while Hoccleve waits until lines 72–73 to supply details pertaining to his extraliterary person ("For ofte whan I/in Westmynstre halle//And eek in Londoun/among the prees wente"), Ashby provides such detail in the first line of his second stanza. This predominance of first-person discourse and density of historically specific detail, while crucial to Hoccleve's purposes, are even more important to Ashby's and are closely related to the other more obvious revisions of Hoccleve's stanzas: viz., the replacement of the general agent of decline, "broun sesoun," with the more specific and active "gret wyndes," and the corresponding relocation of the source of cosmic trouble from a general lack of "stablenesse/in this world" (*Complaint*, 9) to the effects of a specific "gret commaundment of a lord." To put it simply, Ashby takes Hoccleve's complaint about the social isolation following mental illness and turns it into a poem about the physical isolation following political trauma.

One may only surmise how Ashby came across the text of the *Complaint*. Being in similar lines of work, the two poet-clerks may have known one another, although Ashby at the time of Hoccleve's death (1426) had just begun working for Duke Humphrey and did not join the signet until several years later. Perhaps a colleague of Hoccleve's at the privy seal passed on a copy of the latter's poems to the new clerk of the signet, or perhaps the agent of transfer was Humphrey, whom, as we saw in Chapter 3, Hoccleve names in the *Dialogue*, the item that follows the *Complaint* in the linked sequence known collectively as the *Series*. Whatever the route, Hoccleve's influence on Ashby is quite marked and consists of much more than mere verbal echo; as we will see, it infects the very heart of his poetic practice. Furthermore, we may guess that Ashby absorbed some of this influence with regret; for available to him was also the model of (the then much more celebrated) Lydgate, whose influence is equally incontestable, but whose laureate poetics, as we will also see, Ashby could not perfectly replicate.

One of the characteristics of both Lydgate's and Hoccleve's poetic practices is the poet's textualization of himself as himself – his association of his historically specific, extraliterary person with his first-person speaker. Ashby follows – if indeed he does not exceed – his fifteenth-century predecessors in that regard. After naming his place of imprisonment, he goes on to describe exactly what his "enemyes" have done to his property, to explain why they have done it,[26] and to list more of the specific damages that he has suffered. And at the beginning of the fifth stanza, he makes the identification of speaker with extraliterary person unambiguous by declaring, "George Asshby ys my name, that ys greued/By enprysonment a hoole yere and more" (29–30). In providing directly to the reader his full name in the body of the poem, he follows Hoccleve and Lydgate but departs from the precedents of the prison consolation genre. (Boethius and James Stewart never identify themselves in the course of the work; Usk does so only through an acrostic consisting of the head letters of chapters; and Charles d'Orléans only in the guise of exchanges between himself and Venus and/or Cupid – and then quite sparingly). In fact, even in comparison with his Lancastrian models, this blunt self-identification is remarkably emphatic as a direct communication to the reader within the thematic unfolding of the poem (and not in the ascriptive context of, say, an envoy). This act of self-naming unequivocally affirms that the person known as George Ashby is at once empirical author, implied author, and character-narrator. Or – to adapt E. T. Donaldson's famous formulation – with these lines Ashby thoroughly conflates man, poet, and prisoner. From this point on, the poem's "I," no matter how conventional the matter it voices, must be understood as a pointer to a historically concrete person with an existence both inside and outside the text.[27]

Hoccleve's special influence on this form of self-representation becomes plainer in the following two stanzas. Here Ashby first laments,

> Oon thyng among other greueth me sore:
> That myne old acqueintaunce disdeyned me
> To vysyte (36–38)

and next reveals,

> The grettest peyne that .I. suffyr of all
> Is that .I. am put to vnpayable det ... (43–44)

These complaints, as David Lawton has pointed out, are quite characteristically Hocclevean and indeed come close to being a tissue of Hoccleve allusion.[28] This literary pillage, however, does not mean that Ashby's apparently real complaints are mere imitation but rather that Ashby, in trying to evoke the sense of a real person complaining, turns for help to the contemporary poet who more than any other had rendered this sense in English verse. As we saw in the previous chapter, though, Hoccleve's realism, especially by the time he wrote the *Complaint*, was his consolation prize. Hoccleve was unable to occupy plausibly the role of laureate because of the manifest subjection — and, in particular, pecuniary· desire — inherent in his socioeconomic position. He thus renders instead an authorial pose that parades the speaker's extraliterary existence as a plea for money, as well as a claim to authority. The contradictions that this compensatory strategy engenders are at once the basis of his realism and a sign of his failure to be the poet his patrons want him to be. For Ashby — and this is a topic I explore more fully later — this notion of the failed, beggar poet is his greatest Hocclevean inheritance, although in his case this notion responds as much to the purely political as it does to the socioeconomic.

In the next several stanzas of *A Prisoner's Reflections*, we witness the poet's internal struggle with his plight. After the Hocclevean echoes of stanzas six and seven, in the eighth he appeals to God to guide and rule him "to hys most plesaunce" and to help him "to haue humble suffraunce" (55–56). These lines strike one as an attempt to conclude the *prohemium*; his autobiographical exposition apparently completed, he now seems ready to provide the generically expected discourse on consolation. But, as if realizing that for his purposes he needs to place himself on center stage a bit longer, he provides instead a four-stanza mini-autobiography. This passage begins by his stating abruptly, "I gan remembre and revolue in mynde" (57, which echoes the *Regiment*, 15), includes a stanza about his professional writing, and ends with the observation that, though he has had a good life, ultimately "thys welth ys transytory" (84). This last commonplace leads into a series of rather awkward stanzas in which he offers a number of similarly conventional observations on fortune and the will of God, and this series ends suddenly with the final stanza of the *prohemium*, in which Ashby informs us,

> I thynke to wryte of trouble rehersall —
> How hyt may be takyn in pacyence —
> Procedyng theryn for myn acquytall,
> Though I haue no termes of eloquence,
> With that I may conclude perfyte sentence;
> Wherfore I counseyll aftyr wordes thyse,
> Euery man to be lernyd on thys wyse. (113–19)

At this point, the reader understands that the poet offers the observations of the preceding stanzas not for their own sake but rather to represent the ruminations of his creative process, which he now wishes to shape into a publicly digestible text. The relative thematic unity of the following set piece on consolation, as it is manifestly spoken by the same "I" who speaks the more fragmented *prohemium*, suggests the recovery of a unified selfhood. With consolation achieved within, this "I" may authoritatively direct a consolatory ethos to the public.[29]

One may now perceive more precisely how the poem as a whole works. When Ashby says in line 113, "I thynke to wryte," he negotiates the difficult transition from complaint to homily. In the former, autobiographical exposition finds natural expression, since individual experience (no matter how conventional) is the ultimate basis of its authority. In comparison, the authority of homily, although typically mediated by officially sanctioned *auctores*, must ultimately be based on a transcendental source of truth. The transition between the two is especially difficult in this case because Ashby effects it without any change in the nature of the poem's first-person speaker. Unlike Boethius and Usk, he provides no fictional frame to facilitate the transition; the poem contains no interlocutor such as Lady Philosophy or Lady Love who by definition speaks from a position outside the poet's subjective universe with an absolute, allegorical authority.[30] Nor does he supply, as does Hoccleve in the *Complaint*, the avowal of a written source, a text through which the speaker has found consolation and which he thus wishes to share with his readers. Instead, what Ashby goes on to counsel, while conventional and patently derivative, he presents as his own understanding of fortune and his own moral advice. The authority of this set piece thus has its basis neither in an allegorical personification of truth nor in another *auctor* but instead in Ashby's own apparently *extraliterary* experience. The aim of the autobiographical *prohemium*, accordingly, is to invest the poet's extraliterary person with the dignity of the Boethian tradition in order to authorize the experientially based meditation that follows. Conversely, the aim of the meditation, among other things, is to confirm that the George Ashby of the *prohemium* is indeed as wise and selfless under tragic circumstances as was Boethius.

The poet in exile

The complexity of this strategy suggests that what motivated Ashby to write *A Prisoner's Reflections* was not simply that he desired to share the consolation that he had discovered in the face of adversity — although that motive was no doubt present. The poem, in addition, possesses a more calculated purpose, a likely indication of which appears in its closing stanza, which dates and locates its place of composition. This stanza is appended to the envoy, in which Ashby sends off his "lytyll boke .../To folk troubelyd and vexed greuously" (309–10), and which seemingly brings his work to an end with the expected dose of humility – submitting his poem to be corrected by those of "hygh connyng" (327), apologizing to those he has "offendyd in [his] lewdnesse" (333), and affirming his "vertuous entent" (335). This envoy, in turn, immediately follows the conclusion of his 27-stanza sermon, which, after some provocative, though conventional, sentiments (e.g., "Was there euyr lord so gret and so sure,/.../That may not fall in the snare and in the lure/Of trouble" [267–69]), ends humbly with a prayer:

> With feruent loue and feythfull reuerence,
> I beseche the, god, of thy worthynes,
> Yeue me grace
> . . .
> That I may dwell in heuyn at myn ease. Amen. (303–8)

In this context, in which at least two graceful endings have been made, the closing stanza strikes one as an afterthought, a signet clerk's conscientious recording of the extrinsic details of his epistle:

> Wretyn in pryson, in oure lordes date,
> A thowsand foure hundryd syxty and thre,
> Thus occupying me, thys was my fate,
> Besechyng the, our lord god in trynyte,
> To take my makyng in plesure and gre,
> And therto hau mannys benyuolence,
> To thyne owne preysyng, laude and reuerence. Amen. (337–43)

These details, however, are hardly superfluous. The extraliterary existence of the speaker, already to some extent brought back into focus by the personal tone of the envoy, is unmistakably reemphasized here in the information of the first two lines. The prayer occupying the final four lines connects this reemphasis back to the more impersonal sermon, creating a final reminder that the authoritative voice that uttered "Amen" there is the same one as that of the historically specific prisoner uttering it here. Most important, the wording of the third line potentially revises our understanding of all that has preceded. In a perhaps unintended slip, Ashby writes, "thys was my fate" rather than "is," and – assuming that he refers here to the entire time he was "in pryson" – this one instance of the past tense punctures the carefully constructed illusion of his text.

It reveals that the preceding poem, instead of representing an active or just completed search for consolation, may possess instead a quite different nature. Even if one grants the veracity of the statement "Wretyn in pryson" (and there is no obvious reason to doubt it), one must now entertain the possibility that the surviving poem may be a revisited and revised draft — a carefully designed retrospective account of his experience. Such a deferral of the poem's public appearance and its presentation nonetheless as present experience bespeaks a level of premeditation quite beyond that required for the purpose of consolation.[31]

For now, though, let us put aside the question of what this more calculated purpose may be and turn instead to Ashby's two other poems, which I will argue are similarly so calculated. These poems, the *Active Policy of a Prince* and the *Dicta & opiniones diversorum philosophorum*, form the sole contents of CUL MS Mm.IV.42. Although Mary Bateson edits them as independent pieces, they were most likely meant to be read as different parts of a single work. The *Active Policy* consists of a Latin prose preface, a 12-stanza verse prologue, 114 stanzas of advice (subdivided into that pertaining to the past, present, and future), and an undemarcated five-stanza envoy. As John Scattergood has observed, the *Dicta* follows the *Active Policy* directly without an intervening *explicit* or title that appears different from the subheadings of the first piece; the Latin preface opening the manuscript describes both pieces; and the *Active Policy* frequently echoes and at times quotes directly from the *Dicta*. The *Dicta* thus appears to be not an independent poem but instead a kind of appendix for the *Active Policy* — a rather hastily composed (it seems to me) bibliography of *auctores* that lends authority to the advice offered the prince.[32]

The *Dicta* conveys this authority through both its content and its form, which reinforce, respectively, two important and distinguishing aspects of the *Active Policy*: its strikingly specific topicality and the authority it invests in the historically specific person of its poet. Examples of the poem's topicality include the speaker's recommendation that Prince Edward "bryng vp ayen clothe makyng" to "kepe youre Comyns oute of ydelnesse" (527–28); his insistence that "By lawe euery man shold be compellede/To vse the bowe and shetyng for disport" (569–70), i.e., that training in archery ought to be compulsory; and his warning that Edward should "lete neuer temporal Lorde/Be your tresourer ne your Receyvour" (807–8). Each of these recommendations responds to a specific problem in Henry VI's reign: respectively, the

disruption of the cloth industry due to England's tumultuous relationships with its continental neighbors; the lack of military training for the
commons, who were so often drafted for wars both abroad and at home;
and the domination of important government posts by self-interested
barons. Such topicality has led one historian to characterize the poem
as "a remarkably penetrating commentary on English public life" and
"a co-ordinated legislative programme."[33] In providing this sort of advice,
Ashby pushes the boundaries of the genre, in which the authority of
the speaker's recommendations is typically based on their very generality.
The medieval *Fürstenspiegel* author, by relying on such sources of moral
and political platitudes as the *Secreta secretorum*, could claim his advice
is authoritative because it has been so ever since Aristotle gave it to
Alexander. In comparison, much of the advice of the *Active Policy*,
reflective as it is of the troubles of Henry VI's reign, derives from the
specific experiences of one intimately acquainted with, and yet not
responsible for, the direction of Henry's policies — i.e., the poet himself.
Yet, Ashby, as mere clerk of the signet, is a doubtful figure of political
authority. He thus provides an appendix of *auctores* that echoes
his own advice enough to make more palatable the fact that it is,
indeed, his own advice that he is offering.

  If the contents of the *Dicta* thereby make more authoritative the advice
of the *Active Policy*, the form of the *Dicta* underwrites the presumption of
authority invested in the poet's person. In the *Dicta*, Ashby supplies for
each *sentence* the Latin, the name of its *auctor*, and a rhyme royal stanza or
two of translation. By supplying and ascribing the Latin, he demonstrates
his knowledge of classical lore, and by rendering the English in aureate
diction and in a Chaucerian stanza, he demonstrates his command of
high-culture vernacular verse. In addition, his juxtaposition of Latin and
English makes his expansions and modifications obvious, suggesting that
he wished to convey to the learned his active interpretation of his source.
Because we know from the preface that the translator is not an unnamed
scholar whom the poet copies but the poet himself, the conventional
claims that he makes in the *Active Policy* about his lack of learning (as in
stanzas six through eleven) he means to be shown disingenuous by the
Dicta. Hence, even though he claims "I haue not seien scripture/Of many
bookes right sentenciall" (*Active Policy*, 50–51), the implicit counterclaim
of the *Dicta* is that Ashby has seen a great deal; he is no mere scribe, but
an expert scholar.

  For the full significance of these strategies of authorization,
the historical context of this politically topical poem is an obvious

place to look. Its precise date of composition, unfortunately, remains uncertain, as Ashby chose not to versify the year as he did in *A Prisoner's Reflections*. Since throughout the *Active Policy* he seems to presume confidently that Edward will inherit the throne, Bateson restricts this date to the period demarcated by Prince Edward's birth in October 1453 and the Yorkist revolution of 1460, or to the very brief period of Henry's readeption of 1470–71. But there are problems with both of these. In regard to the first, Edward, through most of 1460, would have been only six and thus an unlikely student for a text clearly not addressed to a child. In addition, since Ashby tells us in the poem that he is "Right nygh at mony yeres of foure score" (65), a date before 1460 would make him quite an old man, by medieval standards, at his death in 1475. For those reasons most scholars have tended toward the later date, and yet this one, too – at least on the grounds on which it is usually proposed – is suspect. Not only was the window of opportunity for writing such a poem quite small Henry regained the throne in October and lost it again in April, while Margaret and Prince Edward did not return to England until the evening of the same day that Edward IV defeated the earl of Warwick at Barnet (14 April), but also, for someone who had witnessed as many reversals of fortune as Ashby – including the unlikely alliance of Margaret and Warwick, on which the hopes of Prince Edward's succession were pinned – it seems far-fetched that during this short period he would display so much sincere confidence in regard to the prince's future.

It may be, however, that he is not entirely sincere, a possibility that few have entertained, given the general critical inclination to derogate Ashby's poetic abilities. In support of this possibility, Scattergood – whose work on Ashby is a valuable exception to this inclination – has unearthed evidence that suggests a date of composition of 1463 or soon thereafter. He observes that two stanzas in the *Active Policy* – the one recommending the revival of cloth making mentioned above and the immediately following one, on the importance of enforcing existing sumptuary laws (534–40) – refer to specific petitions of the Commons to Edward IV at the 1463 parliament.[34] Scattergood shows that the attitude of Ashby's stanzas reflects closely that of the corresponding petitions and that the poet has in some cases – e.g., with "ydelnesse" (528) and "progenitours" (540) – even quoted their wording. He further notes that no other sumptuary legislation was passed during Ashby's lifetime and that both the Commons' petition and Ashby's stanza on this topic are explicitly related to concerns about the cloth-making industry. Putting all this together with the information that Ashby supplies in *A Prisoner's Reflections*, Scattergood concludes that Ashby probably wrote the *Active Policy* in prison at about the same time as that poem and that he, like "his more illustrious contemporary, Sir Thomas Malory," turned to literary pursuits as a means for coping with "the enforced idleness of imprisonment."[35]

Yet, even disregarding the "was" in the final stanza of *A Prisoner's Reflections*, which suggests a later date for that poem, we still have reason to suspect a later date for the *Active Policy*. In 1463 Prince Edward was only nine or ten and, moreover, physically far removed from Ashby — he and Margaret were in the field in the north, or, having lost Scottish support, making their long journey into exile, or, having finally reached their destination, lodged far away in Bar.[36] Even if we grant that the poet's confidence in a Lancastrian succession may be feigned, it seems unlikely for him to write such a poem, from prison, at such a time. A somewhat later date for the piece thus seems probable — sometime after the prince was reasonably old enough to be a credible recipient of its advice but before his and Margaret's campaign of April–May 1471 that ended with his death at Tewkesbury.

The evidence so far suggests that the poem was written for Edward while he and Margaret were in exile. Ashby — who most likely was imprisoned "At the ende of Somer … Afore myghelmas" following Towton — probably was not incarcerated much past the "hoole yere and more" he reports in *A Prisoner's Reflections*.[37] In the early 1460s, Edward IV followed a policy of leniency toward most Lancastrians (at least toward those not executed in the field). Since Sir Thomas Tresham, the speaker of the 1459 Coventry parliament of which Ashby was a member, received a pardon in March 1464, it is reasonable to assume that Ashby was also pardoned sometime during this year or shortly thereafter.[38] Although we have no record of Ashby's activities after 1463 until his death in 1475, it is equally reasonable to assume that he, like Tresham, responded to Edward's mercy by rejoining the Lancastrians. Since he had spent the previous 40 years in their employ, it would have been natural, even inevitable, for him to find his way to Bar and resume his job as Margaret's signet clerk — especially because Edward's mercy typically did not extend to a restoration of assets. In the mid-1460s the Lancastrian position was quite weak and hence not favorable to the conception of a poem like the *Active Policy*. But by 1468, with the souring of the relationship between Edward and Warwick and the negotiations between the latter and Louis XI of France, there was reason for renewed optimism. Late in the year, believing military support from Louis for an invasion of England was imminent, Margaret and her entourage relocated to Normandy. At this juncture, with her son now 15 and the English throne both physically and politically closer to him than it had been in years, a poem like the *Active Policy* not only would have been appropriate but also quite calculated.[39]

What I am suggesting by these speculations is that the *Active Policy* was intended not just as advice for a young prince but also as a sophisticated piece of propaganda, encouraged or perhaps even commissioned by Margaret and aimed at making the prince appear as the authentic and fully capable heir to the throne — at the very moment when there was renewed hope that his disinheritance, achieved in principle by Richard of York and in practice by his son Edward IV, might be reversed.[40] Without question Margaret understood the value of such literary propaganda. In 1459, for example, her faction was responsible for the *Somnium vigilantis*, a prose dream vision and debate that argues that the attainders of the Yorkists at the forthcoming Coventry parliament are essential to the safety of the realm.[41] And, more pertinent to Ashby and the *Active Policy*, in her retinue from Towton on was none other than Sir John Fortescue, who produced the most sophisticated propaganda in a period in which such writings flourished.

In addition to his English and Latin refutations of the Yorkist claim to the crown, which he wrote in the early 1460s in Scotland, in a subtler mode Fortescue produced the famous *De Laudibus legum Anglie*. This text, which is above all a celebration of the ideals (if not the actual practices) of English law, is as well a kind of *Fürstenspiegel*. Like Ashby's poem, it is addressed to the Prince of Wales and confidently assumes that he will succeed his father.[42] The picture it paints of the prince as a robust, martially oriented young man, who is nevertheless quite articulate, serves the same purpose that I am attributing to the *Active Policy*. Although structured as a pedagogical drama, Fortescue's tract was clearly intended for a broader audience and thus possesses the triple function of educating both prince and public as well as demonstrating for the latter the merits of the former. It advertises the prince as not only the authentic but also an appropriately talented and educated heir; it demonstrates, in short, that he is ready to receive the crown. Ashby's poem, despite the tendency of scholars to view it principally as evidence of the poet's putative tutorial responsibilities, was conceived along similar lines: it supplies the prince with useful advice; makes policy recommendations a broader audience might appreciate; and paints a picture of the prince as thoughtful, moral, and practical. It even goes as far as to make legislation the Commons proposed to Edward IV appear as precisely the policy Edward, Prince of Wales, will follow.

Ashby's primary model for his poem was not, however, Fortescue's *De Laudibus*. Even if one could demonstrate influence one way or the other or provide hard evidence of Margaret's instigation of both pieces, there remains the much more obvious precedent of Hoccleve's *Regiment of Princes*. Addressed to Henry of Monmouth at a time when his kingly aspirations had placed him in disfavor with his father, Hoccleve's widely disseminated poem, as Derek Pearsall and others have argued, was designed, at least in part, to make this earlier Prince of Wales appear eminently worthy of his inheritance.[43] Ashby, quite sensibly, turned once again to his favorite poet in a bold attempt to depict Edward as the second coming of the ultimate Lancastrian hero.

As we saw in Chapter 3, in the *Regiment*, following his long pseudo-autobiographical prologue, Hoccleve begins the section of advice proper with a lofty address to the prince:

> Hy noble and mighty Prince excellent,
> My lord the Prince, o my lord gracious,
> I, humble servant and obedient
> Unto your estat hy and glorious,
> Of which I am ful tendre and ful gelous,
> Me recommande unto your worthynesse,
> With herte enteer and spirit of meeknesse[.] (2017–23)

Similarly, in the *Active Policy*, Ashby turns from his (apparently factual) autobiographical prologue with the same stance toward his addressee and even with a number of verbal echoes:

> Right & myghty prince and my right goode Lorde —
> Linially comyn of blode royal
> (Bothe of Faders & moders of recorde),
> Occupying by grace celestial
> Thaier Roiaulmes, with grace especial —
> To whom be al honnour and reuerence,
> Dewe to youre high estate and excellence;
>
> I mene, to youre highnesse Edwarde by name,
> Trewe sone & heire to the high maiestie
> Of oure liege lorde Kynge Henry & dame
> Margarete, the Quene — bothe in Charitee
> Euer, though grete was their maiestie,
> Yit they eschewed vengeance and Rigoure,

Shewynge their beneuolence and Favour. (85–98)

In both cases a professional letter writer has expanded the conventional epistolary opening to the highborn into a mini-panegyric, and the aim of this expansion is to reposition the extraliterary person of the speaker, established in the autobiographical prologue, as a poet worthy of praising a prince. In formulating his address in this manner, the poet helps to construct the prince's authority by embedding it in an established discursive tradition, and at the same time he reflexively constructs his own authority. One of the most compact ways to leverage the power of poetic praise, this type of address seeks to produce a circuit of mutual legitimation among poet, prince, and poetic medium.[44]

Ashby, however, requires fourteen lines for this purpose compared with Hoccleve's seven, and almost all the added matter pertains to the authenticity of the prince's royal heritage. This emphasis is apparent with the very first word of the address. Ashby begins with the uncommon usage (in respect to the epistolary addresses that are his model) of the word "right" as meaning "true," and he calls attention to this usage by repeating the word in the same line with its more typical meaning of "very."[45] In the next two lines he expands upon the first meaning in respect to Edward's royal claims through both Henry and Margaret, and in the following stanza he repeats this point with greater specificity, naming all the parties involved and more strongly restating that Edward, "Linially comyn of blode royal," is "Trewe sone & heire to the high maiestie." The motivation behind this added matter is plain. When Hoccleve addressed Prince Henry, Lancastrian rule was well established (if not entirely accepted). In contrast, when Ashby addressed Prince Edward, another Edward was ruling the country, one who had earlier with his father waged a propaganda campaign aimed at establishing the legitimacy of their rival claim to the throne.[46] Consequently, Ashby's panegyrical address has to carry the burden of not only making the prince's authority appear legitimate but also, as in the writings of his colleague-in-exile Fortescue, insinuating the authenticity of the entire Lancastrian dynasty.

The last laureate

Much more may be said about the strategies with which Ashby attempts to depict the prince as both the "right" and "goode" inheritor of the throne — as well as the ways he seeks to account for and amend Lancastrian policy (for example, in the sudden termination of his panegyrical address in the curious and ambiguous observation of Henry's and Margaret's eschewing of "vengeance"). But we have already seen enough of these strategies to understand the centrality of the idea of lineage. In the practice of laureate poetics, one would expect a parallel and mutually reinforcing emphasis on poetic lineage, in which Ashby is to Hoccleve — and the *Active Policy* is to the *Regiment* — as Prince Edward is to Prince Henry. And, beginning with the very first lines of his prologue, Ashby does indeed exhibit a concern with poetic lineage, only here (and throughout the poem), an explicit reference to Hoccleve is conspicuously missing:

> Maisters Gower, Chauucer & Lydgate,
> Primier poetes of this nacion,
> Embelysshing oure englisshe tendure algate,
> Firste finders to oure consolacion
> Off fresshe, douce englisshe and formacion
> Of newe balades, not vsed before,
> By whome we all may haue lernyng and lore. (1—7)

The three names with which Ashby begins his prologue form a parallel with the three names he later gives in the beginning of the advice section. He presents Lydgate, rather than Hoccleve, as heir to Gower's and Chaucer's poetic authority, creating an analogy between that poet and Edward as heir to Henry and Margaret. At the same time, however — while rhymes such as "consolacion"/ "formacion" and the term "embelysshing" are a nod toward Lydgate — the language of this eulogy owes a marked debt to Hoccleve's tributes to Chaucer. Specifically, the uncommon phrase "Firste finders" originates in the *Regiment* in Hoccleve's description of Chaucer as "The firste fyndere of our fair langage" (4978).[47] With Hoccleve's *Fürstenspiegel* very much in mind, Ashby nevertheless chooses Lydgate as the final member of the "Primier poetes of this nacion."

Ashby's naming of the trio is not simply formulaic but rather a meaning-laden construction of a vernacular poetic heritage. Despite his patent debt to Hoccleve and the wide circulation of the *Regiment*, Ashby names Lydgate as heir to Chaucer and Gower, and thus as his own immediate poetic ancestor. He does so because Lydgate, much more than Hoccleve, was in practice (if not in official standing) the poet laureate of the Lancastrian dynasty through his death in 1449. For the purposes of the *Active Policy*, what Ashby needed was a model of vernacular poetic authority thoroughly conflated with political authority in general and Lancastrian interests in particular, but also one that unequivocally descended from a source beyond reproach. One of Lydgate's achievements was that he imagined such a model in the form of an English poet laureate. Ashby, by including Lydgate along with Chaucer and Gower in the opening of the *Active Policy*, constructs a legitimate and unmistakably Lancastrian poetic heritage, the authority of which, as we will shortly see, finds its present embodiment in himself.

As epitomized in Lydgate's practice, a central feature of laureate poetics is the poet's self-representation as a historically specific, empirical embodiment of a timeless, autonomous authority that reflects, but is not reducible to, the parallel embodied authority of the prince. Ashby, as clerk of the signet, was in some ways especially well positioned to textualize such a pose. The signet was the personal seal of the king (or queen) and was used to authenticate correspondence that issued from dictation or direct request. The office of the signet produced letters of a relatively private nature (such as Richard II's command to Lady Ponynges to spend Christmas at court), as well as those that helped to construct the king's public image (such as Henry V's letters from France, addressed to the mayor and aldermen of London, bringing news of his military successes).[48] Such letters, while not properly instruments of governance, are intimately related to the king's person in both its private and public capacities. In effect, a writer for the signet was responsible for producing a textual extension of the royal person in the twin capacities as possessor of an abstract dignity and as historically specific wielder of power. This function is well illustrated by the letter of compliment (such as Richard II's congratulation to Archbishop Courtenay "upon a miracle lately worked at the shrine of St. Thomas"), which J. Otway-Ruthven cites as the single most characteristic product of the signet prior to Edward IV's expansion of its use.[49] Such letters are public acknowledgments of royal favor issued in the form of a private message from one individual to another. They aim to create or to sustain a relationship between the specific person of the sovereign and one of his or her subjects, as well as to be a material instance of royal patronage. In conveying a sovereign presence that is at once private, public, specific, and general, they are a textualization of the sovereign's two bodies. Regardless of their apparent administrative emptiness, they are an essential component of the sovereign's machinery for producing himself or herself as ruler of the realm.

Ashby himself tells us as much about the signet in
A Prisoner's Reflections, when he provides a brief but revealing account
of the relationship that exists between a sovereign and his or her signet
clerks. Recalling his service to Humphrey, Henry VI, and Margaret, he
describes himself as

> Wrytyng to theyr sygnet full fourty yere,
> Aswell beyond the see as on thys syde,
> Doyng my seruyce aswell there as here,
> Nat sparyng for to go ne for to ryde,
> Hauyng pen and Inke euyr at my syde,
> Redy to acomplysshe theyre commandment,
> As truly as .I. coude to theyr entent. (64–70)

At first glance mere autobiographical exposition, this stanza repays close
attention. The first word, "Wrytyng," not only provides a specific, active
image of Ashby's work but is also the topic of the entire seven lines. The
poet signals its importance by positioning it at the head of the line,
leading a vertical list of similarly placed participles, "Doying," "Nat
sparyng," and "Hauyng." Also in the first line he emphasizes his devotion to — and identity with — his work by conflating three
separate appointments into the single "theyr sygnet," which allows him
to give, accurately but also hyperbolically, "full fourty yere" as the
duration of his employment. He spends the next three lines developing
through repetition a sense of both his constant attendance upon his
employer, wherever he or she may choose to travel, and his productivity — playing on the two meanings of "aswell" as "both" and "as
competently."[50] This sense spills over into the next line, in which the
image of Ashby accompanying his lord on either "syde" of the sea
reappears as the image of his "pen and Inke" at his own "syde" wherever
he happens to "ryde." Drawing an analogy between his "seruyce" to his
employers and his writing equipment's service to him, he metaleptically
figures himself as his *sovereign's* "pen and Inke" — i.e., their textual
extension. In the next line he further conveys the nature of his service by
loading the word "commandment" with a double meaning: it is both the
command to him to write and the commanding content of that which he
writes. In the act of writing he obeys one "commandment," and in the
product of his writing he textualizes the "entent" of another (and,
significantly, these two words form the concluding couplet). In the end,
one sees that the import of the entire stanza is largely and neatly captured
by its first and final words: in "Wrytng" the sovereign's "entent," he puts
into text his or her public and private desires.

The importance of this function for the fifteenth-century court is evident in the fact that, relative to the privy seal clerk Hoccleve, Ashby was well remunerated. He was granted two annuities (one of 10 pounds for his position with the king and one of 10 marks when he also began writing for the queen) and a corody at St. Bartholomew's, Smithfield, and he was named constable of Dinevor castle and steward of Warwick. Although this more or less comfortable income did not preclude him from versifying complaints about his finances, he was able to put enough away to purchase Brakespeares, a small estate in Harefield, Middlesex, as early as 1447, and to expand his property there sometime before he died. From the record of an indult that he and his wife received for a portable altar, we know that he achieved the rank of esquire. And, while perhaps other signet clerks were as well compensated, Ashby in particular was clearly valued and trusted. In 1439, he accompanied Secretary Bekynton to Calais on an embassy headed by Cardinal Beaufort, and in 1444 he again journeyed to France as a member of the embassy that brought Margaret of Anjou to England. This latter journey marked the beginning of a close relationship with the formidable queen, which is attested by her mention of him in a personal letter, and which culminated in his being selected an MP (for Warwick) for the queen's parliament at Coventry in 1459.[51]

Returning to the *Active Policy*, we should thus not be surprised — given the hospitable circumstances of his profession, his knowledge of the nascent vernacular poetic tradition, and the task at hand — when Ashby quickly follows up his opening celebration of the English literary triumvirate with a suggestion that he himself is their heir. In the poem's second stanza he focuses explicitly on the idea of poetic heritage by lamenting the apparent cessation of the line after Lydgate. He wishes that God had allowed the poets to live until they had left a true heir, "a personne, lerned & Inuentif,/Disposed aftur youre condicion,/Of fresshe makyng to oure Instruccion" (12–14). In the third stanza, with its initial two lines, "But sithe we all be dedly and mortal,/And no man may eschewe this egression" (15–16), he seems about to offer a replacement heir and, with the "I" at the head of the third line — notably, the first instance of the first-person pronoun — to assume that role himself. At this point, though, he steps back from this assertion and instead asks God to pardon all the "transgression" of the past poets in recompense for the "many a scripture" they "haue englisshede without lesure" (18–21). Tellingly, in this elaborate, elegiac stage-setting, Ashby is once again imitating Hoccleve. In the *Regiment*, at the conclusion of the eulogy of

Chaucer that follows the beginning of the advice text proper, Hoccleve laments that death "mighte han taried hir vengeance a whyle/Til that sum man had egal to thee [Chaucer] be"; acknowledges that, nonetheless, "hir [death's] office needes do moot shee"; accordingly asks God to "reste" Chaucer's "soule"; and then proceeds to fill the poetic office vacated by Chaucer by finally beginning his *Fürstenspiegel*: "Now to my mateere as that I began" (2101–8). Ashby's imitation of these lines in almost precisely the same literary context all but explicitly implies a line of succession from Chaucer to Ashby leading through Hoccleve, which makes it all the more striking that it is Lydgate whom he explicitly figures as playing this mediatory role.

In the next stanza, Ashby returns to where he left off, and this time he names the person who in this context can only be taken as the poetic heir whose nonexistence he has just rather disingenuously declared:

> So I, George Asshby — not comparison
> Making to youre excellent enditing —
> With right humble prayer & orison,
> Pray god that by you I may haue lernyng,
> And, as a blynde man in the wey blondryng,
> As I can, I shall now lerne and practise
> Not as a master but as a prentise. (22–28)

Here Ashby carefully underscores his historically specific identity and, by means of the humility topos, stakes his claim for a poetic inheritance. In the stanza's first line, the first-person pronoun receives the emphasis of the pause we want to put between it and the appositional name. The first syllable of the surname receives its natural stress, but the internal rhyme of the second syllable with "I" turns the entire surname into a spondee, doubly emphasizing it as well as its attachment to the speaking voice of the poem. The participle "Making" beginning the next line receives positional emphasis, and the imperfect rhymes with the pronoun directly above it, the author's surname, and the final word on the same line, "enditing," associate the word with the identity of the poem's *maker*. Paronomastically belying their strictly denotational meaning, these lines call attention to Ashby's act of *making* in the sense of writing poetry. In this stanza, as in the similar eulogies of Chaucer written by Hoccleve and Lydgate, the humility topos means for the most part the opposite of what it says. Ashby is indeed making a "comparison" of his poem to the "excellent enditing" of his predecessors, and, in the very humble insistence on his status as a "prentise," he establishes the idea of poetic succession, the possibility of which he has just denied.

The authority of the laureate tradition, which Ashby has thereby established in the prologue, serves then as the backdrop to the sustained argument, rendered in the form of a *Fürstenspiegel*, for the legitimacy of the Lancastrian royal heritage. In this argument, the *a priori* authority of the Lancastrian poetic heritage functions as a model both of and for the parallel authority of the royal line. Throughout the advice section, the "I" who speaks the counsel is always necessarily that of George Ashby specifically, the historically concrete inheritor of the laureate seat and, like Lydgate before him, poet to a prince. The *Active Policy* in this manner advertises Edward's qualifications by way of advertising Ashby's. Nonetheless, I should emphasize that the *Active Policy* is not *merely* such an advertisement. Despite its propagandistic motives, it remains a poem that gives thoughtful advice to a prince – advice largely concerned with morally proper and politically just practices of wielding power. It is, in this sense, a poem in which its author attempts to speak truth to the powerful and thus to use poetry as a means of making the world a better place.[52] Just like the laureate performances of Ashby's predecessors, if it is in part propaganda, it also submits one of the greatest claims for what poetry can do.

To return, finally, to the question of the calculated purpose of *A Prisoner's Reflections*, one may now see that, in some important respects, the effect of that poem is similar to that of the *Active Policy*, although expressed in a different register. The "I" of the former poem's sermon on patience is a variant of the laureate "I": it signifies at once an abstract voice of moral authority and a historically specific poet. And yet, since this "I" is also, as the *prohemium* relates, that of a prisoner of the Yorkists, it signifies a laureate forced away from the characteristic activities of praise and advice giving and, at least at first, into complaint. If one of the primary burdens of the *Active Policy* is to represent the author as a Lancastrian laureate, a burden of *A Prisoner's Reflections* is to demonstrate how laureate authority, even when subjected to political trauma, may transcend politics. Implicitly, the poem tells the story of how a Lancastrian laureate, unjustly imprisoned, transforms his despair into a consolatory meditation for the benefit of all, regardless of the livery they wear. In short, in *A Prisoner's Reflections* Ashby represents himself as a martyr laureate.

Of course, the poem's transcendence of politics is not entirely sincere, and neither is it the poem's sole nor perhaps even primary purpose.

Ashby's imprisonment is unjust only from a Lancastrian viewpoint. By calling attention to this injustice — and the noble manner in which he copes with it — Ashby helps to fabricate the Lancastrian depiction of the Yorkist revolution as the destruction of an authentic dynasty. Further, if he made his prison poem public at the same time as the *Active Policy* — as I have supposed, in the late 1460s — then, when it appeared, the most famous prisoner in England, Henry VI, was still lodged in the Tower. Ashby in *A Prisoner's Reflections* may hence be a proxy for the incarcerated king. As in his *Fürstenspiegel*, the poet serves as an analogue for a prince, but in this case what he reflects is pious, noble suffering amidst tragic circumstances, a martyr laureate as the *imago* of a martyr king. To the extent that the ethos of patient suffering the poem endorses is meant to pertain to all Christians, *A Prisoner's Reflections* reaches for eternal truth. But, to the extent that this suffering points to a specific political trauma that may still be redressed, the poem is the work of a partisan seeking to manipulate public opinion.

The heir of Hoccleve

Just like both of his Lancastrian poetic predecessors, then, Ashby attempts to combine an underlying propagandistic agenda with assertions of literary and moral authority manifestly invested in his own person. These predecessors, however, took rather different approaches to this task, and despite the fact that Ashby explicitly acknowledges the influence of only Lydgate, in the end, as is perhaps already apparent, he cannot escape his Hocclevean heritage. Although he recognizes in Lydgate's work the more apt model for accomplishing his aims, his socioeconomic location tends to tip the balance in favor of mendicant poetics. His professional situation, while conducive in the ways outlined above to laureate poetics, was in other ways hostile. Like Hoccleve, he was entirely dependent economically on the royal personages who serve as parallels to his authorial pose. His poems are therefore not so much autonomous works with their own specific aims as moments within the dialogue between employee and employer. In addition to their aim of constituting a laureate selfhood, they are also a servant's petitions for preferment. Again like Hoccleve, Ashby possessed neither a social identity nor an institutional source of authority outside that which he obtained from his professional life. Lydgate, in comparison, could exploit his monastic affiliation; by representing himself as the embodiment of an institutional authority distinct from the prince's, he could plausibly serve as a notional analogue of the prince in the realm of literature. The best that administrative clerks like Hoccleve and Ashby could do in this regard was to exploit the *Fürstenspiegel* genre and its tradition of advising princes. Yet these clerks patently fell far short of the self-determination they and their contemporaries would have attributed to the paradigmatic author-figure of this genre, Aristotle. In relying on the authority of genre, Hoccleve and Ashby thus called attention to their subjected position through the very strategy with which they sought to transcend it.

This problem, as we have seen, is in fact endemic to fifteenth-century laureate poetics, infecting even Lydgate's monkish practice of it. There is great tension — even contradiction — between the transcendental claims made in the high-culture poetry of this period and the specific political realities that motivated this poetry. The fifteenth-century laureate, in posing as an analogue of a historically specific sovereign/patron, exposes both the contingent nature of his poetry and the manifest difference between himself and the sovereign whom he addresses. In this period, high-culture vernacular poetry, in claiming what it may neither theoretically nor practically achieve (i.e., absolute truth and autonomous authority), is at once self-assertive and self-defeating. The difference between the Lydgatean and Hocclevean versions of this poetry to a large extent hinges on the different degree to which each poet explicitly recognizes and utilizes the tension inherent in it. Lydgate attempts to channel this tension into rather obsessive rehearsals of the humility topos. In this way he may admit both the contingency of his poetic matter and his own subjection but, at the same time, count on the conventionality of the gesture to ensure that this admission does not interfere with — and indeed even supports — his strategies of poetic elevation and self-aggrandizement. Hoccleve, in contrast, foregrounds the tension, making the fragmentation of poetic selfhood it entails one of his primary thematic preoccupations. In poems such as the *Regiment*, he makes the friction between his self-centered pecuniary desire and the selfless moralism of public poetry a central concern. If Lydgate's poetry records his success at achieving a kind of laureateship that, in the end, fails to be what he thinks it is, much of Hoccleve's poetry makes his failure to be a laureate its very subject matter.

Such a failure is also in one sense what *A Prisoner's Reflections* records, although in this case the failure, as it mimics the condition of the poem's sponsoring dynasty, provides thematic unity. Unlike the speaker of Hoccleve's *Complaint*, the speaker of *A Prisoner's Reflections* is not inherently subjected but instead suffers as a result of specific political circumstances. Facing a common enemy in the Yorkist usurpers, the personal and public in this poem are not in tension but instead almost perfectly aligned. Furthermore, the highly specific nature of the poem's circumstances makes its laureate postures less rather than more problematic. Since the poet in effect tells us that, because of these circumstances, he is unable to be a laureate, his moralistic pronouncements on consolation do not strike us as particularly self-serving, and thus we are not as prone to question their authority. The decisive role of historical contingency in the genesis of the poem, to which the poem itself testifies, is what eventually enables its apparent transcendence of history. In this way the poem may succeed at being at once a historically specific political intervention and a timeless, non-partisan meditation on fortune.

In the *Active Policy*, however — which is an attempt at a more straightforward laureate performance — the problematic nature of both the contingency of Ashby's themes and his subjected position vis-à-vis his addressee are everywhere apparent. We have already witnessed the problem of contingency in the poet's obsessive insistence on the legitimacy of Prince Edward's claim to the throne. This insistence implicitly acknowledges that a basic assumption of the genre — that it is a prince who is in fact being addressed — is not a given but an argument that must be proven. The poem's very generic stance is thus in constant threat of being unmasked as mere propaganda — not the timeless advice of a sage to his prince, but the efforts of a paid writer to certify his patron. In this case, historical contingency has a corrosive effect on the poet's authority, as it points to the possibility that, rather than being autonomous, this authority is merely the shadow of a disenfranchised Lancastrian will to power.

The more characteristically Hocclevean problem, the subjected position of the poet, is evident in the *Active Policy* in its pervasive references to Ashby's economic dependency upon the poem's sponsors. These references, over the course of the nearly 800 lines of the advice section, devolve into self-advertisement that borders on begging, just as the similar references more explicitly so devolve in Hoccleve's *Regiment*. Early on, after a stanza suggesting (reflexively, of course) that a king should "do all thinge with counseil" (281), Ashby uniquely departs from rhyme royal, rendering the following stanza *ababbbcc*. This stanza begins by stating that a king ought "to cherisshe" the virtuous and "to put in grevance" the "vicious" (290–91). But the surplus *b* line, "Yevyng hym rewarde & other expence" (293), is concerned only with the first half of this policy, and as a formal anomaly it calls attention to its reduction of the idea of "cherisshe" to that of payment. This narrowed meaning then forms the topic of the following interstanzaic Latin *sentence*, the first of a number of such *sententiae* scattered throughout the advice section:

> Decet Regem satisfacere/de stipendiis stipendiariis suis;
> Alioquin societas despiciet eum & dominium suum; hec
> Plato.[53]

In the subsequent English stanza, Ashby paraphrases this bit of "Platonic" wisdom, replacing the implied threat contained in "despiciet" with the converse suggestion that reliable payment of wages is needed to ensure the king's *subjects'* moral integrity:

> And paie youre men theire wages & dutee,
> That thei may lyue withoute extorcion —
> And so wol god trouthe & equitee;
> And therfore take hertili this mocion,
> And in their nedys be their proteccion,
> And so shal youre fame encrece & rise,
> And euery man youre pleasire accomplise. (296—302)

If a king pays his men "theire wages," Ashby says here, he will both protect them from the sin of "extorcion" and accrue the side benefit of having his "fame encrece." Behind this pointed but nevertheless generally worded advice stands not only the fact that the speaker himself has received "wages & dutee" from the parents of his addressee but also that one of those grants was at least once suspended. In 1449, Parliament reassumed Ashby's grant of Dinevor, which he had held since 1438 and which he did not regain until 1452. The rather unsubtle hidden message of this stanza, then, is that Ashby, for his work in general and for this poem of "counseil" in particular, desires appropriate and reliable payment.[54]

Ashby repeats this same message, in a somewhat different way, a little over 100 lines later, when he warns,

> if ye wol be Kyng,
>
> . . .
> Ye must subdewe with al suppressyng
> Euery persoune withoute submission
> Pretendyng right to your coronacion,
> Or ellis ye may not regne in seurte
> Nor set youre subiettes in quiete. (415—21)

Committing an apparent non sequitur, he immediately adds,

> And euer remembre olde Sarueyeres,
> Hauyng suche persounes in tendernesse
> That hathe be feithfull & trewe welewyllers
> To thair ligeance withoute feintnesse,
> Suffryng therfore grete peine & butternesse. (422–26)

The first stanza, again despite its general phrasing, points to the most fundamental and quite specific difficulty Prince Edward faced at the time the poem was written, and also signals the very project of the poem, the legitimation of the prince as true heir and the consequent "suppressyng" of the other Edward. The next stanza asks the prince to remember "olde Sarueyeres," a group that must of course include the aged Ashby in particular, whose specific service in this case consists of helping to carry out the advice of the prior stanza by authoring the present poem – and who, as we know from *A Prisoner's Reflections*, has suffered "grete peine & butternesse."

Lest we believe this self-allusion to be accidental, Ashby soon offers another more suggestive instance of it. In a later stanza, after recommending a "Confessour" for the "helthe" of Edward's soul in the first two lines and "a good leche" for the "welthe" of his body in the next (464–66), he spends the final four recommending

> ... a Secretarie withe Inspection –
> Secrete, sad, and of goode Intencion –
> That can accomplisshe your commaundement
> To thonnour and profit of youre entente. (467–70)

He then adds:

> Also chese your servantes of goode draught,
> That wol attente and be seruiable,
> Remembryng with whom thei haue be vpbraught,
> For to suche thei shalbe appliable. (471–74)

Through his grouping of a secretary with a confessor and doctor, Ashby depicts the former as the maintainer of a sovereign's textual body (as distinct from its spiritual or physical manifestations). And, although Ashby was only a secretary's clerk, through intertextual self-allusion he indicates all but explicitly that it is he, specifically, who is currently such a maintainer. He uses here virtually the same couplet to describe the secretary's work that we saw him use in *A Prisoner's Reflections* to describe his own ("Redy to acomplysshe theyre commandment,/As truly as .I. coude to theyr entent" [69–70]), and, in regard to the best servants to "chese," he uses very similar language to that which he used to describe the reasons for his imprisonment ("Because of my draught and my bryngyng vp" [22]). In these lines of putatively general advice, Ashby underscores — at least to a careful reader — the crucial importance of his own employ.

Later, putting aside the theme of his vocation and returning to his poetry and his desire for remuneration, he advises that a king ought to "cherrisshe .../.../In especial suche as be makers;/Thise may exaltat youre name & werkes" (611–14). We know by this point that by "cherrisshe" he means "to pay" and that, among the "makers" who ought to be so rewarded, that of the present poem is indeed primarily concerned with exalting the prince's "name & werkes."[55] Then, near the end of the advice section, after a pair of stanzas on the virtue of listening to good counsel, Ashby proceeds to counsel that annuities that the prince grants "stande withoute resuming," since the "variance" of income caused by such "resumyng" has in the past created trouble for "many folk" (723–29). And, lest we miss that "many" in this case stands for one, he includes a pun on "making" ("A man to be preferred to honour/Of fee or office to his grete making" [730–31]), which here denotes "benefit" but also, through recurrence of the verb "cherish" ("It is nought a man to be cherished/And aftur for povertee perished" [735–36]), points back to the "makers" who exalt the name and works of a prince — i.e., to this present poem and poet. That this coy intratextual self-allusion is no accident becomes apparent in the immediately following stanzas, in which the poet observes that, if a sovereign endeavors to win the admiration of his servants, "Than your seruauntes wol bere oute your fame/ ... /Blissyng you daily with goode hert & free,/Whos worship shal be cronicled sadly" (744–49). Ashby, of course, is an essential member of these "seruauntes" who, by means of well-cherished *makyng*, "wol bere oute" the fame of the prince, and he points also to the present poem as an exemplary vehicle for ensuring that Edward's "worship" will be "cronicled sadly." At this juncture, even if this poem had not begun with an autobiographical prologue that makes quite clear the specific identity of the speaker, one would readily gather that its "I" possesses a striking degree of particularity, and that in this case the authoritative advice this "I" offers cannot be separated from the reward it seeks in exchange.

In demanding this reward, Ashby, like Hoccleve, puts his own desires before those of his patrons; his poem drifts from the work of sage advice giving and legitimizing propaganda into self-advertisement and personal need. Hence, although Ashby at the poem's opening represents himself as the heir of Lydgate, by the end of the advice section it is evident that he is equally, and probably more so, the heir of Hoccleve. If the *Regiment of Princes* — which was completed several years before Lydgate's *Troy Book* — represents the first large-scale attempt at a Lancastrian laureate performance, the *Active Policy* represents the last. The opportunistic politico-literary experiment that these performances demarcate ends much as it began, with an effort full of contradictory motives and generic murkiness. And at the center of both works is a first-person narrator who represents a historically specific poet and administrative clerk, one who cannot aspire to the lofty claims of the high-culture vernacular tradition without also making a request for financial favor — his desire to be "cherisshed." In the end, the martyr laureate of *A Prisoner's Reflections*, when restored to his seat in the *Active Policy*, turns out to be another beggar laureate, a poetic selfhood split between a desire for autonomy and a subjected desire.

CAXTON AND THE DISASSOCIATION OF LAUREATE POETICS

A few years before Ashby's death, Henry VI and his only child Edward were both killed, and the Lancastrian line thus extinguished. A year or so after Ashby's death, the Lydgatean laureateship, while still a force in English letters despite the decline and termination of its sponsoring dynasty, began to acquire a new form through the activities of William Caxton. In 1473, while still in Bruges, Caxton began his career as a printer of English texts with *The Recuyell of the Historyes of Troy*. From this point on, the idea of a laureateship became increasingly reified in the printed book, serving as one commodity among others within the nascent industry of the mass production of cultural objects. No longer only the notional property of a relatively small number of writers and scribes, who deployed the idea for specific literary and political purposes, it became one of the more important items in the publisher's bag of marketing tricks. To a degree, a similar reification was already present in the manuscript-based deployment of the idea, especially in the codicological entrepreneurship of John Shirley, the fifteenth-century Lydgate promoter *par excellence*. But the demands of marketing a number of different, mass-produced texts accelerated the process, leading Caxton regularly to utilize an idea of a laureateship no longer essentially tied, as was Ashby's, to authorial lineage and a distinct set of poetic practices.[56]

This disassociation is well illustrated in the epilogue to Book 2 of Caxton's *Recuyell*, in which the printer mentions Lydgate by name:

And as for the thirde book which treteth of the generall and last destruccioin of Troye, hit nedeth not to translate hit into Englissh for as moche as that worshipfull and religyous man Dan John Lidgate, monke of Burye, dide translate hit but late, after whos werke I fere to take upon me, that am not worthy to bere his penner and ynkehorne after hym, to medle me in that werke.[57]

At first glance, Caxton's strategy of self-authorization, though in prose, appears very similar to that of such early Lydgatean disciples as Benedict Burgh. The surface features are the same: the eulogy of the poetic predecessor, the self-derogation articulated in the very language used by that predecessor in similar situations (e.g., *Troy Book*, 5.3530), and the manifest willingness to do precisely what one claims to "fere to take upon." But Caxton, in contrast with Burgh, is not here assuming a laureate pose; despite the passage's imagery of apprenticeship, Caxton is not seeking to attach laureate authority to his own person as much as he is to the book he has printed. Stylistically, the *Recuyell* is quite far from a Lydgatean text. In order to bolster its authority, Caxton insinuates that it participates in the Lydgatean tradition based simply on the fact that the monk also wrote about Troy. Rather than fully impersonating the master as a poetic disciple would, Caxton as printer, through this brief imitative comment, *extracts* laureate capital from the individual who more than any other possessed it. Once he so disassociates this capital, he makes possible its reinvestment in a variety of different texts by a variety of different authors.

Among the earliest of Caxton's productions in England was the *Book of Curtesye*, a text which must have attracted Caxton because, among other reasons, it itself performs this disassociation, in the interest of recommending to its readers the very sort of texts that Caxton was at that time busy producing.[58] Written sometime after Lydgate's death (1449) and before Caxton's print (1477), this verse courtesy book includes a relatively expansive passage (encompassing lines 309–427 of the poem's total of 532) on the importance of studying the great vernacular poets of the past. In this pantheon, Gower comes first and receives one stanza, which is largely a seven-line amplification of Chaucer's epithet "moral Gower." Chaucer is second, and he receives three stanzas, the first of which is a eulogy that seems almost a caricature of Lydgateanisms:

O Fader and Founder of eternate eloquence,
That eluminede all this oure britaigne;
To sone we lost his lauriate presence,

> O lusty licoure of that fulsome fountaigne;
> Cursed deth, why hast thou this poete slayne,
> I mene Fadir chaucers, mastir Galfride?
> Allas! the while, that euer he from vs diede.[59]

Aside from the term "Fader" — which, as Ethan Knapp has shown, as an epithet for Chaucer originates in Hoccleve's *Regiment*[60] — this stanza strikes one as an attempt to pack as many Lydgatean clichés as possible into seven lines. After dispatching with Chaucer, the next two stanzas are, rather surprisingly, devoted to Hoccleve, making them the only place in all fifteenth-century verse where Hoccleve is explicitly named by someone other than himself. Less surprisingly, the aim of these lines is to depict the *Regiment* as a laureate performance:

> Beholde Oclyff in his translacion,
> In goodly langage and sentence passing wyse,
> Yevyng the prince suche exortacion
> As to his highnesse he coude best devyse
> . . .
>   whos excellent highnesse
> He aduertysede by his writing playne,
> To vertue perteynyng to the nobles
> Of a prince, and berith wyttenesse
> His trety entitlede "of regyment,"
> Compyled of most entier true entent. (351–64)

There is here no evidence of Hoccleve's rambling, self-absorbed prologue, and no indication of the Lancastrian author's social identity as privy seal clerk. Instead, Hoccleve in these stanzas is solely the advisor to a future king, the exhorter of Henry of Monmouth, whom he, with "entier true entent," "aduertysede [i.e., instructed] by his writing playne" in the "vertue perteynyng to the nobles/Of a prince." He is, in short, the laureate he never was.

The next and final vernacular hero is Lydgate, who receives both the place and quantity of honor with five stanzas, and whom the speaker addresses as his "maister":

> Loketh Also vppon dan Iohn lidgate,
> My maister, whilome clepid monke of bury,
> Worthy to be renownede laureate,
> I pray to gode, in blis his soule be mery,
> Synging "Rex Splendens," the heuenly "kery,"
> Among the muses ix celestiall,
> Afore the hieghest Iubiter of all. (365–71)

In this passage, the more personal tone, the lament over his master's death, and the epideictic convection among political, spiritual, and poetic praise would all suggest that the poet of the *Book of Curtesye* has positioned himself in the same way as had earlier Lydgatean disciples.[61] He is now ready — like, for example, Ashby in the *Active Policy* or Burgh in his *Letter* — to figure himself as Lydgate's heir and the culmination of the line of vernacular poets. Instead, however, he declares,

> Lette his owne werkys prayse him and magnifie;
> I dare not preyse, for fere that I offende,
> My lewde langage shuld rather appeyre than amend. (397–99)

Although cloaked in a humility topos that appears consistent with Lydgatean self-aggrandizement, the poet's demurral in this case differs markedly from Lydgate's claim in respect to Chaucer in the *Troy Book*:

> And, for my part, I wil neuer fyne,
> So as I can, hym to magnifie
> In my writynge pleinly til I dye;
> And God, I praye, his soule bring in joie. (3.4260–63)

As I argued in Chapter 2, Lydgate here asserts that "magnifying" Chaucer is the specific aim of his own work, and, by setting up an epideictic relationship between his own poetic activity and his predecessor's, he draws the latter's authority to his own person. In contrast, the poet of the *Book of Curtesye* ascribes the epideictic function to Lydgate's "own werkys." With this gesture, the poet — although he has demonstrated himself to be an avid imitator of Lydgate — assumes a role more like that of Caxton's in *The Recuyell*. In contrast with his contemporary Ashby, for this poet the laureateship is the property of already-existing texts rather than an inheritable status and repeatable practice.

Without knowing more about the circumstances of the *Book*'s composition (and, in particular, the relation between its text and Caxton's print), we can only speculate about the reasons for the poet's attitude toward laureate poetics. One verbal cue, however, suggests that this attitude involves recognition of the historical evolution of the laureateship. When, in praising Lydgate, he does not simply title him laureate but rather "[w]orthy to be renownede laureate," he may be referring to the fact that, by then, the English literary system recognized (if it had not yet itself created) a laureateship as an academic honor — that is, as a concrete institutional marker rather than a notional effect of a set of poetic strategies. Beginning with the academic features of Petrarch's laureation in 1341, the laureateship began to be more and more associated with the university, and, by the second half of the fifteenth century, numerous continental writers had been granted the honor.[62] Hence, for the *Book* author, the laureateship may no longer have been only an idea with which a specific poet is able to legitimate his function and authority, but also a real credentializing power held by an institution, an honor which it may bestow on any number of individuals. To refer to Lydgate as simply a laureate would thus have been a factual error. At best, the monk could now only be worthy of being "renownede" as such — that is, he could only be praised as an author of laureate abilities before a laureateship was in reality obtainable. In his very eulogy of Lydgate, the *Book* poet may hence be acknowledging that the conditions in which his master's laureate poetics most flourished no longer hold.

A suggestion of Benedict Burgh as this poet, although entirely speculative, makes a nicely symmetric conclusion to this chapter on Lydgateanism. Such an attribution is certainly not out of the realm of possibility. In the late 1470s, Burgh was a canon of St. Stephen's in Westminster. There he most likely encountered Caxton, since in 1477 the first of three editions of the poet's *Disticha Catonis*, which Caxton retitled *Parvus Cato, Magnus Cato*, was produced at the printer's Westminster shop. The *Book of Curtesye* is similar in form and intent to the *Disticha*; both consist of practical advice on a variety of topics given by a father figure to his son. Also, Burgh would have been, as we have seen, a ready versifier of the *Book*'s hyperbolic, mimicking praise of "maister" Lydgate. Finally, Caxton's failure to cite the work's author parallels *Parvus Cato, Magnus Cato*, which Caxton also printed without attribution.[63] If Burgh was responsible for the *Book*, however, this effort would stand as a rather sober appraisal of the laureate ambitions he expressed in his *Letter*, since this later work appears to acknowledge that his former strategy of inheriting authority by impersonating his master is obsolete.

But regardless of the identity of the *Book*'s author, without doubt the academic institutionalization of the laureateship that it may signal greatly influenced Caxton, who, having spent much time on the continent and, in particular, within the literary circles of the Burgundian court, would have been quite familiar with the honor. In this sort of laureateship, he encountered the very principle of laureate disassociation: a literary authority that was bestowed on individuals but was also a detachable emblem of cultural capital that might be utilized more generally. Moreover, Caxton benefited from precisely that which hampers the *Book* author. Although academic institutionalization makes the inheritance of laureate authority through imitation problematic, it supplies, conversely, *a priori* authority to those individuals who in fact possess the honor, freeing them from the *need* to produce laureate authority through imitation. And no individual seized this opportunity with more energy and ambition than the laureate who appears as such near the end of Caxton's career in the prologue to the printer's *Eneydos* (1490). Here Caxton asks "Mayster John Skelton, late created poete laureate in the Unyversite of Oxenforde, to oversee and correcte this sayd booke and t'addresse and expowne where as shalle be founde faulte to theym that shall requyre it."[64] At this juncture, Caxton does not need, as he did in his *Recuyell*, to feign anxiety in regard to retracing the steps of a past "renownede" laureate; instead, he may request the assistance of a living possessor of the institutionally bestowed degree. As Lerer has noted, with *Eneydos* Caxton culminates a career that began with another book of Troy, only in the first instance he finds a source of authority in the notional laureateship of Lydgate, whereas in the second he finds it in the actual laureateship of Skelton.[65]

As we will see in the next chapter, for Skelton the academic laureateship and, more especially, the office for which it forms a qualification entail both his departure from a purely Lydgatean style and his reduction of laureate self-representation to egocentricity. In contrast, his contemporaries and competitors Stephen Hawes and Alexander Barclay perceive the academic laureateship as a barrier to their poetic ambitions. While the disassociation of the laureateship does not prevent these two poets from producing capacious extensions of the Lydgatean tradition, it is at least in part responsible for the nostalgia and resentment, respectively, that marks their poems, as well as their idiosyncratic Hocclevean turns. Despite their differences, however, what all three of these early Tudor poets have in common is a point of departure in the Lydgatean tradition, and, notwithstanding the changes they work on it, they carry Lydgatean laureate poetics into the sixteenth century.

CHAPTER 5

The trace of Lydgate: Stephen Hawes, Alexander Barclay, and John Skelton

When Henry Tudor crossed the Channel in 1485 to seize the throne from Richard III, he apparently brought along a poet laureate – Bernard André, the "Blynde Poete" of Toulouse. Unlike any other poet writing for an English king before him (at least that we know of), André, in his role as poet, possessed an unambiguous status at court: he was a well-paid professional, the top man in Henry's troupe of highly educated, foreign-born propagandists. By no later than November 1486, Henry had granted "Bernardo Andreae Poetae Laureato quandam annuitatem," and André would continue in the office underwritten by this grant until his death around 1522, dutifully churning out political paeans, pedagogical works, devotional treatises, and historical encomia for the first two Tudor kings.[1] His laureateship possessed neither the exclusivity nor the status of an official recognition for artistic accomplishment of its modern counterpart; nonetheless, like the latter, it was a very visible position of honor intimately connected with the interests of the State. Henry's establishment of this office, from one perspective, was a tremendous innovation, an importation of a Burgundian practice into an English literary system in which the use of poets for political purposes had been ad hoc, if not haphazard.[2] But from another perspective, Henry simply completed the process begun by his Lancastrian ancestors. As I observed in Chapters 2 and 3, soon after seizing the throne from Richard II, Henry IV invited Christine de Pizan to his court, and, failing to gain the services of this *au courant* continental poet, he relied instead on the insular efforts of Hoccleve and Lydgate. Henry VII, toppling the next Richard, brought his continental poet with him.

What Henry VII achieved over his predecessors in this regard was thus the institutionalization of the formally notional role of the poet laureate, an achievement that was innovative inasmuch as it made official the de facto role first occupied by Hoccleve and Lydgate at the beginning of the century.[3] While Henry was no doubt influenced by the continental

174

fashion of the court laureate, his patronage of writers for high-culture propaganda had the same motives (e.g., the legitimation of a dubious claim to the throne) and resulted in the same products (e.g., eulogies, histories, and devotional verse) as that of the Lancastrians. Before 1485, two generations of poets had possessed ready access to a notional laureateship; Henry, in giving institutional form to this role, was merely recognizing its political efficacy and making use of it somewhat more systematically than his predecessors. Nevertheless — as we saw at the end of the previous chapter with Caxton's reification of the laureateship in his publishing ventures — a concretization of the notional may have far-reaching effects. In this instance, the very visibility of André's role effectively made it impossible for a poet unequivocally to assume a laureate pose without in fact being one of the king's laureates. The royal favor that André achieved, as David Carlson has suggested, made him a standard against which other writers were compelled to measure their success.[4] As long as the laureateship had remained only notional, any poet could more or less legitimately assume the post simply by mimicking the gestures of which it consisted. But by the early sixteenth century, such posturing began to appear absurd for poets who failed to have a position, title, and academic degree similar to André's.

Yet, even for those poets who possessed the appropriate credentials, such as John Skelton, Henry's establishment of the office of poet laureate created ultimately intractable problems. Most significantly, it brought to the foreground the inherent contradiction in the very idea of the role — the simultaneously opposed and interdependent concepts of self-determination and subjection that have troubled the laureateship at least since its incarnation in Petrarch's crowning of 1341. As a notional role, the nature of the laureate's relation to the prince could to some extent remain mystified, and in this dim light claims for self-determination and the autonomy of the poetic enterprise may authentically, if uneasily, be made. The presumption of an analogical relationship with the sovereign does not permit the laureate to be a mere servant; and yet, as official members of his household charged with writing verse, mere servants were precisely what Henry VII's laureates were, no matter how ostentatious they appeared or how highly placed they actually were. Or, to put this another way, in his creation of the office of the poet laureate, Henry completed its conflation with the role of *orator regis*. An early Tudor poet's claim to the former was specious if he lacked official recognition as the latter. But when that recognition was forthcoming, the laureate, as putatively self-determining analogue of the king, was also, as *orator*, a simple extension of the king's voice.

This problem affected the three circles of writers in the early Tudor court in different ways. As I remark in this book's epilogue, it aided the ascendancy of the amateur courtier verse produced by Sir Thomas Wyatt and other "courtly makers." For Erasmus and his fellow humanists, it created a tension, akin to that felt by the poet laureate, between the presumption of a disinterested pursuit of knowledge and the deployment of that knowledge in the interests of the sovereign. Typically, this tension could be contained within a humanist ideology of public service and vented through complex strategies of dissimulation.[5] In the extreme, as in the case of Sir Thomas More, a humanist could terminate his relationship with the sovereign and remain a humanist. For the poets laureate — the looser-knit group around André — the problem was more fundamental: under Henry VII, one failed to be a true laureate if one was not on the king's payroll. In England, since Lydgate, the greater a poet's claim for the cultural importance of his verse, the more crucial it was that that claim be underwritten by the cultural authority of laureate poetics; yet, under Henry VII, official recognition of such poetics was not forthcoming without an institutionalized subjection of poetry to politics.

Of course, the émigré André, whose writings are all in either Latin or French, would not have had the weight of the Lydgatean tradition on his shoulders. But the three most prominent poets writing in English during the reign of Henry VII — Stephen Hawes (c.1475–c.1523), Alexander Barclay (c.1476–1552), and John Skelton (c.1460–1529) — very self-consciously began their careers within this tradition, and, despite the attempt each made in different ways to transcend it, they found themselves ultimately trapped between that tradition's great claims for the poet and poetry and the historical realities of the early Tudor court.[6] Each, in his own fashion, inherited the outlook of the poet laureate and the accompanying understanding of the value of poetic discourse in ways that went well beyond the function André played at court. Because each spent some portion of his career in alignment with the court and some portion alienated from it, each poet's expressions of this outlook and understanding varied over the course of his career. But in all cases laureate self-construction remained a central, if vexed, preoccupation. Indeed, for these authors — and especially for actual court poets Hawes and Skelton — the constitution of a laureate selfhood was even more of a basic concern than it was for their Lancastrian predecessors. Whether marginalized from power or within its orbit but patently subject to it, these early Tudor poets faced the uncomfortable task of reconciling the idealizations of Lydgatean laureate self-representation with their actual, relatively humble roles at court (or, in the case of Barclay, the lack of such a role). In this situation, they more resemble Hoccleve than Lydgate — despite the latter's unmistakable influence on their work and the near complete absence of any echo of the former. In their desire to construct themselves as Lydgatean laureates under conditions in which that construction necessarily appears to some extent inauthentic or absurd, their poetic focus at important moments turns inward, and, just like Hoccleve, they thematize that very desire. For Hoccleve, this desire ultimately fixes on the pecuniary; for these poets, it is expressed as some sort of longing for the ideal laureateship they imagine as once possible. As in the case of George Ashby, these poets strive to be like Lydgate under Hocclevean conditions. But, unlike Ashby, they are scarcely conscious of the Hocclevean strand of the laureate tradition, and so instead are thrown back onto their own resources to discover a manner in which to represent their perceived fall from an ideal. As a consequence, they each render a poetic selfhood that adds new dimensions to the conventions of laureate and beggar.

Hawes was a groom of Henry VII's privy chamber who seems to have gained that position, at least partially, because of his poetic abilities; in this role he possessed an institutionally more intimate relationship with the king than any other English poet before him. But this position was also categorically one of a household servant, lacking completely the differentiated social basis (such as Lydgate's monastic one) needed to found a laureate's claim of self-determination. Accordingly, Hawes's poetic enterprises are marked by explicit longings and narrative analogues for the achievement of a traditional, notional laureateship. Barclay, in comparison, seems to have spent most of his life in a sometimes friendly, sometimes hostile, but always arms-length relationship with the court. As a Benedictine monk during most of his active poetic career (he later seems to have become a Franciscan friar), he was able to assume more authentically the pose of the Lydgatean laureate and to speak on moral, social, and political questions with an authority manifestly different from the king's. Yet, because of the institutionalization of the laureateship, especially in the person of Skelton, this notional pose for Barclay possessed a taint of failure. Consequently, resentment creeps into his verse — a sense that he, as authentic laureate, goes unrecognized as such because an inauthentic laureate occupies the king's office. For Skelton, the occupation of this office, or his barring therefrom, became an obsession spanning his poetic career. Both when in and out of the king's favor, he spent much of his considerable poetic energies either demonstrating or reconstructing his laureate authority. As a result, his English poetry, despite its broad intellectual scope and multiform stylistic virtuosity, ultimately possesses a relative poverty of reference. In their repeated returns to the nature of the laureate speaker, his poems are centered on a self that wishes to keep obscured the inner complexity that would mark an alienation from power. At times, it seems as if a reduction to pure laureate self-gratification is all Skelton seeks, and the strength of his poetry lies in the extent to which he acknowledges, in these very moments, the impossibility of that gratification.

In this chapter I examine moments in the poetic careers of each of these three poets that illustrate particularly well their ties to the Lydgatean tradition, their expansions upon this tradition, and, especially, the manner in which and reasons why novel versions of the beggar laureate surface in their work. This focus casts into relief one facet of these poets' complex relationships with both the literary past and future, and highlights the intercalation of those relationships with the pressures of their historical moment. These poets, in turning back to Lydgate, stumble into a Hocclevean situation that serves as the basis for something new. In the wake of these poets' historically conditioned failures to achieve the lofty aims of laureate verse, the beggar — always a tendency in laureate poetics as the negative image of laureate self-construction — appears in unprecedented ways. The nature of their failures firmly ties these poets to the literary past and yet also, as we will see, provides them with attributes one generally associates with the future. This does not make them merely transitional figures, as they are often labeled, but instead attests to the complex, nonlinear fashion in which a tradition evolves. Rather than representing the last gasp of the medieval at the dawn of the modern era or — to say the same thing in a different way — the first breath of the Renaissance in the stagnant air of the Middle Ages, the work of these poets testifies more generally to the dialectical inevitability inhering in the politico-cultural practice of a literary tradition. Their work illustrates the paradox that, to the extent that poetry, because of its political utility, becomes more explicitly one weapon among others in the king's arsenal, it becomes increasingly impossible to practice it in the manner most useful to the king. The day of Lydgatean poetics, as the quasi-official set of gestures of high-culture English verse, begins to set with these three poets not because a Renaissance sensibility eclipses it, but because the very success of Lydgateanism eventually brings about its own demise.

STEPHEN HAWES

The brief account that John Bale, writing in 1557, supplies of Hawes's life reads like an outline for the biography of an ideal poet laureate, a man who nurtured his God-given gift in the cradle of the university and was later recognized by his sovereign for his merit alone. Hawes was, Bale writes, "eager from his youth to develop his mind through humane studies," and, when the opportunity arose, traveled "to various universities in different countries to seek to become a man of letters." Having achieved this, he dedicated "all his life and utterance to demonstrating that he was, as it were, an example of virtue." Eventually, his merit was brought to the attention of the king, and Henry VII "called him to his court, to his inner chamber and private counsels, on the sole recommendation of his virtue."[7] In this portrait, Bale idealizes the relation between literary pursuit and public service. Instead of depicting the willing subjection of poet to prince for reasons of economic opportunism or political expedience — i.e., more or less the situation of André — he portrays Hawes as the disinterested counselor *par excellence*, more loyal to the virtue that inheres in his specific person than to the pleasures of the king.

These idealizations notwithstanding, however, Bale could not refer to Hawes as laureate because, patently, he was not one. In all his alleged university training he failed, somehow, to gain the appropriately titled degree. More crucially, when he did achieve a place at court, it was not, as in the case of André, as *poeta laureatus*, but, as Hawes himself advertises, as "one of the gromes of the moost honorable chaumber of our souerayne lorde kynge Henry the .vii.''[8] This role, as indicated by Hawes's (or his printer's) repeated publication of it, possessed both social stature and — more important — the suggestion of intimacy with the king. Although it was lower in status than knight of the body or gentleman of the privy chamber (an office later created by Henry VIII), it nonetheless promoted its occupant as one who potentially had the ear of the king on a frequent basis. And yet, it also made plainly evident Hawes's position as a household servant. In his identity as a gentleman attendant upon the king's body, his complete dependence upon his master and the immense imbalance in status and power in their relationship was readily visible to all. More so than Hoccleve or Ashby, and precisely because of his closer proximity to the king, Hawes possessed little institutional authority outside of that provided by the sovereign, and, as in the case of the earlier poets, to invoke the sovereign's authority is at the same time to advertise one's subjection.

Hawes's poetry, nonetheless, indicates that he believed that the poetic enterprise ought to transcend the political relationships in which it is produced and to possess an intrinsic authority that resides in its own aim and tradition. This aim, as Bale puts it (cued by the title of Hawes's earliest work), is to make manifest an *exemplum virtutis*, and perhaps there is some truth to the claim that Hawes owed his position at court to his ability to textualize models of virtue — "above all," as Anthony à Wood writes, "for his most excellent vein in poetry."[9] For Hawes, the literary tradition that most embodied this aim was Lydgateanism. Wood mentions, as an illustration of Hawes's "prodigious memory," the remarkable feat of his being able to "repeat by heart most of our English poets; esp. John Lydgate, a monk of Bury[.]"[10] But we need not imagine Hawes reciting by rote all 36,365 lines of the *Fall of Princes* to understand how central the figure of this Lancastrian poet was in his conception of poetry. Every poem that Hawes published begins with a meditation on poetry in which Lydgate figures more or less prominently. Especially and consistently in his prologues, Hawes locates in the past ideal poetic practices and the poets engaged in them, and he explicitly seeks to position his own work in continuity with — and even as a fulfillment of — this history. In these prologues, Lydgate stands as Hawes's most proximate and ideal predecessor. Although Hawes has been called "the most Lydgatean of the English Chaucerians" on stylistic grounds, Lydgate, as A. S. G. Edwards points out, is far more important to Hawes as model for what a poet and his poetry should be.[11]

Hawes appears to downplay Lydgate's importance only in his first published poem, *The Example of Vertu* (1503–1504). This poem, to achieve its goal of exemplifying virtue, attempts to be a kind of *summa* of late medieval verse — containing, among other things, a moral allegory, a romance narrative, a debate, and a visionary journey to heaven and hell, all of which are centered around the development of a first-person narrator named Vertu. The work begins with a four-stanza prologue that possesses logical symmetry, in which the first stanza's reflections on the "famous draughtes of poetes eloquent" (2) take the form, in the fourth stanza, of the English triumvirate of "Gower ... Chauser ... Lydgat" (22–26). Sandwiched between these are two stanzas about Hawes himself, predictably in the guise of a humility topos: "I, now symple and moost rude ... It fereth me sore for to endyte;/But at auenture I wyll now wryte" (8–14). By means of the conventional tactic of framing one's self-derogation with eulogies of one's predecessors, he implicitly claims a place in the tradition of high-culture English poetry for himself and the quite ambitious 2100 lines of verse that follow.

Lydgate's role in this prologue seems at first limited to his membership in the triumvirate, but a few details suggest his greater significance. Hawes states in the first stanza that "the custume of antyquyte" was "to contryue" books for "the profyte of humanyte" (4–7) and then, in the third stanza, asserts that *he* in particular "wyll now wryte for to fulfyll/ Saynt Powles wordes and true sentement:/'All that is wryten is to oure document' " (19–21). In this way he conjoins a classical sense of the public profit of writing with a Christian insistence on true *sentence* and thereby suggests that, with this poetic effort, he becomes a Christian version of the great civilizing poets of antiquity. Tellingly, by describing himself as "very blynde in the poetys art" (15), he slyly appropriates for this project the notion of the laureateship by alluding to André, the blind poet who was Henry's laureate at the very time Hawes was writing. Yet, with this allusion, a disjunction threatens to surface between the idealized laureateship Hawes claims and the actual laureateship of André, a disjunction Hawes attempts to negotiate through the figure of Lydgate, who, alone among the triumvirate, receives the crucial epithet "vertuous." With this single word, Hawes connects his poetic predecessor with the allegorical hero of his poem, who stands in turn for both the essence of Hawes's poetics and, at least at times, Hawes himself.

Hawes's *Pastime of Pleasure* (1505–1506), totaling close to 6000 lines, resembles in many ways a greatly expanded revision of *The Example of Vertu*, except in this case the hero of the work carries the more romantic name Graunde Amoure, and his love object, rather than *Example's* Clennes, is Labell Pucell.[12] In the eight-stanza prologue to this work, Hawes puts his earlier obscurity aside and makes explicit his high regard for, and desire to perpetuate, Lydgatean laureate poetics. He begins with a three-stanza panegyrical address first to his "Ryyght myghty prynce & redoubted souerayne" (1) Henry VII and then to the latter's son, "Noble pryuce [*sic*] Henry," who "dyscendeth by ryghtfull lyne" (15–16). In the next stanza, he then asks his king "to accepte ... This lytell boke," despite his humble admission, "Nothyng I am experte in poetry/As the monke of Bury, floure of eloquence" (23–27). Once again, Hawes uses logical symmetry to convey his message, only in this case he makes his parallels more specific: Henry VII is the royal father, while Lydgate is the poetic one; praise of Henry and his son "by ryghtfull lyne" is doubled by praise of the "monke of Bury" and the inverse praise of Hawes's self-derogation. In this way he forges an implicit claim to be rightful heir of the Lydgatean tradition vis-à-vis the presumed legitimacy of the Tudor dynasty, and, lest his royal reader miss this dynastic implication, he goes on to remind the king that Lydgate wrote in the time

> Of your predecessour, the .v. kynge henry;
> Vnto whose grace he dyde present
> Ryght famous bokes, of parfyte memory,
> Of his faynynge with termes eloquent,
> Whose fatall fyccyons are yet permanent —
> Grounded on reason, with clowdy fygures,
> He cloked the trouthe of all his scryptures. (29–35)

With this mention of Henry V, the most renowned English king of the recent past, Hawes underscores the parallel between royal and poetic lineage and, at the same time, presents an idealized portrait of the relationship between poet and prince. The message is plain: to be a king like Henry V, one must have a poet like Lydgate — not a servant who pens verses upon command, but a "floure of eloquence" who presents the king "Ryght famous bokes ... Grounded on reason." And, of course, assuming that Hawes wished his book to be included in this category, this very prologue performs precisely such an act of presentation. In short, this prologue seeks to educate its reader in the very laureate poetics that it enacts.

The remainder of the prologue is extensively self-referential, albeit indirectly so, cloaked by a description of a poetics of cloaking that is characteristically Hawes's. As Lois Ebin has shown, Hawes uses a consistent set of terms to refer to poetry and how it operates, some of which are present in the stanza quoted above (e.g., "fatall fyccyons," "clowdy fygures," "cloked ... trouthe," and "scryptures").[13] While the basic concepts these terms denote were fairly commonplace, in Hawes's hands they also connote a notion of occulted prophetic utterance that simultaneously signals his affiliation with, and advertises his personalization of, the Lydgatean poetic project. For Hawes, the *locus classicus* of this understanding of poetry was likely the prologue to Lydgate's *Isopes Fabules*, which, as we saw in Chapter 2, similarly begins with reflections on the ancients, and, in particular, on "þe poete laureate/ Callyd Isopus" who "In fables rude includyd gret prudence/And moralytees full notable of sentence" (MP II, 8–9, 20–21).[14] In a characteristic move, after a four-stanza celebration of this past laureate and his poetics, Lydgate concludes his prologue with four stanzas about himself, humbly excusing his presumption and his lack of "floures of eloquence" (35), but managing to name himself in the process. Hawes, correctly reading Lydgate's self-derogation as inverted self-celebration, attributes to him, as quoted above, precisely the "floures of elloquence" that the monk denies. Just as Lydgate praises Aesop in order to make claims for his own work, Hawes, substituting Lydgate for Aesop, praises the monk in order to assert the authority of his own brand of poetics and, further, to place it in contiguity with the English laureate tradition.

Hawes makes this self-assertion more explicit as the prologue proceeds. Immediately following his description of Lydgate as having "cloked the trouthe of all his scryptures," he laments,

> The lyght of trouthe I lacke connynge to cloke,
> To drawe a curtayne I dare not to presume,
> Nor hyde my mater with a mysty smoke:
> My rudenes connynge doth so sore consume
> Yet, as I maye, I shall blowe out a fume
> To hyde my mynde vnderneth a fable,
> By conuert colour, well and probable. (36–42)

Couched within this self-abnegation is a bold claim for his own poetic accomplishment. In addition to the curious fact that in the final three lines of this stanza he asserts a willingness to do exactly what in the first four lines he denies possessing the "connynge" for, Hawes indicates here the two-pronged maneuver by which he ultimately substitutes himself for his predecessor. First, as he well knew, the cloaking of truth – a poetics that he represents as passing directly from Lydgate to himself by repeating its description in lines 35 and 36 with "he" and "I" as respective subjects – is in fact not at all typical of Lydgate's method. Lydgate's greatest works – the *Life of Our Lady*, the *Troy Book*, and the *Fall of Princes* – are manifestly more direct conduits of "trouthe." In comparison, a relatively small fraction of the monk's work makes use of the fabular/allegorical method that characterizes the blend of romance and moral allegory of Hawes's own poems. Second, Hawes's emphasis on Lydgate's "faynynge" (32) – which here means the composing of original verse – stands in contrast with Lydgate's more typical role as translator, as the monk himself represents it in the *Isopes Fabules* prologue. In a later eulogy of Lydgate in the same work, Hawes uses the synonymous "contrive," which in this instance he explicitly distinguishes from translation: "And after hym [i.e., Chaucer], my mayster Lydgate,/The monke of Bury, dyde hym well apply/Bothe to contryue and eke to translate" (1338–40).[15] Hawes's poems, although largely patchworks of conventions from the English and Burgundian high-culture vernacular traditions, are neither presented as, nor in fact, translations. Revealingly, while Lydgate excuses his Aesopian "translacion" "bycause of ignoraunce" (43–44), Hawes, in the stanza immediately following the one above, apologizes for the "ignoraunce" of his "fayned fable" (43–44) and goes on to state,

> To folowe the trace and all the parfytenesse
> Of my mayster Lydgate, with due exercyse,
> Suche fayned tales I do fynde and deuyse. (47–49)

What at first may seem like mere Lydgatean imitation thus turns out to be Hawes's introjection of his own poetics — and himself — into the Lydgatean tradition. Just as his predecessor presented "bokes" to Henry V, Hawes, "to folowe the trace and all the parfytenesse/Of [his] mayster Lydgate" presents his own "fayned tales" of cloaked truth to Henry VII. As his suggestive image conveys, Hawes does not merely imitate his master, but, by following in his trace — i.e., walking in his footsteps — he replaces the monk's person with his own.[16]

The prologues to Hawes's short poems — *The Conuercyon of Swerers* and *A Ioyfull Medytacyon* (both 1509, the latter written for Henry VIII's coronation) — work in much the same way. Both begin with reflections upon the poets of "olde antyqutye" (line 2 of each); both parade out the "monke of bery" (*Conuercyon*, 23; *Medytacyon*, 8) as the exemplary English poet in this tradition; both refer in some way to the proper political role of the laureate; and in both Hawes casts aspersions on himself as an act of humble self-aggrandizement. The prologue to Hawes's final poem, the 938-line *Conforte of Louers* (1510–11), appears at first glance quite similar, especially to that of *The Example of Vertu*, the four-stanza structure of which it shares. But in fact this later prologue contains subtle differences that throw more light on the nature and causes of Hawes's idiosyncratic and proto-Spenserian Lydgateanism. While it begins with a meditation on "gentyll poetes," its first stanza, unlike that of the other prologues, moves directly to a statement of Hawes's own poetics:

> The gentyll poetes vnder cloudy fygures
> Do touche a trouth and cloke it subtylly.
> Harde is to construe poetycall scryptures —
> They are so fayned & made sentencyously.
> For som do wryte of loue by fables pryuely,
> Some do endyte vpon good moralyte
> Of chyualrous actes done in antyquyte. (1–7)

Notable here is Hawes's use of present tense; he refers not to poets of "antyquyte" but to present poets who write "Of chyualrous actes done in antyquyte." Any reader of Hawes's earlier poems would immediately recognize this self-referentiality, as the poet had, in the collectively nearly 9000 lines of the *Example* and *Pastime*, quite definitively made it his particular project to "touche a trouth" by writing about both "loue" and "chyualrous actes." (And, just to ensure that this allusion to his earlier work is not missed, he mentions "fables and storyes" that have been "pastymes pleasaunt" in the first line of the following stanza.) Seven years after he wrote about the "custume of antyquyte" in the first stanza of the *Example*, he implies in the opening of the *Conforte* that that custom has been fully revived in his own practice.

As in the prologue to that earlier poem, Hawes quickly makes his self-assertions explicit, here as there proclaiming his identity as one of the "gentyll poetes" through the ruse of denying it. In this later instance, however, he places this denial in the context of the early Tudor court and specifically in its institutionalization of culture production, submitting himself to his readers' "grete gentylnes,/As none hystoryagraffe nor poete laureate −/But [one who] gladly wolde folowe the makynge of Lydgate" (19−21). As Alistair Fox has pointed out, Hawes here is not merely feigning modesty in denying an identity as a "hystoryagraffe" or "poete laureate." In contrast with what was only a hint in the *Example* prologue, he quite explicitly acknowledges that he does not hold the position of André − who possessed the title of king's historiographer as well as laureate.[17] Equally explicitly, *against* this institutionally concrete office, Hawes places the notional laureateship of the Lydgatean tradition. Not only does he suggest that there is a difference between the "makynge of Lydgate" and that of Henry VII's "poete laureate" (a difference he underscores by positioning name and title as stanza-ending rhyme pair), but he also expresses his opinon of the superiority of the former "makynge," which he "gladly wolde folowe."

Nonetheless, in the next stanza, we realize retrospectively that the "gladly" of the preceding comment denotes longing rather than enthusiasm, and that the subjunctive "wolde" refers to a scenario that is no longer a possibility:

> Fyrst noble Gower moralytees dyde endyte,
> And after hym Cauncers grete bokes delectable −
> Lyke a good phylosophre − meruaylously dyde wryte;
> After them Lydgate, the monke commendable,
> Made many wonderfull bokes moche profytable.   .

> But syth they are deed, & theyr bodyes layde in chest,
> I pray to god to gyue theyr soules good rest. (22–28)

After being left out of every prologue Hawes had written since the *Example*, Gower and Chaucer rejoin Lydgate in the *Conforte* in the same position as in the earlier poem, the fourth and concluding stanza of the prologue. In the *Example*, each *auctor* appears simply as the celebrated object of an apostrophe, and the three together operate as an authorizing agent whose "connynge," Hawes boldly proclaims, he "now vse[s]" (27–28). In contrast, as is apparent in the syntactical construction of "Fyrst ... And after hym ... After them," it is the historical line of descent that is important to Hawes in the *Conforte*. And revealingly, this line of descent does not reach the prologue's speaker: intervening between Lydgate – the final and, for Hawes, most accomplished member of the triumvirate – and the "I" of the poem is the blunt fact that these poets of the past "are deed, & theyr bodyes layde in chest." Lerer suggests that this line and the one that follows allude to Chaucer's Clerk's eulogy of "Fraunceys Petrak, the lauriat poete": "He is now deed and nayled in his cheste;/I prey to God so yeve his soule reste" (4.29–31).[18] But Hawes's remarks may be an allusion to an allusion, as they also echo closely his favorite and more proximate predecessor's eulogy of Chaucer in the *Life of Our Lady*: "Pray for hym – that liethe nowe in his cheste –/To god above, to yeve his saule reste" (2.1654–55).[19] Either way, with this allusion Hawes wistfully depicts himself as at least twice removed from the golden age, standing before the graves of those who themselves stood before graves of the great. His concluding prayer, although an entirely conventional ending for a eulogy, in the context of his previous work suggests disenfranchisement. Instead of asserting his inheritance of the triumvirate's "connynge," as in his earlier prologue, he may only pray for their souls.

In fact, the newly formed court of Henry VIII, containing what was by then the long-established role of the official poet laureate, had no room for the notional presumptions of poets like Hawes: as the body of the poem relates, upon the accession of the second Henry Tudor, Hawes had lost his place at court. For him, not only was the ideal of a Lydgatean laureateship lost to the past, but now gone also was the shadow of it he held as a poetically inclined groom of the chamber. Not coincidentally, the *Conforte* is a poem of consolation that is at times heavily – if obliquely – autobiographical. From this poem we receive details of Hawes's ouster that we do not learn from his mere disappearance from court records. And among the many coded revelations he offers — e.g., "Aboue .xx. woulues dyde me touse and rent" (163) — he makes one mechanism of his downfall relatively clear, which is that his poems were used against him:

> Some had wened for to haue made an ende
> Of my bokes before they hadde begynnynge;
> But all vayne they dyde so comprehende —
> Whan they of them lacke vnderstandynge,
> Vaynfull was & is theyr mysse contryuynge.
> Who lyst the trouthe of them for to ensue,
> For the reed and whyte they wryte full true. (183–89)

The gist of these syntactically tortured lines seems to be that a court faction had construed Hawes's "bokes" as somehow disloyal to the Tudor "reed and whyte" and had thus sought to suppress them. This interpretation is confirmed by Hawes's interlocutor's response in the next stanza, which also implies that his enemies, while obviously not successful at eliminating his books, did succeed at alienating him from the court:

> "Well," says this lady, "I haue perceueraunce
> Of your bokes whiche that ye endyte.
> So as ye saye is all the cyrcumstaunce
> Vnto the hyghe pleasure of the reed and the whyte,
> Which hath your trouth and wyll you acquyte.
> Doubte ye no thynge, but at the last ye maye
> Of your true mynde yet fynde a Ioyfull daye." (190–96)

The very existence of this dramatized, official confirmation of the pro-Tudor sentiment of Hawes's "bokes" suggests that the poet felt he needed to defend himself. Moreover, the future tense of "acquyte" and the conditionality of the "Ioyfull daye" that he only "maye ... finde" indicate that this very poem is a plea for the reinstatement that he is here imagining. The implication of all this — which must have been devastating to Hawes — is that, inasmuch as his prior writings were construed as disloyal, they utterly failed to be the laureate performances that he had so self-consciously framed them to be.

   In the *Conforte*, the poet's manifest failure to sustain a notional laureateship adds a new dimension to an already person-centered poetics. Lest a reader doubt that the "bokes" in question have much to do with the empirical Stephen Hawes, the poet later, through the voice of his imagined love object Labell Pucell, identifies one of these "bokes" as none other than his longest, most ambitious, and best-known work: "Of late I sawe aboke of your makynge/Called the pastyme of pleasure, which is wondrous" (785–86). And despite his redeployment of the character Pucell, as well as the lover-narrator persona Grande Amour, from this earlier, "wondrous" book, in the *Conforte* Hawes's entire coextensiveness with the first-person speaker is, for the most part, never in question. Relating the tale of Grande Amour's impossible love for the princess Pucell, the poem's elaborate and fantastical narrative strikes one as part bitter allegorical commentary on the early Tudor court and part coded fantasy of (incomplete) self-gratification. As in Hoccleve's poetry, thwarted laureate desire becomes an essential feature of the poet's self-representation, appearing as a longing for that which will most efface the difference between his current circumstances and the laureateship as he imagines it. For Hoccleve, this effacing agent was money, a plentitude of which would — or so he wished to think — obscure his actual economic subservience to his prince/employer, allowing him take up an unproblematically analogical laureate pose. For Hawes, the effacing agent is the reestablishment of an intimate relationship with the sovereign — a bond of friendship between intellectual equals that would obscure the actual social, political, and economic bonds that both enable and compel the subservient friendship offered by a groom of the chamber.

In the *Conforte*, Hawes dramatizes his desire for such a relationship, but, following his strategy of expressing "trouthe" under "cloudy fygures," he substitutes *amor* for *familiaritas*. In place of Henry VIII, he puts the king's sister Mary Tudor in the guise of Labell Pucell; in place of an alienated former servant, he puts the poet-lover Grande Amour of lowly social status; in place of a frustrated laureateship, he puts an unrequited love.[20] Seen in this light, the poem's story of a lamenting lover dreaming about attainment of chivalric honor and a confessional colloquy with his beloved may be read as Hawes's fantasy of, respectively, royal recognition of his poetic prowess and verbal intimacy with the young king. At the end of the poem, Hawes appears to recognize this fantasy as such. Pucell, "promest to a myghty lorde" (861), cannot be won. Despite whatever poetic achievement Hawes may attain, "a myghty lorde" — i.e., a sovereign's equal (and the specific reference here is to Charles of Castile, later Emperor Charles V)[21] — he may never become. The best he can imagine for himself in consolation is a royal admission of his worthiness for the role he desires, even while that role is denied him; as Pucell says,

Yf fortune wolde, for the payne ye haue taken,
I wolde graunt you loue — but it may nothynge auayle:
My loue is past, it can not be forsaken. (897—99)

Pucell admits that Hawes/Amour deserves royal "loue," but it is too late: that love has been bestowed upon others. The early Tudor court has given the lie to Hawes's laureate ambitions, and at the end of the poem, which also turns out to be the end of his poetic career, all Hawes may do is turn to superlunary powers and await ultimate justice — to "abyde the Iugment" of "Venus and fortune" (920).

This depiction of his plight and the strategies he uses to convey it are, while quite marked and urgently expressed in the *Conforte*, present in different degrees in his other poems as well. In the *Example* and *Pastime* especially, narratives of achievement of external reward and internal self-actualization at many points become Hawes's self-commentary on his poetic and sociopolitical ambitions. Hawes flags this self-commentary by explicitly occupying his protagonist's first-person voice. An early instance of this occurs in the *Example*, when Dame Sapyence remarks to Vertu, "Of myn owne chaumbre ye shall be grome" (403). This bald self-reference aims both notionally and practically to elevate Hawes's position at court. If, in the world outside the poem, he is a groom of the king's chamber, in the world inside the poem he becomes a groom of the chamber of wisdom itself — i.e., a poet laureate in training. Further, Dame Sapyence adds, "For and ye wyll theym [her commandments] well obserue,/A moche better rome ye do deserue" (405—6). If Hawes, these lines imply, is dutifully successful in the world inside the poem — i.e., if the poem itself is successful — then he may expect a "moche better rome," which, in the world outside the poem, would be a social and political promotion, perhaps to something like a laureateship. With the peculiar logic of laureate poetics, in which the notional and the empirical are interimplicated, Hawes here makes virtually explicit this poem's underlying petitionary function. Given such moments as these, readers are understandably confused when Vertu, in the end, turns out to be not Hawes but Henry VII, and the love object Clennes, Elizabeth of York.[22] In fact, this confusion reflects the very analogical aim of Hawes's laureate self-construction: Vertu, at the end of the poem, is for Hawes a personification of the principle of accomplished worthiness, upon which both laureateship and kingship are independently founded. By way of this conflated prosopopoeia, he is claming that, when reduced to their essences, king and laureate are identical entities.

In the *Conforte*, Hawes places this claim under scrutiny and anguishes over its very absurdity, even while holding onto a fantasy of its realization. In the process, the author-centered poetics that was already part of the Lydgatean tradition becomes charged with a narrative of erotic failure that serves as an analogy for the poet's alienation from power. The resulting coded autobiographical poem, in which erotic pursuit and political jockeying are interchangeable, represents something new in English verse, and is not far from what Wyatt would soon make, in a very different poetic form, his conventional *modus operandi*.[23] Yet, even while Hawes held his position at court, he could not but have been acutely aware that this position was neither what he imagined Lydgate's to be, nor even what André's in fact was. Like Hoccleve before him, precisely because Hawes's social circumstances belied the claims inherent in laureate poetics, his personal history becomes a crucial element of his poetry. In this regard, Hawes does indeed, as some have claimed, look forward to Spenser in a more than superficial way, as it is the latter poet's inability to analogize perfectly his sovereign that provides one of his key creative tensions.[24] But Spenser offsets the fundamental difference between himself and his female sovereign by claiming continuity with a line of male poets, the most paradigmatic of whom being Virgil. Hawes, by the time he wrote the *Conforte*, was faced with unbridgeable discontinuity along both poetic and sociopolitical dimensions. For this early Tudor poet, the Lydgatean literary tradition and the relationship with a sovereign that it presupposes were both, in 1510, "deed" and "layde in chest."

ALEXANDER BARCLAY

If Hawes's obsession with the figure of Lydgate belies the essential differences in their historical situations, Barclay's reluctance to acknowledge this Lancastrian precursor belies the many similarities between his and Lydgate's careers. Shortly after he published his initial literary effort, Barclay became, like Lydgate was, a Benedictine monk. Also like him, he proceeded to make a name for himself as poet by rendering into English verse some of the most esteemed Latin texts of his day, and, in so doing, he forged, like his predecessor, ecclesiastical and poetic identities that were mutually reinforcing. In sum, as a morally, spiritually, and politically authoritative poet-monk who wrote for a secular audience of nobles and lesser aristocrats (an identity prominently on display in a woodcut presentation scene Richard Pynson used for three of his books),[25] Barclay resembled in many ways — and more so than any other early Tudor poet — a latter-day Lydgate. As Harold Bloom has taught us, we may read his silence in regard to his fifteenth-century precursor as his acute awareness of his debt.

Barclay's personal history, however, also differs from Lydgate's in key ways. He was most likely Scottish, and thus would have been something of an outsider in respect to the English aristocracy among whom he sought his patrons.[26] More significant, the alignment of Church and State in the early sixteenth century was not what it was in the early fifteenth. Barclay's Benedictine conservatism was out of step with various court and clerical factions and, ultimately, with the king. Further, like Hawes, he had to compete with officially recognized poet-clerics such as André and Skelton. He did manage to secure a number of friends and patrons among the rich and powerful, including such figures as, among the aristocracy, Thomas Howard, duke of Norfolk; Richard, earl of Kent; and Sir Giles Alington; and, among the clerisy, William Cornish, Master of the Chapel Royal; William Crane, Cornish's successor in that post; and John Kyte, chaplain and sub-dean of the Chapel. But his work — and the name attached to it — never became the cultural and political commodity that Lydgate's did. And although Barclay, who was born around the same time as Hawes in the 1470s, survived the tumults of the Reformation to die an old man in 1552, his literary career, which began late (with the 1508 *Ship of Fools*), also ended early. At some point in the early 1520s, he seems to have put aside his monk's habit and become a Franciscan friar. No longer a member of Lydgate's religious order, he seems to have abandoned as well his ambition to become part of the order of English laureates.

Two references to Barclay in the historical record, taken together, chart the rise and fall of this monk-turned-friar. The first occurs in a letter from Sir Nicholas Vaux to Cardinal Wolsey, dated 10 April 1520. Vaux was in Calais making preparations for that spectacular meeting between Henry VIII and Francis I known as the Field of Cloth and Gold, which was orchestrated by Wolsey ostensibly to celebrate the peace between the two nations. He requests that Wolsey send over, among others, "Maistre Barkleye the Blacke monke and poete, to devise histoires and convenient raisons to florisshe the buildings and banquet house withal."[27] His choice of words here are happily rich in connotation. By "histoires" he probably means verses to accompany a "representation of historical events in a tableau or a tapestry" (MED *historie* n. [1(d)]), but the term also then possessed its modern meaning of a "systematic account of past events"

(MED *historie* n. [1(b)]). This word thus neatly captures what Vaux likely perceived as Barclay's desirable dual identity as paid propagandist and authoritative monastic writer. Similarly, by "raisons" Vaux probably refers to a "written sentence or verse; a motto, esp. one engraved, embroidered, or inscribed upon something" (MED *resoun* n. [2] 9a). But the word also carried more profound meanings, including a "principle, fundamental ground of something, essential character, essence" (MED *resoun* n. 5[a]). In Vaux's usage these terms were, in short, euphemisms. What he wanted from Barclay was ultimately quite crassly political, but, in asking for it, he made sure that he tipped his hat to the monastic authority that Barclay embodied.

As the object of Vaux's request, Barclay achieved a status resembling Lydgate's when the latter was receiving official charges for such pieces as *The Soteltes at the Coronation Banquet of Henry VI* (1432).[28] Like Lydgate an authoritative "Blacke monke" and renowned author of ponderous volumes of learned verse, Barclay now also resembled his predecessor in being a sought-after propagandist, one who could provide apt ornamental words for state occasions. At this time, Skelton was out of favor with Wolsey and living within sanctuary at Westminster Abbey. From Vaux's letter, one may infer that, with Skelton's place at court vacated, Barclay's star had risen. Yet, not more than eight years later, as evident in a letter from Herman Rinck to Wolsey dated 4 October 1528, it had quite precipitously fallen. Rinck contemptuously refers to a group of religious exiles, "William Roy, William Tyndale, Jerome Barlow, Alexander Barclay, and their adherents, formerly Observants of the order of St. Francis, but now Apostates," who, along with "many other rebels of the King's grace, ought to be arrested, punished, and delivered up on account of Lutheran heresy."[29] This change in status seems so remarkable that some have doubted that this Alexander Barclay is our poet. One possibility, as R. J. Lyall has argued from subsequent letters to Wolsey and the facts of Barclay's later ecclesiastical career, is that Barclay's exile was not, as the others' were, for apostasy but rather for a rigid orthodoxy that alienated him from Wolsey.[30] Regardless of the precise circumstances, though, Barclay's hope for a career as a court poet, if he even maintained one, was apparently now dashed — a supposition confirmed by the absence of any surviving work after 1523. Again, the contrast with Skelton is telling: in the same year that Rinck wrote his letter, Skelton — having made amends with Wolsey and consequently restored to his position at court — wrote his vicious, Wolsey-prompted anti-reform poem, *A Replycacion Agaynst Certyane Yong Scolers Abjured of Late.*

Barclay's problem was twofold. On the one hand, despite being more suitable for the role of Lydgatean laureate than someone like Hawes, he could not compete with those who claimed institutional, rather than merely notional, laureate identity. His practice of laureate poetics and updating the source texts of laureate performance were not enough to obtain court favor in a literary system that included the likes of Skelton and André. On the other hand, he remained resolutely tied to a Lydgatean ideal of the noble place and function of poetry and the poet – an ideal that was patently unrealizable in the early Tudor court. Like Lydgate, he wished to understand himself as moral and spiritual advisor rather than as versifying political henchman. In short, he neither was fully able nor fully desired to be what a laureate was in the early Tudor court. His resemblance to Lydgate, when paired with these practical and dispositional barriers to a fully realized reenactment of the latter's poetics, resulted in poetic passages possessing a character at once self-confident and resentful. In comparison with Hawes, he displays little nostalgia for a past in which notional laureates held sway; his social location and relative success as poet probably convinced him that he had in fact inherited Lydgate's mantle. But he could not ignore the reality that some poets, whom he perceived as less than ideal laureates, had achieved an institutional recognition denied him, and his consequent resentment over this denial appears in his poems as an infrequent but consistent series of polemics aimed at Skelton in particular and laureates in general. Overall, these polemics create an impression of Barclay as an anti-laureate laureate – an authoritative monk who is quite willing to leverage his social identity in a circuit of mutual legitimization with those in political power, but who also habitually (and more explicitly than does Lydgate) puts court and cloister in opposition.

This self-conflicted poetics takes intricate and elaborate form in Barclay's best-known efforts, the *Ship of Fools* and the *Eclogues*.[31] But in regard to the former, what initially most strikes one about this 113-chapter work is its incredible ambition, especially given that it was Barclay's debut. With his inaugural foray into the realm of public verse, Barclay attempted nothing less than to trump Lydgate's *magnum opus*, the *Fall of Princes*. Like that work, the *Ship* is a loose translation of an erudite, monumental effort by an *au courant* continental author – the Alsatian *Narrenschiff* of Sebastian Brant (1494), putatively by way of Jacob Locher's official Latin translation, the *Stultifera navis*, the text of which Barclay supplies alongside his English.[32] Both Lydgate's *Fall* and Barclay's *Ship* are encyclopedic in design and scope and represent an attempt at a comprehensive account of the moral dimensions of human existence. Both poets, it has been fairly claimed, have scrubbed their sources of much (if not all) of their proto-humanistic elements in order to present a moralistic *summa* of a more traditional outlook.[33] Unique to Barclay's version of the *Ship* — and famously a feature of Lydgate's *Fall* — is a chapter/envoy structure, in which the translator systematically reserves to himself a space to summarize, comment on, and add to the matter that has come before. Barclay also imitates the weariness topos to which Lydgate (or Bochas) in the *Fall* is frequently prone. Finally, in the chapter of the *Ship* that takes up the very matter of the *Fall*, "Of the mutabylyte of fortune," he comes closer than he does anywhere else to acknowledging explicitly his precursor. After noting that the "most peryll is in *hyest* dignyte" and "howe many men *Royall*/Hath fortune dryuyn downe into aduersyte," he encourages one to "rede Bochas" to "se playne/The fall of prynces, wryten ryght compendeously."[34] His phrase "The fall of prynces" cannot but have recalled Lydgate's widely disseminated English version of Boccaccio's *De casibus virorum illustrium*, as Barclay chooses the precise words that Lydgate uses to translate Boccaccio's title.[35] Certainly not coincidentally, Lydgate's ponderous work was issued by Pynson just 14 years before Barclay saw his *Ship* through the same press.[36] In occluding his true poetic model with the name of the latter's own *auctor*, Barclay (again, as Bloom has taught us) insinuates that he wants not so much, like Hawes, to follow in Lydgate's trace, as to efface his belated position altogether and in an essential way to occupy Lydgate's place. Perhaps it was no mere coincidence that, shortly after publishing the *Ship*, Barclay gave this literary occupation a social and spiritual reality by entering Lydgate's Benedictine order.

"Occupation" is as well the most apt term for describing how Barclay practices that essential gesture of laureate poetics, self-representation as an authoritative, historically specific poet. While making plain his role as translator, Barclay, beginning with the quite elaborate introductory apparatus, does not hesitate to put his person into the shoes of his *auctor*. Before the poem proper begins, he names himself no less than seven times — in titles or subtitles, twice in verse, and twice in prose. In comparison, the first appearance of Brant's name in the English sections of the work is buried near the end of the first of two prose prologues — after two introductory sections of verse entitled "Alexander Barclay excusynge the rudenes of his translacion" and "Barclay the translatour tho [*sic*] the Foles."[37] And even this reference to Brant is framed in such a way as to privilege the role of the most recent "translatour," since Barclay also mentions the subsequent Latin and French versions of Brant's work and, in an elaborately auctorial passage, claims to have built his *Ship* out of them all. On the one hand, Barclay depicts himself in this passage (pp. 145–47) as the last in a long line of poetic defenders of "vertue" against "vyce," a line beginning with "Dant Florentyne and Francis Petrarche, Poetes heroycal," and recently revived in "Mayster Sebastian Brant" and "his Disciple," "one called James Locher." On the other hand, the hierarchy such a line potentially predicates between "composer" and "translatours" is remarkably flattened. Instead of appearing as just another agent for the dissemination of Brant's great "Inuencion," Barclay appears as an equal member of a group of moral authorities, each of whom (in the most ideal conception of laureate poetic service) wishes "to redres the errours and vyces" of his respective community, from Dante's Florence, to Brant's "Almayne," to Barclay's "Royalme of Englonde." That this is a group of peers, rather than masters and disciples, Barclay underscores by his insistence that the Alsatian, Latin, and French texts (and presumably his own) "agreeth in sentence" despite being "threfolde in langage." He calls attention to his membership in this group not only by naming himself in their company but also by insisting – as he does in several other places – that his version of the *Ship* represents a kind of culmination of the prior ones, drawn from "thre Langages" rather than a mere translation of a translation.[38]

In the poem proper, Barclay furthers his co-option of the auctorial role by consistently violating the formal boundary between chapter and envoy, embedding details in the former that align its narratorial "I" with his own, well before the subtitle of the latter, which often names Barclay, and which ostensibly demarcates the space to which his voice has been restricted. Such a violation occurs in the very first chapter, in which the narrator observes that, "For if one can flatter and bere a hawke on his Fyst,/He shal be made Person of Honyngton or of Clyst" (p. 162.13–14). Honiton and Clyst, as David Anderson notes, refer to well-endowed livings near Ottery St. Mary, where at the time Barclay served as pedagogue to choir boys at the collegiate church.[39] These details, the first examples of Barclay's habitual geographical adaptation of his source, not only relocate Brant's work from Alsace to England but also – as local allusions scarcely the most accessible to a wide English audience – point to Barclay's historical specificity. In this way, they assist Barclay's seizure of the narratorial "I" from Brant and his translators and effect an occupation of the first person all the more significant in this initial chapter because of its confessional nature (it begins, "I Am the firste fole of all the hole nauy" [p. 159.1]).

This self-referential localization of his source is one of Barclay's favorite tactics of laureate self-construction. But he makes use of many other such tactics as well, such as versified self-naming (e.g., p. 259.11) and aureate epideictic passages. The latter is well illustrated by the long envoy to the chapter entitled "Of the great myght and power of Folys," which celebrates Henry VIII as the epitome of those few ideal individuals who have "myght and power" and yet succeed at *not* being a fool. The combined effect of all these tactics is to make the specific person of the named narrator, just as in Lydgate's *Fall*, repeatedly rise to the surface of an immense sea of moralism. The reader never forgets that it is the monk of Bury who voices the inevitable doom of illustrious men throughout history, and just so the reader never loses sight of the fact that it is Barclay, cleric of Ottery, who anatomizes the fools on his *Ship*.

But another, rather different, impression that one receives, especially near the end of the work, is a sense of the speaker's dissatisfaction with the possibilities available to him as a Lydgatean laureate in the world of Skelton and André. This dissatisfaction appears both positively, in the form of coded petitions for advancement, and negatively, in disparagement of Skelton. A positive instance occurs relatively early, in the concluding stanza of the envoy celebrating king "Harry" mentioned above. By praising his newly crowned king specifically for promoting clerics "of wysdome and science" (p. 493.5), Barclay — then a simple school chaplain — puts in a plea for his own advancement, on the basis of the "wysdome and science" of the very poem that contains this plea. Since at the beginning of the immediately preceding stanza he proclaims that, under the reign of Henry VIII, "all Englonde [is] lawreat" (p. 492.17), the implication is that the nation will remain "lawreat" if Henry, among other things, promotes cleric-poets such as himself to positions supporting such laureate performances as the present one. Less subtly, in the chapter entitled "The descripcion of a wyse man," he expresses his hope that "the noble royalme of Englonde auaunce/In our dayes men of vertue and prudence," and that "men of wysdome were brought out of the scolys/And after theyr vertue set in moste hye degre" (p. 778.89, 15–16). A few lines later he becomes more specific in regard to which particular "men of wysdome" in the "scolys" he refers:

> Wysedome shall men auaunce vnto honour:
> So Barclay wyssheth and styll shall tyll he dye

Parfytely pray to god our creatour
That vertuous men and wyse may haue degree
(As they ar worthy) of lawde and dygnyte —
But namely to his frende, bysshop by name,
Before all other desyreth he the same. (p. 780.8—14)

By claiming that he seeks the advancement of someone else —
"his frende, bysshop by name" — Barclay avoids a blatant, Hocclevean
petition for his own reward of "degree ... of lawde and dygntye" that the
act of self-naming in this context would otherwise convey. In the next
stanza, however, we learn that this friend, a certain John Bishop of Exeter,
"was the first ouersear of this warke," and that his great act of wisdom
was to give "vnto his frende ... his aduysement" for the *Ship* "nat to
suffer to slepe styll in the darke,/But to be publysshyd abrode and put
to prent" (p. 778.89, 15—16). As it turns out, the principal basis of
Bishop's merit is that he possesses the wisdom to see the great value of
Barclay's "warke." Bishop's advancement, then, should manifestly be on
the coattails of Barclay's own.

Barclay insinuates in these passages that the health of the realm is
threatened by the dearth of traditional cleric-poets, and in particular
himself, in posts of eminence. For him, this dearth is the result of the
institutional conditions under which a poet like Skelton, who possesses
the appropriately named credentials, is qualified, while one like himself,
who more purely perpetuates the Lydgatean tradition, is kept from court
(notwithstanding his later invitation to the Field of Cloth of Gold).
Barclay's resentment in this regard is understandably focused on Skelton,
the most preeminent English poet of the day, whose sense of poetic
propriety was so different from Barclay's, even while his general outlook
was quite similar. We receive an early hint of this resentment in the
chapter entitled "Of the prowde and vayne bostynge of Folys,"
when among these vain boasters Barclay includes "Some other
Crowned as Poetis lawreat" (p. 543.1). But the most explicit
reference occurs in the final stanza of the work's final chapter, Barclay's
own "brefe addicion of the syngularyte of some new Folys," just before
the work's benedictory ballad to Mary. After a rather long and detailed
defense of his *Ship*, he concludes by describing quite specifically the kind
of work to which it is opposed:

Holde me excusyd: for why my wyll is gode
Men to induce vnto vertue and goodnes.
I wryte no Iest ne tale of Robyn hode,

Nor sawe no sparcles ne sede of vyciousnes.
Wyse men loue vertue, wylde people wantones.
It longeth nat to my scyence nor cunnynge
For Phylyp the Sparowe the (Dirige) to synge. (p. 841.15–21)

Skelton's *Phyllyp Sparowe* — a virtuoso blend of satire, sex, and liturgy — was, for Barclay, far from a laureate performance, and brought the high-culture Lydgatean tradition down to the level of a "tale of Robyn hode." In contrast, the *Ship*, designed as it was "to induce [its readers] vnto vertue and goodnes," is, Barclay claims, a true instance of such a performance, despite its poet not being among those "Crowned as Poetis lawreat." Perhaps, also, there is something here in addition to a sentiment of resentful superiority. At the time that Barclay wrote these lines, Skelton was likely still in Diss and seeking a place back at court. Barclay may well have been attempting to preempt Skelton's reappointment by making a case for himself as a better candidate.

But regardless of the actual circumstances surrounding the *Ship*, Barclay's next poetic endeavor, the *Eclogues*, suggests that he was not unequivocally enthusiastic about gaining such a position. Barclay began writing this sequence of five eclogues perhaps as early as 1509 and most likely completed them, after much revision, in 1514.[40] Although smaller in scale than the *Ship*, this work, the first instance of pastoral eclogues in English, is plainly as ambitious. His source for his first three eclogues is Aeneas Sylvius Piccolomini's *Miseriae curialium* and, for his final two, Mantuan's fifth and sixth eclogues, respectively. But Barclay expands upon his sources tremendously; according to John Schultz, there are about 45,500 words in the *Eclogues* to his sources' 14,830.[41] Although some of this expansion results from the inevitable amplification of Englished Latin, Barclay's changes are so extensive that this work is in many respects no more a translation than is Chaucer's *Troilus and Criseyde*. This is especially the case with the first three eclogues, which transform Piccolomini's prose epistolary polemic against court culture into a sequence of pastoral dialogues in couplets. Such a reworking allows Barclay to localize, self-referentially, the entire work in one stroke by setting it in the English countryside, somewhere near his monastery in Ely, where he lived after taking his vow.[42] In addition, it allows him to introject his person into the verse in several different guises — in particular, as both narrator and the bitter, moralistic shepherd Cornix, who, like Barclay, "in youth in Croidon towne did dwell" (1.389).

For the *Eclogues*, however, more important than these tactics of personalization is the opposition between courtier and cleric that informs the entire work and that shows Barclay confronting the fact that a monkish laureate, in the early sixteenth century, was becoming a contradiction in terms. In the opening of the first eclogue, when the youthful Coridon complains about the hardships of a shepherd's life and declares that, "to the Court nowe will I get me playne" (1.329), we can expect — from the conventional association of shepherds with clerics — an argument from the older and wiser Cornix for the superiority of the pasture. And, indeed, this argument occupies the whole of the first three eclogues. In a few places this takes the positive form of eulogies for the great ecclesiastics of Barclay's day — especially ones with Ely ties, such as John Morton, bishop of Ely from 1479 to 1486 and subsequently Archbishop of Canterbury ("shepheard Morton" [3.459]); John Alcock, Morton's successor at Ely through 1500 ("the gentle Cocke whiche sange so mirily" [3.470]); and Roger Westminster, prior at Ely from 1478 to 1500 ("Shepheard Roger," whose "death was mourned from Ely forty mile" [3.494, 508]).[43] But for the most part, Barclay, following Piccolomini, pursues this argument negatively, emphasizing both the physical unpleasantness and moral emptiness of the life of the courtier.

The relevance of this critique to Barclay's own position and aspirations becomes plain in the second eclogue, in one passage of which (2.291–318) Cornix argues at length that the court corrupts wise men and in particular encourages them to falsify their language. At court, Cornix claims, "men of wisedome," instead of speaking "playne veritie," must "cloke the truth, their princes to content" (2.291, 302, 295) — an operation that, in contrast with Hawes, was for Barclay not one of the prime virtues of poetry. In particular, "poetes or oratours ornate," in their "orisons before some great estate" (2.297–98), must speak with "spice of adulation" (2.304), and, revealingly, Barclay has changed here Piccolomini's "Philosophi" to high-style "poetes."[44] A poet who goes to court, this passage insists, necessarily becomes a mere prince-pleaser who conforms his verse to the whims of the sovereign, regardless of the virtue of those whims. It is impossible within Henry VIII's court, the implication is, for Barclay to be the kind of poet he wishes to be. Even those greatest products of monkish poets — "true histories of actes auncient" — are "falsely turned, some princes to content" (2.309–10). Presumably, an epic and epideictic history such as Lydgate's *Troy Book* would, if written for the early Tudor court, be rendered as "newe histories . . . fayned of the olde,/With flattery paynted and lyes manyfolde" (2.313–14). All that

a "good scholer without promotion [i.e., Barclay],/Hearing suche glosed
communication" may do, since he "[d]are not be so bolde [the court
poet's] lying to gainsay" is "laugh in his minde" (2.315–18) at such
courtly abuse of letters – a bitter laughter which is in large part what his
first three eclogues express.

This bitterness derives from the fact that Barclay, self-righteously
depicting his willing disassociation from the court, nonetheless feels
dissatisfied at being an outsider. This latter sentiment he signals near the
end of the third eclogue. Having run through Piccolomini's treatise, he –
as expected – has Coridon admit the rightness of Cornix's argument:
"Beleue me Cornix, thou turned hast my minde;/Farewell all courting,
adewe pleasour vnkinde" (3.757–58). A few lines later, however, in verses
original to Barclay, Coridon once more returns to the question of court
versus pasture, formulating it in this instance as a dilemma:

> But tell me, Cornix, one thing or we departe,
> On what maner life is best to set my harte?
> In court is combraunce, care, payne, and misery,
> And here is enuy, ill will and penury. (3.811–14)

This last line recalls the opening complaints, uttered by Cornix as well as
Coridon, about the hardships of pastoral life and, importantly, makes it
clear that these hardships are not just physical but also moral. All is not
well in the pasture. Despite Cornix's affirmative reply – "Liue still a
shepheard, for playnly so will I" (3.818) – one senses that Barclay realizes,
while it is no longer possible to be a true Lydgatean court poet, neither
can he be a poet of the stature he desires without a relationship with the
court. The "enuy" Coridon mentions here is perhaps Barclay's own.

It is thus certainly no coincidence that Barclay positions as
the following eclogue Mantuan's fifth,[45] which is fundamentally
a poet's complaint about the lack of economic support for his work.
Following generic convention, Barclay complains also about
inadequate secular support of the clergy – as when his character
Minalcas speaks of the sorry state of his fields and his "poore flocke"
(4.105). Yet Minalcas, unlike the shepherds of the previous eclogues,
is represented throughout as a famed poet, who was "wont to sing
full merily,/And to lye piping oftetime among the floures" (4.40–41).
He is, to be precise, both poet and cleric, and he believes that to be
successful as the former requires the patronage of the wealthy.
This patronage is represented by Minalcas's interlocutor Codrus,
to whom at one point Minalcas petitions,

Make thou me iocunde, helpe me with cloth and foode,
Clothe me for winter with pilche, felt and hoode.
Auoyde all charges, let me sit in my cell,
Let worldly wretches with worldly matters mell.
Succoure my age, regarde my heares gray,
Then shalt thou proue and see what thing I may:
Then shalt thou finde me both apt to write and sing. (4.383–89)

Sitting in his "cell," without having to "mell" in "worldly matters," this
now monkish poet will again be "apt to write and sing" once he has
adequate "cloth and foode." And, lest we miss the note of self-
aggrandizement in this assertion of aptitude, a few lines later he supplies
as one example of a similarly well-provided shepherd none other than
"Titerus" who "liued vnder Mecenas" — i.e., Virgil, who "songe of
fieldes and tilling of the grounde,/Of shepe, of oxen, and battayle did he
sounde" (4.410–14).[46]

Moreover, that Barclay is neither slavishly imitating his source nor
simply asking for "cloth and foode" to support his writing becomes clear
in the second half of the eclogue. Beginning at line 536, even though
Minalcas has just insisted that he does not wish for a place at "the court
of Rome" (4.519) but rather only "a liuing sufficient and small" (4.515),
he and Codrus nonetheless enter into a detailed discussion about the
contemporary relationship between poets and princes. Codrus suggests
that Minalcas celebrate the martial deeds of "mightie princes," who, as
"worthy rulers of fame and name royall,/Of very reason ought to be
liberall" (4.538–40). Minalcas's negative response is threefold: princes
these days do not appreciate poetry ("For in this season, great men of
excellence/Haue to poemes no greater reuerrence/Then to a brothell or els
a brothelhouse" [4.553–55]); and, even if they did, they would not
seek the services of a poet so destitute ("Howe should a Poet — poore,
bare, and indigent —/Indite the actes of princes excellent" [4.571–72]);
and, in any event, for the most part they are no longer suitable objects of
poetic praise ("If Poetes should their maners magnify,/They were
supporters of blame and lechery" [4.597–98]). Codrus replies that
some true noble heroes do remain, in particular "the sonnes of noble
lorde Hawarde [i.e., Thomas Howard, duke of Norfolk]" (621). Minalcas
acknowledges the worthiness of the Howards, yet he reiterates that most
princes remain ignorant of the value of poetry: "Ful litle they force for to
delate their fame,/That other realmes may laude or prayse their name . . .
And some be vntaught and learned no science,/or els they disdyane hye
stile of eloquence" (4.645–46, 653–54). We begin to suspect that Barclay

has adapted this entire passage for a very specific audience, and, when Minalcas then proceeds to supply an intricately crafted allegorical elegy for the duke's son Edward (who, as Lord High Admiral, was killed in an encounter with the French in 1513),[47] this suspicion is confirmed. This passage in general and the elegy in particular (the originality of which Barclay underscores by having Minalcas twice attribute its authorship to Cornix, his alter ego from the first three eclogues [4.797–98, 1135–36]) stand as a coded tutorial, directed at Edward's grieving father, regarding the value of poetry. Barclay's point is that truly virtuous and heroic nobles ought to be the subject of poems by truly virtuous and eloquent poets – and that, in order for Edward to be recognized as the former, Barclay must be recognized as the latter.

Before Barclay supplies this elegy of more than 300 lines (4.823–1134),[48] however, he must explain why he is writing from the position of begging rather than laureate poet – "poore, bare, and indigent" rather than already officially recognized and well patronized. He contends, through Minalcas, that dubious entertainers, such as "Iugglers and Pipers, bourders and flatterers," have managed to "good Poetes forth of all courtes chase" (4.665–69). But even worse, he continues, are the court laureates, and he goes on to supply the most mean-spirited and detailed critique of Skelton in his entire oeuvre:

> Another thing yet is greatly more damnable:
> Of rascolde poetes yet is a shamfull rable,
> . . .
> Then is he decked as Poete laureate,
> When stinking Thais made him her graduate
> . . .
> They laude their verses, they boast, they vaunt and iet,
> Though all their cunning be scantly worth a pet
> . . .
> Thus bide good Poetes oft time rebuke and blame,
> Because of other which haue despised name.
> And thus for the bad the good be cleane abiect,
> Their art and poeme counted of none effect. (4.679–714)

Although bad and good poets are given in the guarded plural here, the personal nature of the enclosing passage and a remark in the *Eclogues'* general prologue (quoted below) ensure that the underlying singular references will be evident to the careful reader.[49] Barclay, according to his own testimony, is not at court because Skelton – "decked as Poete laureate" and certainly among those who most "laude their [own] verses ... boast ... vaunt and iet" — occupies the place he deserves. As one of the "good Poetes," Barclay must abide "rebuke and blame" and tolerate his work being "counted of none effect." In this context, the elegy that follows stands as both an example of the kind of "art and poeme" that ought to be composed by a laureate and a plea for Barclay's advancement to a place similar to the one occupied by Skelton. Indeed, as if to underscore this double-edged strategy, he in fact provides not one but *two* examples of true laureate performances. Before he is interrupted by Codrus, Minalcas manages to utter four ballad stanzas of aureate, moralistic verse (beginning, "As medoes paynted with floures redolent" [4.759]). Codrus's impatience with this sort of verse ("Ho there Minalcas, of this haue we ynough,/. . . ./Tell somewhat els, wherein is more conforte" [4.791—95]) should probably be read as a negative illustration of how Barclay wishes his ideal audience (the duke of Norfolk) to respond. But it also conveys the inhospitable climate for a poet of Barclay's predilections and his knowledge that the only sure way to please a patron like Norfolk is to offer poetic monuments to his descendants.

At this point, Barclay has come full circle from the stance he assumes at the outset of his *Eclogues*. In the work's general prologue, he explicitly denies any desire for Skelton's officially recognized status — instead being content with the knowledge that he is keeping true to his monastic identity while at the same time walking in the poetic footsteps of Virgil, Petrarch, and Mantuan:

> But of their writing, though I ensue the rate,
> No name I chalenge of Poete laureate.
> That name vnto them is mete and doth agree,
> Which writeth matters with curiositee.
> Mine habite blacke accordeth not with grene,
> Blacke betokeneth death as it is dayly sene;
> The grene is pleasour, freshe lust and iolite —
> These two in nature hath great diuersitie.
> Then who would ascribe, except he were a foole,
> The pleasaunt laurer vnto the mourning cowle?
> Another rewarde abideth my labour,
> The glorious sight of God my sauiour. (1.103—114)

As we know from Skelton's *Agenst Garnesche*, as *orator regis* Skelton wore robes of "wyght and grene" (3.139), the colors of the royal livery. Barclay here insists that, while his writing has the same value as that of past laureates ("though I ensue the rate"), he has no desire for an official post such as Skelton's, preferring instead to remain true to his Benedictine "habite blacke," which "accordeth not with grene." With the term "curiositee," Barclay aptly describes both Skelton's ingenious formal dexterity and the idle vanity for which he believes it is deployed;[50] in contrast, Barclay writes not for his own "pleasour" but as spiritual labor aimed at winning the "glorious sight of God." Yet, by the fourth eclogue, Barclay seems intent on redeeming the term "laureate." Following his initial four-stanza example of a laureate performance, he uses the term four times in a space of less than 250 lines, each instance with a positive, albeit somewhat different, meaning.[51] Although only the last of these is associated with a writer rather than a warrior ("Tully laureate" [4.1091]), the principle of epideictic poetry that governs this passage necessitates that a laureate victor receive adequate praise only from a laureate singer. While Barclay may still wish to keep wearing his "habite blacke," he no longer seems reluctant to receive a "pleasaunt laurer."

What is more, Barclay fully owns this ambivalence. He knows that he has, by his fourth eclogue, written the sort of paean "swetely saused with adulation" (2.294) that he condemns in the second. Although he most likely believes this paean to be truthful, he knows that such truth, in this context, is indistinguishable from "flattery paynted and lyes manyfolde" (2.314). He dramatizes these mixed feelings at the end of this eclogue, which follows but expands upon Mantuan. After Minalcas completes his performance of the elegy for Howard, Codrus, thoroughly impressed, pledges that he will "well rewarde [Minalcas's] songe" (4.1144). But a few lines later, upon Minalcas's request for this reward, Codrus quickly exits, offering only a "dieu te garde" (4.1151). With the substitution of Barclay for Minalcas and royal patronage for Codrus, what the reader encounters here is Barclay's double realization that he cannot be the poet he wishes to be without the offer of such patronage, and neither can he be that poet if he were to accept it. Although he understands himself as a more authentic and morally qualified Lydgatean than Skelton, in the end he cannot and, more importantly, does not wish to "chalenge" the name "of Poete laureate." After completing the *Eclogues*, Barclay continued to write poetry for six or so more years, ceasing suddenly some time after his invitation to the Field of Cloth and Gold. We will likely never know for certain why he ended his poetic career,[52] but from the *Eclogues'* depiction of his dilemma, we may plausibly suppose that he concluded that his laureate desires were no longer good for his soul.

JOHN SKELTON

The ups and downs of Skelton's court career have been well documented by William Nelson, H. L. R. Edwards, and, more recently, Greg Walker.[53] For present purposes, two aspects of this career are most relevant. First, there is the fact that there were, indeed, some significant downs. Early on, there were the loss of his royal tutorship and his subsequent rustication to the rectorship at Diss soon after his pupil, Henry Tudor, became heir apparent upon the death of his older brother Arthur in 1502.[54] Restored to court in the early years of the reign of his former pupil (c.1512) and given the title *orator regis*, he just a few years later experienced a seven-year exile from court favor (1516–23), some of which he spent within sanctuary at Westminster Abbey, and which seems largely the result of his having antagonized Cardinal Wolsey.[55] In addition, even while he held his court position, he was not, perhaps, as eminent a figure as has been supposed. Walker argues that scholars, mistaking Skelton's self-aggrandizement for his actual status, have glossed over the evidence that suggests that his first stint at court was primarily as tutor rather than poet, and that his second stint as *orator regis* may have been merely "a limited commission to provide propaganda for the war" against France and Scotland.[56]

Second, despite its low points, Skelton's court career was the single most essential element of his poetic identity. Its importance may be observed in everything from his choice of topics, the development of his style, his habit of dating his poems to the year of his entrance into the king's service,[57] to his thoroughgoing self-advertisement as poet laureate. In regard to this last feature, many critics have been quick to point out that, in the early sixteenth century, the title of poet laureate was a mere academic degree held by any number of individuals. Yet, the fact remains that no other Englishman before Skelton — other than the obscure John Kay — laid explicit claim to the title.[58] More important, this title plainly held great significance for Skelton himself. As Stephen Dickey has calculated, of the 37 works of Skelton's appearing in John Scattergood's edition, 21 somehow proclaim their author to be "Skelton laureate," and, of these, 11 contain this epithet in the poem proper. In addition, 6 of the poems that do not contain this epithet refer to Skelton's laureateship in some other manner, leaving only 10 works that do not explicitly name its author as laureate.[59] For contemporary readers, this pervasive self-advertisement must have made the author's name and title virtually synonymous — an effect which at least one fellow poet, as we have seen, especially resented.[60]

What is more, this epithet or its referential equivalent is no mere titular attempt at self-authorization but — as evident in works spanning his entire career — a crucial element of most of Skelton's poems' thematic centers. In his earliest surviving English poem (1489) — an elegy for Henry Percy, earl of Northumberland (who was killed by a mob angry at Henry VII's war tax) — the thematic work that this epithet performs is apparent in the very heading that follows the Latin preface: "Skelton Laureat Upon the Dolorus Dethe and Muche Lamentable Chaunce of the Mooste Honorable Erle of Northumberlande." Here Skelton, by positioning his poetic identity on one end of the heading and his object of praise on the other, and joining subject and object with a lofty description of the poetic matter, lays out schematically the epideictic circuit that he exploits throughout the poem's 31 rhyme royal stanzas. The two implicit claims of this heading are that only a laureate may adequately lament an honorable earl, and that the stature of both will be represented and produced by the aureate elegy that follows. As the subsequent opening stanzas of the poem make evident, Skelton, early in his career, was already a master of these characteristic features of Lydgatean poetics:

> I wayle, I wepe, I sobbe, I sigh ful sore
> The dedely fate, the dolefulle destenny
> Of hym that is gone, alas, withoute restore,
> Of the blode royall descendinge nobelly;
> Whos lordshepe doutles was slayne lamentably
> Thorow treson, ageyn hym compassyd and wrought,
> Trew to his prince in word, in dede, and thought.
>
> Of hevenly poems, O Clyo, calde by name
> In the college of musis goddes hystoriall,
> Adres the to me, whiche am both halt and lame,
> In elect uteraunce to make memoryall!
> To the for succour, to the for helpe I kall,
> Myne homely rudnes and drighnes to expelle
> With the freshe waters of Elyconys welle.
>
> Of noble actis auncyently enrolde
> Of famous princis and lordis of astate,
> By thy report ar wonte to be extolde,
> Regestringe trewly every formare date;
> Of thy bounte after the usuall rate
> Kyndle in me suche plente of thy nobles,
> Thes sorowfulle ditis that I may shew expres. (1–21)

These three stanzas efficiently deploy many Lydgatean tactics: a centralized, named "I"; the epideictic linking of aristocratic and poetic aura; an assertion of poetry's memorializing function; and an invocation of Clio couched in a humility topos that means the opposite of what it literally says. As a whole, in fact, this poem is the purest Lydgatean performance in Skelton's oeuvre – which suggests that he soon realized that, to continue to succeed at court, the tradition he inherited had to be adapted rather dramatically.[61]

In what seems to be the first poem he wrote after being sent to Diss, *Ware the Hauke* (c.1505), Skelton deploys an apparently very different set of poetic strategies – ones that, while equally aimed at laureate self-construction, would ultimately prove better suited for such purposes when he later regained a place at court. Probably unhappy about his removal, Skelton was not likely to find in his new surroundings a worthy object on which to lavish aureate praise. Instead, he finds much to ridicule – a literary operation that, though the inverse of praise, operates in a homologous fashion:

> I shall you make relacyon
> By way of apostrofacyon
> Under supportacyon
> Of your pacyent tolleracyon,
> How I, Skelton laureat,
> Devysed and also wrate
> Uppon a lewde curate,
> A parson benyfyced
> But nothynge well advysed.
> He shall be as now nameles,
> But he shall not be blameles,
> Nor he shal not be shameles;
> For sure he wrought amys
> To hawke in my church of Dys. (29–42)

The aureate terms of the first four lines of this passage (which the reader retrospectively understands as parodic) lead naturally into an act of self-naming, but subsequently, instead of an object of praise, there is an object of blame – the "nameles" "lewde curate" who stands in rhymed contra-distinction to the named "Skelton laureat." The parson, constructed as an object of utter contempt, reflexively constructs his condemner as a voice of moral authority. Precisely by being *not* "blameles," the object of this poem helps to constitute the speaker's authority in the same way – but with inverse polarity – as the named earl of Northumberland does

in *Upon the Dolorus Dethe*. As Skelton surely knew, epideictic poetry since
its classical origins has included both praise and blame, and the circuit
that it brings into being among poetic subject, object, and medium may
operate efficiently in either mode. The Lydgatean tradition, in fact,
contains abundant examples of blame poetry (for example, Lydgate's
A Ballade of Jak Hare; Hoccleve's *Remonstrance against Oldcastle*; and, in
a more generalized fashion, most of Barclay's *Ship of Fools*). Skelton,
however, was the first in this tradition to make this face of epideixis so
fundamental to his poetics.[62]

Upon his return to court, Skelton put the formal innovations
and generic adaptations he had developed during his rustication to
productive if unspectacular work in his new role as *orator regis*. In a short
space, he turned out a series of poems possessing the straightforward aims
of professional vituperation and direct self-advertisement; these include
Agaynst the Scottes (1513), *Agenst Garnesche* (1514), *Against Dundas*, and
Against Venemous Tongues (both 1515–16). That he quickly became in this
period (and perhaps even prior to it) personally associated with venomous
blame poetry is evident in Barclay's peculiar about-face in the fourth of his
Eclogues. After Barclay's own vituperative remarks about the laureates who
"laude their verses ... boast and iet" he realizes that blaming Skelton is
tantamount to imitating him and semi-recants the use to which he has just
put his verse:

> It is not seeming a Poete one to blame,
> All if his hauour hath won diffamed name.
> And though such beastes pursue me with enuy,
> Malgre for malice, that payment I defye. (4.733–36)

Characteristically taking the moral high road, Barclay contends that a
"Poete" should not waste his verses on blame, even if the object of attack
deserves such treatment – and here, in the context of his having just
contemptuously referred to one who is "decked as a Poete laureate," we
should understand "Poete" to denote a more authentic, if unofficial,
laureate. The implication is that, for Barclay, Skelton has achieved success
only at the cost of denigrating the very medium that forms the basis of
that success.

Skelton must have, at least at times, felt similarly. His career contains
moments that express a much loftier sense of the nature and purpose of
poetry – as well as his ambition to create such poetry – than is apparent
in such efforts as the entertaining but shallow *Agenst Garnesche*. For
example, in the *Bowge of Courte* (1498) and in his long morality play

Magnyfycence (1515–16), written, respectively, before and after his time at Diss, Skelton shows both a willingness and an ability to turn verse into a forum for grappling with the moral complexities of court life. More revealing, as *orator regis* the name he wore in gold letters on his green and white robes was Calliope, the muse of epic poetry, his devotion to whom he makes clear in the little poem he wrote most likely in celebration of his new position. I quote the English verses of this poem in full, not only to convey the excessively — and unprecedentedly — blatant nature of Skelton's laureate self-construction, but also because they neatly exemplify his essentially Petrarchan understanding of the poetic enterprise:

> Why were ye Calliope, embrawdered with letters of golde?
> Skelton Laureate, *Orator Regius*, maketh this aunswere etc.
>
> Calliope,
> As ye may se,
> Regent is she,
>   Of poetes al,
> Whiche gave to me
> The high degre
> Laureat to be
>   Of fame royall;
>
> Whose name enrolde
> With silke and golde
> I dare be bolde
>   Thus for to were.
> Of her I holde
> And her housholde;
> Though I waxe olde
>   And somdele sere,
>
> Yet is she fayne,
> Voyde of disdayn,
> Me to retayne
>   Her serviture.
> With her certayne
> I wyll remayne
> As my soverayne
>   Moost of pleasure. (1–24)

Epic poetry, with its "Regent" muse, is for Skelton the highest form of poetry, and it is to this form that a laureate "Of fame royall" ought to be dedicated. Such a poet, although necessarily associated with a prince, owes his true feudal obligations only to his muse, whose "serviture" he "wyll remayne."[63] In the vision of this short lyric, a poet laureate works autonomously, writing epic poems under the auspices, but not under the control, of the laureating sovereign.

But Skelton never had an opportunity to write his *Africa*; instead, as I have noted, upon his return to court, the aptitude for blame poetry that he had sharpened at Diss was put to work attacking the king's (or, in some cases, his own) enemies. With the early Tudor institutionalization of the laureateship, poetry, by the second decade of the sixteenth century, had become manifestly just one political weapon among others, and the poet laureate consequently less a notional analogue of the prince than one of his flesh-and-blood henchmen. In the Lancastrian era, Henry V, at least according to Lydgate, had seen in poetry a reflection of his eminence as well as a tool for persuasion. While poetry under Henry VIII also could possess this dual function, its instrumental half was much plainer for all to see. Under these conditions, Skelton, in order to maintain his faith in the good work that poetry may accomplish, sought, as one critic has put it, to refigure his henchman role into a "Juvenalian scourge of hypocrisy, shoddy scholarship, and failed idealism."[64] He sought, that is, to elevate the status of the blame poet so that he could serve both Calliope and his king, and be a loyal servant to the latter without making a mockery of the former.

The extravagant claims that he expresses in *Calliope* are not, however, easily reconciled with the utterly subordinate role he held in the play of power and personality that characterized Henry VIII's court. The idea of the Petrarchan/Lydgatean laureate, which to a large extent informed Skelton's sense of self-importance, was much too big to fit into the small institutional box of the king's *orator regis*. More concretely, with the ascendance of Wolsey shortly after Skelton's return to court, Skelton was confronted with an embodiment of real political power in the person of a lowborn cleric like himself — a commoner who was not merely a *notional* double of the sovereign, but a *practicing* one. In comparison with Wolsey, Skelton was an exceedingly marginal figure, and thus it is perhaps no surprise that Skelton's lofty sense of his own and his poetry's importance somehow earned the ire of the Cardinal. This antagonism eventually led to Skelton's exile from court and hence the effective decoupling of his poetic project from its alignment with power. Living in sanctuary, Skelton found himself faced with a situation much like Hawes's in *The Conforte of Louers*. With his laureate desire so patently thwarted, that very desire became even more persistently the topic of his verse. For Hawes (and, before him, for Hoccleve), this desire appears most acutely, as we have seen, as a longing for that which will enable or restore the poet's laureateship. In Skelton's case this was the removal of Wolsey, who figures, in the triptych of poems he wrote during his Westminster exile, as an imposing barrier between his laureate wisdom and the ear of the king.

As one would expect in these circumstances, in each of these poems the poet's voice and authority are fundamentally at issue. Yet, by focusing on a specific and powerful opponent, Skelton is able, unlike Hawes, to continue to fashion a poetically operative claim for an analogical relation to the king. Making use of the blame structure of his court polemics, he constructs an epideictic circuit through the contention that he and the king have a common enemy in the king's chancellor. As Greg Walker points out, Skelton wrote his first anti-Wolsey poem, *Speke Parott* (1521), when a rift between Henry and Wolsey suggested the possibility of the latter's removal.[65] Skelton's derogation of the chancellor in this case was thus an attempt to elevate himself notionally to the status of an advisor authoritative and intimate enough to confirm the king's doubts about his highest-ranking official. In this work as well as its two siblings, Skelton, by means of a triangulation of himself, Wolsey, and the king, reasserts his laureate status in adverse circumstances and, at the same time, reins in the tendency of thwarted laureate desire to express itself autobiographically. His laureate self-construction – rather than mutating, as for Hawes and Hoccleve, into abject narratives of longing – finds instead avenues of expression in, on the one hand, denunciation of Wolsey (i.e., blame that stands in for and operates inversely as praise of the king) and, on the other, conspicuous display of poetic virtuosity.

It is primarily within the space of this virtuosity that Skelton tackles the pressing questions of voice and authority. Limited to this space, these questions are able to admit the crisis that has raised them, even while still leading to claims for an intrinsic laureate authority – albeit the strength of these claims diminishes with each subsequent poem. In *Speke Parott* – which is generally acclaimed as Skelton's masterpiece – the poet finds in the titular figure a near perfect expression of his situation. In the poem's first two stanzas, he neatly exploits the allusive multivalence of the parrot to capture the conceptual and practical contradictions of his current status. In the second of these stanzas, the speaker depicts himself as a caged pet surrounded by "greate ladyes of estate" (i.e., courtiers), a pet who, for "an almon or a date" (i.e., tokens of noble largesse), speaks what is to them brilliant nonsense (i.e., this very poem, a multilingual patchwork of allusion, artfully stitched together in the guise of a parrot's unknowing mimicry). Portrayed in this fashion, a poet laureate is nothing more than a learned but inconsequential entertainer. In the first stanza, however, Parott is quite a bit more: "a byrde of Paradyse,/By Nature devysed of a wonderowus kynde." "Paradyse" may be read here, as Fox and others argue, as Henry's court, and the first stanza thence as narrating Skelton's removal therefrom.[66] But paradise can also be understood more literally, as an expression of what Skelton, following the Petrarchan/Lydgatean tradition, considered to be the transcendental nature of his poetic gift and the timelessness of his work, which, after his death, like Parott's body, "dothe not putrefy" (213).[67]

These conflicting self-depictions are well represented by the poem as a whole. On the one hand, what strikes us is its macaronic pyrotechnics — its wily play of linguistic surfaces — and, relative to this, profounder intentions seem secondary. On the other hand, the poem repeatedly insists on the presence of underlying pith, as in the following lines from the "Lenvoy royall":

> For trowthe in parabyll ye wantonlye pronounce,
> Langagys divers; yet undyr that dothe reste
> Maters more precious than the ryche jacounce ... (364–66)

Near the end of the poem, Parott's interlocutor Galathea asks him to reveal this pith not in wanton "parabyll" but "trew and playne" (448), and, in the poem's final 10 stanzas, he complies. This long-awaited "trowthe" turns out to be a moralistic, rather conventional account of the world gone awry, at the center of which is an agon between Wolsey, the "braggyng bocher" (485), and Skelton as wise laureate.[68] Only with the removal of Wolsey, the butcher's son, and the return of the "popagay royall" (446 and elsewhere) — who, like Skelton in his capacity as *orator regis*, is draped in "emerawde grene" (16) — can poetry once again speak plainly and the world be set back on its proper course. Given the tenor and straightforward manner of this conclusion, one retrospectively recognizes the oblique, fractured voice of the rest of the poem as, at least in part, a formal expression of the deflation of Skelton's laureate status, the marginalization of his authority in favor of Wolsey's.[69]

The other two anti-Wolsey poems grapple with the same issues, but employ rather different modes of virtuosity for doing so. In *Collyn Clout* (1521–22), Skelton leaves behind the multivalent self-representation of *Speke Parott* in favor of a more coherent and conventionally recognizable alter ego. Perhaps dissatisfied with the practical ineffectiveness of the earlier poem, in the first 46 lines of *Collyn Clout* Skelton laments the

inability of his writing to produce change (e.g., "What can it avayle . . .
bokes to compyle/Of dyvers maner style,/Vyce to revyle/And synne to
exyle?" [1–13]). He then introduces his new strategy by way of a second
take on "My name is . . .":

> And yf ye stande in doute
> Who brought this ryme aboute,
> My name is Collyn Cloute.
> I purpose to shake oute
> All my connynge bagge,
> Lyke a clerkely hagge.
> For though my ryme be ragged,
> Tattered and jagged,
> Rudely rayne-beaten,
> Rusty and mothe-eaten,
> Yf ye take well therwith
> It hath in it some pyth. (47–58)

With this metastylistic association of the persona Collyn with Skelton's
idiosyncratic, "[t]attered and jagged" verse form, the author calls
attention to his gesture of putting on a mask. Consequently, although
Skelton wears this mask throughout the remainder of the poem's
1265 lines, the reader never forgets that the work as a whole represents the
author's attempt to forge a more efficacious literary strategy. As it turns
out, the very character of this mask exacerbates Skelton's problem.
Collyn's voice is that of the common everyman and therefore by
definition cannot approach the ideal of analogizing the prince's. While
Parrot in all his multivalence can still be a "popagay royall," the very
coherence of the Collyn mask demands that it stand for a figure in some
essential way different from the laureate who wears it. By putting on this
mask, Skelton therefore signifies a more definitive loss of status than he is
willing to do in *Speke Parott*, probably in the hope that such a gesture,
through its appeal to a more comprehending reading public, would more
effectively help him to regain that status. The aim of the Collyn persona,
in short, is to make itself unnecessary.

Skelton ends *Collyn Cloute* with a Latin epilogue that, in its bemoaning
of the decline of the "gens Anglica" ("English race") that formerly held
the "Laurus honoris" ("laurel crown of honor") (epi. 7), all but explicitly
laments the diminution of his own laurels. Feeling, perhaps, that in this
poem he had too much conceded his fall from the king's grace, in the
subsequent *Why Come Ye Nat to Courte* (1522) he returns as himself —
specifically, as a former laureate insider, now relegated to the role of

gadfly. The very question from which the poem takes its title presumes that its author *should* be at court, but, as he goes on to explain, he has willingly removed himself because of its moral turpitude and according lack of appreciation for him. The historical specificity of the poem's first-person voice, which throughout authoritatively answers a catechism of one-line questions, is unmistakably signaled near the beginning and at the very end of the poem through the same Latin couplet, "Hec vates ille/De quo loquntur mille" ("About these things the famous bard of whom a thousand speak") (29–30).[70] The crisis of voice and authority that he addresses in the prior two poems, largely through experiments in persona and form, he makes here his poem's explicit topic. This is probably as close as Skelton could come to reoccupying his prior role without in fact being restored to his office. He assumes the same authorial pose as he does in, say, *Agaynst the Scottes*, but he has redirected blame from the king's enemies to his chancellor, and instead of defending the king's interests, he is defending his own. Yet this pose, while better approximating the speaker of his *orator regis* phase, represents a great diminishment from one that may be equated with a "byrde of Paradyse." In seeking the most direct route to the recovery of his former status by the closest imitation of his former institutional practice, he has unavoidably (and maybe unwittingly) emphasized the vitiated nature of the only laureateship he may in fact possess. In *Why Come Ye*, Skelton succeeds in rendering a laureate poetics largely indistinguishable from that of his officially sponsored laureate performances, and this suggests that, in Henry VIII's court, the institutionalization of the laureateship scarcely differs from its marginalization.

Nonetheless, a desire for the institutionalized role of laureate is precisely what animates these three anti-Wolsey poems – and not simply a desire for the removal of Wolsey, which, as I have argued, is only the avenue through which the former desire finds expression. These poems, I repeat, are not so much interested in deposing Wolsey as they are in using their insistence on that deposition as a substitute source of laureate legitimation.[71] Once we understand that Skelton's antipathy toward Wolsey possesses this functional nature, we do not find so startling his sudden about-face in respect to the Cardinal in the "Lautre Envoy" to the *Garlande or Chapelet of Laurell* (published 1523), in which the "Cardineum dominum ... Legatum a latere" appears alongside "Henricum octavum" as the honorific recipients of the poem (1587–90). As is surely evident by now, Skelton's poetic interests, no matter what the explicit topic of a work may be, almost always include self-interests.

The oppositional epideictic relay he deploys in the anti-Wolsey poems to bolster his laureate claims in lieu of an institutional affiliation thus may easily — and even predictably — become a relay of praise, once that affiliation has, through the cardinal's intervention, been restored. What remains essential in either case is the centrality of Skelton's laureate selfhood. In the Wolsey-dominated English court of the early 1520s, such a selfhood necessarily had to be constructed in some relationship with the cardinal. This fact alone, regardless of what other extenuating circumstances there may have been, explains the presence of Wolsey in the envoy to this poem, which stands as the single most elaborate (if sometimes ironic) instance of self-celebration in the English poetic canon.

In this multifaceted work, Skelton recounts a dream vision in which he travels to the court of Fame and — at the urging of Pallas and before an audience of the most eminent poets of the past — receives his laurel crown. As a whole, this poem is a virtual encyclopedia of the devices of laureate self-construction. Among other things, it opens with an aureate astrological periphrasis ("Arectyng my syght toward the zodyake" [1]); contains several instances of self-naming (as when Fame recounts Pallas's "ryall commaundement" that "Skelton shulde have a place" in Fame's court and reports that, indeed, "regestred is his name/With laureate tryumphe" [58–63]); describes a long parade of past poets, which culminates in the English triumvirate (each member of which engages in a polite, mutually complimentary dialogue with the author); includes a series of exemplary epideictic lyrics for the countess of Surrey and her entourage; and records a ponderous autobibliography. This poem is, in short, a superbly excessive and remarkably self-focused laureate performance. It is also, apparently, a composition that spans most of Skelton's career, as he seems to have developed it in three stages: in c.1492, c.1495, and c.1523, at which point he published it.[72] He therefore likely revisited this monument to himself one final time before making it public, just months after writing *Why Come Ye*, and this timing probably reflects his exuberance at his restoration to court and his sense that his long career was nearing its end. He celebrates this moment with a poem that is literally his crowning achievement: it both narrates his crowning and serves itself as a textualized version of the crown, the poem bringing into being that which it describes. As A. C. Spearing remarks about the point in which the English triumvirate, upon seeing the garland made by the ladies, concedes that Skelton's "lawrell was the goodlyest/ That ever they saw, and wrought it was the best" (1113–14), "one begins to suspect that 'the laurel' has come to refer not just to the garland Skelton as dreamer is wearing but also to the poem called after it which Skelton as poet is writing."[73] If, in this instance, crown and poem are one, then so must be title and poet. The formerly descriptive epithet "Skelton laureate" has, in this context, become a mere tautology.

A thorough reading of this over-1600-line poem would doubtlessly help to flesh out the portrait of early sixteenth-century laureate poetics that this chapter has sought to draw.[74] But even from the few comments I have provided, one may gather that the *Garlande* represents not only a culmination of this poetics but also an evolutionary endpoint. By in effect making himself both epideictic object and subject, Skelton has brought the self-aggrandizing element of laureate poetics from its typical position as a partially occluded mechanism of legitimation into the foreground as the poem's *raison d'être*. Once this point in the trajectory of laureate poetics has been reached, one may fairly wonder if it may any longer plausibly be deployed to any other end.

Even in this poem, however — and well before the appearance of Wolsey in the *Lautre Envoy* — the actual social conditions of laureate practice intrude, and the figure of the poet as prince-pleaser (or, in this case, princess-pleaser) must be accounted for. When early on Fame asks, "With laureat tryumphe why Skelton sholde be crownde" (217), it is not enough for Skelton to depict his fellow laureates as testifying to his worthiness; he must also provide examples of his work — exemplary instances of actual laureate performances. Specifically, he must supply panegyrical verse for the countess of Surrey and her ladies, in exchange for which they bestow upon him the laurel garland that he depicts them as weaving. In a telling recapitulation of the logic of Boccaccio's *Trattatello* — or, for that matter, Petrarch's laureation address — Skelton bluntly juxtaposes lofty claims for the nature and value of poetry with an unrepentant portrayal, or even actual instance, of its sociopolitical function. That he was aware of some incompatibility in this juxtaposition is apparent in the fact that, as the series of panegyrics proceeds, he more and more assumes the upper hand. Not only is his praise of the ladies, as many have observed, subtly equivocal and thus at once a critique of contemporary laureate practice and a form of self-praise (in respect to his poetic ingenuity),[75] but also, by the last two lyrics, the sole basis of his praise becomes merely that these particular ladies are helping to make his laurel — that is, his praise becomes unmistakably reflexive, turning his ostensible epideictic object into a placeholder for himself. The irony that this entails may well be his underhand strategy for reasserting the autonomy of his laureate practice at its seemingly most servile moment. Yet, even at best, this strategy is a symptom of the narrow confines of his laureate self-determination (and, at worst, it results in self-parody). In the end — or, specifically, in the *Lautre Envoy* — Skelton cannot escape the institutional conditions that underwrite his laureate claims. In this postscript he bows "pronus" (1587) before the king and the previous object of his most vitriolic verse. And, as if that bow alone were not enough, he concludes by holding out his hand to Wolsey, petitioning him for a prebend, the promise of which most likely led to his return to court under the cardinal's auspices:

> et fiat memor ipse precare
> Prebendae, quam promisit mihi credere quondam,
> Meque suum referas pignus sperare salutis
> Inter spemque metum.
>
> and beg him to remember
> the prebend he promised to commit to me,
> and give me cause to hope for the pledge of his favour.
> Between hope and dread. (1590–93)

With the verb *precor*, Skelton, at the end of this poetic monument to himself, admits that he — like all those before him writing in the Lydgatean tradition — cannot suppress the beggar within the laureate.

In what was most likely his final poem, *A Replycacion agaynst Certayne Yong Scolers Abjured of Late* (1528), the contradiction within laureate poetics appears in such extreme form as to be an almost poignant statement of Skelton's inability to escape it. This poem, most basically, serves as a vernacular, literary mouthpiece for the official condemnation of the heresy exposed in the 1527 trials of Cambridge scholars Thomas Arthur and Thomas Bilney. Yet, by including among the orthodoxies that the heretics allegedly denied an insistence on the divine nature of the poet's inspiration, Skelton finds a reason to devote the last quarter of this poem's 400 or so lines to the most impassioned and theologically far-reaching defense of poetry written in English to that time. In these lines, Skelton asserts, in effect, that God "maketh his habytacion" in "poetes laureate" (376, 358). Surely no greater claim, in a Christian culture, could be made for the transcendental nature of the laureateship.[76] Nonetheless, framing this poem are stark indications of early Tudor laureate practice. At the poem's head stands a panegyrical address from "Skeltonis laureatus" to "Cardinali meritissimo … princip[i] sacerdotum [i.e., Wolsey]" — an address so ostentatiously ornate that it makes the poet's remarks at the end of the *Garlande* seem insulting in comparison, and which has led at least one critic to suspect that it represents Skelton's tongue-in-cheek acknowledgment of the fact of his being "bought" by the cardinal.[77] Similarly, in the poem's Latin epilogue, after Skelton concludes, "reor ergo poetas/Ante alios omnes divine flamine flatos" ("therefore, I think that poets, before all others, are filled with divine inspiration"), he adds, "sic Caesar, maximus heros/Romanus, celebres semper coluere poetas" ("thus Caesar, the greatest of Roman heroes, always honoured famous poets") (epi. 6–10). At the end of this poem, after recapitulating his greatest claim for poets and poetry, he cannot resist including a tactful, flattering reminder to Henry VIII that Skelton, as famous poet, ought to receive honor from England's "Caesar." As it turns out, the most sweeping, passionate defense of poetry ever mounted by this official laureate is sandwiched between an obsequious salute to his former archenemy and a dunning note to his king.

As we have seen in the preceding chapters, this give-and-take between – or, more precisely, interimplication of – the transcendental and instrumental appears in some form throughout the Lydgatean tradition. But because Skelton, more so than any other poet in this tradition, was recognized institutionally as what he claimed to be notionally, he, more than others, had to grapple directly with the contradictions contained within laureate poetics. If, for the monk Lydgate, who was never fully identifiable as a court poet, these contradictions could remain largely mystified, and if Hoccleve simply allowed himself to be overwhelmed by them, Skelton, by his very appointment at court, could not but attempt to make sense of them. And this requirement ensured that a basic endeavor of many (if not most) of his poems was his own constitution as laureate. His selfhood is, consequently, a pervasive topic of his verse, but ultimately the selfhood that he most typically renders is – notwithstanding the moral agons that critics such as Stanley Fish have found in it – rather shallow. Only when his identity as court poet was somehow threatened did Skelton probe deeper into his interior, but the overriding concern of the resulting poems to reclaim that identity inevitably led him back to that volatile but nonetheless desired epithet, "Skelton laureate."

A year or so after *A Replycacion* was published, the old laureate died, and with him went one of the final practitioners – if not at all the final influence – of the continuous tradition that began with Lydgate more than a century earlier.[78] Hawes had died some years before, and Barclay had ceased writing verse. In the same year as Skelton's death, Wolsey was dismissed by Henry VIII for failing to gain a papal annulment of Henry's marriage to Catherine of Aragon, and the next year he also was dead. Great change was afoot, and in the fourth decade of the sixteenth century the literary convention of personalized anticourt sentiment — much exercised in Hawes's *Conforte*, Barclay's *Eclogues*, and Skelton's *Bowge* — would combine with an aristocratic inwardness to produce, in the work of Wyatt, verse that may at first appear strikingly different from that which immediately preceded it. Yet, as the careers of the three poets discussed in this chapter suggest, change was inevitable, even apart from the failure of Wolsey and the talents of Wyatt. Years before the dissolution of the monasteries, Lydgatean laureate poetics — by realizing in actuality what it had initially only imagined — had emptied itself of much of its native authority.

Epilogue: Sir Thomas Wyatt: anti-laureate

At various moments throughout this book, I have gestured toward Spenser as a latter-day Lydgatean, and hence a natural conclusion would be to revisit this gesture and, in particular, to consider the ways in which Spenser refashions laureate poetics to suit his specific circumstances and, more generally, ushers it into early modernity. Yet, such a consideration, done thoroughly, bespeaks not so much a terminus for this project as the beginning of a new one, and hence, for practical reasons, cannot be pursued here. Moreover, there are pressing literary historical reasons to focus this epilogue elsewhere — ones that are strikingly evident in the opening of E. K.'s *Epistle* in *The Shepheardes Calender* (1579), in which E. K. celebrates Chaucer as "the olde famous Poete," the onomastic twin of Virgil in their shared cognomen Tityrus, while he mentions Lydgate merely as Chaucer's admiring "scholler." Similarly, in the first gloss to *Januarye*, E. K. acknowledges Skelton's coinage of the pseudonym "Colin Cloute" but, in identifying Spenser's source, quickly passes over the English laureate in favor of Clément Marot.[1] In the fifty years that had elapsed between Skelton's death and Spenser's publication of *The Shepheardes Calender*, Tudor poets had learned to publicize their origins as occurring anywhere but in fifteenth-century England. In fact, this general suppression happened rather suddenly, decades before Spenser's birth, in the very court in which Skelton practiced his trade. To suggest, as I have done in this book, that Spenser is a Lydgatean poet thus implies that Lydgateanism somehow went "underground" in the later years of Henry VIII's reign, persisting in the very poets who most identified themselves otherwise and who created the sixteenth-century poetic premises upon which Spenser built his career. The first of these poets was Sir Thomas Wyatt, and hence it is with him that I conclude.

When Wyatt arrived at the court of Henry VIII in 1516 to serve as Sewer Extraordinary, he was only about 13.[2] Among the more colorful figures he would have encountered at that time was Skelton, who in his mid-fifties was busy churning out pieces appropriate to his office as *orator regis*. We may only guess what the young Wyatt thought about this stout, egocentric priest arrayed in green and white robes emblazoned in gold with the name Calliope. Surely he must have associated Skelton with the laureateship, the possession of which, as we have seen, Skelton went to great lengths to promote. But Wyatt never mentions him or in any way alludes to his poetry. In contrast, he unmistakably records his debt to his and Skelton's common vernacular ancestor, Chaucer. Whether he silently imitates the Ricardian poet, as in his lyric "If thou wilt mighty be" (which takes as its model Chaucer's Boethian "Truth"), or explicitly alludes to, for example, "Syr Thopas" and "Pandare," he makes plain his appreciation for the fourteenth-century poet and implicitly casts himself as his sixteenth-century follower.[3] Correspondingly, Wyatt's lack of acknowledgment of the vernacular poetry of the intervening century suggests that, for him, fifteenth-century poetry in general and the laureate performances of Skelton in particular were an aberrant branch of the native tradition, an unfortunate detour from the path first blazed in the late fourteenth century. One may fairly infer that, for Wyatt, English poetry was ripe to be reborn. Such indeed is how George Puttenham, writing not quite sixty years after Wyatt's death, famously characterizes Wyatt's and the earl of Surrey's contributions to the native tradition. Celebrating them in the same manner that fifteenth-century poets praise Chaucer, he pronounces them "the first reformers of our English meetre and stile"; in comparison, Skelton, merely "vsupring the name of a Poet Laureat," is "but a rude rayling rimer," whose habits of verse are to be categorically shunned by those who wish to be poets of the newly reformed tradition: "in our courtly maker we banish them vtterly."[4] Conventional accounts of English literary history have typically echoed Puttenham's assessment, seeing little relationship between Wyatt's achievements and the work of the adjoining generation of poets, understanding the former instead as at once the deferred fulfillment of Chaucer's promise and the brilliant eclipse of fifteenth-century Chaucerianism.

Although by most accounts Wyatt's achievements are relatively modest in comparison with those of such later sixteenth-century figures as Spenser, he retains immense importance because of this literary historical narrative — that is, his presumed status as the first poet of the

English Renaissance. And, as often as this status has been questioned, it remains resilient for a number of reasons, most prominent being, perhaps, its institutionalization in the period-based structure of scholarship, university curricula, and anthologies. Medievalists have at times, and especially of late, registered complaints about this structure in general and the presumed discontinuity of the early Tudor period in particular, countering assumptions that privilege early modern poetry over the medieval verse it supposedly overcomes and that locate in the sixteenth century points of cultural origin that are in fact largely adaptations of cultural phenomena of earlier periods. Both the recent Cambridge and Oxford histories of medieval English literature, for example, include studies of Wyatt, and the Oxford history in particular – James Simpson's *Reform and Cultural Revolution* – positions itself as a thoroughgoing critique of conventional distinctions between late medieval and early Renaissance (although it retains a less conventional distinction in its basic argument). In a more institutional vein, Derek Pearsall has published a textbook anthology of English writing that forges a new period of literary history by joining the later portion of the Middle Ages and the earlier portion of the Renaissance, covering a range of texts spanning Chaucer and Spenser. Nonetheless, few have attempted to argue for continuity between Wyatt and his most immediate poetic predecessors, the first generation of Tudor poets discussed in Chapter 5. Most students of late medieval English poetry, as wary as they may be of categorical periodization, would likely agree with the judgment Pearsall offers in his anthology's headnote to this second-generation Tudor poet: though the literary historical rupture that Puttenham imagined, in a wider view, cannot be borne out, "Wyatt, at least, *is* different."[5] Since throughout this book I have maintained a claim for the ongoing significance of fifteenth-century laureate poetics – a significance that persists beyond one terminus of the tradition with the death of Skelton – Wyatt's apparent difference requires at least brief investigation. If a preliminary case can be made for Wyatt's participation in the dynamics of laureate and beggar, then this epilogue may become, in a sense, a prologue for another study that would, beginning with a more thorough consideration of this poet, trace the vicissitudes of laureate poetics across the putative medieval/Renaissance divide, through Spenser, and into the modern era.

While there are many ways in which Wyatt has been distinguished from his most immediate predecessors, a commonly adduced one is reflected in the contrast with which I began this book – between, that is,

Chaucer's third-person and Wyatt's first-person renderings of Petrarchan lyric subjectivity. As Pearsall succinctly puts it, in these and other instances Wyatt's authorial self-representation seems to possess "the character of a 'real' person."[6] Just how and why Wyatt's self-representation seems to evoke this character has, of course, no simple answer, and, indeed, this question, in one form or another, has been one of the most frequently debated about the poet. Nonetheless, Stephen Greenblatt's chapter on Wyatt in *Renaissance Self-Fashioning*, because of its wide influence, may fairly stand as a representative response to this question from the perspective of early modern studies.[7] Wyatt's verse, as Greenblatt observes, is no less conventional than that of his predecessors or less reliant on source texts. Rather than innovation in these respects, it is the play of similarity and difference — between Wyatt's own historically specific situation and those of convention and his sources — that enables a literary selfhood to emerge that plausibly presents itself as corresponding to the empirical Sir Thomas Wyatt. As Greenblatt puts it, "He rehearses the familiar tropes and stale paradoxes, parades the appropriate proverbs and turns of phrase, assumes the expected poses, and yet convinces us again and again of the reality of his pain and disillusionment" (p. 137).

This strategy — in which the putatively real arises out of a literary engagement with the already given — may be found in a variety of Wyatt's poems and especially in the aforementioned adaptations of Petrarch's Italian lyrics. To consider only perhaps the most famous example, in "Whoso list to hounte," Wyatt adapts Petrarch's "Una candida cerva" to the predatory world of Henry VIII's court — returning, for instance, the Italian inscription on the white doe's collar, "Libera farmi al mio Cesare parve" ("It has pleased my Caesar to make me free"), to the traditional tale's blunt fact of a hind's possession: "for Cesars I ame[.]"[8] In the historical context of Wyatt's version, the name Caesar irresistibly becomes associated with Henry, and this association in turn localizes the poem's "I" as well as the woman corresponding to the hind (long assumed to refer to Anne Boleyn). In the journey from one language to another — or, in other cases, in the imperfect reproduction of convention — Wyatt adds thematic and formal distortions that strike one as the genuine footprint of a specific author/translator's desire. By creating the impression that his literary givens become overwhelmed and hence partially transformed by the presence of real passion, these distortions stand as markers of an empirical author, indices of the unique individual who may authentically sing,

"Who list her hount I put him owte of dowbte,/As well as I may spend his tyme in vain" (9–10).

These distortions, moreover, signal not just the agency of a historically specific author but also, as Greenblatt argues, his lack of agency: they convey the external forces that are ultimately responsible for the passionate warping of his source material, forces that, most character-istically, take the form of the absolute incontestability of royal power. In "Whoso list to hounte," the power of Caesar stands as an unmovable object in the path of the fulfillment of the author's erotic desire, and it is within the space opened up by this frustrated desire that the excessive nature of the author's passions becomes visible. According to Greenblatt, in general, "power over sexuality produces inwardness" (p. 125), and, in the case of "Whoso list to hounte," with the three words "Cesars I ame," "The intimation of power spreads backward like a stain through the preceding lines, so that the whole poem comes to be colored by it" (p. 146). In this poem, Wyatt's selfhood appears as the cross-product of a mutually constitutive opposition between erotic desire and political power. With erotic relationships thereby politicized and political ones eroticized, private discourse of the self blurs into public discourse of the polity. "[I]f we grasp the extent to which Wyatt and others like him were defined by their relation to power, the extent to which they were at once attracted and repelled by Henry VIII and the world he represented," Greenblatt writes, "we grasp more readily in their poetry the heightened awareness of techniques of self-presentation and concealment" (pp. 142–43).[9]

These two aspects of Wyatt's poetry — its insinuation that the speaker is the "real" Sir Thomas Wyatt and the psychological inwardness resulting from its oppositional relation to power — are thus by many accounts (again assuming that we may take Greenblatt to be representa-tive) what makes his verse most fundamentally different from that of the preceding century.[10] Yet, as I hope this book has made plain, little of what I have summarized here in respect to Wyatt could not also be said in some fashion about the fifteenth-century tradition that he supposedly supersedes. Lydgate's work largely consists of personalization of received material — the innovations of the Ricardian poets, French and Latin source texts, and convention of a number of different flavors. Like Wyatt, Lydgate adapts this material in such a way that one is often compelled to associate his first-person speakers with his empirical person. An ambi-valent, oppositional relation to power similar to Wyatt's is also evident in Lydgate's work, although it is Lydgate's contemporary, Hoccleve, who more profoundly leverages this relation to render a textualization of his interiority, most obviously in the *Series*. Indeed, there are several parallels between Hoccleve (or, more precisely, the Hocclevean tradition) and Wyatt in this regard. As John Watkins has pointed out, Wyatt, as a relatively new member of the aristocracy (his father having been knighted by Henry VII), must have been acutely conscious of the fact that he owed his social identity to the Tudor court.[11] In this respect he resembled, albeit on a step up the social scale, Stephen Hawes, who, as we saw in the preceding chapter, became starkly Hocclevean when he lost the favor of Henry VIII. Because of their complete dependence on the court, these poets delve deepest into themselves when alienated from power, and they achieve the resulting textualizations of interiority by speaking of the sociopolitical in the language of personal desire. For Hoccleve, this desire was primarily pecuniary, and, for Hawes and Wyatt, erotic; but for all three poets this desire demarcates an interior that has at its center a prince who denies its satisfaction.

In the immediate poetic context of the court Wyatt joined in 1516, therefore, his literary achievements were, in many respects, hardly unprecedented. In particular, in Lydgatean laureate poetics and its Hocclevean mendicant secret sharer, he would have encountered a mature set of conventions through which an author represents himself as both historically specific poet and individual subjected to royal power. From this perspective, the arguments for Wyatt's difference from the preceding generation of poets appear instead as arguments for his sameness. Nonetheless, a side-by-side comparison of the work of, say, Skelton with that of Wyatt, while yielding more similarities than one might expect, would also still convince most readers that, to echo Pearsall, Wyatt *is* different. If we cannot anymore assume that these differences derive from a wholly innovative Renaissance self-fashioning, perhaps, at least, we can rest with the obvious. First, much more than any Lydgatean or Hocclevean poet, Wyatt is steeped in, and largely (if not exclusively) focuses on, the culture of *fin' amor*. Second, the small scale of his varied formal repertoire — and the density of his deployment of it — supports for the most part lyric performance rather than the larger-scale efforts typical of the laureates. Nowhere in his surviving oeuvre, with one exception mentioned below, do we find anything remotely resembling such long-winded tomes as the *Troy Book* or the *Regiment of Princes*. And third, throughout his career he shows little concern with celebratory political monuments (the production of which forms the most instrumental role of the laureate) or with pleading for financial favor (the symptom of the laureate's beggarhood).[12] Altogether, one may fairly conclude that these surface differences in theme and form are consistent enough as to be virtually categorical. Indeed, even to refer to his collected poems as a "career" is misleading if not merely a misnomer, and this sense of inappropriateness suggests the basic motivation behind his differences. Wyatt, to put it simply, was self-consciously an amateur poet, and as such his verse had to be manifestly distinguishable from that of court professionals such as Skelton.[13] With the institutionalization of the office of poet laureate, Lydgateanism, as we saw in the preceding chapter, became a patently professional endeavor. Wyatt first arrived at court not as a poet — or, for that matter, any sort of intellectual — but as a sewer, a sort of dinner attendant. Although as such he was a fellow member of the king's household, he owed his presence there not, as Skelton did, to his abilities at the function he performed, but to his aristocratic heritage. His status was most crucially a function of his birth, while, in contrast, Skelton's meritorious position was at once elevating and *déclassé*.

The imperative of class distinction, then, encouraged Wyatt to distinguish himself from the early Tudor Lydgateans — an imperative he must have felt all the more strongly given his family's relatively new aristocratic status. For him, it was not wholly acceptable — as it had been for Anthony Woodville, second earl Rivers, in the reign of Edward IV — to perform literary work too closely resembling that of those who, in his time, had become staff professionals.[14] Instead, in his habits of composition he fell back on the more traditional marker of cultured aristocracy, the lyrical amorous complaint that for centuries had served the elite as a demonstration of their facility with language and their deep capacity for refined sentiment. In this light, the differences between him and the Lydgateans appear more regressive than forward-looking. In comparison with the formal pyrotechnics and thematic versatility of Skelton, the topics on which Wyatt dwells and the forms in which expresses himself (notwithstanding his landmark importation of Italian lyric forms) are relatively narrow. Still, to declare Wyatt's work regressive in comparison with Skelton's seems odd, and this intuition brings us to at least one of the reasons for Wyatt's pivotal status: his difference from the Lydgateans lies not so much in his techniques of self-representation but in how he *redeploys* the techniques of the preceding generation in a more class-appropriate literary discourse. The fact that this latter discourse would, to a greater extent than the laureate discourse of the Lydgateans, pervade the verse of the modern era helps to explain his stronger resonance with us, even while keeping firm his multifaceted ties to the literary past.

To understand the motivation behind Wyatt's redeployment of Lydgatean poetics, we need only recall that in 1527, two years before Skelton's death, Queen Catherine asked not the aging laureate but the young courtier to perform the laureate duty of translating Petrarch's *De remediis utriusque fortunae*.[15] As this request suggests, with the ever-expanding scope of the English government and the consequent demand for intellectual labor, the functional difference at court between cleric and university-educated aristocrat, especially in regard to their capacity for the production of cultural capital, was becoming increasingly obscure.[16] This tendency is already evident in Woodville's literary activities of the 1470s and would culminate in the sixteenth century in the work of such figures as Sir Philip Sidney. Wyatt, however, was among the first aristocrats to be tapped to perform a laureate duty in an English court that included actual professional laureates. In one sense, the queen's request represented a great opportunity for him to distinguish himself from his peers, any number of whom could fill the more traditional offices he held in the 1420s (i.e., Esquire of the Royal Body, Clerk of the King's Jewels), and perhaps even perform similarly well on the diplomatic journeys he made to France and Italy. Wyatt's intellectual and literary strengths no doubt set him apart from his crowd of fellow courtiers, and hence it was in his interest to use these strengths, much as a poet laureate would, to curry the favor of the powerful. Yet, in another sense, to fulfill the queen's request and render into English Petrarch's morally authoritative Latin text would — because of the inevitable association of such tasks with figures like Skelton and Barclay — risk a diminution of his status. To distinguish himself through his facility with literature was one thing, but to lower himself was something else.

Wyatt wisely sidestepped the queen's request, offering polite excuses for not pursuing Petrarch's laureate performance and instead translating the *Quyete of Mynde* of Plutarch.[17] He was, nonetheless, made well aware of the opportunity his facility with literature presented, and he eventually discovered a means to negotiate the narrow passage between laureate poetics on the one hand and *fin' amor* on the other. As I have claimed, he needed to differentiate himself from the laureates principally for reasons of class. Yet, the poetics of *fin' amor* in its traditional form was also not perfectly suited to his purposes — and also for reasons of class. The very point of this poetics was not to distinguish aristocrats from their peers but to demonstrate their sameness. Cultured amorous complaint served as a marker of the aristocracy precisely because all aristocrats voiced it in more or less the same manner. As the large amount of surviving anonymous verse of this sort suggests, its intent was not to call attention to one's historical specificity, but to demonstrate oneself as adept at reproducing convention and as capable of depths of passion as any other aristocrat — up to and including the royalty. For example, as we saw in Chapter 4, the lyrics attributed to the duke of Suffolk bestow upon their first-person speaker a class rather than individual identity. In the one lyric in which this speaker does supply the specific names of Chaucer and Lydgate, his aim is to critique the literary discourse he understood the latter poet as promulgating: against Lydgate's self-identifying laureate poetics, he places his own discourse of love poetry composed by anonymous aristocratic amateurs. If Wyatt had possessed a noble status like Suffolk's, perhaps his corpus would have more wholly consisted of this sort of love poetry. But as a second-generation aristocrat, he needed to make the most out of whatever opportunities presented themselves for consolidating his position at court (at least among other courtiers, if not necessarily in respect to the king, who was not likely the intended audience for his poems). Poetically, this meant calling attention to his own person even while reproducing the poetics of anonymity.

Wyatt thus saw sociopolitical utility in some of the strategies of laureate poetics, but only if he could render these strategies in a mode appropriate to his rank. How he accomplished this poetic class adjustment is readily apparent in such lyrics as "Whoso list to hounte." On the surface, the object of praise or blame in this poem is, as expected in the tradition of *fin' amor*, an erotic one; but at a deeper level it is, as in a laureate performance, his prince. Just like a laureate, Wyatt sets up an equation between his prince and himself, but unlike in laureate practice and more in line with the conventions of *fin' amor*, this equation is based on erotic competition rather than on analogous spheres of authority. While many of Wyatt's other amorous complaints do indeed serve the traditional function of declaring, "I am like everyone else of my rank," this and several others — typically his most famous ones — work in the opposite direction. In these, he constructs a fraught triangulation of himself, a feminine erotic object, and his king that resembles structurally the epideictic circuit of the laureate; like that circuit, it declares, "I, specifically, am like my king" (as an erotic competitor) even while acknowledging subjection (as loser). Thus, as it happened, although he indeed turned to Petrarch, the archetypical poet laureate, for reasons of distinction, he did so by carefully replacing Petrarch's laureate self-aggrandizement with a self-depiction, at once more specific and more ambivalent, as the prince's unhappy foil.[18]

That a laureate nevertheless remains submerged within this self--depiction is evident already in the verse of Wyatt's poetic successor, Surrey,[19] and more explicitly in the series of verse eulogies composed shortly after Wyatt's death (1542) by England's first literary historian, John Leland. In these eulogies, Wyatt's longtime friend does not hesitate, in essence, to rewrite Skelton's *Calliope* with Wyatt as the muse's chosen crown prince:

> Not long ago the Muses, as they sat
> Beside the Castalian spring, a garland made
> Of ivy, with its usual berries decked.
> And when the crown was finished they discussed
> Which man should wear it at the poets' feast
> As a reward. Calliope, the first
> Of the virgin choir, decided in these words:
> "The learned Wyatt is worthy of this gift."[20]

Though Leland — like Puttenham, and, indeed, Surrey, to whom this series of eulogies is dedicated — associated Wyatt with Chaucer rather than with his fifteenth-century successors, he nonetheless easily imagines the achievements of Wyatt's career in precisely the terms idealized by early Tudor court professionals Hawes and Skelton. Moreover, rather remarkably, in the final eulogy before the concluding two-verse "Epitaphium," Leland seems to go out of his way to acknowledge the role of the prince in Wyatt's poetic imagination:

> There was a ring which gleamed on Wyatt's finger,
> Set with an agate upon which was carved
> The head of Julius, used for sealing letters.
> The image of Caesar, spur to highest virtue,
> Aided the inborn genius of Wyatt. (p. 269)

As if recalling Petrarch's claim in his laureation address, that "Caesars and poets move toward the same goal, though by different paths,"[21] Leland figures a perfect symbiosis between poet and prince: imperial power does not turn poet into servant but instead supplies authority to his "letters" ("chartis"); the "image of Caesar" ("Caesaris . . . imago") does not subjugate Wyatt but serves rather as an encouragement or "spur" ("calcar") to his "inborn genius" ("Ingenitas . . . vires animosque") — that is, it scaffolds his autonomous poetic excellence.

And yet, against such lyrics as "Whoso list to hounte," we cannot help but read Wyatt's ring instead as a kind of livery or even brand, the sign of power that bestows authority only by also marking possession.[22] If it signifies "inborn genius" through imperial corroboration, it at the same time announces, "Cesars I ame." Just as in Petrarch's address, the most transcendentalizing of laureate claims always also reveal the subjection to power that both enables and vitiates them.

To conclude, an essential component of Wyatt's literary achievement was his fusion of techniques of Lydgateanism with the detailed anatomy of subjectivity provided by the tradition of *fin' amor*, thereby melding historical specificity with psychological depth. To perform this feat, he needed to have in place a century-long, authoritative laureate tradition, which he could co-opt by appearing to oppose. Further, with the subsequent arrival of the English Reformation, the individualistic aspect of this co-option took on the added dimension of Protestant theology; and with the consequent diminishment of the cleric-poet − the social identity of whom was so important to laureate poetics − Wyatt's transformation of the tradition begun by the monk of Bury achieved some amount of literary-historical decisiveness. Yet, as Leland's eulogies reveal, Wyatt's accomplishments, so seemingly different from the literature of the first generation of Tudor poets, arose not *ex nihilo* or as a phoenix from the ashes of a decadent tradition, but rather through a dialectical engagement with the then still reigning authoritative mode of poetry, the Lydgateanism of the fifteenth century.

The aim of this book has been to offer an amplified understanding of fifteenth-century English poetry's literary historical significance, and, to that end, to investigate the development and impact of what I have termed laureate poetics. At the beginning and now at the end of this book (and in much of the middle), I have argued that an essential feature of this poetics is the poet's self-representation as a historically specific, empirical author. In the course of examining the role this feature plays in the poetry of the period, I have also implied that the reasons that this sort of self-representation becomes normative little resemble those that many associate with it − e.g., as a device for in some way thematizing interiority for its own sake, or, more simply, for self-expression. I have claimed, rather, that in the fifteenth century poets began attaching their historically specific persons to authoritative first-person speakers, foremost among other reasons, as a good faith trope of power. This trope, although its form and significance differ with each poet who deploys it, always possesses somewhere in its semantic field the desire of an English monarch to see himself, in various guises of cultural reflection, as a more pure and original sovereign than the one whom he has displaced. But, just as this desire may never be fully satisfied, this trope, through its inability to coincide with its idealizations, inevitably shows itself to be a ruse. The author posing as laureate must at some point acknowledge that he will never quite be the laureate he imagines, and, as we have seen, in many instances this acknowledgment transforms laureate poetics into its mendicant other, to disclose in full view the beggar that always lurks within. In this very failure to achieve an ideal, however, a resistance to power and — in the space opened up through that resistance — something resembling an expression of interiority become literary possibilities. In the early sixteenth century, when laureate poetics in all its imperfection became institutionalized, Wyatt sought to oppose laureate self-construction even while exploiting its constitutive elements. In this way he became, as a well-positioned and influential anti-laureate, the revisionary point of origin for a subsequent tradition of lyric self-expression that stretches from Surrey to the present.[23]

As Leland's eulogies indicate, however, this tradition, despite the conceptual strength it gained from the Reformation, has never rid itself of its laureate dialectical other. Most obviously, just a half-century after its inauguration, its not-so-suppressed other was auspiciously reinvented in the work of Spenser, who may be said to project Wyatt's psychological depth into the vastness of Lydgatean space. From Spenser onward, one can trace an unbroken line of poets having some relation to laureate poetics, reaching as far as to Wordsworth (and hence to us) by way of his reading of Milton's reading of Spenser. In his old age and soon to become England's official laureate, Wordsworth, the most paradigmatic of English Romantics, finds himself writing verse the nature of which would easily win the approval of Lydgate and his patron, Henry V. As he declares in the ninth of his *Sonnets Upon the Punishment of Death*,

> Speaking through Law's dispassionate voice the State
> Endues her conscience with external life
> And being, to preclude or quell the strife
> Of individual will, to elevate
> The groveling mind, the erring to recall,
> And fortify the moral sense of all.[24]

Only an authoritative poet who embodies state power could write such lines — that is, a post-monarchal laureate, whether notional or actual, who substitutes "the State" for the role before played by the prince. That this poet is the same one who wrote *Tintern Abbey* suggests that, in English poetry, one should never be surprised to find a Lydgatean laureate buried within a singer of subjectivity. Lydgate, of course, is not quite a constitutive figure of English literary history in the same way that Chaucer or Wordsworth is. But I hope that this book has shown that he permanently altered this history's course by putting into place a relationship betwen poets and power that, even to this day, haunts English poetry's greatest claims to being something other than mere words.

Notes

INTRODUCTION: LAUREATES AND BEGGARS

1 Seth Lerer, *Chaucer and His Readers: Imagining the Author in Late-Medieval England* (Princeton: Princeton University Press, 1993), p. 5. Subsequent references are given by page number in the text.

2 Paul Strohm, "Hoccleve, Lydgate and the Lancastrian Court," in *The Cambridge History of Medieval English Literature*, ed. David Wallace (Cambridge: Cambridge University Press, 1999), pp. 640–61 (p. 659).

3 David Lawton, "Dullness and the Fifteenth Century," *ELH* 54 (1987), 761–99 (775). Perhaps more than any other single study, this densely suggestive article has encouraged the ongoing critical re-examination of fifteenth-century English literature.

4 It remains a matter of debate whether James Stewart was in fact the author of the *Kingis Quair* and, likewise, whether Charles d'Orléans or a translator was responsible for the English verse containing his name, although at present most critics accept the authorship of each. For a recent review of the debates and evidence, see Joanna Summers, *Late-Medieval Prison Writing and the Politics of Autobiography* (Oxford: Clarendon Press, 2004), Chapter 2 on James (pp. 60–89) and Chapter 3 on Charles (pp. 90–107).

5 See Anne Middleton, "The Idea of Public Poetry in the Reign of Richard II," *Speculum* 53 (1978), 94–114.

6 Richard Helgerson, *Self-Crowned Laureates: Spenser, Jonson, Milton and the Literary System* (Berkeley: University of California Press, 1983).

7 Louis Adrian Montrose, "The Elizabethan Subject and the Spenserian Text," in *Literary Theory/Renaissance Texts*, ed. Patricia Parker and David Quint (Baltimore: Johns Hopkins University Press, 1986), pp. 303–40.

8 These objections and others noted later notwithstanding, let me acknowledge here at the outset a general debt to Lerer's important work.

I   LAUREATE POETICS

1 This glances at David Wallace's influential reading of this admittedly ambiguous prologue; see *Chaucerian Polity: Absolutist Lineages and*

Associational Forms in England and Italy (Stanford: Stanford University Press, 1997), pp. 261–98. For a rather different reading, see Christopher Cannon, *The Making of Chaucer's English: A Study of Words* (Cambridge: Cambridge University Press, 1998), pp. 148–49 and p. 171.

2 According to the *MED*, before Lydgate the sole use of the word "laureate" in English, in reference to a poet, is that of Chaucer's Clerk (see *laureate* adj.). Subsequent to the accession of Henry IV, this usage suddenly becomes quite common, with the numerous instances in Lydgate's work no doubt setting the example.

3 For an English translation of the laureation address, see Ernest Hatch Wilkins, *Studies in the Life and Works of Petrarch* (Cambridge, Mass.: The Mediaeval Academy of America, 1955), pp. 300–13; all subsequent citations are to this translation and given in the text by page number. For the Latin, see *Scritti Inediti di Francesco Petrarca*, ed. Attilio Hortis (Trieste: Tipografia del Lloyd Austro-Ungarico, 1874), pp. 311–28. Virgil's lines are from *Georgics* 3.291–92, and Wilkins renders them, "But a sweet longing urges me upward over the lonely slopes of Parnassus." For an account of Petrarch's laureation address congruent with the one I offer here, see Larry Scanlon, "Poets Laureate and the Language of Slaves: Petrarch, Chaucer, and Langston Hughes," in *The Vulgar Tongue: Medieval and Postmedieval Vernacularity*, ed. Nicholas Watson and Fiona Somerset (University Park: Pennsylvania State University Press, 2003), pp. 231–33. I owe thanks to Professor Scanlon for providing me with an advance copy of his work.

4 In this poem, a poet-figure or *scop* alternates between providing long lists of rulers, tribes, and heroes and recalling moments in which he has received gifts for just this kind of activity – the implication being that, if the powerful wish to be memorialized in verse, they must pay for the service. See *Widsith*, ed. Kemp Malone, 2nd edn (Copenhagen: Rosenkilde and Bagger, 1962). I am not the first to mention *Widsith* in the context of Petrarch's laureation address; J. B. Trapp, in his highly informative survey of the history of the laureateship, discusses this *scop* in the first few pages of his study: see "The Poet Laureate: Rome, *Renovatio* and *Translatio Imperii*," in *Rome in the Renaissance: The City and the Myth*, ed. P. A. Ramsey (Binghamton: Medieval and Renaissance Texts and Studies, Center for Medieval and Early Renaissance Studies, 1982), pp. 93–130. *Widsith* also has a significant cameo early on in Peter Dronke's magisterial *The Medieval Lyric*, 3rd edn (Cambridge: D. S. Brewer, 1996), pp. 17–25, which suggests that this *scop* has achieved an almost emblematic status in respect to the idea of the poet as praise-making servant to a prince.

5 For Petrarch's dependence on, for example, the Visconti, see Wallace, *Chaucerian Polity*, esp. pp. 53–54 and pp. 267–70. For his ecclesiastical career, see Wilkins, *Life and Works*, pp. 3–32. As Trapp shows, the subjection of the laureate to the interests of the laureating prince, while somewhat mystified in Petrarch's case, became quickly evident in the lives of his successors.

6 I cite Wallace's translation of excerpts of the *Trattatello* in A. J. Minnis and A. B. Scott, with David Wallace (eds.), *Medieval Literary Theory and Criticism c.1100–c.1375: The Commentary Tradition* (Oxford: Clarendon Press, 1988), p. 494 and p. 498, respectively. Subsequent citations are to this translation and given in the text by page number. I have deleted references to the paragraph numbers in the Italian text, for which see *Opere in versi, Corbaccio, Trattatello in laude di Dante, prose latine, epistole*, ed. Pier Giorgio Ricci (Milano: R. Ricciardi, 1965). Boccaccio completed the first version of this extended eulogy of Dante between 1351 and 1355 and wrote two other versions before 1373; see *Medieval Literary Theory*, p. 434, and Wallace, *Chaucerian Polity*, p. 271.

7 For Wallace's discussion of this story, see *Chaucerian Polity*, p. 117 and p. 271.

8 For a translation, see *Boccaccio on Poetry: Being the Preface and the Fourteenth and Fifteenth Books of Boccaccio's "Genealogia Deorum Gentilium,"* trans. Charles G. Osgood (Indianapolis: Bobbs-Merrill Company, 1956), pp. 21–32. All subsequent citations are to this translation and given in the text by page number. For the Latin, see *In Defense of Poetry: Genealogia deorum gentilium liber XIV*, ed. Jeremiah Reedy (Toronto: Pontifical Institute of Mediaeval Studies, 1978).

9 Paul Strohm has been at the forefront of this effort. See, for example, his *England's Empty Throne: Usurpation and the Language of Legitimation, 1399–1422* (New Haven: Yale University Press, 1998).

10 The functional necessity of misrecognition is a premise that appears throughout Bourdieu's writings. For a brief introduction to his work, see Pierre Bourdieu and Loïc J. D. Wacquant, *An Invitation to Reflexive Sociology* (Chicago: University of Chicago Press, 1992). In my adaptation of Bourdieu's term "cultural capital" I mean to designate any cultural products associated with, and hence legitimizing, naturalizing, and distinguishing, the nobility. This capital is distinct from political capital, by which I mean those practices and artifacts that are *explicitly* recognized as legitimating political power (such as coronation ceremonies).

11 For the significance of Richard's epitaph, see Michael J. Bennett, "The Court of Richard II and the Promotion of Literature," in *Chaucer's England: Literature in Historical Context*, ed. Barbara A. Hanawalt (Minneapolis: University of Minnesota Press, 1992), pp. 3–20 (p. 16). Bennett's essay was written in response to studies such as V. J. Scattergood, "Literary Culture at the Court of Richard II," in *English Court Culture in the Later Middle Ages*, ed. V. J. Scattergood and J. W. Sherborne (London: Duckworth, 1983), pp. 29–46, which expresses doubts about the extent and significance of Richard's encouragement of literary production. For a view akin to Bennett's but more cautiously formulated, see A. J. Minnis, with V. J. Scattergood and J. J. Smith, *Oxford Guides to Chaucer: The Shorter Poems* (Oxford: Clarendon Press, 1995), pp. 9–35. My account of the Ricardian court's attitude toward literary production owes a debt to all three of these studies.

12 Paul Strohm, *Hochon's Arrow: The Social Imagination of Fourteenth-Century Texts* (Princeton: Princeton University Press, 1992), p. 82. For the roots of the Lancastrian obsession with "image" in John of Gaunt's ambitions, see Lynn Staley, "Gower, Richard II, Henry of Derby, and the Business of Making Culture," *Speculum* 75 (2000), 68—96.

13 For a study of the differences between Ricardian and Lancastrian poetic practice along these lines, see Robert Epstein, "Chaucer's Scogan and Scogan's Chaucer," *Studies in Philology* 96 (1999), 1—21.

14 For the textual ramifications of the reactionary response to Lollardy, see Strohm, *Empty Throne*, esp. Chapter 2, pp. 32—62, and Chapter 5, pp. 128—52. For the officially sanctioned shift toward English, see John H. Fisher, *The Emergence of Standard English* (Lexington: University Press of Kentucky, 1996), pp. 16—35. For the changing nature of the reading public, see Paul Strohm, "Chaucer's Fifteenth-Century Audience and the Narrowing of the 'Chaucer Tradition,'" *Studies in the Age of Chaucer* 4 (1982), 3—32. For humanism in England, see, in respect to fifteenth-century poetry, Lois A. Ebin, *Illuminator, Makar, Vates: Visions of Poetry in the Fifteenth Century* (Lincoln: University of Nebraska Press, 1988), and, more generally, Roberto Weiss, *Humanism in England during the Fifteenth Century*, 2nd edn (Oxford: Blackwell, 1957).

15 Not only the fact of Petrarch's laureation but also the ideas that it carried had likely become familiar among the English literati by the early fifteenth century. Lydgate explicitly records his awareness of the event as early as the *Troy Book* (begun 1412), and, by the end of his career, in his adaptation (via a French intermediary) of Boccaccio's *De casibus virorum illustrium*, he is working at some depth with *trecento* ideas of the poet and poetry. Larry Scanlon, "Lydgate's Poetics: Laureation and Domesticity in the *Temple of Glass*," in *John Lydgate: Poetry, Culture, and Lancastrian England*, ed. James Simpson and Larry Scanlon (Notre Dame: University of Notre Dame Press, 2006), has speculated that Petrarch's very laureation address influenced Lydgate's *Temple of Glas*, a poem which many have taken to predate the *Troy Book*. More generally, James G. Clark, "Thomas Walsingham Reconsidered: Books and Learning at Late-Medieval St. Albans," *Speculum* 77 (2002), 832—60, has documented the existence of a late medieval English Benedictine community passionately interested in classical accounts of the poet and poetry. Lydgate may thus have obtained some of his notions about the laureateship via this community and hence indirectly from many of the same sources as Petrarch, in addition to what he more obviously took from Chaucer.

16 In Chaucer's case, as is well known, the poet's initial departure from the norms of the native tradition comes about through his exploitation of the norms of another tradition — namely, those of the French *dit*. To some extent, Wyatt's case, through his exploitation of Petrarch's *Rime sparse*, is analogous, although a basic contention of this book is that some of the most prominent "imported" aspects of Wyatt's verse were already well established in the high-culture English poetic tradition of the fifteenth century.

17 In the last decade or so, much has been written about this strategy. The seminal work is A. J. Minnis, *Medieval Theory of Authorship: Scholastic Literary Attitudes in the Later Middle Ages*, 2nd edn (Philadelphia: University of Pennsylvania Press, 1988). More recently, see Trevor Ross, *The Making of the English Literary Canon: From the Middle Ages to the Late Eighteenth Century* (Montreal: McGill-Queen's University Press, 1998), esp. pp. 23–84, and, for the pose of the historian specifically, Peter Damian-Grint, *The New Historians of the Twelfth-Century Renaissance: Inventing Vernacular Authority* (Woodbridge: Boydell Press, 1999), pp. 41–42 and passim. The term "auctorial" I take from Ross.

18 *Brut*, ed. W. R. J. Barron and S. C. Weinberg (Harlow: Longman Group Limited, 1995), line 1; *The Chronicle*, ed. Idelle Sullens (Binghamton: Center for Medieval & Early Renaissance Studies, 1996), lines 1–5.

19 Leo Spitzer, "Note on the Poetic and the Empirical 'I' in Medieval Authors," *Traditio* 4 (1946), 414–22. Spitzer's influential (and, recently, often criticized) argument does not distinguish among linguistic traditions and makes rather difficult-to-swallow categorical claims. I deploy it only in the limited sense described above.

20 For this point, see Siegfried Wenzel, *Preachers, Poets, and the Early English Lyric* (Princeton: Princeton University Press, 1986).

21 This is presumably the entire poem, cited from Carleton Brown (ed.), *English Lyrics of the XIIIth Century* (Oxford: Clarendon Press, 1932), no. 8.

22 This is, of course, the full title of the poem commonly referred to as *Tintern Abbey*.

23 This is the poem's first stanza, cited from *English Writings of Richard Rolle Hermit of Hampole*, ed. Hope Emily Allen (Oxford: Clarendon Press, 1931). For a summary of the attribution issues surrounding Rolle's lyrics, see Rosemary Woolf, *The English Religious Lyric in the Middle Ages* (Oxford: Clarendon Press, 1968), pp. 380–82. For the methods and significance of Rolle's self-aggrandizement, see Nicholas Watson, *Richard Rolle and the Invention of Authority* (Cambridge: Cambridge University Press, 1991).

24 In this formulation I draw on the reworking of Spitzer in Judson Boyce Allen, "Grammar, Poetic Form, and the Lyric Ego: A Medieval *A Priori*," in *Vernacular Poetics in the Middle Ages*, ed. Lois A. Ebin (Kalamazoo: Medieval Institute Publications, 1984), pp. 199–226.

25 This is the famous formulation of the monastic ideal of selfhood in Caroline Walker Bynum, *Jesus as Mother: Studies in the Spirituality of the High Middle Ages* (Berkeley: University of California Press, 1982), p. 87.

26 So argues Thomas C. Stillinger, *The Song of Troilus: Lyric Authority in the Medieval Book* (Philadelphia: University of Pennsylvania Press, 1992), p. 3 and passim.

27 See *The Owl and the Nightingale: Text and Translation*, ed. Neil Cartlidge (Exeter: University of Exeter Press, 2001), esp. lines 187–214 and 1745–80, and, for the question of the poem's authorship, pp. xiv–xv.

28 George Kane, *The Autobiographical Fallacy in Chaucer and Langland Studies* (London: University College London, 1965), p. 15.

29 I use the masculine possessive pronoun here (and throughout) meaningfully; in Ricardian poetry the narratorial personae and generic individuals they signify are in practice – with a few notable exceptions – strictly male.

30 Admittedly, this is a simplified account of the so-called *Retraction* (and an equally easy deployment of the categories made famous by E. T. Donaldson). As is typical of the crucial moments in the *Canterbury Tales*, enough ambiguity lingers to suggest an opposite reading – for example, that the *Retraction* is part of the *Tales'* fiction and thus person, poet, and pilgrim are fundamentally irreconcilable.

31 With this observation, I offer qualified assent to Gregory B. Stone's argument in *The Death of the Troubadour: The Late Medieval Resistance to the Renaissance* (Philadelphia: University of Pennsylvania Press, 1994).

32 The semantic range and thematic function of Chaucer's "I" are notoriously complex topics; here I am referring principally only to one of the more pointed and tantalizing aspects of this "I" – the one that repeatedly draws the reader toward the notion of Chaucer's person only to frustrate that quest with dazzling ambiguity. Minnis has aptly termed this elusiveness Chaucer's "poetic of reticence": see *Shorter Poems*, pp. 31–33. Interestingly, as John M. Bowers has noted, while Chaucer himself expresses this reticence, his early fifteenth-century scribes, in renderng this particular passage, do not: see "Two Professional Readers of Chaucer and Langland: Scribe D and the HM 114 Scribe," *Studies in the Age of Chaucer* 26 (2004), 113–46. Moreover, Stephen Partridge (in personal communication, 3 July 2005) believes that the marginal identifications of Chaucer here and elsewhere are authorial, which, if so, would nudge Chaucer's habits of self-representation closer to Gower's (for which, see below).

33 Dante, as is well known, preemptively provides a defense of this act in his *Convivio*, but in the process confirms the late medieval normative bias against authorial self-identification in vernacular poetry: see Dante Alighieri, *Dante's Il Convivio (The Banquet)*, trans. Richard H. Lansing (New York: Garland Publishing, 1990), bk 1 ch. 2. In claiming that Chaucer's parallel act of self-naming in the *House of Fame* may not hold much more significance than intertextual critique, I do not mean to narrow the significance of his more general strategies of self-representation in the poem.

34 For one recent argument for the Man of Law as a Gower figure, see Richard Axton, "Gower – Chaucer's Heir?" in *Chaucer Traditions: Studies in Honour of Derek Brewer*, ed. Ruth Morse and Barry Windeatt (Cambridge: Cambridge University Press, 1990), pp. 21–38. Although we will probably never know for certain the precise textual relationship between the *Man of Law's Tale* and the *Confessio*, the introduction to the former must clearly be taken as some kind of comment on Gower's work – and a parodic, gently ridiculing one would be right in line with what we expect from Chaucer from his stance toward other poets.

35 For Chaucer's likely immediate audience, see Paul Strohm, *Social Chau* (Cambridge, Mass.: Harvard University Press, 1989), pp. 47–83.

36 For Gower's and Langland's implied audiences, see Middleton, "Publi Poetry," and her "The Audience and Public of 'Piers Plowman,'" in *Middle English Alliterative Poetry and Its Literary Background: Seven Essays*, ed. David Lawton (Cambridge: D. S. Brewer, 1982), pp. 101–23.

37 Anne Middleton, "William Langland's 'Kynde Name': Authorial Signature and Social Identity in Late Fourteenth-Century England," in *Literary Practice and Social Change in Britain, 1380–1530*, ed. Lee Patterson (Berkeley: University of California Press, 1990), pp. 15–82 (p. 42).

38 Middleton, "'Kynde Name,'" p. 36. See also James Simpson, "The Power of Impropriety: Authorial Naming in *Piers Plowman*," in *William Langland's "Piers Plowman": A Book of Essays*, ed. Kathleen M. Hewett-Smith (New York: Routledge, 2001), pp. 145–65.

39 Middleton, "Audience and Public," p. 119.

40 Cited from *Piers Plowman: The B Version*, ed. George Kane and E. Talbot Donaldson (London: Athlone Press, 1975), 15.152. The entire set of Langland's signatures is conveniently given by Middleton, "'Kynde Name,'" pp. 79–82.

41 See Middleton, "'Kynde Name,'" p. 16.

42 I cite lines 1 and 374–75 from the edition in *The English Works of John Gower*, ed. G. C. Macaulay, EETS e.s. 81–82 (London: Kegan Paul, Trench and Trübner, 1900–1901). All subsequent citations of Gower's English poems are from this edition and given by line number and, for the *Confessio*, book. For the ambivalent stance Gower assumes toward his king in this poem, see the penetrating study by Frank Grady, "The Lancastrian Gower and the Limits of Exemplarity," *Speculum* 70 (1995), 552–75.

43 See A. J. Minnis, "De Vulgari Auctoriate: Chaucer, Gower and the Men of Great Authority," in *Chaucer and Gower: Difference, Mutuality, Exchange*, ed. Robert F. Yeager (Victoria: University of Victoria, 1991), pp. 36–74.

44 This is the first stanza of the envoy to *Ballade to King Henry VI upon His Coronation*, no. 31, MP II, lines 121–28.

45 Lawton, "Dullness," 781. One of the mysteries of the fifteenth-century reception of Ricardian poetry is why Gower, whose association with Chaucer was well known and whose *Confessio* was widely available, had so little comparative influence, of the obvious sort, on the Chaucerian poets. For a survey of this influence, see Derek Pearsall, "The Gower Tradition," in *Gower's "Confessio Amantis": Responses and Reassessments*, ed. A. J. Minnis (Cambridge: D. S. Brewer, 1983), pp. 179–97. Recently, however, more pervasive influences of the less obvious sort have been uncovered. Hoccleve's role as a *Confessio* scribe was first brought to light in A. I. Doyle and M. B. Parkes, "The Production of Copies of the *Canterbury Tales* and the *Confessio Amantis* in the Early Fifteenth Century," in *Medieval Scribes, Manuscripts & Libraries*, ed. M. B. Parkes and Andrew G. Watson (London: Scolar Press, 1978), pp. 163–210, and his debt to Gower studied in

Charles R. Blyth, "Thomas Hoccleve's Other Master," *Mediaevalia* 16 (1993), 349–59. Lydgate's debt to Gower, I believe, marks his entire career, although it only becomes fully explicit in the *Fall of Princes*. In this late work (completed 1438), Lydgate includes a version of the story of Canacee partially derived from the *Confessio* — and, as Larry Scanlon, *Narrative, Authority, and Power: The Medieval Exemplum and the Chaucerian Tradition* (Cambridge: Cambridge University Press, 1994), pp. 335–36, has argued, one of Constantine — and offers as well an expanded rendition of Chaucer's epithet, "In moral mateer ful notable was Goweer" (9.3410). But Maura Nolan, *John Lydgate and the Making of Public Culture* (Cambridge: Cambridge University Press, 2005), shows Gower's *Confessio* to be the conceptual touchstone for Lydgate's earlier work, the *Serpent of Division* (probably 1422) and makes a case for the Ricardian poet's influence on Lydgate's *Henry VI's Triumphal Entry into London* (1432) (see pp. 43–52 and 219–33, respectively). Nolan also provides a penetrating examination of Lydgate's engagement with the *Confessio* in the *Fall of Princes* in "Lydgate's Literary History: Chaucer, Gower, and Canacee," *Studies in the Age of Chaucer* 27 (2005), 59–92. For other accounts of Gower's influence congruent with the one I am suggesting, see Ross, *English Literary Canon*, p. 39, and Robert Epstein, "'At the Stremes Hed of Grace': Representations of Prince and Poet in Late Medieval English Court Poetry" (Ph.D. dissertation, Princeton University, 1995), esp. pp. 83–100.

46 Middleton, "Public Poetry," 99 and 109. This double movement, in which the first-person speaker is simultaneously individualized and emptied of individuality, occurs as well in Gower's *Confessio*; but a demonstration of this point is beyond the scope of this study.

47 For a recent, penetrating discussion of this differentiation, see Scott-Morgan Straker, "Deference and Difference: Lydgate, Chaucer, and the *Siege of Thebes*," *Review of English Studies* n.s. 52 (2001), 1–21.

48 For example, see John M. Ganim, *Style and Consciousness in Middle English Narrative* (Princeton: Princeton University Press, 1983), p. 104. For a discussion of this moment in the *Siege* more congruent with mine, see Stephanie Trigg, *Congenial Souls: Reading Chaucer from Medieval to Postmodern* (Minneapolis: University of Minnesota Press, 2002), pp. 94–95.

PART II: THE FIRST LANCASTRIAN POETS

1 See John Fyler's note to this passage in *Riverside*, p. 983.

2 *Hoccleve's Works: The Minor Poems*, ed. Frederick J. Furnivall and I. Gollancz, rev. by Jerome Mitchell and A. I. Doyle, EETS e.s. 61 and 73 (London: Oxford University Press, 1970), p. xxxviii.

3 Lee Patterson, "'What is Me?': Self and Society in the Poetry of Thomas Hoccleve," *Studies in the Age of Chaucer* 23 (2001), 437–70 (437). Perhaps, too, in an academic culture saturated with employment anxiety and, in particular, the "publish or perish" relation of one's writing to one's

livelihood, Hoccleve's self-mocking, self-regarding, but genuinely anxious professional and pecuniary obsessions resonate with a profundity less visible in more tenure-plentiful times. What could be more a propos (and postmodern) than to write self-consciously, in the interest of economic security, about a poet who wrote self-consciously in the interest of economic security?

2   JOHN LYDGATE: THE INVENTION OF THE ENGLISH LAUREATE

1 W. B. Yeats, *Essays* (New York: Macmillan, 1924), pp. 458–49. Cited in Helgerson, *Self-Crowned Laureates*, p. 48.
2 For Gower's collar and grant of wine, see John Hines, Nathalie Cohen, and Simon Roffey, "*Iohanannes Gower, Armiger, Poeta*: Records and Memorials of His Life and Death," in *A Companion to Gower*, ed. Siân Echard (Cambridge: D. S. Brewer, 2004), pp. 23–41 (p. 26). For Lydgate's annuity, see *Biobib*, pp. 36–39, and, for the pertinent documents, appendix nos. 14–29. The reason given for Lydgate's initial grant is, as Pearsall translates, "for good service to the king's [Henry VI's] father and uncles now deceased, to Humphrey, duke of Gloucester, and to the king" (p. 36).
3 Marshe printed the *Troy Book* in 1555, and Tottel and Wayland both produced editions of the *Fall of Princes* in 1554: see *Biobib*, p. 71 *and* p. 80. For a fascinating account of Tottel's and Wayland's competing editions of the *Fall* and, more generally, of the resurgence of Lydgate publications in Marian England, see John J. Thompson, "Reading Lydgate in Post-Reformation England," in *Middle English Poetry: Texts* and *Traditions: Essays in Honour of Derek Pearsall*, ed. A. J. Minnis (Woodbridge: York Medieval Press, 2001), pp. 181–209.
4 This amount of verse doubles that which survives of Shakespeare's, and triples Chaucer's; see Derek Pearsall, *John Lydgate* (London: Routledge & Kegan Paul, 1970), p. 4.
5 For Lydgate's "patronage networks," see the "Laureate Lydgate" chapter in Pearsall, *John Lydgate*, pp. 160–91. Admittedly, in a number of instances the sole attestation to a patron's identity is an annotation by fifteenth-century scribe and proto-publisher John Shirley. As argued by Julia Boffey and A. S. G. Edwards, "'Chaucer's Chronicle,' John Shirley, and the Canon of Chaucer's Shorter Poems," *Studies in the Age of Chaucer* 20 (1998), 201–18, some of Shirley's notes strain credibility, and one suspects that in several cases the anecdotes they report have more "marketing pizzazz" than ascriptive authority. Nonetheless, Lydgate himself records his patron's identity in verse in enough cases to suggest that most of those indicated by Shirley are credible. And, in any event, the overall picture of the extent of Lydgate's patronage remains the same whether or not one includes the Shirlean evidence.

6 For Lerer's supposition, see *Chaucer and His Readers*, p. 51. For the likely restrictions on Lydgate's movements, see *Biobib*, 21–22, where Pearsall argues against the common assumption that the poet spent long intervals outside the cloister.

7 For this now widely accepted understanding of the relationship between court poetry and aristocratic distinction, see Richard Firth Green, *Poets and Princepleasers: Literature and the English Court in the Late Middle Ages* (Toronto: University of Toronto Press, 1980), esp. pp. 101–34.

8 For Paston and the *Temple of Glas*, see Pearsall, *John Lydgate*, p. 18; for the Rushall Psalter, see Thorlac Turville-Petre, "Poems by Chaucer in John Harpur's Psalter," *Studies in the Age of Chaucer* 21 (1999), 301–13; for the Percy codex, see Carol M. Meale, "Patrons, Buyers and Owners: Book Production and Social Status," in *Book Production and Publishing in Britain 1375–1475*, ed. Jeremy Griffiths and Derek Pearsall (Cambridge: Cambridge University Press, 1989), pp. 201–238 (pp. 213–14); for the "utilitarian" appeal of Lydgate's didactic works, see, in the same anthology, Julia Boffey and John J. Thompson, "Anthologies and Miscellanies: Production and Choice of Texts," pp. 279–315 (esp. p. 297); and, for an analysis of the circulation and appeal of one of these didactic works, see Claire Sponsler, "Eating Lessons: Lydgate's 'Dietary' and Consumer Conduct," in *Medieval Conduct*, ed. Kathleen Ashley and Robert L. A. Clark (Minneapolis: University of Minnesota Press, 2001), pp. 1–22.

9 Lydgate's poem on Humphrey's and Jacqueline's marriage is known as *On Gloucester's Approaching Marriage*, no. 36 in MP II. His poem on Margaret, known as *Verses for Queen Margaret's Entry into London*, was thought lost by MacCracken in MP I, p. xl, but was later found and edited by Carleton Brown, "Lydgate's Verses on Queen Margaret's Entry into London," *Modern Language Review* 7 (1912), 225–34, and a fragment from a different manuscript was subsequently printed by Robert Withington, "Queen Margaret's Entry into London, 1445," *Modern Philology* 13 (1915), 53–57. Although Brown confidently affirms Stow's attribution of the poem to Lydgate, this attribution has since been questioned, first in a comment of MacCracken's reported by Withington, "Queen Margaret's Entry," 54–55, and more recently and expansively in Gordon Kipling, "The London Pageants for Margaret of Anjou: A Medieval Script Restored," *Medieval English Theatre* 4 (1982), 5–27, whose argument against Lydgate's authorship, while strongly formulated, is to me still inconclusive. Even if Lydgate did not write this poem, his relationship with Suffolk is well attested by the duke's support of his petition for a new letters patent in 1441 (see *Biobib*, pp. 38–39 and appendix no. 19).

10 A work perhaps not as entirely mundane as it seems, as argued by Maura Nolan, "Lydgate's Worst Poem: The *Tretise for Lavandres*" (paper presented at the International Congress on Medieval Studies, Kalamazoo, 7 May 2005).

11 See *Biobib*, pp. 68–84.

12 Doyle and Parkes, "Production of Copies," 201. For the activities of the so-called Lydgate scribe – who produced at least nine manuscripts of Lydgate's poetry and seems to have been based in Bury – see A. S. G. Edwards and Derek Pearsall, "The Manuscripts of the Major English Poetic Texts," in *Book Production*, ed. Griffiths and Pearsall, pp. 257–78 (p. 264 and p. 268), and Kathleen L. Scott, "Lydgate's Lives of Saints Edmund and Fremund: A Newly-Located Manuscript in Arundel Castle," *Viator* 13 (1982), 335–66 (360–66).

13 The fullest account of Shirley is Margaret Connolly, *John Shirley: Book Production and the Noble Household in Fifteenth-Century England* (Aldershot: Ashgate, 1998). Debate persists as to whether Shirley's activities resembled more that of a hobbyist or a commercial publisher (or librarian); Connolly leans toward the former, while A. S. G. Edwards, "John Shirley and the Emulation of Courtly Culture," in *The Court and Cultural Diversity: Selected Papers from the Eighth Triennial Congress of the International Courtly Literature Society*, ed. Evelyn Mullally and John Thompson (Cambridge: D. S. Brewer, 1997), pp. 309–17, leans toward the latter.

14 For this point, see Julia Boffey, *Manuscripts of English Courtly Love Lyrics in the Later Middle Ages* (Cambridge: D. S. Brewer, 1985), esp. pp. 13–19.

15 Pearsall, *John Lydgate*, p. 207. *Proverbs of Lydgate* is STC 17026. For discussion, see Alexandra Gillespie, "'These proverbes yet do last': Lydgate, the Fifth Earl of Northumberland, and Tudor Miscellanies from Print to Manuscript," *Yearbook of English Studies* 33 (2003), 215–32. The use of Lydgate by early English printers, as Gillespie shows, is considerably more nuanced than my brief remarks can convey; see also Gillespie's "The Lydgate Canon in Print from 1476 to 1534," *Journal of the Early Book Society* 3 (2000), 59–93.

16 This is the title in *Poems*, from which edition I take all citations. The poem is no. 49 in MP I and entitled there *Ballade at the Reverence of Our Lady, Qwene of Mercy*. Other scholars of Lydgate's poetry have, in different ways, described what I am calling Lydgate's habit of personalization, especially in respect to Chaucer's poetry. A. C. Spearing, *Medieval to Renaissance in English Poetry* (Cambridge: Cambridge University Press, 1985), for example, has made the argument in Bloomian terms, as has, more recently, Daniel T. Kline, "Father Chaucer and the *Siege of Thebes*: Literary Paternity, Aggressive Deference, and the Prologue to Lydgate's Oedipal Canterbury Tale," *The Chaucer Review* 34 (1999), 217–35.

17 The pertinent lines of *Troilus and Criseyde* are 5.1849–55, and those of the *Complaynt of a Lovere's Lyfe*, 400–6. Norton-Smith edits the *Complaynt* in *Poems*; in MP II it is no. 3 and carries the title *The Complaint of the Black Knight*. For the allusions among these works, see Norton-Smith's note in *Poems*, p. 143.

18 For "redresse" see the MED's three meanings for *redressen* v. For "stile," see *stile* n.(2) meanings (a), (b), and (c), which cover denotations from "writing instrument," to "subject matter," to "elaborate, ornamented style"; for each

of these the MED supplies an example from Lydgate's *Troy Book*. This pun on *stile* is one Lydgate's favorites, he no doubt finding its conflation of his person (via the metonymy with his pen) and his aureate style much suited to his purposes.

19 Norton-Smith finds another echo of *Troilus and Criseyde* (viz., 2.1–10: see *Poems*, p. 144) in this invocation. If this is the case, then it not only makes the association with Chaucer so much the firmer, but also – as Lydgate would then have displaced this invocation from its more appropriate context of a historical romance to the less appropriate one of a devotional panegyric – makes its self-referential quality that much more apparent.

20 For a discussion of the generic versus specific poetic "I," see Chapter 1. I do not mean to claim here that first-person specificity is uniformly characteristic of Lydgate's poetic practice; in fact, he frequently makes use of a purely generic "I." In addition – as David Lawton, *Chaucer's Narrators* (Cambridge: D. S. Brewer, 1985), reminds us – one cannot assume that first-person pronouns are referentially consistent even in the same work, much less across works. Nonetheless, as the instances cited in this chapter and later indicate, Lydgate makes use of first-person specificity with such regularity – especially in his most prominent works – that it is fair to cite this feature as a central element of his poetics.

21 Norton-Smith observes that, although "Skeat and Schirmer put forward the view that the *Commendation* owed much of its structure and diction to Chaucer's *ABC*," in fact the poem "little resembles Chaucer's poem or Deguileville's original prayer," especially since the "personal tone and style of the speaker is radically different" (*Poems*, p. 144). Lydgate translated the whole of *La pelerinage* for the earl of Salisbury in 1426; interestingly, when he reaches the place of Deguileville's prayer, he promises to include the "translacion" of the "noble poete off Breteyne," his "mayster Chaucer," but instead all surviving manuscripts supply only a lacuna; see *The Pilgrimage of the Life of Man*, ed. F. J. Furnivall and Katherine B. Locock, EETS e.s. 77, 83, 92 (London: Kegan Paul, Trench, Trübner & Co., 1899–1904), lines 19751–90. For a speculative discussion of this moment in manuscript history, see John J. Thompson, "After Chaucer: Resituating Middle English Poetry in the Late Medieval and Early Modern Period," in *New Directions in Later Medieval Manuscript Studies: Essays from the 1998 Harvard Conference*, ed. Derek Pearsall (Woodbridge: York Medieval Press, 2000), pp. 183–98. I am grateful to Professor Thompson for bringing this article to my attention.

22 For the sources and analogues of the *Commendation*, see *Poems*, p. 144.

23 See Ernst Robert Curtius, *European Literature and the Latin Middle Ages*, trans. Willard R. Trask (Princeton: Princeton University Press, 1990), esp. pp. 154–59, and, for Averroes's influence on late medieval poetic theory, O. B. Hardison Jr., *The Enduring Monument: A Study of the Idea of Praise in Renaissance Literary Theory and Practice* (Chapel Hill: University of North Carolina Press, 1962), pp. 34–36 and passim.

24 Joel Fineman, *Shakespeare's Perjured Eye: The Invention of Poetic Subjectivity in the Sonnets* (Berkeley: University of California Press, 1986), p. 5. Cf. Hardison, *The Enduring Monument*, p. 30.

25 Epideictic heightening, in other words, is a version of the Derridean supplement: a superfluity that somehow comes to stand for the essence of that to which it is added. See Jacques Derrida, *Of Grammatology*, trans. Gayatri Chakravorty Spivak (Baltimore: Johns Hopkins University Press, 1974), pp. 144–45.

26 *Shakepeare's Perjured Eye*, p. 7, p. 13, emphases in the original.

27 *Misericordias domini in eternum cantabo*, MP I, no. 15, lines 5–6.

28 Walter F. Schirmer, *John Lydgate: A Study in the Culture of the XVth Century*, trans. Ann E. Keep (Berkeley: University of California Press, 1961), for example, asserts that the monk's poetry "reaches its zenith in his hymns of praise" (p. 188), and, more generally, Pearsall observes that he "raised almost to the level of new modes of invention" the "desire to amplify, to heighten and to idealise" that late medieval epideixis shared with "classical panegyric" (Pearsall, *John Lydgate*, p. 144).

29 Hardison Jr., *The Enduring Monument*, p. 30.

30 For example, Ganim finds Lydgate's aim in the *Siege of Thebes* to be "rhetorical in the most didactic sense, not mimetic or even narrative" (*Style and Consciousness*, p. 112). Similarly, Pearsall finds that, in the *Troy Book*, "Lydgate systematically subdues the narrative to non-narrative purposes" (*John Lydgate*, p. 129).

31 In glossing over the difference between poetry and writing more generally, I follow Lydgate himself. With just one prose work in his entire oeuvre (the *Serpent of Division*), it is fair to assume that, in defending past "writyng" in general, he is thinking of present poetry in particular. Incidentally, as Bergen points out in his notes (p. 205), this entire passage on writing and writers is original to Lydgate. Lois Ebin discusses this passage and the one I subsequently quote from the *Life of Our Lady* in *Illuminator*, p. 24; my understanding of Lydgate's trope of illumination owes a debt to this study. Lydgate no doubt takes this trope from Chaucer's clerk's remark about "Fraunceys Petrak, the lauriat poete" who "Enlymyned al Ytaille of poetrie" (4.31–33), which Hoccleve first reapplies to Chaucer in the *Regiment* (1974) – see Robert F. Yeager, "Death is a Lady: *The Regement of Princes* as Gendered Political Commentary," *Studies in the Age of Chaucer* 26 (2004), 147–93 (179–80). But with Lydgate the trope reaches unparalleled elaboration and significance.

32 In this discussion and elsewhere, I am not, obviously, using the term "aureate" in the narrow sense of an enrichment of poetic language through the importation of Latin diction. (For a useful discussion of this sense, see Lydgate's *Poems*, pp. 192–95). Instead, following the work of critics such as Lerer and Ebin – and, more importantly, Lydgate himself – I take the term to denote at once this diction, a more general mode of poetry, and the idealized nature of that which this poetry describes. Further, I do not mean to

suggest that Lydgate, as is sometimes thought, *habitually* freights his verse with aureation. He is instead rather selective in this regard, deploying aureation typically only when it is thematically relevant, as in this passage from the *Life of Our Lady*. In comparison, he renders vast stretches of works such as the *Siege of Thebes* in an unadorned middle style appropriate to purposes of narration.

33 This formulation of the reflexivity of poetic memorialization is very close to the one Petrarch himself provides in his laureation address, as discussed in Chapter 1.

34 The ideal in epideictic poetry is traditionally figured as brilliant specularity; see Fineman, *Shakespeare's Perjured Eye*, p. 13.

35 For a brief history of this very old convention, see Curtius, *European Literature*, pp. 83—85.

36 For the monastic ideal of selfhood and Spitzer, see Chapter 1.

37 As demonstrated by J. C. Laidlaw, "Christine de Pizan, the Earl of Salisbury and Henry IV," *French Studies* 36 (1982), 129—43, from which study I draw much of the historical information that follows. Christine herself records Henry's overtures and the manner in which she finessed them to secure the return of her son in her 1405 *Avision-Christine*. See *L'Avision-Christine: Introduction and Text*, ed. Sister Mary Louis Towner (New York: AMS, 1969), pp. 164—66, and, for an English translation, *Christine's Vision*, trans. Glenda K. McLeod (New York: Garland Publishing, Inc., 1993), pp. 120—21. For a summary of the passage, see Charity Cannon Willard, *Christine de Pizan: Her Life and Works* (New York: Persea Books, 1984), pp. 164—65. For the *Epistre*, see *Epistre Othea*, ed. Gabriella Parussa (Geneva: Librarie Droz, S. A., 1999). For this work's ambitious formal complexity, see Mary Ann Ignatius, "Manuscript Format and Text Structure: Christine de Pizan's *Epistre Othea*," *Studies in Medieval Culture* 12 (1978), 121—24.

38 *Epistre Othea*, lines 10—12.

39 See *Lydgate and Burgh's Secrees of Old Philisoffres*, ed. Robert Steele, EETS e.s. 66 (London: Kegan Paul, Trench, Trübner & Co., 1894). For a brief history of the *Secreta secretorum*, see Steele's introduction, pp. vii—xiv.

40 For Scrope's translation (of which he made more than one version), see *The Epistle of Othea*, ed. Curt F. Bühler, EETS o.s. 264 (London: Oxford University Press, 1970). For a wide-ranging investigation of the popularity of the *Epistre* and other works by Christine in England in the second half of the fifteenth century, see Jennifer Summit, *Lost Property: The Woman Writer and English Literary History, 1380—1589* (Chicago: University of Chicago Press, 2000), pp. 61—107.

41 See Laidlaw, "Christine de Pizan," 137—40. The entrepreneurial Christine more than once reissued her *Epistre* with a dedication to a different noble personage. Parussa, who accepts Laidlaw's argument about Henry IV, prints all these dedications in an appendix to her edition. The following citations of the Harley 219 dedication are to this appendix and given in the text by line number.

42 Cf. Green's brief comment on this topic in *Poets and Princepleasers*, p. 179. As notes Fisher, *Emergence*, p. 21, in this same period Henry granted Gower his annual two pipes of wine and doubled Chaucer's annuity. Cultural intervention was, it seems, high on the king's agenda in the shaky early days of his reign.

43 This version of the dedication is in fact filled with acts of naming, and Christine goes out of her way to call attention to this feature through her repetition of the word "nommee" either by itself or as part of another word: e.g., in lines 1, 12, 19, and 20. In addition, the "grand vois" that she associates both with the prince of "haute renommee" (1–2) and herself – as the "petite clochete" ("little bell") that a "grand vois sonne" (38) – could mean "name" as well as "sound," "authority," or "utterance": see Algirdas Julien Greimas, *Dictionnaire d l'ancien Francais: Le Moyen Âge* (Paris: Larousse, 1992), *vois*, n.f. Although she also names herself in the other versions of the dedication, none of these are as self-conscious of the act of naming. Strikingly, moreover, the Harley 219 dedication is the only one in which she does *not* explicitly name her dedicatee. Given the antipathy she later expresses toward Henry, one suspects that this play of naming and not naming was her subtle way of signaling Henry's usurpation of the position that should be held by the true "Roy noble."

44 For one especially lucid discussion of this strategy, see Maureen Quilligan, *The Allegory of Female Authority: Christine de Pizan's "Cité des dames"* (Ithaca: Cornell University Press, 1991), pp. 11–68.

45 For the prerequisite of a legitimizing agent's differing basis of authority, see Scanlon, *Narrative*, p. 311.

46 *L'Avision-Christine*, p. 165; *Christine's Vision*, pp. 120–21.

47 C. David Benson, "Prudence, Othea and Lydgate's Death of Hector," *The American Benedictine Review* 26 (1975), 115–23, was, I believe, the first to demonstrate Lydgate's use of the *Epistre*. See also Benson's *The History of Troy in Middle English Literature: Guido delle Colonne's "Historia Destructionis Troiae" in Medieval England* (Woodbridge: D. S. Brewer, 1980), pp. 124–29. Benson contends that Christine's influence on Lydgate extends beyond this episode and is visible in the monk's poem-long preoccupation with the theme of prudence versus willfulness.

48 Pearsall prints this letter in *Biobib*, appendix no. 8.

49 According to Laidlaw, Christine's son returned to England "at the very end of 1401 or, more probably, in the first half of 1402" ("Christine de Pizan," 133), which is thus the latest date for her to have sent manuscripts to Henry IV in the hope of securing this return. If we follow Christopher Allmand, *Henry V* (London: Methuen, 1992), pp. 7–8, and put Prince Hal's birth in September 1386, then the prince would have turned fifteen just months before Jean de Castel left for France.

50 For the events of 1410–13, see Allmand, *Henry V*, pp. 43–58. For the relationship of the *Troy Book* to Lancastrian politics, see, among other studies, Alan S. Ambrisco and Paul Strohm, "Succession and Sovereignty in

Lydgate's Prologue to *The Troy Book*," *The Chaucer Review* 30 (1995), 40–57; Lee Patterson, "Making Identities in Fifteenth-Century England: Henry V and John Lydgate," in *New Historical Literary Study: Essays on Reproducing Texts, Representing History*, ed. Jeffrey N. Cox and Larry J. Reynolds (Princeton: Princeton University Press, 1993), pp. 69–107; and Christopher Baswell, "*Troy Book*: How Lydgate Translates Chaucer into Latin," in *Translation Theory and Practice in the Middle Ages*, ed. Jeanette Beer (Kalamazoo: Medieval Institute Publications, 1997), pp. 215–37.

51 See MED *wel* adv. 18 (b) and 5a (b), respectively.

52 That this is not exactly what the prince received with the *Troy Book*, when its sentiment is considered as a whole, has been well argued by James Simpson, *Reform and Cultural Revolution* (Oxford: Oxford University Press, 2002), pp. 77–103, with reference to the somewhat earlier alliterative *Destruction of Troy*.

53 For a thorough discussion of Lydgate's historicism in the *Troy Book*, see Benson, *History of Troy*, pp. 97–129. For Guido, see *Historia destructionis Troiae*, ed. Nathaniel Edward Griffin (Cambridge, Mass.: The Mediaeval Academy of America, 1936), which is translated in *Historia destructionis Troiae*, trans. Mary Elizabeth Meek (Bloomington: Indiana University Press, 1974).

54 For the nature and wide influence of the *Polychronicon*, see John Taylor, *The "Universal Chronicle" of Ranulf Higden* (Oxford: Clarendon Press, 1966). The first chapter of the first book of Higden's opus may have served as another source for Lydgate's defense of history writing in the *Troy Book* prologue. As Trevisa translates, Higden asserts, "Writnge of poetes is more worthy to preisynge of emperoures þan al þe welþe of þis worlde. . . .": see *Polychronicon Ranulphi Higden Monachi Cestrensis; Together with the English Translations of John Trevisa and of an Unknown Writer of the Fifteenth Century*, ed. Churchill Babington (London: Longman & Co., 1865), vol. I, p. 1. For Lydgate's knowledge of the *Polychronicon* and his use of Trevisa's translation in the *Troy Book*, see A. S. G. Edwards, "The Influence and Audience of the *Polychronicon*: Some Observations," *Proceedings of the Leeds Philosophical and Literary Society, Literary and Historical Section* 17 (1980), 113–19 (115), and R. A. Dwyer, "Some Readers of John Trevisa," *Notes and* Queries 212 (1967), 291–92.

55 For Paris's authorial self-identification, see Andrew Galloway, "Writing History in England," in *Cambridge History*, ed. Wallace, pp. 255–83 (p. 269).

56 For this tradition of historicism, its crucial role in English culture, and Lydgate's transformative deployment of it in the service of Lancastrian legitimation, see Christopher Cannon, "Monastic Productions," in *Cambridge History*, ed. Wallace, pp. 316–48 (esp. pp. 340–48).

57 See MED *enacten* v., meanings 2 and 3.

58 See Lerer, *Chaucer and His Readers*, pp. 45–49.

59 For Henry V's totalizing identification of himself with his nation, see Patterson, "Making Identities," p. 87.

60 That is, Lydgate's focus on Chaucer as a rhetorician does not necessarily mean, as has been often assumed, that he understood the achievement of his predecessor solely in these terms, but rather that lavish rhetoric was simply the most convenient and legible means to associate his verse with his predecessor's. For a like-minded account (but to different ends) of Lydgate's praise of Chaucer, see Cannon, *Chaucer's English*, pp. 185–87.

61 See MED *magnifien* v. 4, 1 (a), 1 (b), and 2 (a), respectively. For similar conclusions about this passage, see Baswell, "How Lydgate Translates," p. 230, and Nicholas Watson, "Outdoing Chaucer: Lydgate's *Troy Book* and Henryson's *Testament of Cresseid* as Competitive Imitations of *Troilus and Criseyde*," in *Shifts and Transpositions in Medieval Narrative: A Festschrift for Dr. Elspeth Kennedy*, ed. Karen Pratt (Cambridge: D. S. Brewer, 1994), pp. 89–108 (p. 95).

62 The occasional basis of much of Lydgate's poetry has often been noticed; indeed, in some sense, "all his poetry is occasional poetry" (Pearsall, *John Lydgate*, p. 5). For a discussion of how this occasionality relates to his transcendentalizing poetics similar to the one I am putting forward, see Lois A. Ebin, *John Lydgate* (Boston: Twayne, 1985), p. 91.

63 No. 28 in MP II.

64 For the manner in which this poem approaches its impossible political task and how it ultimately expresses the very opposite of its manifest intentions, see Patterson, "Making Identities," pp. 89–93. A further explanation of the unusual nature of this and other poems written by Lydgate during Henry VI's minority is offered by Nolan, who notes that the "idea of *representation*, the notion that the king literally embodied the realm, was a crucial one during the minority, when it was deployed precisely to compensate for the absence of an adult king" (*Public Culture*, p. 6; for *Pedigree* specifically, see also pp. 73–74). Laureate poetics, which supplies a double for the king in the person of the poet laureate, thus became at once more awkward and more urgent when Lancastrian authority had a child at its center.

65 Pearsall, *John Lydgate*, p. 256.

66 I cite the edition of this poem in Carleton Brown and G. V. Smithers (eds.), *Religious Lyrics of the XIVth Century*, 2nd edn (Oxford: Clarendon Press, 1957), by line number in the text.

67 No. 14 in MP I. Although the references to the speaker's old age in these opening lines are conventional, from them the poem is usually assumed to be late.

68 Acknowledging the strangeness of this poem's cross-purposes, Pearsall writes, "It is difficult to think of anyone who could have been so ignorant of the Paternoster and at the same time so appreciative of Lydgate's literary pyrotechnics. It looks like a *tour de force*" (Pearsall, *John Lydgate*, p. 258).

69 For Humphrey's status and activities during this time, see M. H. Keen, *England in the Later Middle Ages: A Political History* (London: Routledge,

1973), pp. 416–17, as well as V. J. Scattergood, *Politics and Poetry in the Fifteenth Century* (London: Blandford Press, 1971), pp. 150–51, and *Biobib*, pp. 32–33. For a more recent account of Humphrey's influence on the *Fall*, see Nigel Mortimer, *John Lydgate's "Fall of Princes": Narrative Tragedy in its Literary and Political Contexts* (Oxford: Clarendon Press, 2005), pp. 51–94.

70 Weiss, *Humanism*, p. 42.

71 For the *Humfroidos*, see Pearsall, *John Lydgate*, pp. 225–26.

72 For the manner in which Lydgate manipulates his praise of first Chaucer and then Humphrey to the end of his own self-authorization, see Scanlon, *Narrative*, pp. 322–49 and esp. pp. 327–28.

73 For this rising and Humphrey's response to it, see Ralph A. Griffiths, *The Reign of King Henry VI: The Exercise of Royal Authority, 1422–1461* (Berkeley: University of California Press, 1981), pp. 139–40.

74 Lawton, "Dullness," 770.

75 For an elaboration of a similar, if much more nuanced, point, see Paul Strohm, *Politique: Languages of Statecraft between Chaucer and Shakespeare* (Notre Dame: University of Notre Dame Press, 2005), pp. 89–104.

76 See, for example, Scott-Morgan Straker, "Rivalry and Reciprocity in Lydgate's *Troy Book*," *New Medieval Literatures* 3 (1999), 119–47. Straker's position, along with that of Simpson, may be contrasted with those of Pearsall and Ambrisco and Strohm, who understand Lydgate's laureate performances as for the most part propagandistic in intent, if not always in execution. For a view somewhere between these poles, see Colin Fewer, "John Lydgate's *Troy Book* and the Ideology of Prudence," *The Chaucer Review* 38 (2004), 229–45.

77 Cf. Nolan's identification of a "shadow narrative" running through Lydgate's work, "whereby a dominant discourse or logic is paired with its opposite and maintained in a constant and irresolvable tension": "'Now wo, now gladnesses': Ovidianism in the *Fall of Princes*," *ELH* 71 (2004), 531–58 (553).

78 Montrose, "The Elizabethan Subject," p. 323.

79 No. 24 in MP II.

80 For Marie's work, with a facing-page translation, see *Fables*, trans. Harriet Spiegal (Toronto: University of Toronto Press, 1987). All citations are from this edition and given by line number in the text. I have also consulted *The Fables of Marie de France: An English Translation*, trans. Mary Lou Martin (Birmingham, Ala.: Summa Publications, Inc., 1984). For Lydgate's dependence on Marie, see the excellent chapter on *Isopes Fabules* in Edward Wheatley, *Mastering Aesop: Medieval Education, Chaucer, and His Followers* (Gainesville: University Press of Florida, 2000), pp. 124–48. Wheatley speculates that Lydgate's elevation of Aesop into a laureate may be the result of his confusion of the Greek fabulist with Romulus, a legendary Roman emperor/translator whose epistle accompanies the Latin text of the fables used in the medieval grammar school curriculum (*Mastering Aesop*, pp. 126–27). But Marie plainly distinguishes Romulus from Aesop in her

prologue, and, as Wheatley himself shows, the latter, as a subject of a "mestre" (a term Marie supplies twice in 40 lines), is unambiguously designated a slave (*Mastering Aesop*, pp. 25–26). Hence, given also what we have seen of Lydgate's poetic practice elsewhere, Aesop's novel laureateship in the monk's prologue seems less likely a mistake than his strategic adaptation of his source to suit his particular needs.

81 The translation is Martin's, with the substitution of the more literal "clerks" for her "writers."

82 A good example of Lydgate's manipulation of his source in this regard is his rendition of the fable of the wolf and crane. In this fable, a wolf gets a bone stuck in his throat, promises a crane a great reward if she pulls it out, and then reneges on this promise, asserting that the crane is lucky simply to be alive after placing her neck between his teeth. Lydgate's wolf, in comparison with Marie's, is much more a king-figure, since, for example, the events take place in a "court" (773) over which the wolf presides. And, while Marie's brief moral emphasizes general feudal abuse – the broken promises of a "mal seignur" (33) – throughout his rendition Lydgate associates the wolf specifically with a tyrant who oppresses the poor of his nation; in his moral, for example, he soberly observes, "Prayer of princes is a commaundement,/ The poure obayethe, they dare none othar do,/Presept of tyrantes is so vyolent,/Who-evar sey nay, nede it muste be so" (813–16). For Wheatley's discussion of this fable, see *Mastering Aesop*, p. 133.

3 THOMAS HOCCLEVE: BEGGAR LAUREATE

1 Burrow gives 1367 as the most likely year of Hoccleve's birth, which would make him Lydgate's elder by a mere four years: see *ThomasH*, p. 2.

2 See, for example, the introduction to *Selections from Hoccleve*, ed. M. C. Seymour (Oxford: Clarendon Press, 1981), and William Calin, *The French Tradition and the Literature of Medieval England* (Toronto: University of Toronto Press, 1994), p. 399.

3 Strohm, *Empty Throne*, pp. 145–46, asserts Hoccleve's orthodoxy in no uncertain terms. Others, such as Nicholas Perkins, *Hoccleve's "Regiment of Princes": Counsel and Constraint* (Cambridge: D. S. Brewer, 2001), have found him to be more consciously critical of the established powers for whom he wrote. As will become apparent, I do not find that Hoccleve's complicity in the Lancastrian project of legitimation excludes the possibility of intentional dissent.

4 For the dating of the *Regiment*, see below; for the *Troy Book*, see *Biobib*, p. 18; for the *Remonstrance against Oldcastle*, see *ThomasH*, p. 21; for *A Defence of Holy Church*, see Lydgate, *Poems*, pp. 150–51; for the *Series*, see *ThomasH*, pp. 26–28; for *On Gloucester's Approaching Marriage*, see *Biobib*, pp. 22–23.

5 As I recounted in the previous chapter, the prince had some form of contact with Lydgate early in the poet's career, while both were at Oxford in 1398. He would have heard about Hoccleve – and perhaps even have

met him — through his activities on the king's council after 1409. The keeper of the privy seal during this time, John Prophet, was in the same period also a member of the king's council: see Derek Pearsall, "Hoccleve's *Regement of Princes*: The Poetics of Royal Self-Representation," *Speculum* 69 (1994), 386–410. See also, for the relation of the *Regiment* to Prince Hal's attempts to distinguish himself from his father, Yeager, "Death is a Lady."

6 For the political motives behind Humphrey's patronage of writers, especially Italian humanists, see Weiss, *Humanism*, esp. pp. 40–42, and Scattergood, *Politics and Poetry*, esp. pp. 142–43.

7 See, for example, Hoccleve, *Selections*, p. xiii, and Strohm, "Hoccleve, Lydgate," pp. 643–44.

8 Hoccleve's political poems, in addition to the *Regiment* and *Remonstrance against Oldcastle*, are nos. 4, 5, 6, and 8 in pt. 1 and no. 9 in pt. 2 of *Minor Poems*. (The *Remonstrance against Oldcastle* is Seymour's title; in *Minor Poems*, the piece is named *Address to Sir John Oldcastle*.) According to Burrow, all these poems date between 1413 and 1416, except for the earlier *Regiment* and the *Balade on King Henry V*, which, as I note below, must be dated in 1421 or later. But Burrow, "Thomas Hoccleve: Some Redatings," *Review of English Studies* 46 (1995), 366–72, argues also that Hoccleve's mental illness occurred in 1414 rather than the more commonly adduced 1416, which would place at least two of Hoccleve's so-called laureate productions after his mental illness, including the *Remonstrance against Oldcastle* (written "in the summer of 1415" — see *ThomasH*, pp. 21–22).

9 See, for example, Lawton, *Chaucer's Narrators*, p. 160 n. 6. Hoccleve comes nearest to detailing a specific commission in an envoy addressed to Edward, second duke of York, which he includes as a freestanding poem in his holograph Huntington Library MS HM III, a manuscript compiled late in life. He also vaguely alludes to what may have been a commission in the section of the *Series* known as the *Dialogue*; but, as we will see, this allusion — even if it refers to an actual commission — plays a rather different function than the detailed accounts that Lydgate supplies.

10 It has been argued that the prince commissioned Lydgate's *Life of Our Lady* around 1416, which, if correct, would nicely, if circumstantially, corroborate the argument about the lapse of Hoccleve's proto-laureateship. But the date of this work and even the extent of the prince's involvement in the project are still topics of debate: see *Biobib*, pp. 19–20. If, however, Hoccleve's illness took place, as Burrow proposes, in 1414, then Lydgate's *Defence of Holy Church*, perhaps written at about that time (see Norton-Smith's note in Lydgate's *Poems*, pp. 150–51), may be taken as evidence of a shift in patronage — one which Hoccleve sought to counter with his *Remonstrance against Oldcastle*.

11 See *ThomasH*, p. 28 and *Minor Poems*, pt. 2 no. 9. This poem appears in Huntington Library MS HM 744, which, like HM III, is a holograph Hoccleve compiled late in life, most likely after 1422 (*ThomasH*, p. 30).

Interestingly, it is the sole political poem in this manuscript, and one of just three secular poems.

12 Sylvia Wright, "The Author Portraits in the Bedford Psalter-Hours: Gower, Chaucer, and Hoccleve," *British Library Journal* 18 (1992), 190–201. Subsequent citations are given in the text by page number.

13 Manuscript portrait identification is a tricky business. In her 1992 essay, Wright, in regard to what she apparently considers Lydgate's surprising *absence* from the Psalter-Hours, notes that, while there are "six portraits of Benedictines in the manuscript," none of these "can be connected with Lydgate either by context or resemblance to the three known portraits elsewhere" ("Author Portraits," p. 200). In a more recent essay ("The *Gesta Henrici Quinti* and the Bedford Psalter-Hours," in *The Court and Cultural Diversity*, ed. Mullally and Thompson, pp. 267–85), however, she finds "[t]he fleshy face of the Benedictine monk John Lydgate ... appears twice" (p. 268). Further, in the first essay she detects three portraits of Hoccleve, while in the second she reduces this to one, noting instead "[t]wo further portraits are modeled after the Gower portrait formula" (p. 269). Doubt may even be cast on the identity of this single portrait, as the one Wright uses for comparison — the kneeling figure in the presentation scene in London, BL MS Arundel 38, a lavish copy of the *Regiment* — may not in fact depict Hoccleve. Kathleen L. Scott, *Later Gothic Manuscripts, 1390–1490*, 2 vols., A Survey of Manuscripts Illuminated in the British Isles 6 (London: Harvey Miller Publishers, 1996), vol. 2, pp. 158–60, labels the Arundel illustration a "gift-giving" scene, and identifies the kneeling figure as John Mowbray. Her argument, however, is far from definitive. Perkins, who reviews all the evidence, judges it "problematic" (*Hoccleve's "Regiment,"* pp. 116–17); and Burrow, guessing Scott to believe that Hoccleve was "too humble a figure to be so represented," claims the opposite — see "Hoccleve and the 'Court,'" in *Nation, Court, and Culture: New Essays on Fifteenth-Century English Poetry*, ed. Helen Cooney (Dublin: Four Courts Press, 2001), pp. 70–80 (p. 74 n. 18).

14 Pearsall points out that the three known recipients of early presentation copies of the *Regiment* — John Mowbray, second duke of Norfolk; John, duke of Bedford; and (perhaps) Edward, second duke of York — were each to different degrees political opponents of Prince Henry. The *Regiment* seems likely, then, to have been part of the prince's program to "cement relationships with possibly doubtful friends" (Pearsall, "Hoccleve's *Regement*," 396).

15 My observations in this and the following paragraph echo those made in my "Hoccleve and the Apprehension of Money," *Exemplaria* 13 (2001), 173–214 (180–83).

16 See the appendix of documents in *ThomasH*, pp. 33–49.

17 Lines 13–22 of the edition and translation of Christine's poem in *Poems of Cupid, God of Love*, ed. Thelma S. Fenster and Mary Carpenter Erler (Leiden: E. J. Brill, 1990). All subsequent citations are from this volume and given in the text by line number.

18 For a summary of this *querelle* and the role that the *Epistre* played in it, see Fenster's and Erler's introduction to *Poems of Cupid*, pp. 3–19.

19 See F.227–31 or G.253–57 in the *Legend*, where the God of Love attacks Chaucer for having translated the "Romaunce of the Rose" in "pleyn text."

20 In regard to the literary savvy of Hoccleve's audience and the poet's awareness of this, Fenster and Erler remark, "Hoccleve does not, then, wish to make Christine's poem available to an English audience: rather he provides an English work parallel to the French one, for an audience which could appreciate both" (*Poems of Cupid*, p. 167). In this, Hoccleve was again modeling his practice on Chaucer's, whose *Book of the Duchess*, for example, was similarly targeted at an audience that was fully aware of his literary debts. For a study of Hoccleve's Chaucerianism in the *Epistre*, see Roger Ellis, "Chaucer, Christine de Pizan, and Hoccleve: *The Letter of Cupid*," in *Essays on Thomas Hoccleve*, ed. Catherine Batt (London: Centre for Medieval and Renaissance Studies, Queen Mary and Westfield College, University of London, 1996), pp. 19–54. Ellis also comments on the wit of Hoccleve's translation techniques in this poem in the introduction to his edition (*"My Compleinte"*), pp. 36–41.

21 For this double impersonation, or, as he terms it, ventriloquism, see Ethan Knapp, *The Bureaucratic Muse: Thomas Hoccleve and the Literature of Late Medieval England* (University Park: Pennsylvania State University Press, 2001), pp. 45–75 and esp. p. 59.

22 Hoccleve's account of the response to his *Epistre* occurs in the *Dialogue*, 750–91. For a summary of the critical debate regarding the *Epistre*'s attitude toward women, see Karen A. Winstead, "'I am al othir to yow than yee weene': Hoccleve, Women, and the *Series*," *Philological Quarterly* 72 (1993), 143–55 (143–44).

23 As Patterson remarks in his discussion of this poem, "But within the context of the Lancastrian household, dominated by Henry's understandable anxiety about disloyalty and betrayal, would ambiguity have been highly prized?" ("'What is Me,'" 452).

24 Although Hoccleve was following Christine in giving the poem this bureaucratic shape, Fenster and Erler suggest that "it must have seemed a pleasant conceit to present this elegant transmutation of the matter of his workaday life" (*Poems of Cupid*, p. 168).

25 As Patterson succinctly puts this point, "These lines could hardly have amused the king" ("'What is Me,'" 452).

26 For the historical circumstances and date of the *Male regle*, see *ThomasH*, pp. 14–15.

27 For the moral authority that Hoccleve derives from the act of begging, see Scanlon, *Narrative*, esp. pp. 307–8, and Judith Ferster, *Fictions of Advice: The Literature and Politics of Counsel in Late Medieval England* (Philadelphia: University of Pennsylvania Press, 1996), pp. 137–59.

28 See Eva M. Thornley, "The Middle English Penitential Lyric and Hoccleve's Autobiographical Poetry," *Neuphilologische Mitteilungen* 3 (1967), 295–321.

29 The *Male regle* survives in full only in the holograph HM III.

30 This revised extract appears in Canterbury Cathedral Archives Register O, ff. 406v—407r: see Marian Trudgill and J. A. Burrow, "A Hocclevean Balade," *Notes and Queries* 243 (1998), 178—80. As his religious lyrics attest, Hoccleve was an adept practitioner of devotional poetics, and hence it is not surprising that even his parody of this poetics could be appreciated by a reader preferring to take it seriously.

31 See Middleton, "Public Poetry."

32 For the manner in which Henry's financial straits show up in Hoccleve's poetry, see Ferster, *Fictions of Advice*, pp. 137—59; Patterson, "'What is Me,'" 454—56; and Meyer-Lee, "Apprehension." For a rather different view of the royal doubling Hoccleve's begging performs, see Robert Epstein, "Prisoners of Reflection: The Fifteenth-Century Poetry of Exile and Imprisonment," *Exemplaria* 15 (2003), 159—98 (182), who sees the pose of beggar as inversely constitutive of an idealized royal subjectivity.

33 For an analysis of the term "crauour" in this regard, see Knapp, *Bureaucratic Muse*, pp. 41—42, and, for Knapp's argument about the mutual interdependence of the poem's petitionary and penitential modes (to which my reading of the *Male regle* owes a general debt), the encompassing chapter, pp. 17—43. See also J. A. Burrow, "Autobiographical Poetry in the Middle Ages: The Case of Thomas Hoccleve," *Proceedings of the British Academy* 68 (1982), 389—412 (esp. 409), and, more generally, Perkins, *Hoccleve's "Regiment"*, pp. 34—48.

34 See J. A. Burrow, "Hoccleve and the Middle French Poets," in *The Long Fifteenth Century: Essays for Douglas Gray*, ed. Helen Cooper and Sally Mapstone (Oxford: Clarendon Press, 1997), pp. 35—49 (esp. pp. 44—49), where he juxtaposes the *Male regle* with a similar poem by Deschamps. See also Calin, *The French Tradition*, pp. 399—418. Another likely influence is the goliardic poets, whose stratagem of linking moral authority to begging anticipates Hoccleve's; see Jill Mann, "Satiric Subject and Satiric Object in Goliardic Literature," *Mittellateinisches Jahrbuch* 15 (1980), 63—86.

35 For these dates, see Pearsall, "Hoccleve's *Regement*," 386—88. Burrow more or less concurs, believing that Hoccleve presented his poem to the prince "in the last months of this period, or shortly thereafter" (*ThomasH*, 18).

36 In this respect one may contrast Hoccleve with his predecessor Gower, who had completed his ambitious works of public poetry in French and Latin before composing Book 7 of the *Confessio*.

37 See, in particular, Perkins, *Hoccleve's "Regiment"*; Ferster, *Fictions of Advice*, pp. 137—59; and Scanlon, *Narrative*, pp. 299—322.

38 Scanlon, *Narrative*, p. 309. For the enclosing discussion, see pp. 308—10, to which this present paragraph is indebted. See also Epstein, "Chaucer's Scogan," who, after citing the same passage from Scanlon's study, observes, "It is precisely this kind of direct address to royal patrons that distinguishes

Hoccleve's fifteenth century from Chaucer's era and marks the differences between Ricardian and Lancastrian poetics" (13).

39 As Scanlon remarks, "Like any good dedication to a *Fürstenspiegel* this one is flowery and obsequious, so flowery and obsequious, in fact, one tends not to notice that its subject is almost entirely Hoccleve" (Scanlon, *Narrative*, p. 309). Additionally, the very form and style of these stanzas, which follow rather closely the epistolary conventions for a petition to the highborn, point to Hoccleve in his role as privy seal clerk.

40 One instance of such implicit begging occurs in the advice text section entitled "De regis prudencia"; revealingly, the faithful payment of annuities is the very first example Hoccleve supplies of kingly prudence (4789–95). Hoccleve here versifies as general advice the sentiment that he has already given as the poem's specific motive, using the same two words — "yeerly guerdoun" — to describe annuities in general as he used to describe his own just 400 lines or so earlier. Most remarkable, he has gone as far as to threaten an unspoken "hate" as the inevitable result of the suspension of his annuity, and, lest the reader miss the specificity of this threat, he describes this hate's nonverbal nature with a near homophone for his place of work — "undir pryvee silence" almost explicitly enunciating "in the privy seal." There is perhaps no better example, in all Hoccleve's verse, of how the subjection of his beggar poetics leads to not servile complicity but to resistance and even outright hostility. For a wide-ranging study of the *Regiment* that takes as its point of departure this very paronomasia, see Sarah Tolmie, "The *Prive Scilence* of Thomas Hoccleve," *Studies in the Age of Chaucer* 22 (2000), 281–309.

41 For various positions on this question, see the studies of the *Regiment* cited above, as well as James Simpson, "Nobody's Man: Thomas Hoccleve's *Regement of Princes,*" in *London and Europe in the Later Middle Ages*, ed. Julia Boffey and Pamela King (London: Centre for Medieval and Renaissance Studies, Queen Mary and Westfield College, University of London, 1995), pp. 149–80; Simpson's revisited account of the *Regiment* in *Reform*, pp. 204–14; and Anna Torti, *The Glass of Form: Mirroring Structures from Chaucer to Skelton* (Cambridge: D. S. Brewer, 1991), pp. 87–106. Perhaps closest to the view taken here is that of Antony J. Hasler, "Hoccleve's Unregimented Body," *Paragraph* 13 (1990), 164–83. Although articulated in a psychoanalytic idiom, Hasler's account likewise sees the two halves of the poem as at once mutually reinforcing and in competition, drawing our attention to the paradoxical tensions of what he calls the "thoughty text" and painting a deeply ambivalent picture of the relation between poet and patron.

42 For this point, and for a detailed analysis of the latter three moments, see Knapp, *Bureaucratic Muse*, pp. 107–27. For a discussion of how the Chaucer portrait bears on this section of the advice text, see Perkins, *Hoccleve's "Regiment,"* pp. 114–21.

43 See Pearsall, "Hoccleve's *Regement*," 387 n. 5, and Allmand, *Henry V*, p. 386.

44 These titles are from *Minor Poems*. Ellis, in his recent edition of the *Series*, offers titles with more manuscript basis, but I retain the older ones for convenience.

45 J. A. Burrow, "Hoccleve's *Series*: Experience and Books," in *Fifteenth-Century Studies*, ed. Robert F. Yeager (Hamden: Archon Books, 1984), pp. 259–73 (p. 260). For a similar but more theorized account of the poem, see James Simpson, "Madness and Texts: Hoccleve's *Series*," in *Chaucer and Fifteenth-Century Poetry*, ed. Julia Boffey and Janet Cowen (London: King's College London, 1991), pp. 15–29.

46 See, for example, Patterson, "'What is me,'" and George MacLennan, *Lucid Interval: Subjective Writing and Madness in History* (Leicester: Leicester University Press, 1992), pp. 21–23.

47 For the relative paucity of reference to Hoccleve as author in the textual record, see Lee Patterson, "Beinecke MS 493 and the Survival of Hoccleve's *Series*," in *Old Books, New Learning: Essays on Medieval and Renaissance Books at Yale*, ed. Robert G. Babcock and Lee Patterson (New Haven: Beinecke Rare Book and Manuscript Library, 2001), pp. 80–92 (pp. 88–89), and John M. Bowers, "Thomas Hoccleve and the Politics of Tradition," *The Chaucer Review* 36 (2002), 352–69, who also speculates more generally on the reasons for Hoccleve's feeble reception.

48 This only apparently superfluous digression on coin clipping functions as a crucial link to the pecuniary obsessions of his earlier poems. See Meyer-Lee, "Apprehension," 203–11.

49 See Burrow's edition of the *Dialogue*, p. 104. For a similar point about this gloss, see David Watt, "'I this book shal make': Thomas Hoccleve's Self-Publication and Book Production," *Leeds Studies in English* 34 (2003), 133–60 (150–51).

50 See Burrow's note to line 561, pp. 101–2.

51 See Summit, *Lost Property*, esp. pp. 71–81.

52 For the importance of recursivity in Hoccleve's poetics, see Knapp, *Bureaucratic Muse*, pp. 109–11. For a reading of this passage in the *Series* that, *contra* mine, sees in Hoccleve's depiction of Humphrey a genuine indication of the poet's subjective reintegration, see Epstein, "Prisoners of Reflection," 192–93.

53 See *ThomasH*, 26–27.

54 Patterson, "Beinecke MS 493," p. 86.

55 In the holograph Durham University Library MS Cosin V.iii.9, which Hoccleve copied late in life, at the end of *Jonathas and Fellicula* Hoccleve uniquely dedicates either the *Series* as a whole or this tale in particular to "my lady of Westmerland" (734 in Ellis's edition of the *Series*), i.e., Humphrey's aunt Joan Nevill, daughter of John of Gaunt by Katherine Swynford and second wife of Ralph Nevill, earl of Westmorland. As Patterson remarks, "Lady Westmerland had persuaded the earl to strip his eldest son of his inheritance for the benefit of the eldest of *her* sons. How could Hoccleve have thought it appropriate to dedicate this tale, which describes a woman

persuading a man to part with his inheritance and then being savagely punished, to this particular woman?" ("Beinecke MS 493," p. 87).

56 This is the basic contention of Fineman's *Shakespeare's Perjured Eye*; see pp. 1–2.

PART III: FROM LANCASTER TO EARLY TUDOR

1 Thomas Freeman, *Rvbbe, and a Great Cast. Epigrams* (London: T. Montforde, 1614), STC 11370. Cited from EEBO, accessed 21 February 2003. I quote the first four lines of no. 14 in the second half of the diptych, *Rvnne, and a Great Cast*. For the epigrams celebrating the poets I list, see, also in the second half, nos. 69, 84, 93, 96, 62, and 94.

2 *The Kingis Quair*, ed. John Norton-Smith (Oxford: Clarendon Press, 1971), lines 1374–77. For the pervasive influence of, in particular, Lydgate's *Temple of Glas* on this poem, see Norton-Smith's introduction, pp. xii–xiii.

3 See *The Kingis Quair*, p. 83.

4 LYDGATEANISM

1 The title of Burgh's poem is from E. P. Hammond (ed.), *English Verse Between Chaucer and Surrey* (Durham: Duke University Press, 1927), where the piece appears on pp. 189–90; all citations are given by line number to this edition, to which I add punctuation. The *Letter* is also printed in Lydgate and Burgh, *Secrees*, pp. xxxi–xxxii. There do exist a few encomia of living English poets that predate Burgh's (e.g., Usk's and Gower's of Chaucer), but these are quite different in scope and form.

2 There do exist, however, a number of earlier *implicit* critiques of fellow poets — for example, Chaucer's Man of Law's tongue-in-cheek remarks on Gower's "wikked ensample of Canacee" (2.78). *A Reproof to Lydgate* is again Hammond's title, although I cite the text in William de la Pole, *The "Suffolk" Poems*, ed. Johannes Petrus Maria Jansen (Groningen: Universiteitsdrukkerij, 1989). For convenience, I give both Jansen's line numbers — which run continuously through the 20 poems in Oxford, Bodleian Library MS Fairfax 16 that have been attributed to Suffolk — and those of Hammond, who edits just the single lyric (*English Verse*, pp. 200–201). In a few instances I have modified Jansen's punctuation. For the attribution to the duke of Suffolk, see below.

3 Hammond, *English Verse*, p. 188. See also Lydgate and Burgh, *Secrees*, pp. xvii–xviii.

4 Pearsall gives 1430 as the date by which Lydgate's priorate had certainly ended, but he also believes that the poet continued to reside at the priory until the royal visit to Bury at Christmas, 1433; see *Biobib* pp. 24–55 and pp. 32–34.

5 For the date of the *Disticha Catonis*, see Max Förster, "Die Burghsche Cato-Paraphrase," *Archiv für das Studium der neueren Sprachen und*

Literaturen 115 (1905), 298—323 (298), in which article Förster edits the *Parvus Cato* and the first three books of the *Cato Major*. For the final book of the latter and extensive textual and linguistic notes, see Max Förster, "Die Burghsche Cato-Paraphrase," *Archiv für das Studium der neueren Sprachen und Literaturen* 116 (1906), 25—40.

6 See Pearsall, *John Lydgate*, p. 168, for a convenient summary of these patronage relationships. The two poems listed are nos. 23 and 37, respectively, in MP I.

7 See *Biobib*, p. 49 n. 98.

8 Alternative explanations of the *Letter* are possible, of course. It may, for instance, have been written much later, perhaps not long before Lydgate's death and Burgh's subsequent completion of the *Secrees*. If this is the case, then Burgh's connections with the Bourchier family may have led him to Lydgate, rather than vice versa. This scenario has some support from internal evidence, as the *Disticha Catonis* is nowhere near as Lydgatean as the *Letter* or Burgh's portion of the *Secrees*.

9 The reference to "Bocase" in line 21 of the *Letter* suggests that Burgh at least knew of the *Fall of Princes*, the work which preoccupied Lydgate through most of the 1430s.

10 *The "Suffolk" Poems*, p. 13. See also Hammond, *English Verse*, pp. 198—99, and *Biobib*, p. 39.

11 See H. N. MacCracken, "An English Friend of Charles of Orléans," *PMLA* 26 (1911), 142—80, in which article he also prints all the poems, French as well as English, that he believes Suffolk wrote. The long-debated attribution has recently been taken up by Derek Pearsall, "The Literary Milieu of Charles of Orléans and the Duke of Suffolk, and the Authorship of the Fairfax Sequence," in *Charles d'Orléans in England (1415—1440)*, ed. Mary-Jo Arn (Cambridge: D. S. Brewer, 2000), pp. 145—56, who decides it impossible to draw any final conclusions. Jansen, after reviewing all the evidence, concludes that, while the author cannot be determined with any certainty, Suffolk remains the most "attractive candidate" (*The "Suffolk" Poems*, p. 30).

12 For the manuscript ascription of the patron of *Virtues of the Mass*, see MP I, p. 97.

13 For the patron of *Pilgrimage*, see *Biobib*, pp. 27—28 and p. 46 n. 61. For *On the Departing*, see the edition in *Poems*, pp. 4—6, along with Norton-Smith's notes, pp. 119—22.

14 Pearsall, *John Lydgate*, p. 162. Pearsall observes further, "As a great East Anglian landowner, Suffolk was constantly associated with Bury, and sat on commission several times with William Curteys, Lydgate's abbot." For the document recording Suffolk's support of Lydgate's grant, see *Biobib*, p. 62.

15 MacCracken, in respect to the phrase "my penne enlumyne," observes, "This is certainly a burlesque of Lydgate's style" ("An English Friend," 149). He also detects other less obvious but equally pointed echoes of Lydgate's stylistic tics. *Contra* MacCracken, Jansen believes that the term "enlumyne" was "not a very uncommon figure of speech" (*The "Suffolk" Poems*, p. 127),

but his example of Osbern Bokenham's usage is not very convincing, since Bokenham was also very pointedly imitating Lydgate.

16 For Baret, see *Biobib*, p. 38; and, for the text of the Suffolk-endorsed petition (dated November 1441), *Biobib*, p. 62.

17 Translations based on this French source are known as *The Dicts and Sayings of the Philosophers*, for which, see Cameron Louis, "Proverbs, Precepts, and Monitory Pieces," in *A Manual of the Writings in Middle English, 1050–1500*, ed. Albert E. Hartung, 11 vols. (Hamden: Connecticut Academy of Arts and Sciences, 1967–, vol. IX, pp. 2957–3048 (pp. 2976–78).

18 The lone possible exception, of which I am aware, is a poem that survives in the Welles Anthology, for which see *The Welles Anthology: MS. Rawlinson C. 813: A Critical Edition*, ed. Sharon L. Jansen and Kathleen H. Jordan (Binghamton: Medieval and Renaissance Texts and Studies, 1991), pp. 110–14. This eight-stanza poem begins, "Musyng vppon the mutabilite/off worldlye changes and grett vnstablenes," and provides a brief *de casibus* meditation on the falls of Eleanor Cobham, John, duke of Somerset, and Duke Humphrey. By mentioning "bokas tragedye" (line 10), the poem's author ensures an association with Lydgate's *Fall of Princes*. And yet, as Nicholas Perkins, "Musing on Mutability: A Poem in the Welles Anthology and Hoccleve's *The Regement of Princes*," *Review of English Studies* 50 (1999), 493–98, argues, the poem's echoes of the opening of Hoccleve's *Regiment* "comprise a palpable debt to Hoccleve's poem" (497). As it was apparently written in the 1460s, the poem's appearance coincides with Ashby's known period of active versifying, and it utilizes strategies and evokes an elegiac Lancastrian sympathy that resemble Ashby's. Perhaps it is not an exception to Ashby's singularity but instead one of Ashby's other compositions that have been lost in the haze of anonymity.

19 *Ingulph's Chronicle of the Abbey of Croyland*, ed. and trans. Henry T. Riley (London: Henry G. Bohn, 1854), p. 425.

20 For the biographical information in this paragraph and elsewhere, in addition to Ashby's poems, I am indebted to the following sources: Summers, *Prison Writing*, pp. 142–44; John Scattergood, "George Ashby's *Prisoner's Reflections* and the Virtue of Patience," *Nottingham Medieval Studies* 37 (1993), 102–9; Scattergood, "The Date and Composition of George Ashby's Poems," *Leeds Studies in English* n.s. 21 (1990), 167–76; J. Otway-Ruthven, *The King's Secretary and the Signet Office in the XV Century* (Cambridge: Cambridge University Press, 1939); Josiah C. Wedgwood and Anne D. Holt, *History of Parliament: Biographies of the Members of the Commons House 1439–1509* (London: His Majesty's Stationery Office, 1936), pp. 21–22; and Sir Leslie Stephen and Sir Sidney Lee (eds.), *The Dictionary of National Biography* (London: Oxford University Press, 1949), vol. I, pp. 636–37. Scattergood dates Ashby's birth "shortly before 1385" ("*Prisoner's Reflections*," 103), which he derives from his dating of the *Active Policy of a Prince* in 1463 and the fact that Ashby claims in this poem to be near 80. As I argue below,

I would date the poem somewhat later, thus pushing Ashby's birth up a few years.

21 This point is made forcefully and at length by Summers, *Prison Writing*, pp. 142–69. Summers's book appeared at the same time as the initial publication of much of the Ashby material in this chapter, and, although we examine Ashby's poetry in respect to somewhat different literary traditions and toward different ends, many of our conclusions are in full accord.

22 For a survey of this genre, see — in addition to Summers, *Prison Writing* — Julia Boffey, "Chaucerian Prisoners: The Context of the *Kingis Quair*," in *Chaucer and Fifteenth-Century Poetry*, ed. Boffey and Cowen, pp. 84–102. For a study of authorial self-representation that encompasses Charles's, James's, and Ashby's contributions to the genre, as well as thematically similar efforts by Hoccleve and the duke of Suffolk, see Epstein, "Prisoners of Reflection."

23 In addition, following the *explicit*, there is a single (most likely spurious) stanza comparing "Pryson" to a "sepulture." The headings to each of the sections are in the same hand as the text of the poem, the manuscript's principal scribal hand. For the paleographical details and contents of this manuscript, see Trinity College, Cambridge University, *Manuscript Trinity R.3.19: A Facsimile*, introduction by Bradford Y. Fletcher (Norman: Pilgrim Books, 1987), pp. xv–xxxi. See also Fletcher's "An Edition of MS R.3.19 in Trinity College, Cambridge: A Poetical Miscellany of c.1480" (Ph.D. dissertation, University of Chicago, 1973), esp. pp. 399–400, where, in lieu of re-editing Ashby's poem, Fletcher provides notes for and corrections to the standard edition in *George Ashby's Poems*, ed. Mary Bateson, EETS e.s. 76 (London: Kegan Paul, Trench, Trübner, 1899). For a study of this manuscript and the related Trinity College, Cambridge MS R.3.21, see Linne R. Mooney, "Scribes and Booklets of Trinity College, Cambridge Manuscripts R.3.19 and R.3.21," in *Middle English Poetry: Texts and Traditions: Essays in Honour of Derek Pearsall*, ed. A. J. Minnis (Woodbridge: York Medieval Press, 2001), pp. 241–66. All citations of Ashby are from Bateson's edition and given in the text by line number. For a quite emended edition of *A Prisoner's Reflections*, see F. Holthausen, "Ashby-Studien II," *Anglia. Zeitschrift für Englische Philologie* 45 (1921), 77–91.

24 Marring an otherwise fluid stanza (by mid-century standards), the rhyme "singler" with "ther" is admittedly horrid. Holthausen, "Ashby-Studien II," emends the latter word to "der," which works better stylistically and thematically.

25 See Lawton, "Dullness," 771–74, and Epstein, "Prisoners of Reflection," 193–98. Summers claims also the influence of the anonymous *Lament of a Prisoner*, which, for reasons she outlines, Ashby may have thought Chaucer's: see *Prison Writing*, pp. 156–58, and, for the poem, E. P. Hammond (ed.), "Lament of a Prisoner against Fortune," *Anglia. Zeitschrift für Englische Philologie* 32 (1909), 481–90.

26 "Because of my draught [glossed in the wordlist as "education"] and my bryngyng vp ["nurture"]/I haue suffryd thys and other spoylyng" (22–23). Obviously, his education alone would not have been responsible for his "spoylyng." He is hence rather obliquely referring to his specific vocational "bryngyng vp" in various Lancastrian households – and perhaps also to the production of propagandistic writings that this education fostered and that have either not survived or are not attributed to him ("draught" could also mean, among other things, "a treatise": see MED *draught* n. 9 [a], [c], and [d]).

27 Seemingly to emphasize this aspect of the speaker, the scribe has added marginal pointers in several key places. Next to line eight, in which Ashby names his prison, the scribe has written in red, "Nomen prisone"; next to line 29, "Nomen Prisonarii." Other pointers include "Spoliacio Prisonarii" next to the stanza about Ashby's "draught," "Lamentacio prisonarii" next to the one about his acquaintances not visiting him (discussed below), and "Seruicium Prisonarii" next to the one about his service to Humphrey, Henry VI, and Margaret (57–63). Significantly, these are the only marginal annotations in the poem; there are none in the ensuing, rather impersonal sermon.

28 See Lawton, "Dullness," 773. In respect to the first passage, compare Hoccleve's *Complaint*, 64–70 (and, for line 36, the *Dialogue*, 100–1); in respect to the second, compare the numerous passages in the *Male regle* and the prologue to the *Regiment of Princes* in which Hoccleve complains about his financial situation (for examples of which, see Chapter 3). Summers suggests that Ashby's stanza on his "det" may refer to the nominal reason for his incarceration (as the Fleet housed many debtors); nonetheless, she holds it most likely, as do I, that the ultimate reason was political: see *Prison Writing*, p. 143.

29 That this intended public may have included a rather specific party is suggested by a possible pun on the word "acquytall." In the context of these stanzas, which meditate upon the punishments of God, this word carries a primary meaning of "faithful conduct," i.e., the spiritually appropriate attitude and behavior he ought to maintain in the face of adversity. But, given the dramatic situation of the poem as a whole, the less common meaning of "release ... from an accusation" is probably also present: see MED *aquitaille* n. 1 and 2. Ashby may have hoped that this poem – among its other purposes – would lead his jailers to see the injustice of their act.

30 Cf. Summers, *Prison Writing*, pp. 154–55.

31 This supposition does not hang on a single word; even if Ashby had written "thys is my fate," a deeper level of premeditation may, of course, still be present. The use of the past tense only makes this level more likely.

32 See Scattergood, "Date and Composition," 171–74, and cf. Summers, *Prison Writing*, p. 144. My own inspection of the manuscript confirms Scattergood's observations.

33 Arthur B. Ferguson, *The Articulate Citizen and the English Renaissance* (Durham: Duke University Press, 1965), p. 89, p. 111. I should note that what is striking about this poem's topicality is not that topicality per se, since versified commentaries on public policy abound in the fifteenth century, the greatest example of which is the *Libelle of Englyshe Polycye*. Rather, what is unusual is that this topicality appears in an explicitly framed *Fürstenspiegel*, which by its nature is an address of one known individual to another. In other words, while unsigned topical poems were by no means uncommon, signed ones — for obvious reasons in such a violently retributive time — were virtually unheard of.

34 See Scattergood, "Date and Composition," 168–71. Scattergood supplies excerpts of the pertinent petitions in his essay.

35 Scattergood, "Date and Composition," 174.

36 For Margaret's and Edward's movements in 1463, see J. J. Bagley, *Margaret of Anjou: Queen of England* (London: Herbert Jenkins Ltd., 1948), pp. 146–54. Margaret and Edward left Scotland for Flanders by early August and, with nowhere else to go, made their way to Bar by winter.

37 Although Ashby's name does not appear on the list of those attainted in the November parliament following Towton, this set of attainders is notorious both for its size and for its number of individuals of relatively low birth: see J. R. Lander, "Attainder and Forfeiture, 1453 to 1509," *Historical Journal* 4 (1961), 119–51 (144). In addition, another list of those attainted — *Annales rerum Anglicarum*, in *Letters and Papers Illustrative of the Wars of the English in France during the Reign of Henry the Sixth, King of England*, ed. Joseph Stevenson, Rolls series 22, 2 vols. (London: Longman, Green, Longman, Roberts, and Green, 1864), vol. II, pt. 2, pp. 778–79 — while it also does not contain Ashby's name, lists more individuals than those in the parliamentary record and concludes with an unnamed "xlij. plures." Alternatively, Ashby's absence from these lists may reflect his nominal charge as debtor. Ashby himself seems to describe the effects of his attainder when he complains in *A Prisoner's Reflections* of his "spoylyng," which left him with neither "dyssh, neyther cup" (23–24). It is possible, however, that Ashby remained at large until September 1462, which also fits with the "yere and more" he claims to have been incarcerated. In this case, his imprisonment would have occurred just before Margaret's October invasion from France.

38 For Tresham, see Charles Ross, *Edward IV* (New Haven: Yale University Press, 1997), pp. 67–68.

39 For Margaret's and Edward's movements during their exile, see Bagley, *Margaret of Anjou*, pp. 155–221. Margaret's optimism in 1468 proved premature, and she eventually returned to Bar. But by June–July 1470 she was negotiating through Louis her reconciliation with Warwick, who invaded England in September. Invited to Paris by Louis in October after news of Warwick's success reached him, she set sail for England in March. Although Ashby could have written the *Active Policy* anytime between 1463 and 1471,

1468 strikes me as most probable for the reasons outlined above. (Summers, arguing from the sources Ashby must have used, also believes he completed it after leaving the Fleet; see *Prison Writing*, pp. 145–46.) Nonetheless, my following interpretation of the *Active Policy*, while made more likely by this date, does not depend on it, as anytime after Prince Edward's inheritance was first threatened (no later than the 1455 battle of St. Albans) a literary intervention in this regard is entirely plausible.

40 In regard to Margaret's possible role in the project, it is noteworthy that in his preface Ashby lists, as his motivation for composing the work, the "bona voluntate" ("good will") that he has toward the queen before that which he has toward Edward. Given Margaret's control over the prince's affairs and her single-minded obsession with his royal inheritance, it seems all but certain that she at least instigated the writing of her signet clerk's *Fürstenspiegel*.

41 The *Somnium vigilantis* has been edited by J. P. Gilson — see "A Defence of the Proscription of the Yorkists in 1459," *English Historical Review* 26 (1911), 512–25 — and insightfully discussed by Margaret Kekewich, "The Attainder of the Yorkists in 1459: Two Contemporary Accounts," *Bulletin of the Institute of Historical Research* 55 (1982), 25–34. Gilson believes that the *Somnium* was most likely written subsequent to the Coventry parliament, but Kekewich persuasively argues that its aim was to move Henry VI away from his tendency toward mercy prior to this parliament. For a recent study of the *Somnium's* political theory, see Strohm, *Politique*, 12–17.

42 See *De Laudibus Legum Anglie*, ed. and trans. S. B. Chrimes (Cambridge: Cambridge University Press, 1942). Puzzlingly, in his opening paragraph Fortescue locates himself and the prince in exile in Bar and yet puts the king's imprisonment in the past tense and does not mention whether at that time he has been restored to the throne. (For reflections on this ambiguous temporality, see Strohm, *Politique*, pp. 142–43, who prefers to term Fortescue's writings "situated" rather than propagandistic.) This leads Chrimes to favor a date of composition after October 1470 but before early 1471, i.e., in the period after Henry's restoration but before the exiles began their journey back to England (pp. lxxxvii–lxxxviii). But, as Chrimes observes, Fortescue plausibly may have written the work anytime after "late in the second half of 1467, probably not before early 1468" (p. lxxxvi). The range of possible dates for Fortescue's tract thus coincides with the range of most probable dates I have given for Ashby's similarly conceived *Active Policy*.

43 Pearsall, "Hoccleve's *Regement*."

44 For a similar assessment of this moment in Hoccleve's poem, see Scanlon, *Narrative*, p. 309.

45 On no manuscript evidence that I can perceive, Bateson — perhaps believing such wordplay was beyond Ashby — emends this line to include the word "high" after the initial "right," thus obscuring the poet's clever use of multiple meanings. Although her emendation makes the address more

conventional, it also adds an 11th syllable to the line, when Ashby regularly uses 10. For a brief notice of Ashby's "overwhelming sense of threatened royal lineages" in this poem, see Simpson, *Reform*, p. 225.

46 See Alison Allan, "Yorkist Propaganda: Pedigree, Prophecy and the 'British History' in the Reign of Edward IV," in *Patronage, Pedigree and Power in Later Medieval England*, ed. Charles Ross (Gloucester: Alan Sutton, 1979), pp. 171—92.

47 For an insightful discussion of the ambiguities of this phrase, see Knapp, *Bureaucratic Muse*, pp. 121—22.

48 For Richard's and Henry's letters, see Otway-Ruthven, *King's Secretary*, pp. 42, 46. All factual information about the signet in this paragraph comes from this study.

49 Otway-Ruthven, *King's Secretary*, pp. 50, 42.

50 See MED *wel* adv. 18(b) and 5a, respectively.

51 For the reference to Ashby in Margaret's letter, see *Letters of Queen Margaret of Anjou and Bishop Beckington and Others*, ed. Cecil Monro (Westminster: Camden Society, 1863), p. 114. This letter, possibly addressed to none other than Alice Chaucer, thanks the addressee for her service to "our servant George Ashby, Clerk of our Signet" (quoted by Bateson in *George Ashby's Poems*, v). From the nature of this letter collection's contents, Otway-Ruthven has speculated that the entire collection, which is preserved in a single manuscript, may have been produced by Ashby himself, making it his parallel to Hoccleve's *Formulary* (*King's Secretary*, pp. 119—20). If that is the case, Ashby's decision to include a mention of himself may possess the same crypto-autobiographical motive that Knapp sees in Hoccleve's self-references in the *Formulary*; see Knapp, *Bureaucratic Muse*, pp. 29—36.

52 Lawton, "Dullness," 770, considers this motive to be a general characteristic of fifteenth-century Chaucerian poetry.

53 "It is proper that a king pay the wages of those under his employ; otherwise, the people will look down upon him and his dominion." The manuscript has "Docet" rather than "Decet"; the latter is Bateson's suggested emendation. For the same sentiment, see Hoccleve's *Regiment*, lines 4789—95.

54 The relatively sloppy composition of this stanza, in which six of seven lines begin with "And," suggests further that it, the Latin, and the extra line in the preceding stanza, may represent late, hasty revisions. (In the manuscript, the Latin and its English paraphrase are concatenated at the top of a page and appear as one extended stanza.) Perhaps Ashby felt that he was not sufficiently getting his point across.

55 Simpson has called attention to the Hoccleveaen nature of these lines, noting in addition how pathetically futile they are, given that Ashby's patron is in exile; see *Reform*, p. 225.

56 For a brief account of how the necessity of marketing affected Caxton's techniques of constructing literary authority, see David R. Carlson, "Chaucer, Humanism, and Printing: Conditions of Authorship in

Fifteenth-Century England," *University of Toronto Quarterly* 64 (1995), 274–88. See also Seth Lerer, "William Caxton," in *Cambridge History*, ed. Wallace, pp. 720–38, which is a revised version of his chapter on Caxton in *Chaucer and His Readers*, pp. 147–75.

57 Cited from *Caxton's Own Prose*, ed. N. F. Blake (London: André Deutsch Ltd., 1973), p. 99. For a much more detailed account of Caxton's production of literary authority in the *Recuyell* than I can offer here, see William Kuskin, "Reading Caxton: Transformations in Capital, Authority, Print, and Persona in the Late Fifteenth Century," *New Medieval Literatures* 3 (1999), 149–83. See also Kuskin's "Caxton's Worthies Series: The Production of Literary Culture," *ELH* 66 (1999), 511–51, and N. F. Blake, "John Lydgate and William Caxton," *Leeds Studies in English* n.s. 16 (1985), 272–87.

58 Lerer, whose comments on the *Book of Curtesye* have guided mine, suggests that it functions for Caxton as a kind of program statement: "The assessments of the *Book of Curtesye* provided Caxton with the aesthetic criteria and social functions of vernacular authorial writing, and his editions were calibrated to conform to its precepts" ("William Caxton," p. 726). Early in his career, needing to establish himself as a legitimate purveyor of high-culture English literature, Caxton does not stray far from texts with relatively straightforward associations with the Lydgatean tradition. In addition to texts by Lydgate himself, Caxton's first phase is replete with works by the monk's disciples or predecessors. For example, in 1476 he prints Lydgate's *The Churl and the Bird* and *The Debate of the Horse, Sheep and Goose*, Burgh's *Disticha Catonis*, and Chaucer's *Canterbury Tales*; in 1477, Lydgate's *Temple of Glas* and *Stans puer ad mensam* and Chaucer's *Anelida and Arcite* and *Parliament of Fowls*; in 1478, Chaucer's *Boece*; in 1482, the Lydgatean *Court of Sapience*; in 1483, Gower's *Confessio Amantis* and Chaucer's *Troilus and Criseyde* and *House of Fame*; and, in 1484, Lydgate's *Life of Our Lady*. For these dates, see N. F. Blake, "William Caxton," in *Authors of the Middle Ages: English Writers of the Late Middle Ages: Nos. 7–11*, ed. M. C. Seymour (Aldershot: Variorum, 1996), pp. 57–63. That some of these texts derived from the same set of manuscript booklets that contains Ashby's *A Prisoner's Reflections* (as argued by Mooney, "Scribes and Booklets") adds yet another note of pathos to the signet clerk's poetic career, as thus his emaciated attempt to replicate a Lydgatean laureateship was shortly followed by his exclusion from the extension of Lydgateanism into the era of print.

59 Cited from *Caxton's Book of Curtesye*, ed. Frederick J. Furnivall, EETS e.s. 3 (London: N. Trübner & Co., 1868), lines 330–36 of the text from Oxford, Oriel College MS 79. As Furnivall shows in his preface (relying on analysis by Skeat), the likely earlier Oriel text, though substantially the same, is superior to Caxton's (see pp. vi–vii). All subsequent citations are given by line number to this text. Furnivall also supplies Caxton's text on the facing page and that of Oxford, Balliol College MS 354 at the page bottom. For bibliographical information on this work, see Jonathan Nicholls,

The Matter of Courtesy: Medieval Courtesy Books and the Gawain-Poet
(Woodbridge: D. S. Brewer, 1985), pp. 191–92.

60 See Knapp, *Bureaucratic Muse*, pp. 108–9.

61 The lament technically occupies the first three stanzas of the paean to
   Lydgate, which, as they share a refrain in their last line, form a ballad (see, in
   the edition's preface, Skeat's comments, quoted by Furnivall, p. vi). Caxton's
   text lacks the second stanza, which more than the others mimics Lydgate's
   laments for Chaucer.

62 For a perceptive overview of the history of the laureateship, see Trapp,
   "The Poet Laureate."

63 Strangely, in Caxton's own *Caton* – a translation of a prose commentary
   based on the Latin *Disticha* that he published in 1484, after Burgh's death –
   he does mention Burgh and his English version of the *Disticha*, and yet he
   nowhere indicates that he has printed by then three editions of the work. For
   a brief discussion of Caxton and Burgh, see Blake's notes to *Caton* in *Caxton's
   Own Prose*, p. 131.

64 *Caxton's Own Prose*, p. 80.

65 See Lerer, *Chaucer and His Readers*, p. 151. My argument about Caxton and
   the laureateship in this paragraph owes a debt to this study and Lerer's later
   essay, "William Caxton."

5   THE TRACE OF LYDGATE: STEPHEN HAWES, ALEXANDER
    BARCLAY, AND JOHN SKELTON

 1 The full text of this grant survives in the records of Henry's privy purse;
   see Albert Frederick Pollard, *The Reign of Henry VII from Contemporary
   Sources*, 3 vols. (London: Longmans, Green and Co., 1914), vol. II,
   pp. 233–34, from which source also comes the epithet "Blynde Poete."
   For recent studies of André, see David R. Carlson, *English Humanist
   Books: Writers and Patrons, Manuscript and Print, 1475–1525* (Toronto:
   University of Toronto Press, 1993), pp. 60–81; and Daniel Hobbins,
   "Arsenal MS 360 as a Witness to the Career and Writings of Bernard
   André," *Humanistica Lovaniensia* 50 (2001), 161–98. For the nature of
   André's oeuvre, see David R. Carlson, "The Writings of Bernard André
   (c.1450–c.1522)," *Renaissance Studies* 12 (1998), 229–50. Other foreign-
   born writers employed by Henry VII include Pietro Carmeliano and
   Giovanni and Silvestro Gigli. For an overview of the work and roles of
   these writers, see William Nelson, *John Skelton, Laureate* (New York:
   Columbia University Press, 1939), pp. 4–39.

 2 This is the view of Gordon Kipling, *The Triumph of Honour: Burgundian
   Origins of the Elizabethan Renaissance* (The Hague: Leiden University Press,
   1977); see esp. pp. 16–20.

 3 According to Kipling, Henry VII's interventions into other aspects of high
   culture were also noteworthy for just this tendency toward institutionalization: see "Henry VII and the Origins of Tudor Patronage," in *Patronage in*

the Renaissance, ed. Guy Fitch Lytle and Stephen Orgel (Princeton: Princeton University Press, 1981), pp. 117–64.

4 David R. Carlson, "Reputation and Duplicity: The Texts and Contexts of Thomas More's Epigram on Bernard André," *ELH* 58 (1991), 261–81 (262).

5 Carlson, "Reputation and Duplicity," esp. 270–72, shows how the internecine verbal battles among early Tudor writers – in this case, between the humanist Thomas More and the laureate André – were a product of just this tension between claims of intellectual disinterest and practices of political interest.

6 Unless otherwise specified, in this chapter I draw all biographical and bibliographical information about these three poets from, respectively, *Stephen Hawes: The Minor Poems*, ed. Florence W. Gluck and Alice B. Morgan, EETS o.s. 271 (London: Oxford University Press, 1974), pp. xi–xiv (henceforth cited as Gluck and Morgan); *Eclogues of Alexander Barclay*, ed. Beatrice White, EETS o.s. 175 (London: Oxford University Press, 1938), pp. i–liv; and *John Skelton: The Complete English Poems*, ed. John Scattergood (New Haven: Yale University Press, 1983), pp. 17–19. All citations of Hawes's poetry, except for his *Pastime of Pleasure*, are from Gluck and Morgan; all citations of Barclay's *Eclogues* are from White; and all citations of Skelton (including translations of his Latin) are from Scattergood. I have added punctuation to Gluck and Morgan and modified that of Barclay's *Eclogues*.

7 See John Bale, *Scriptorum illustrium maioris Brytanniae* (Basle: Apud I. Oporinum, 1557), p. 632, reprinted in Gluck and Morgan, pp. xi–xii. I quote the translation of Bale's Latin from A. S. G. Edwards, *Stephen Hawes* (Boston: Twayne Publishers, 1983), p. 1.

8 This note follows the table of contents of *The Example of Vertu;* see Gluck and Morgan, p. 2. Similar notes, with slight variations of wording, accompany most of Hawes's other poems.

9 Anthony à Wood and Philip Bliss, *Athenæ Oxonienses* (New York: Burt Franklin, 1967), p. 1, col. 9. At least one piece of external evidence survives that would appear to corroborate this claim – a record of payment of ten shillings in 1506 "for a ballet that he gave to the kings grace in rewarde": see Edwards, *Stephen Hawes*, p. 2.

10 Wood and Bliss, *Athenæ Oxonienses*, p. 1, cols. 9–10.

11 The quotation is from Spearing, *Medieval to Renaissance*, p. 224; for Edwards's discussion of Hawes and Lydgate, see *Stephen Hawes*, pp. 14–20.

12 All citations of the *Pastime* are from *The Pastime of Pleasure*, ed. William Edward Mead, EETS o.s. 173 (London: Oxford University Press, 1928). I have supplied punctuation and modernized long "s."

13 See Ebin, *Illuminator*, pp. 133–62.

14 In respect to his specific terminology, Hawes perhaps got more from the prologue to Lydgate's popular *Churl and the Bird*. There Lydgate describes more explicitly the methodology of "poetes laureate," who "Bi dirk parables ful conveyent ... write wondirful liknessis,/And vndir covert kepte

hem silf ful cloos" (MP II, 15–30). But only in the prologue to *Isopes Fabules* does Lydgate clearly relate this methodology to the mode of self-presentation that proves so important to Hawes.

15 See MED *fainen* v. 2(a) and *feining* ger. 2(a), and *contreven* v. 2[a]. Hawes repeats this dual description of the monk's activities in the prologue to *The Conuercyon of Swerers*, 24.

16 See MED *trace* n.(1). Hawes's use of the noun spans the first three major meanings: 1(c), "folwen… ~, to follow (someone's) example, emulate (someone's) way of life or actions"; 2(b), "a mark or sign left by the passage or presence of something"; and 3(a), "A footstep." Obviously fond of this multivalent image, Hawes repeats it twice more in the course of the poem: near the end of the above-mentioned eulogy of Lydgate (1395) and, tellingly, in the work's very last stanza (5812).

17 Alistair Fox, *Politics and Literature in the Reigns of Henry VII and Henry VIII* (Oxford: Basil Blackwell, 1989), p. 64. Fox would like to see a reference to Skelton here as well, but Skelton was most likely still in Diss at this point — see Greg Walker, *John Skelton and the Politics of the 1520s* (Cambridge: Cambridge University Press, 1988), pp. 43–46. André received the additional title of king's historiographer probably in 1500, when he began work on the *Vita Henrici Septimi* — see Hobbins, "Arsenal MS 360," 176.

18 Seth Lerer, *Courtly Letters in the Age of Henry VIII* (Cambridge: Cambridge University Press, 1997), pp. 50–51.

19 I owe this suggestion to Lauryn S. Mayer.

20 For the evidence that suggests (to me convincingly) that Pucell in this poem is to be identified with Mary Tudor, see the note in Gluck and Morgan, p. 154. Fox, rather than understanding the erotic to be standing in for the sociopolitical, believes instead that they coexist — that is, he believes that Hawes was in fact in love with Mary Tudor, and that in the *Conforte* Hawes seeks consolation for both the loss of his court position and the impossibility of his amorous suit (see *Politics and Literature*, p. 56). I find it more likely, given the well-established romance convention of the lower-born suitor, that Hawes was seizing on an allegorical vehicle the tenor of which would be more or less obvious to his readers. For similar comments on this point and, more generally, about Hawes's relationship with and uses of the literary past, see Simpson, *Reform*, pp. 180–83.

21 As Gluck and Morgan note (p. 152), Princess Mary was engaged to Charles from 1507 to 1514, at which point she married Louis XII of France.

22 For these identifications, see especially lines 2032–94.

23 These similarities between the *Conforte* and Wyatt's poetry have not gone unnoticed; see, for example, Colin Burrow, "The Experience of Exclusion: Literature and Politics in the Reigns of Henry VII and Henry VIII," in *Cambridge History*, ed. Wallace, pp. 793–820 (p. 797).

24 For the role of Queen Elizabeth in Spenser's strategies of self-representation, see, among other studies, Montrose, "The Elizabethan Subject." Although early modernists and medievalists alike are typically skeptical of Hawes's

influence on Spenser, for an exception, see Carol V. Kaske, "How Spenser Really Used Stephen Hawes in the Legend of Holiness," in *Unfolded Tales: Essays on Renaissance Romance*, ed. George M. Logan and Gordon Teskey (Ithaca: Cornell University Press, 1989), pp. 119–36.

25 For a reproduction of this woodcut, which was not a likeness of Barclay but which Pynson used exclusively for Barclay's books, see David R. Carlson, "Alexander Barclay," in *Sixteenth-Century British Nondramatic Writers. First Series*, ed. David A. Richardson, Dictionary of Literary Biography 132 (Detroit: Gale Research Inc., 1993), pp. 36–47 (p. 37). For a discussion of the woodcut, see Carlson's "Alexander Barclay and Richard Pynson: A Tudor Printer and His Writer," *Anglia* 113 (1995), 283–302 (296–97).

26 Scholars disagree about Barclay's national origin; if not a Scot, he was probably an English native of Scottish heritage.

27 J. S. Brewer (ed.) *Letters and Papers, Foreign and Domestic, of the Reign of Henry VIII*, 21 vols. (London: Longman & Co., and Trübner & Co., 1872), vol. III, p. 259.

28 See MP II, no. 30.

29 See Brewer (ed.), *Letters and Papers*, vol. IV, p. 2083. I quote White's translation of Rinck's Latin (*Eclogues*, p. xlii).

30 See R. J. Lyall, "Alexander Barclay and the Edwardian Reformation 1548–52," *Review of English Studies* 20 (1969), 455–61.

31 This poetics appears elsewhere in Barclay's oeuvre as well; for a particularly straightforward example, see lines 1–133 in *The Life of St. George*, ed. William Nelson, EETS o.s. 230 (London: Oxford University Press, 1955). In a short space, this passage evolves from an aureate, self-naming address to Thomas Howard, duke of Norfolk; to instructions to this patron on the proper relations between poets and princes; to complaint about "raylynge poetes" (113) and, in particular, "he which is lawreat [i.e., Skelton]" (118); to a self-serving, falsely humble assertion that he will "wryte," with the help of "glorious mary," in "accorde" with his "degree" (123, 121, 126).

32 Also perhaps like the *Fall*, the source of which was not in fact Boccaccio's Latin but Laurent de Premierfait's French, the primary source of the *Ship* may really have been Pierre Rivière's French translation of Locher, *La Nef des folz du monde*; see Edelgard DuBruck, "Barclay's Veritable Source: A *Ship of Fools* by Pierre Rivière," *Michigan Academician* 4 (1971), 67–75. DuBruck disputes the conclusions of Aurelius Pompen, *The English Versions of "The Ship of Fools"* (London: Longmans, Green and Co., 1925), pp. 309–10, who contends that, while Barclay drew on Rivière, he relied mostly on Locher.

33 For Lydgate's "medievalizing" of Boccaccio's *De casibus*, see Pearsall, *John Lydgate*, pp. 223–54. (For different views, see Strohm, *Politique*, pp. 89–104, and Nolan, "Lydgate's Literary History.") For Barclay's retrograde transformation of Brant's *Narrenschiff*, see the introduction to the most recent edition of the *Ship*, "A Critical Edition of Alexander Barclay's *Ship of Fools* (1509)," ed. David Rollin Anderson (Ph.D. dissertation, Case Western

Reserve University, 1974). Strohm, Nolan, and many others have persuasively described the interpretative pitfalls of epochal assumptions that categorically distinguish medieval from Renaissance; nonetheless, it is difficult to avoid the conclusion that Lydgate and Barclay both possessed a high regard for traditional ways of thinking.

34 Cited from Anderson's edition, p. 347, lines 16–18, and p. 348, lines 1–2, emphases added. All subsequent citations of the *Ship* are to this edition and given in the text by page and line number. The punctuation is mine. I have also consulted *The Ship of Fools*, ed. T. H. Jamieson (Edinburgh: William Paterson, 1874), and, through EEBO, examined Pynson's 1509 edition (STC 3545), accessed 9 April 2003.

35 For Lydgate's title, see Bergen's note in the *Fall of Princes*, vol. I, p. ix. Lydgate at first refers to Boccaccio's work as "the fall of nobles" (e.g., 1.51), but later – initially with reference to Chaucer's monk's *De casibus* – uses "the fall of pryncis" (e.g., 1.249).

36 Pompen notes the relevance of Pynson's print of the *Fall* in *English Versions*, p. 98.

37 The prominence of Barclay's name in these opening pages is well attested by Jamieson's edition, which reproduces many of the features of Pynson's. Although Brant's and Locher's names do appear several times in the Latin prefatory matter that Jamieson does not reproduce, this material is, properly speaking, Locher's rather than Barclay's and is presented as such. In the material that appears as other than mere reprinting, Barclay's name is by far the most prevalent.

38 This insistence on the multiplicity of the *Ship*'s sources appears as early as Pynson's notice, immediately following the opening Latin dedication to Thomas Cornish: "This present Boke named the Shyp of folys of the worlde was translated in the college of saynt mary Otery in the counte of Deuonshyre, out of Laten, Frenche, and Doche into Englysshe tonge by Alexander Barclay Preste" (p. 136). This claim is at best misleading and at worst a lie: although some debate remains as to whether the "Laten" or the tellingly unattributed "Frenche" was Barclay's primary source, all agree that he took little and most likely nothing from the "Doche."

39 See Barclay, "A Critical Edition," pp. 849–50.

40 All surviving copies of the *Eclogues* before Cawood's 1570 edition (STC 3546, a volume that also includes the *Ship of Fools* and the *Mirrour of Good Manners*) are partial and, as Carlson puts it, "evidently derivative rather than authorized, reprints rather than first editions" ("A Tudor Printer," 298; see also *Eclogues*, ed. White, pp. lvi–lx). The earliest is Wynkyn de Worde's edition of just the fifth eclogue in c.1518.

41 John Richie Schultz, "The Method of Barclay's Eclogues," *Journal of English and Germanic Philology* 32 (1933), 549–71 (551).

42 For a good discussion of the nature, consistency, and extensiveness of Barclay's localization of the *Eclogues*, see Schultz, "Barclay's Eclogues," 565–67.

43 For these identifications, see White's introduction, *Eclogues*, pp. xx–xxiv.

44 I cite Piccolomini's Latin from White's edition. A few lines below, Barclay renders Piccolomini's "Philsophorum … Poëtarum" as "Philosophers, Poetes, and Oratours" (2.331). Apparently, for Barclay these roles were functionally similar; each involved a wise, elegant user of language who, ideally, served the interests of the State by speaking "playne veritie" to the prince.

45 We do not know for certain the order in which Barclay composed the individual eclogues. But White makes a strong case from internal evidence and print history that Barclay probably wrote them and certainly intended them to appear in the order in which they stand: see *Eclogues*, pp. lvi–lx.

46 In this allusion he follows Mantuan, who was himself a (Carmelite) monk.

47 See White's comments in *Eclogues*, pp. xxiv–xxv.

48 Barclay entitles this elegy "The description of the Tovvre of vertue and honour, into the which the noble Hawarde contended to enter by worthy actes of chiualry" (interlinear, following 4.822). White contends that its inspiration is the *Temple d'honneur et de vertu* of Jean Lemaire de Belges (see her comparison of the works in *Eclogues*, pp. 258–62). But R. J. Lyall, "Tradition and Innovation in Alexander Barclay's 'Towre of Vertue and Honoure,'" *Review of English Studies* n.s. 23 (1972), 1–18, disagrees, finding that Barclay takes only the title and a few details from the *Temple d'honneur*. Lyall, in fact, sees Lydgate's *Fall of Princes* as a more significant influence. Carlson supposes it was originally an independent piece ("Alexander Barclay," p. 42), which, if the case, makes Barclay's redeployment of it in the context of this eclogue all the more revealing of his pedagogical intentions.

49 I am assuming that these lines were written after Skelton had returned to court in 1512–13, which is likely, given Edward Howard's death in 1513.

50 For these meanings of "curiositee," see MED *curiousite* n. 1(a) and 2(b), respectively.

51 See 4.862, 919, 1073, and 1091.

52 For one speculation on this matter, see Candace Barrington, "'Misframed Fables': Barclay's Gower and the Wantonness of Performance," *Mediaevalia* 24 (2003), 195–225.

53 Nelson, *John Skelton*; H. L. R. Edwards, *Skelton: The Life and Times of an Early Tudor Poet* (London: Jonathan Cape, 1949); and Walker, *John Skelton*.

54 Although the matter has not been conclusively settled, most scholars believe that Skelton left court for Diss against his wishes. Fox, holding to the minority viewpoint, believes that the poet left of his own will because of his acute perception of the court's inherently corrupting influence, as Skelton documents in his 1498 *Bowge of Courte* (see Fox, *Politics and Literature*, pp. 25–36). But casting doubt on this supposition are the five years or so that elapsed between the completion of the *Bowge* and Skelton's departure from court, as well as the poet's unmistakable eagerness to return upon Henry VIII's accession in 1509.

55 Walker calls attention to the full duration of Skelton's Westminster exile, during which time he wrote some of his greatest poems – but not, apparently, in any official capacity (*John Skelton*, pp. 47–49). Fox supplies a detailed but somewhat speculative explanation of the origins of the poet's feud with Wolsey in *Politics and Literature*, pp. 131–55.

56 Walker, *John Skelton*, p. 50.

57 For this dating system and the poems in which it appears, see Scattergood's note to the end of *A Lawde and Prayse Made for Our Sovereigne Lord the King* in *John Skelton*, p. 420.

58 John Kay translated *The Siege of Rhodes* into English prose for Edward IV in 1482, in the beginning of which text he calls himself the king's "humble poete lawreate": see *The Siege of Rhodes* (London?: J. Lettou? and W. de Machlinia?, 1482), STC 4594, accessed via EEBO, 9 April 2003. See also Nelson, *John Skelton*, p. 40.

59 Stephen Dickey, "Seven Come Eleven: Gambling for the Laurel in *The Bowge of Courte*," *Yearbook of English Studies* 22 (1992), 238–54 (238). Dickey counts 37 works in Scattergood's edition by enumerating each of the separate poems in such collective entries as *Dyuyers Baletys and Dyties Solacyous*. We cannot be sure, of course, that the titular instances of the epithet are the work of the poet and not the printer (or scribe), although A. S. G. Edwards, "Skelton's English Poems in Print and Manuscript," *Trivium* 31 (1999), 87–100, believes it likely that Skelton exerted influence in this respect in the printed editions produced in his lifetime. Moreover, the sheer consistency of the manner in which Skelton mentions his laureateship and the frequency with which he does – often repeating it several times in the same work, in Latin as well as in English – suggest that such titles, even when not the work of the author, imitate closely his strategies of self-representation.

60 This synonymy, as Lerer points out, is similar to that achieved much more famously by Petrarch and, moreover, had a similarly exclusionary impact on other poets: see Lerer, *Chaucer and His Readers*, p. 179.

61 To say that this poem is quintessentially Lydgatean is not, however, to say that it lacks complexity, a distinct perception of its political valences and aims, and even self-doubt – all of which have been demonstrated persuasively for the poem by Kevin J. Gustafson, "Rebellion, Treachery and Poetic Identity in Skelton's *Dolorous Dethe*," *Neophilologus* 82 (1998), 645–59.

62 Closely related to this aspect of his poetics, but beyond the scope of this study, is Skelton's development of his characteristic verse form, the "Skeltonics" exemplified in the above passage from *Ware the Hauke*. For a sustained argument about the crucial importance for Skelton of the question of style, see Stanley E. Fish, *John Skelton's Poetry* (New Haven: Yale University Press, 1965).

63 For this point, see Burrow, "Experience of Exclusion," p. 799.

64 Vincent Gillespie, "Justification by Faith: Skelton's *Replycacion*," in *The Long Fifteenth Century*, ed. Cooper and Mapstone, pp. 273–311 (p. 283).

65 Walker, *John Skelton*, p. 89.

66 Fox, *Politics and Literature*, pp. 158–60. See also Spearing, *Medieval to Renaissance*, p. 268.

67 In addition, as Skelton's later refrain (which begins, "Syn Dewcalyons flodde" [455 and following]) indicates, in the mythographical horizon of this poem stands an allusion to Psyttacus, the wise son of Deucalion and Pyrrha and grandson of Prometheus. In his old age, Psyttacus asked the gods to remove him from everyday affairs. They complied, turning him into a parrot. Skelton probably encountered the story of Psyttacus in Boccaccio's *De genealogia deorum*. Fox, *Politics and Literature*, p. 159, supplies a translation of the relevant passage.

68 Skelton's presence is signaled throughout this passage not only through the fact that it is Parott who is speaking but also through the allusion to Pysttacus repeated in each of these stanzas' refrain.

69 For a similar — and more detailed — account of *Speke Parott*, see Greg Walker, "'Ordered Confusion'?: The Crisis of Authority in Skelton's *Speke Parott*," *Spenser Studies* 10 (1992), 213–28.

70 It may be noted here that, for the most part, the Latin that appears in Skelton's otherwise vernacular poetry has a much more integral relationship with the English than the two have in, say, Gower's. In the latter's English poems, the Latin represents an entirely distinct discourse, in which, for example, the author may appear as himself but understood as categorically different from the first-person speaker of the English verse. In contrast, in Skelton's poetry, while the Latin is often used to make more direct and authoritative statements, its voice is, in most cases, not essentially different from that of the English.

71 Walker makes a similar point when accounting for the inconsistency of Skelton's criticism of Wolsey in *Speke Parott* and *Why Come Ye*: see *Persuasive Fictions: Faction, Faith and Political Culture in the Reign of Henry VIII* (Aldershot: Scolar Press, 1996), p. 69.

72 For a detailed outline of these stages, see Appendix 1 in *The Latin Writings of John Skelton*, ed. David R. Carlson, *Studies in Philology* 88 (1991), pp. 1–125 (102–109).

73 A. C. Spearing, *Medieval Dream-Poetry* (Cambridge: Cambridge University Press, 1976), p. 217.

74 For one such reading, see David A. Loewenstein, "Skelton's Triumph: The *Garland of Laurel* and Literary Fame," *Neophilologus* 68 (1984), 611–22.

75 See, for example, Fish, *John Skelton's Poetry*, pp. 228–30, and Loewenstein, "Skelton's Triumph," 617.

76 As Gillespie remarks, "Here, perhaps for the first time explicitly in all his writings, Skelton is able to conflate his laureate status with his perception of his role as the priest-prophet-poet" ("Justification by Faith," p. 293). See also Jane Griffiths, "A Contradiction in Terms: Skelton's 'effecte energiall' in *A Replycacion*," *Renaissance Studies* 17 (2003), 55–68, who concludes that in this passage Skelton presents the poet "as the figure of God on earth" (68).

77 See Fox, *Politics and Literature*, p. 204. The Latin epigraph appears without line numbers on p. 372 in Scattergood's edition.

78 Lydgate's *Fall of Princes* had a longer afterlife than Lydgateanism more generally, having an impact on, in particular, the *Mirror of Magistrates*; for this and other texts, see Strohm, *Politique*, 104–10.

EPILOGUE: SIR THOMAS WYATT: ANTI-LAUREATE

1 See *The Yale Edition of the Shorter Poems of Edmund Spenser*, ed. William A. Oram et al. (New Haven: Yale University Press, 1989), p. 13 and pp. 32–33.

2 See Kenneth Muir, *Life and Letters of Sir Thomas Wyatt* (Liverpool: Liverpool University Press, 1963), p. 4.

3 Among the several investigations of Wyatt's complex relation to Chaucer and the significance of that relation in respect to Henrician politics, see John Watkins, "'Wrastling for this world': Wyatt and the Tudor Canonization of Chaucer," in *Refiguring Chaucer in the Renaissance*, ed. Theresa M. Krier (Gainesville: University Press of Florida, 1998), pp. 21–39; and Lerer, *Courtly Letters*, Chapter 5, esp. pp. 166–77. Both studies discuss the influence of "Truth" on Wyatt's poetry and the allusions mentioned above, which occur in nos. CV at line 50 and CVII at line 75 in *Collected Poems of Sir Thomas Wyatt*, ed. Kenneth Muir and Patricia Thomson (Liverpool: Liverpool University Press, 1969), a volume I henceforth refer to as M&T and from which I take all citations of Wyatt's poetry.

4 *The Arte of English Poesie*, ed. Gladys Doidge Willcock and Alice Walker (Cambridge: Cambridge University Press, 1936), p. 60 (bk. 1, ch. 31), p. 84 (bk. 2, ch. 9). I have modernized long "s."

5 Derek Pearsall (ed.), *Chaucer to Spenser: An Anthology of Writings in English 1375–1575* (Oxford: Blackwell Publishers Ltd, 1999), p. 607, emphasis in the original. Patricia Thomson, who has examined in detail the aesthetic overlap between Wyatt and Skelton, arrives at essentially the same conclusion: see her "Wyatt and Surrey," in *English Poetry and Prose, 1540–1674*, ed. Christopher Ricks (London: Barrie and Jenkins, 1970), pp. 19–40. Even Lerer, *Courtly Letters*, who so richly explores the complexities of an early Tudor literary culture that includes Hawes and Skelton as well as Wyatt, tends to read Wyatt directly against the precedent of Chaucer rather than against his immediate predecessors.

6 *Chaucer to Spenser*, p. 607. Pearsall here is comparing the self-representational strategies of Wyatt and Charles d'Orléans. According to him, while Charles's "poetic persona is a painted picture, conventionally coloured, in two dimensions[,] Wyatt's is a bold sculpted relief, surprising, individual, dramatic" (p. 608).

7 Stephen Greenblatt, *Renaissance Self-Fashioning from More to Shakespeare* (Chicago: University of Chicago Press, 1980), Chapter 3, pp. 115–56. Subsequent citations of Greenblatt are to this study and given in the text

by page number. By singling out Greenblatt as representative, I do not mean to imply the existence of critical consensus. Like all seminal studies, Greenblatt's has had its share of naysayers and correctives: see, for example, Jonathan V. Crewe, *Trials of Authorship: Anterior Forms and Poetic Reconstruction from Wyatt to Shakespeare* (Berkeley: University of California Press, 1990), esp. Chapter 1 on Wyatt, pp. 23—47.

8 Line 11 of no. 190 in *Petrarch's Lyric Poems: The "Rime sparse" and Other Lyrics*, ed. and trans. Robert M. Durling (Cambridge, Mass.: Harvard University Press, 1976), which I henceforth cite as *Rime*. Wyatt's version is no. 7 in M&T, and I cite line 13. For a different, but not wholly incongruent, reading of Wyatt's adaptation of Petrarch in this lyric, see Crewe, *Trials of Authorship*, pp. 37—45.

9 Cf. Spearing, *Medieval to Renaissance*, who asserts, "If we are to grasp the full weight of the lyrics, we need perhaps to read them as part of the same body of work as the satires, and to recognize that for Wyatt private and public life are different faces of the same experience" (p. 310).

10 Among the many other critics whom one may cite to corroborate this, see Perez Zagorin, "Sir Thomas Wyatt and the Court of Henry VIII: The Courtier's Ambivalence," *Journal of Medieval and Renaissance Studies* 23 (1993), 113—41, e.g., in his remark about "The piller pearisht" (M&T 236): "Although this sonnet is an imitation of Petrarch's *Rime*... it resounds with authentic personal feeling" (123 n. 44). For a nuanced, sustained investigation of the circumstances and mechanisms that produce this effect, see Stephen Merriam Foley, *Sir Thomas Wyatt* (Boston: Twayne Publishers, 1990), esp. the second chapter, "Signatures," pp. 34—56.

11 See Watkins, "'Wrastling,'" p. 22 and pp. 26—27.

12 For this point, see Spearing, *Medieval to Renaissance*, p. 279. Simpson locates the reasons for Wyatt's formal choices in the absolutist political conditions of Henrician England: see *Reform*, pp. 155—60 and, more generally, the encompassing Chapter 4, pp. 121—90. One possible politically motivated occasional poem firmly in the Wyatt canon is M&T 104, the odd, unfinished "Jopas' Song" that concludes the Egerton manuscript.

13 He was, more precisely, a "serious amateur," a term Richard Helgerson uses to describe poets such as Donne, who produced their work as amateurs but who wrote with an intensity that belied the putatively recreational nature of their verse: see *Self-Crowned Laureates*, p. 39. Although Helgerson focuses on early modern poets of the generations following Wyatt, my depiction of Wyatt's location in the "literary system" of his day owes much to this study.

14 Woodville's literary enterprises include the translations *The Dictes and Sayings of the Philosophers* (which was also translated by Ashby) and the *Moral Proverbs* of Christine de Pizan, both among the very earliest products of Caxton's English press: see *Caxton's Own Prose*, nos. 29 and 77, and, for a brief discussion of Woodville, Ross, *Edward IV*, pp. 97—98.

15 See Muir, *Life and Letters*, pp. 9—10.

16 See Spearing, *Medieval to Renaissance*, p. 280.

17 For this translation and Wyatt's dedication to Catherine, in which he explains why he abandoned the first task, see M&T Appendix B, pp. 440–63.

18 For this point, see Burrow, "Experience of Exclusion," p. 810.

19 See W. A. Sessions, "Surrey's Wyatt, Autumn 1542 and the New Poet," in *Rethinking the Henrician Era: Essays on Early Tudor Texts and Contexts*, ed. Peter C. Herman (Urbana: University of Illinois Press, 1994), pp. 168–92. Sessions remarks that the "gesture of self-laureation" assumed by the earl in his 1542 elegy for Wyatt (which Surrey uncharacteristically allowed to be printed) may have been "learned from the close family friend, John Skelton, who may have been his tutor" (p. 192 n. 34).

20 I cite Muir's translation of Leland's Latin in *Life and Letters*, p. 268; subsequent references are given in the text by page number. For the original, see John Leland, *Naeniae in mortem Thomae Viati equitis incomparabilis* (London: R. Wolfe, 1542), STC 15446, accessed via EEBO, 28 June 2004. For discussion, see Sessions, "Surrey's Wyatt"; Simpson, *Reform*, p. 124; and Foley, *Sir Thomas Wyatt*, esp. pp. 29–32 and p. 97.

21 I cite the translation of Petrarch's Latin in Wilkins, *Life and Works*, p. 309.

22 Foley, who also conjoins readings of this elegy and "Whoso list to hounte," comes to a similar conclusion: see *Sir Thomas Wyatt*, pp. 97–100.

23 According to Helgerson, the first anti-laureate who understood himself as such was Alexander Pope, who needed the first official laureate, Dryden, as his foil; see *Self-Crowned Laureates*, p. 11. Wyatt's confrontation with the laureate-credentialed Skelton forms an earlier, differently inflected parallel.

24 Cited from *Wordsworth: Poetical Works*, ed. Thomas Hutchinson and Ernest de Selincourt (Oxford: Oxford University Press, 1936), lines 9–14. Wordsworth composed this set of sonnets during 1839–40. He accepted the laureateship in 1843.

Works cited

Alighieri, Dante, *Dante's Il Convivio (The Banquet)*, trans. Richard H. Lansing, New York: Garland Publishing, 1990.

Allan, Alison, "Yorkist Propaganda: Pedigree, Prophecy and the 'British History' in the Reign of Edward IV," in *Patronage, Pedigree and Power in Later Medieval England*, ed. Charles Ross, Gloucester: Alan Sutton, 1979, pp. 171–92.

Allen, Judson Boyce, "Grammar, Poetic Form, and the Lyric Ego: A Medieval *A Priori*," in *Vernacular Poetics in the Middle Ages*, ed. Lois A. Ebin, Kalamazoo: Medieval Institute Publications, 1984, pp. 199–226.

Allmand, Christopher, *Henry V*, London: Methuen, 1992.

Ambrisco, Alan S. and Strohm, Paul, "Succession and Sovereignty in Lydgate's Prologue to *The Troy Book*," *The Chaucer Review* 30 (1995), 40–57.

Annales rerum Anglicarum, in *Letters and Papers Illustrative of the Wars of the English in France during the Reign of Henry the Sixth, King of England*, ed. Joseph Stevenson, Rolls Series 22, 2 vols., London: Longman, Green, Longman, Roberts, and Green, 1864, vol. 2, pt. 2.

Ashby, George, *George Ashby's Poems*, ed. Mary Bateson, EETS e.s. 76, London: Kegan Paul, Trench, Trübner, 1899.

Axton, Richard, "Gower — Chaucer's Heir?," in *Chaucer Traditions: Studies in Honour of Derek Brewer*, ed. Ruth Morse and Barry Windeatt, Cambridge: Cambridge University Press, 1990, pp. 21–38.

Bagley, J. J., *Margaret of Anjou: Queen of England*, London: Herbert Jenkins Ltd., 1948.

Bale, John, *Scriptorum illustrium maioris Brytanniae*, Basle: Apud I. Oporinum, 1557.

Barclay, Alexander, *The Ship of Fools*, ed. T. H. Jamieson, Edinburgh: William Paterson, 1874.

  Eclogues of Alexander Barclay, ed. Beatrice White, EETS o.s. 175, London: Oxford University Press, 1938.

  The Life of St. George, ed. William Nelson, EETS o.s. 230, London: Oxford University Press, 1955.

  "A Critical Edition of Alexander Barclay's *Ship of Fools* (1509)," ed. David Rollin Anderson, Ph.D. dissertation, Case Western Reserve University, 1974.

Barrington, Candace, "'Misframed Fables': Barclay's Gower and the Wantonness of Performance," *Mediaevalia* 24 (2003), 195–225.

Baswell, Christopher, "*Troy Book*: How Lydgate Translates Chaucer into Latin," in *Translation Theory and Practice in the Middle Ages*, ed. Jeanette Beer, Kalamazoo: Medieval Institute Publications, 1997, pp. 215–37.

Bennett, Michael J., "The Court of Richard II and the Promotion of Literature," in *Chaucer's England: Literature in Historical Context*, ed. Barbara A. Hanawalt, Minneapolis: University of Minnesota Press, 1992, pp. 3–20.

Benson, C. David, "Prudence, Othea and Lydgate's Death of Hector," *The American Benedictine Review* 26 (1975), 115–23.

The History of Troy in Middle English Literature: Guido delle Colonne's "Historia Destructionis Troiae" in Medieval England, Woodbridge: D. S. Brewer, 1980.

Blake, N. F., "John Lydgate and William Caxton," *Leeds Studies in English* n.s. 16 (1985), 272–87.

"William Caxton," in *Authors of the Middle Ages: English Writers of the Late Middle Ages: Nos. 7–11*, ed. M. C. Seymour, Aldershot: Variorum, 1996, pp. 1–68.

Blyth, Charles R., "Thomas Hoccleve's Other Master," *Mediaevalia* 16 (1993), 349–59.

Boccaccio, Giovanni, *Opere in versi, Corbaccio, Trattatello in laude di Dante, prose latine, epistole*, ed. Pier Giorgio Ricci, Milano: R. Ricciardi, 1965.

Boccaccio on Poetry: Being the Preface and the Fourteenth and Fifteenth Books of Boccaccio's "Genealogia Deorum Gentilium", trans. Charles G. Osgood, Indianapolis: Bobbs-Merrill Company, 1956.

In Defense of Poetry: Genealogia deorum gentilium liber XIV, ed. Jeremiah Reedy, Toronto: Pontifical Institute of Mediaeval Studies, 1978.

Boffey, Julia, *Manuscripts of English Courtly Love Lyrics in the Later Middle Ages*, Cambridge: D. S. Brewer, 1985.

"Chaucerian Prisoners: The Context of the *Kingis Quair*," in *Chaucer and Fifteenth-Century Poetry*, ed. Boffey and Cowen, pp. 84–102.

Boffey, Julia and Cowen, Janet (eds.), *Chaucer and Fifteenth-Century Poetry*, London: King's College London, 1991.

Boffey, Julia and Edwards, A. S. G., "'Chaucer's Chronicle,' John Shirley, and the Canon of Chaucer's Shorter Poems," *Studies in the Age of Chaucer* 20 (1998), 201–18.

Boffey, Julia and Thompson, John J., "Anthologies and Miscellanies: Production and Choice of Texts," in *Book Production*, ed. Griffiths and Pearsall, pp. 279–315.

Bourdieu, Pierre and Wacquant, Loïc J. D., *An Invitation to Reflexive Sociology*, Chicago: University of Chicago Press, 1992.

Bowers, John M., "Thomas Hoccleve and the Politics of Tradition," *The Chaucer Review* 36 (2002), 352–69.

"Two Professional Readers of Chaucer and Langland: Scribe D and the HM 114 Scribe," *Studies in the Age of Chaucer* 26 (2004), 113–46.

Brewer, J. S. (ed.), *Letters and Papers, Foreign and Domestic, of the Reign of Henry VIII*, 21 vols., London: Longman & Co., and Trübner & Co., 1872.

Brown, Carleton, "Lydgate's Verses on Queen Margaret's Entry into London," *Modern Language Review* 7 (1912), 225–34.

(ed.), *English Lyrics of the XIIIth Century*, Oxford: Clarendon Press, 1932.

Brown, Carleton and Smithers, G. V. (eds.), *Religious Lyrics of the XIVth Century*, 2nd edn, Oxford: Clarendon Press, 1957.

Burrow, Colin, "The Experience of Exclusion: Literature and Politics in the Reigns of Henry VII and Henry VIII," in *Cambridge History*, ed. Wallace, pp. 793–820.

Burrow, J. A., "Autobiographical Poetry in the Middle Ages: The Case of Thomas Hoccleve," *Proceedings of the British Academy* 68 (1982), 389–412.

"Hoccleve's *Series*: Experience and Books," in *Fifteenth-Century Studies*, ed. Robert F. Yeager, Hamden: Archon Books, 1984, pp. 259–73.

Thomas Hoccleve, Aldershot: Variorum, 1994.

"Thomas Hoccleve: Some Redatings," *Review of English Studies* 46 (1995), 366–72.

"Hoccleve and the Middle French Poets," in *The Long Fifteenth Century*, ed. Cooper and Mapstone, pp. 35–49.

"Hoccleve and the 'Court,'" in *Nation, Court, and Culture: New Essays on Fifteenth-Century English Poetry*, ed. Helen Cooney, Dublin: Four Courts Press, 2001, pp. 70–80.

Bynum, Caroline Walker, *Jesus as Mother: Studies in the Spirituality of the High Middle Ages*, Berkeley: University of California Press, 1982.

Calin, William, *The French Tradition and the Literature of Medieval England*, Toronto: University of Toronto Press, 1994.

Cannon, Christopher, *The Making of Chaucer's English: A Study of Words*, Cambridge: Cambridge University Press, 1998.

"Monastic Productions," in *Cambridge History*, ed. Wallace, pp. 316–48.

Carlson, David R., "Reputation and Duplicity: The Texts and Contexts of Thomas More's Epigram on Bernard André," *ELH* 58 (1991), 261–81.

"Alexander Barclay," in *Sixteenth-Century British Nondramatic Writers. First Series*, ed. David A. Richardson, *Dictionary of Literary Biography* 132, Detroit: Gale Research Inc., 1993, pp. 36–47.

English Humanist Books: Writers and Patrons, Manuscript and Print, 1475–1525, Toronto: University of Toronto Press, 1993.

"Alexander Barclay and Richard Pynson: A Tudor Printer and His Writer," *Anglia* 113 (1995), 283–302.

"Chaucer, Humanism and Printing: Conditions of Authorship in Fifteenth-Century England," *University of Toronto Quarterly* 64 (1995), 274–88.

"The Writings of Bernard André (c.1450–c.1522)," *Renaissance Studies* 12 (1998), 229–50.

Caxton's Book of Curtesye, ed. Frederick J. Furnivall, EETS e.s. 3, London: N. Trübner & Co., 1868.

Caxton, William, *Caxton's Own Prose*, ed. N. F. Blake, London: André Deutsch Ltd., 1973.

Chaucer, Geoffrey, *The Riverside Chaucer*, ed. Larry D. Benson, 3rd edn, Boston: Houghton Mifflin Company, 1987.

Christine de Pizan, *L'Avision-Christine: Introduction and Text*, ed. Sister Mary Louis Towner, New York: AMS, 1969.

The Epistle of Othea, ed. Curt F. Bühler, trans. Stephen Scrope, EETS o.s. 264, London: Oxford University Press, 1970.

Christine's Vision, trans. Glenda K. McLeod, New York: Garland Publishing, Inc., 1993.

Epistre Othea, ed. Gabriella Parussa, Geneva: Librarie Droz, S.A., 1999.

Christine de Pizan and Hoccleve, Thomas, *Poems of Cupid, God of Love*, ed. Thelma S. Fenster and Mary Carpenter Erler, Leiden: E. J. Brill, 1990.

Clark, James G., "Thomas Walsingham Reconsidered: Books and Learning at Late-Medieval St. Albans," *Speculum* 77 (2002), 832–60.

Connolly, Margaret, *John Shirley: Book Production and the Noble Household in Fifteenth-Century England*, Aldershot: Ashgate, 1998.

Cooper, Helen and Mapstone, Sally (eds.), *The Long Fifteenth Century: Essays for Douglas Gray*, Oxford: Clarendon Press, 1997.

Crewe, Jonathan V., *Trials of Authorship: Anterior Forms and Poetic Reconstruction from Wyatt to Shakespeare*, Berkeley: University of California Press, 1990.

Curtius, Ernst Robert, *European Literature and the Latin Middle Ages*, trans. Willard R. Trask, Princeton: Princeton University Press, 1990.

Damian-Grint, Peter, *The New Historians of the Twelfth-Century Renaissance: Inventing Vernacular Authority*, Woodbridge: Boydell Press, 1999.

Derrida, Jacques, *Of Grammatology*, trans. Gayatri Chakravorty Spivak, Baltimore: Johns Hopkins University Press, 1974.

Dickey, Stephen, "Seven Come Eleven: Gambling for the Laurel in *The Bowge of Courte*," *Yearbook of English Studies* 22 (1992), 238–54.

Doyle, A. I. and Parkes, M. B., "The Production of Copies of the *Canterbury Tales* and the *Confessio Amantis* in the Early Fifteenth Century," in *Medieval Scribes, Manuscripts & Libraries*, ed. M. B. Parkes and Andrew G. Watson, London: Scolar Press, 1978, pp. 163–210.

Dronke, Peter, *The Medieval Lyric*, 3rd edn, Cambridge: D. S. Brewer, 1996.

DuBruck, Edelgard, "Barclay's Veritable Source: A *Ship of Fools* by Pierre Rivière," *Michigan Academician* 4 (1971), 67–75.

Dwyer, R. A., "Some Readers of John Trevisa," *Notes and Queries* 212 (1967), 291–92.

Ebin, Lois A., *John Lydgate*, Boston: Twayne, 1985.

Illuminator, Makar, Vates: Visions of Poetry in the Fifteenth Century, Lincoln: University of Nebraska Press, 1988.

Edwards, A. S. G., "The Influence and Audience of the *Polychronicon*: Some Observations," *Proceedings of the Leeds Philosophical and Literary Society, Literary and Historical Section* 17 (1980), 113–19.

Stephen Hawes, Boston: Twayne Publishers, 1983.

"John Shirley and the Emulation of Courtly Culture," in *The Court and Cultural Diversity*, ed. Mullally and Thompson, pp. 309—17.

"Skelton's English Poems in Print and Manuscript," *Trivium* 31 (1999), 87—100.

Edwards, A. S. G. and Pearsall, Derek, "The Manuscripts of the Major English Poetic Texts," in *Book Production*, ed. Griffiths and Pearsall, pp. 257—78.

Edwards, H. L. R., *Skelton: The Life and Times of an Early Tudor Poet*, London: Jonathan Cape, 1949.

Ellis, Roger, "Chaucer, Christine de Pizan, and Hoccleve: *The Letter of Cupid*," in *Essays on Thomas Hoccleve*, ed. Catherine Batt, London: Centre for Medieval and Renaissance Studies, Queen Mary and Westfield College, University of London, 1996, pp. 19—54.

Epstein, Robert, "'At the Stremes Hed of Grace': Representations of Prince and Poet in Late Medieval English Court Poetry," Ph.D. dissertation, Princeton University, 1995.

"Chaucer's Scogan and Scogan's Chaucer," *Studies in Philology* 96 (1999), 1—21.

"Prisoners of Reflection: The Fifteenth-Century Poetry of Exile and Imprisonment," *Exemplaria* 15 (2003), 159—98.

Ferguson, Arthur B., *The Articulate Citizen and the English Renaissance*, Durham: Duke University Press, 1965.

Ferster, Judith, *Fictions of Advice: The Literature and Politics of Counsel in Late Medieval England*, Philadelphia: University of Pennsylvania Press, 1996.

Fewer, Colin, "John Lydgate's *Troy Book* and the Ideology of Prudence," *The Chaucer Review* 38 (2004), 229—45.

Fineman, Joel, *Shakespeare's Perjured Eye: The Invention of Poetic Subjectivity in the Sonnets*, Berkeley: University of California Press, 1986.

Fish, Stanley E., *John Skelton's Poetry*, New Haven: Yale University Press, 1965.

Fisher, John H., *The Emergence of Standard English*, Lexington: University Press of Kentucky, 1996.

Fletcher, Bradford York, "An Edition of MS R.3.19 in Trinity College, Cambridge: A Poetical Miscellany of c.1480," Ph.D. dissertation, University of Chicago, 1973.

Foley, Stephen Merriam, *Sir Thomas Wyatt*, Boston: Twayne Publishers, 1990.

Förster, Max, "Die Burghsche Cato-Paraphrase," *Archiv für das Studium der neueren Sprachen und Literaturen* 115 (1905), 298—323.

"Die Burghsche Cato-Paraphrase," *Archiv für das Studium der neueren Sprachen und Literaturen* 116 (1906), 25—40.

Fortescue, Sir John, *De Laudibus Legum Anglie*, ed. and trans. S. B. Chrimes, Cambridge: Cambridge University Press, 1942.

Fox, Alistair, *Politics and Literature in the Reigns of Henry VII and Henry VIII*, Oxford: Basil Blackwell, 1989.

Freeman, Thomas, *Rvbbe, and a Great Cast. Epigrams*, London: T. Montforde, 1614.

Galloway, Andrew, "Writing History in England," in *Cambridge History*, ed. Wallace, pp. 255–83.

Ganim, John M., *Style and Consciousness in Middle English Narrative*, Princeton: Princeton University Press, 1983.

Gillespie, Alexandra, "The Lydgate Canon in Print from 1476 to 1534," *Journal of the Early Book Society* 3 (2000), 59–93.

"'These proverbes yet do last': Lydgate, the Fifth Earl of Northumberland, and Tudor Miscellanies from Print to Manuscript," *Yearbook of English Studies* 33 (2003), 215–32.

Gillespie, Vincent, "Justification by Faith: Skelton's *Replycacion*," in *The Long Fifteenth Century*, ed. Cooper and Mapstone, pp. 273–311.

Gilson, J. P. (ed.), "A Defence of the Proscription of the Yorkists in 1459," *English Historical Review* 26 (1911), 512–25.

Gower, John, *The English Works of John Gower*, ed. G. C. Macaulay, EETS e.s. 81–82, London: Kegan Paul, Trench and Trübner, 1900–1901.

Grady, Frank, "The Lancastrian Gower and the Limits of Exemplarity," *Speculum* 70 (1995), 552–75.

Green, Richard Firth, *Poets and Princepleasers: Literature and the English Court in the Late Middle Ages*, Toronto: University of Toronto Press, 1980.

Greenblatt, Stephen, *Renaissance Self-Fashioning from More to Shakespeare*, Chicago: University of Chicago Press, 1980.

Greimas, Algirdas Julien, *Dictionnaire d l'ancien Francais: Le Moyen Âge*, Paris: Larousse, 1992.

Griffiths, Jane, "A Contradiction in Terms: Skelton's 'effecte energiall' in *A Replycacion*," *Renaissance Studies* 17 (2003), 55–68.

Griffiths, Jeremy and Pearsall, Derek (eds.), *Book Production and Publishing in Britain 1375–1475*, Cambridge: Cambridge University Press, 1989.

Griffiths, Ralph A., *The Reign of King Henry VI: The Exercise of Royal Authority, 1422–1461*, Berkeley: University of California Press, 1981.

Guido delle Colonne, *Historia destructionis Troiae*, ed. Nathaniel Edward Griffin, Cambridge, Mass.: The Mediaeval Academy of America, 1936.

Historia destructionis Troiae, trans. Mary Elizabeth Meek, Bloomington: Indiana University Press, 1974.

Gustafson, Kevin J., "Rebellion, Treachery and Poetic Identity in Skelton's *Dolorous Dethe*," *Neophilologus* 82 (1998), 645–59.

Hammond, E. P. (ed.), "Lament of a Prisoner against Fortune," *Anglia. Zeitschrift für Englische Philologie* 32 (1909), 481–90.

(ed.), *English Verse Between Chaucer and Surrey*, Durham: Duke University Press, 1927.

Hardison Jr., O. B., *The Enduring Monument: A Study of the Idea of Praise in Renaissance Literary Theory and Practice*, Chapel Hill: University of North Carolina Press, 1962.

Hasler, Antony J., "Hoccleve's Unregimented Body," *Paragraph* 13 (1990), 164–83.

Hawes, Stephen, *The Pastime of Pleasure*, ed. William Edward Mead, EETS o.s. 173, London: Oxford University Press, 1928.

Stephen Hawes: The Minor Poems, ed. Florence W. Gluck and Alice B. Morgan, EETS o.s. 271, London: Oxford University Press, 1974.

Helgerson, Richard, *Self-Crowned Laureates: Spenser, Jonson, Milton and the Literary System*, Berkeley: University of California Press, 1983.

Higden, Ranulf, *Polychronicon Ranulphi Higden Monachi Cestrensis; Together with the English Translations of John Trevisa and of an Unknown Writer of the Fifteenth Century*, ed. Churchill Babington, London: Longman & Co., 1865.

Hines, John, Cohen, Nathalie, and Roffey, Simon, "*Iohanannes Gower, Armiger, Poeta*: Records and Memorials of His Life and Death," in *A Companion to Gower*, ed. Siân Echard, Cambridge: D. S. Brewer, 2004, pp. 23–41.

Hobbins, Daniel, "Arsenal MS 360 as a Witness to the Career and Writings of Bernard André," *Humanistica Lovaniensia* 50 (2001), 161–98.

Hoccleve, Thomas, *Hoccleve's Works: The Minor Poems*, ed. Frederick J. Furnivall and I. Gollancz, rev. by Jerome Mitchell and A. I. Doyle, EETS e.s. 61 and 73, London: Oxford University Press, 1970.

Selections from Hoccleve, ed. M. C. Seymour, Oxford: Clarendon Press, 1981.

Thomas Hoccleve's Complaint and Dialogue, ed. J. A. Burrow, EETS o.s. 313, Oxford: Oxford University Press, 1999.

Thomas Hoccleve: The Regiment of Princes, ed. Charles R. Blyth, Kalamazoo: Medieval Institute Publications, 1999.

"*My Compleinte*" *and Other Poems*, ed. Roger Ellis, Exeter: University of Exeter Press, 2001.

Holthausen, F., "Ashby-Studien II," Anglia. Zeitschrift für Englische Philologie 45 (1921), 77–91.

Ignatius, Mary Ann, "Manuscript Format and Text Structure: Christine de Pizan's *Epistre Othea*," *Studies in Medieval Culture* 12 (1978), 121–24.

Ingulph's Chronicle of the Abbey of Croyland, ed. and trans. Henry T. Riley, London: Henry G. Bohn, 1854.

James I, King of Scotland, *The Kingis Quair*, ed. John Norton-Smith, Oxford: Clarendon Press, 1971.

Kane, George, *The Autobiographical Fallacy in Chaucer and Langland Studies*, London: University College London, 1965.

Kaske, Carol V., "How Spenser Really Used Stephen Hawes in the Legend of Holiness," in *Unfolded Tales: Essays on Renaissance Romance*, ed. George M. Logan and Gordon Teskey, Ithaca: Cornell University Press, 1989, pp. 119–36.

Kay, John, *The Siege of Rhodes*, London?: J. Lettou? and W. de Machlinia?, 1482.

Keen, M. H., *England in the Later Middle Ages: A Political History*, London: Routledge, 1973.

Kekewich, Margaret, "The Attainder of the Yorkists in 1459: Two Contemporary Accounts," *Bulletin of the Institute of Historical Research* 55 (1982), 25–34.

Kipling, Gordon, *The Triumph of Honour: Burgundian Origins of the Elizabethan Renaissance*, The Hague: Leiden University Press, 1977.

"Henry VII and the Origins of Tudor Patronage," in *Patronage in the Renaissance*, ed. Guy Fitch Lytle and Stephen Orgel, Princeton: Princeton University Press, 1981, pp. 117–64.

"The London Pageants for Margaret of Anjou: A Medieval Script Restored," *Medieval English Theatre* 4 (1982), 5–27.

Kline, Daniel T., "Father Chaucer and the *Siege of Thebes*: Literary Paternity, Aggressive Deference, and the Prologue to Lydgate's Oedipal Canterbury Tale," *The Chaucer Review* 34 (1999), 217–35.

Knapp, Ethan, *The Bureaucratic Muse: Thomas Hoccleve and the Literature of Late Medieval England*, University Park: Pennsylvania State University Press, 2001.

Kuskin, William, "Caxton's Worthies Series: The Production of Literary Culture," *ELH* 66 (1999), 511–51.

"Reading Caxton: Transformations in Capital, Authority, Print, and Persona in the Late Fifteenth Century," *New Medieval Literatures* 3 (1999), 149–83.

Laȝamon, *Brut*, ed. W. R. R. Barron and S. C. Weinberg, Harlow: Longman Group Limited, 1995.

Laidlaw, J. C., "Christine de Pizan, the Earl of Salisbury and Henry IV," *French Studies* 36 (1982), 129–43.

Lander, J. R., "Attainder and Forfeiture, 1453 to 1509," *Historical Journal* 4 (1961), 119–51.

Langland, William, *Piers Plowman: The B Version*, ed. George Kane and E. Talbot Donaldson, London: Athlone Press, 1975.

Lawton, David, *Chaucer's Narrators*, Cambridge: D. S. Brewer, 1985.

"Dullness and the Fifteenth Century," *ELH* 54 (1987), 761–99.

Leland, John, *Naeniae in mortem Thomae Viati equitis incomparabilis*, London: R. Wolfe, 1542.

Lerer, Seth, *Chaucer and His Readers: Imagining the Author in Late-Medieval England*, Princeton: Princeton University Press, 1993.

Courtly Letters in the Age of Henry VIII, Cambridge: Cambridge University Press, 1997.

"William Caxton," in *Cambridge History*, ed. Wallace, pp. 720–38.

Letters of Queen Margaret of Anjou and Bishop Beckington and Others, ed. Cecil Monro, Westminster: Camden Society, 1863.

Loewenstein, David A., "Skelton's Triumph: The *Garland of Laurel* and Literary Fame," *Neophilologus* 68 (1984), 611–22.

Louis, Cameron, "Proverbs, Precepts, and Monitory Pieces," in *A Manual of the Writings in Middle English, 1050–1500*, ed. Albert E. Hartung, 11 vols., Hamden: Connecticut Academy of Arts and Sciences, 1967–, vol. IX, pp. 2957–3048, 3349–404.

Lyall, R. J., "Alexander Barclay and the Edwardian Reformation 1548–52," *Review of English Studies* 20 (1969), 455–61.

"Tradition and Innovation in Alexander Barclay's 'Towre of Vertue and Honoure,'" *Review of English Studies* n.s. 23 (1972), 1—18.

Lydgate, John, *The Pilgrimage of the Life of Man*, ed. F. J. Furnivall and Katherine B. Locock, EETS e.s. 77, 83, 92, London: Kegan Paul, Trench, Trübner & Co., 1899—1904.

Troy Book, ed. Henry Bergen, EETS e.s. 97, 103, 106, 126, London: Kegan Paul, Trench and Trübner, 1906—1935.

The Minor Poems of John Lydgate, Part I: The Religious Poems, ed. H. N. MacCracken, EETS o.s. 107, London: Oxford University Press, 1911.

Siege of Thebes, ed. Axel Erdmann and Eilert Ekwall, EETS e.s. 118, 125, London: Kegan Paul, Trench and Trübner, 1911, 1930.

The Fall of Princes, ed. Henry Bergen, EETS e.s. 121—24, London: Oxford University Press, 1923—27.

The Minor Poems of John Lydgate, Part II: The Secular Poems, ed. H. N. MacCracken, EETS o.s. 192, London: Oxford University Press, 1934.

A Critical Edition of John Lydgate's Life of Our Lady, ed. Joseph A. Lauritis, Ralph A. Klinefelter, and Vernon F. Gallagher, Pittsburgh: Duquesne University, 1961.

Poems, ed. John Norton-Smith, Oxford: Clarendon Press, 1966.

Lydgate, John and Burgh, Benedict, *Lydgate and Burgh's Secrees of Old Philisoffres*, ed. Robert Steele, EETS e.s. 66, London: Kegan Paul, Trench, Trübner & Co., 1894.

MacCracken, H. N., "An English Friend of Charles of Orléans," *PMLA* 26 (1911), 142—80.

MacLennan, George, *Lucid Interval: Subjective Writing and Madness in History*, Leicester: Leicester University Press, 1992.

Mann, Jill, "Satiric Subject and Satiric Object in Goliardic Literature," *Mittellateinisches Jahrbuch* 15 (1980), 63—86.

Mannyng, Robert, *The Chronicle*, ed. Idelle Sullens, Binghamton: Center for Medieval & Early Renaissance Studies, 1996.

Marie de France, *The Fables of Marie de France: An English Translation*, trans. Mary Lou Martin, Birmingham, Ala.: Summa Publications, Inc., 1984.

Fables, trans. Harriet Spiegel, Toronto: University of Toronto Press, 1987.

Meale, Carol M., "Patrons, Buyers and Owners: Book Production and Social Status," in *Book Production*, ed. Griffiths and Pearsall, pp. 201—38.

Meyer-Lee, Robert J., "Hoccleve and the Apprehension of Money," *Exemplaria* 13 (2001), 173—214.

Middleton, Anne, "The Idea of Public Poetry in the Reign of Richard II," *Speculum* 53 (1978), 94—114.

"The Audience and Public of 'Piers Plowman,'" in *Middle English Alliterative Poetry and Its Literary Background: Seven Essays*, ed. David Lawton, Cambridge: D. S. Brewer, 1982, pp. 101—23.

"William Langland's 'Kynde Name': Authorial Signature and Social Identity in Late Fourteenth-Century England," in *Literary Practice and Social Change in Britain, 1380–1530*, ed. Lee Patterson, Berkeley: University of California Press, 1990, pp. 15–82.

Minnis, A. J., *Medieval Theory of Authorship: Scholastic Literary Attitudes in the Later Middle Ages*, 2nd edn, Philadelphia: University of Pennsylvania Press, 1988.

"De Vulgari Auctoriate: Chaucer, Gower and the Men of Great Authority," in *Chaucer and Gower: Difference, Mutuality, Exchange*, ed. Robert F. Yeager, Victoria: University of Victoria, 1991, pp. 36–74.

Minnis, A. J. with Scattergood, V. J. and Smith, J. J., *Oxford Guides to Chaucer: The Shorter Poems*, Oxford: Clarendon Press, 1995.

Minnis, A. J. and Scott, A. B., with Wallace, David (eds.), *Medieval Literary Theory and Criticism c.1100–c.1375: The Commentary Tradition*, Oxford: Clarendon Press, 1988.

Montrose, Louis Adrian, "The Elizabethan Subject and the Spenserian Text," in *Literary Theory/Renaissance Texts*, ed. Patricia Parker and David Quint, Baltimore: Johns Hopkins University Press, 1986, pp. 303–40.

Mooney, Linne R., "Scribes and Booklets of Trinity College, Cambridge Manuscripts R.3.19 and R.3.21," in *Middle English Poetry: Texts and Traditions: Essays in Honour of Derek Pearsall*, ed. A. J. Minnis, Woodbridge: York Medieval Press, 2001, pp. 241–66.

Mortimer, Nigel, *John Lydgate's "Fall of Princes": Narrative Tragedy in its Literary and Political Contexts*, Oxford: Clarendon Press, 2005.

Muir, Kenneth, *Life and Letters of Sir Thomas Wyatt*, Liverpool: Liverpool University Press, 1963.

Mullally, Evelyn and Thompson, John (eds.), *The Court and Cultural Diversity: Selected Papers from the Eighth Triennial Congress of the International Courtly Literature Society*, Cambridge: D. S. Brewer, 1997.

Nelson, William, *John Skelton, Laureate*, New York: Columbia University Press, 1939.

Nicholls, Jonathan, *The Matter of Courtesy: Medieval Courtesy Books and the Gawain-Poet*, Woodbridge: D. S. Brewer, 1985.

Nolan, Maura, "'Now wo, now gladnesses': Ovidianism in the *Fall of Princes*," *ELH* 71 (2004), 531–58.

John Lydgate and the Making of Public Culture, Cambridge: Cambridge University Press, 2005.

"Lydgate's Literary History: Chaucer, Gower, and Canacee," *Studies in the Age of Chaucer* 27 (2005), 59–92.

"Lydgate's Worst Poem: The *Tretise for Lavandres*," paper presented at the International Congress on Medieval Studies, Kalamazoo, 7 May 2005.

Otway-Ruthven, J., *The King's Secretary and the Signet Office in the XV Century*, Cambridge: Cambridge University Press, 1939.

The Owl and the Nightingale: Text and Translation, ed. Neil Cartlidge, Exeter: University of Exeter Press, 2001.

Patterson, Lee, "Making Identities in Fifteenth-Century England: Henry V and John Lydgate," in *New Historical Literary Study: Essays on Reproducing Texts, Representing History*, ed. Jeffrey N. Cox and Larry J. Reynolds, Princeton: Princeton University Press, 1993, pp. 69–107.

"Beinecke MS 493 and the Survival of Hoccleve's *Series*," in *Old Books, New Learning: Essays on Medieval and Renaissance Books at Yale*, ed. Robert G. Babcock and Lee Patterson, New Haven: Beinecke Rare Book and Manuscript Library, 2001, pp. 80–92.

"'What is Me?': Self and Society in the Poetry of Thomas Hoccleve," *Studies in the Age of Chaucer* 23 (2001), 437–70.

Pearsall, Derek, *John Lydgate*, London: Routledge & Kegan Paul, 1970.

"The Gower Tradition," in *Gower's "Confessio Amantis": Responses and Reassessments*, ed. A. J. Minnis, Cambridge: D. S. Brewer, 1983, pp. 179–97.

"Hoccleve's *Regement of Princes*: The Poetics of Royal Self-Representation," *Speculum* 69 (1994), 386–410.

John Lydgate (1371–1449): A Bio-bibliography, Victoria: University of Victoria, 1997.

"The Literary Milieu of Charles of Orléans and the Duke of Suffolk, and the Authorship of the Fairfax Sequence," in *Charles d'Orléans in England (1415–1440)*, ed. Mary-Jo Arn, Cambridge: D. S. Brewer, 2000, pp. 145–56.

(ed.), *Chaucer to Spenser: An Anthology of Writings in English 1375–1575*, Oxford: Blackwell Publishers Ltd., 1999.

Perkins, Nicholas, "Musing on Mutability: A Poem in the Welles Anthology and Hoccleve's *The Regement of Princes*," *Review of English Studies* 50 (1999), 493–98.

Hoccleve's "Regiment of Princes": Counsel and Constraint, Cambridge: D. S. Brewer, 2001.

Petrarch, Francis, *Scritti Inediti di Francesco Petrarca*, ed. Attilio Hortis, Trieste: Tipografia del Lloyd Austro-Ungarico, 1874.

Petrarch's Lyric Poems: The "Rime sparse" and Other Lyrics, ed. and trans. Robert M. Durling, Cambridge, Mass.: Harvard University Press, 1976.

Pollard, Albert Frederick, *The Reign of Henry VII from Contemporary Sources*, 3 vols., London: Longmans, Green and Co., 1914, vol. II.

Pompen, Aurelius, *The English Versions of "The Ship of Fools,"* London: Longmans, Green and Co., 1925.

Puttenham, George, *The Arte of English Poesie*, ed. Gladys Doidge Willcock and Alice Walker, Cambridge: Cambridge University Press, 1936.

Quilligan, Maureen, *The Allegory of Female Authority: Christine de Pizan's "Cité des dames,"* Ithaca: Cornell University Press, 1991.

Rolle, Richard, *English Writings of Richard Rolle Hermit of Hampole*, ed. Hope Emily Allen, Oxford: Clarendon Press, 1931.

Ross, Charles, *Edward IV*, New Haven: Yale University Press, 1997.

Ross, Trevor, *The Making of the English Literary Canon: From the Middle Ages to the Late Eighteenth Century*, Montreal: McGill-Queen's University Press, 1998.

Scanlon, Larry, *Narrative, Authority, and Power: The Medieval Exemplum and the Chaucerian Tradition*, Cambridge: Cambridge University Press, 1994.

"Poets Laureate and the Language of Slaves: Petrarch, Chaucer, and Langston Hughes," in *The Vulgar Tongue: Medieval and Postmedieval Vernacularity*, ed. Nicholas Watson and Fiona Somerset, University Park: Pennsylvania State University Press, 2003, pp. 220–56.

"Lydgate's Poetics: Laureation and Domesticity in the *Temple of Glass*," in *John Lydgate: Poetry, Culture, and Lancastrian England*, ed. James Simpson and Larry Scanlon, Notre Dame: University of Notre Dame Press, 2006.

Scattergood, V. J. (John), *Politics and Poetry in the Fifteenth Century*, London: Blandford Press, 1971.

"Literary Culture at the Court of Richard II," in *English Court Culture in the Later Middle Ages*, ed. V. J. Scattergood and J. W. Sherborne, London: Duckworth, 1983, pp. 29–46.

"The Date and Composition of George Ashby's Poems," *Leeds Studies in English* n.s. 21 (1990), 167–76.

"George Ashby's *Prisoner's Reflections* and the Virtue of Patience," *Nottingham Medieval Studies* 37 (1993), 102–09.

Schirmer, Walter F., *John Lydgate: A Study in the Culture of the XVth Century*, trans. Ann E. Keep, Berkeley: University of California Press, 1961.

Schultz, John Richie, "The Method of Barclay's Eclogues," *Journal of English and Germanic Philology* 32 (1933), 549–71.

Scott, Kathleen L., "Lydgate's Lives of Saints Edmund and Fremund: A Newly-Located Manuscript in Arundel Castle," *Viator* 13 (1982), 335–66.

Later Gothic Manuscripts, 1390–1490, 2 vols., A Survey of Manuscripts Illuminated in the British Isles 6, London: Harvey Miller Publishers, 1996.

Sessions, W. A., "Surrey's Wyatt: Autumn 1542; and the New Poet," in *Rethinking the Henrician Era: Essays on Early Tudor Texts and Contexts*, ed. Peter C. Herman, Urbana: University of Illinois Press, 1994, pp. 168–92.

Simpson, James, "Madness and Texts: Hoccleve's *Series*," in *Chaucer and Fifteenth-Century Poetry*, ed. Boffey and Cowen, pp. 15–29.

"Nobody's Man: Thomas Hoccleve's *Regement of Princes*," in *London and Europe in the Later Middle Ages*, ed. Julia Boffey and Pamela King, London: Centre for Medieval and Renaissance Studies, Queen Mary and Westfield College, University of London, 1995, pp. 149–80.

"The Power of Impropriety: Authorial Naming in *Piers Plowman*," in *William Langland's "Piers Plowman": A Book of Essays*, ed. Kathleen M. Hewett-Smith, New York: Routledge, 2001, pp. 145–65.

Reform and Cultural Revolution, Oxford: Oxford University Press, 2002.

Skelton, John, *John Skelton: The Complete English Poems*, ed. John Scattergood, New Haven: Yale University Press, 1983.

The Latin Writings of John Skelton, ed. David R. Carlson, *Studies in Philology* 88 (1991), pp. 1–125.

Spearing, A. C., *Medieval Dream-Poetry*, Cambridge: Cambridge University Press, 1976.

Medieval to Renaissance in English Poetry, Cambridge: Cambridge University Press, 1985.

Spenser, Edmund, *The Yale Edition of the Shorter Poems of Edmund Spenser*, ed. William A. Oram et al., New Haven: Yale University Press, 1989.

Spitzer, Leo, "Note on the Poetic and the Empirical 'I' in Medieval Authors," *Traditio* 4 (1946), 414–22.

Sponsler, Claire, "Eating Lessons: Lydgate's 'Dietary' and Consumer Conduct," in *Medieval Conduct*, ed. Kathleen Ashley and Robert L. A. Clark, Minneapolis: University of Minnesota Press, 2001, pp. 1–22.

Staley, Lynn, "Gower, Richard II, Henry of Derby, and the Business of Making Culture," *Speculum* 75 (2000), 68–96.

Stillinger, Thomas C., *The Song of Troilus: Lyric Authority in the Medieval Book*, Philadelphia: University of Pennsylvania Press, 1992.

Stone, Gregory B., *The Death of the Troubadour: The Late Medieval Resistance to the Renaissance*, Philadelphia: University of Pennsylvania Press, 1994.

Straker, Scott-Morgan, "Rivalry and Reciprocity in Lydgate's *Troy Book*," *New Medieval Literatures* 3 (1999), 119–47.

"Deference and Difference: Lydgate, Chaucer, and the *Siege of Thebes*," *Review of English Studies* n.s. 52 (2001), 1–21.

Strohm, Paul, "Chaucer's Fifteenth-Century Audience and the Narrowing of the 'Chaucer Tradition,'" *Studies in the Age of Chaucer* 4 (1982), 3–32.

Social Chaucer, Cambridge, Mass.: Harvard University Press, 1989.

Hochon's Arrow: The Social Imagination of Fourteenth-Century Texts, Princeton: Princeton University Press, 1992.

England's Empty Throne: Usurpation and the Language of Legitimation, 1399–1422, New Haven: Yale University Press, 1998.

"Hoccleve, Lydgate and the Lancastrian Court," in *Cambridge History*, ed. Wallace, pp. 640–61.

Politique: Languages of Statecraft between Chaucer and Shakespeare, Notre Dame: University of Notre Dame Press, 2005.

Summers, Joanna, *Late-Medieval Prison Writing and the Politics of Autobiography*, Oxford: Clarendon Press, 2004.

Summit, Jennifer, *Lost Property: The Woman Writer and English Literary History, 1380–1589*, Chicago: University of Chicago Press, 2000.

Taylor, John, *The "Universal Chronicle" of Ranulf Higden*, Oxford: Clarendon Press, 1966.

Thompson, John J., "After Chaucer: Resituating Middle English Poetry in the Late Medieval and Early Modern Period," in *New Directions in Later Medieval Manuscript Studies: Essays from the 1998 Harvard Conference*, ed. Derek Pearsall, York: York Medieval Press, 2000, pp. 183–98.

"Reading Lydgate in Post-Reformation England," in *Middle English Poetry: Texts and Traditions: Essays in Honour of Derek Pearsall*, ed. A. J. Minnis, Woodbridge: York Medieval Press, 2001, pp. 181–209.

Thomson, Patricia, "Wyatt and Surrey," in *English Poetry and Prose, 1540–1674*, ed. Christopher Ricks, London: Barrie and Jenkins, 1970, pp. 19–40.

Thornley, Eva M., "The Middle English Penitential Lyric and Hoccleve's Autobiographical Poetry," *Neuphilologische Mitteilungen* 3 (1967), 295–321.

Tolmie, Sarah, "The *Prive Scilence* of Thomas Hoccleve," *Studies in the Age of Chaucer* 22 (2000), 281–309.

Torti, Anna, *The Glass of Form: Mirroring Structures from Chaucer to Skelton*, Cambridge: D. S. Brewer, 1991.

Trapp, J. B., "The Poet Laureate: Rome, *Renovatio* and *Translatio Imperii*," in *Rome in the Renaissance: The City and the Myth*, ed. P. A. Ramsey, Binghamton: Medieval and Renaissance Texts and Studies, Center for Medieval and Early Renaissance Studies, 1982, pp. 93–130.

Trigg, Stephanie, *Congenial Souls: Reading Chaucer from Medieval to Postmodern*, Minneapolis: University of Minnesota Press, 2002.

Trinity College, Cambridge University, *Manuscript Trinity R.3.19: A Facsimile*, introduction by Bradford Y. Fletcher, Norman: Pilgrim Books, 1987.

Trudgill, Marian and Burrow, J. A., "A Hocclevean Balade," *Notes and Queries* 243 (1998), 178–80.

Turville-Petre, Thorlac, "Poems by Chaucer in John Harpur's Psalter," *Studies in the Age of Chaucer* 21 (1999), 301–13.

Walker, Greg, *John Skelton and the Politics of the 1520s*, Cambridge: Cambridge University Press, 1988.

  "'Ordered Confusion'?: The Crisis of Authority in Skelton's *Speke, Parott*," *Spenser Studies* 10 (1992), 213–28.

  Persuasive Fictions: Faction, Faith and Political Culture in the Reign of Henry VIII, Aldershot: Scolar Press, 1996.

Wallace, David, *Chaucerian Polity: Absolutist Lineages and Associational Forms in England and Italy*, Stanford: Stanford University Press, 1997.

  (ed.), *The Cambridge History of Medieval English Literature*, Cambridge: Cambridge University Press, 1999.

Watkins, John, "'Wrastling for this world': Wyatt and the Tudor Canonization of Chaucer," in *Refiguring Chaucer in the Renaissance*, ed. Theresa M. Krier, Gainesville: University Press of Florida, 1998, pp. 21–39.

Watson, Nicholas, *Richard Rolle and the Invention of Authority*, Cambridge: Cambridge University Press, 1991.

  "Outdoing Chaucer: Lydgate's *Troy Book* and Henryson's *Testament of Cresseid* as Competitive Imitations of *Troilus and Criseyde*," in *Shifts and Transpositions in Medieval Narrative: A Festschrift for Dr. Elspeth Kennedy*, ed. Karen Pratt, Cambridge: D. S. Brewer, 1994, pp. 89–108.

Watt, David, "'I this book shal make': Thomas Hoccleve's Self-Publication and Book Production," *Leeds Studies in English* 34 (2003), 133–60.

Wedgwood, Josiah C. and Holt, Anne D., *History of Parliament: Biographies of the Members of the Commons House 1439–1509*, London: His Majesty's Stationery Office, 1936.

Weiss, Roberto, *Humanism in England during the Fifteenth Century*, 2nd edn, Oxford: Blackwell, 1957.

The Welles Anthology: MS. Rawlinson C. 813: A Critical Edition, ed. Sharon L. Jansen and Kathleen H. Jordan, Binghamton: Medieval and Renaissance Texts and Studies, 1991.

Wenzel, Siegfried, *Preachers, Poets, and the Early English Lyric*, Princeton: Princeton University Press, 1986.

Wheatley, Edward, *Mastering Aesop: Medieval Education, Chaucer, and His Followers*, Gainesville: University Press of Florida, 2000.

Widsith, ed. Kemp Malone, 2nd edn, Copenhagen: Rosenkilde and Bagger, 1962.

Wilkins, Ernest Hatch, *Studies in the Life and Works of Petrarch*, Cambridge, Mass.: The Mediaeval Academy of America, 1955.

Willard, Charity Cannon, *Christine de Pizan: Her Life and Works*, New York: Persea Books, 1984.

William de la Pole, duke of Suffolk, *The "Suffolk" Poems*, ed. Johannes Petrus Maria Jansen, Groningen: Universiteitsdrukkerij, 1989.

Winstead, Karen A., "'I am al othir to yow than yee weene': Hoccleve, Women, and the *Series*," *Philological Quarterly* 72 (1993), 143–55.

Withington, Robert, "Queen Margaret's Entry into London, 1445," *Modern Philology* 13 (1915), 53–57.

Wood, Anthony à and Bliss, Philip, *Athenæ Oxonienses*, New York: Burt Franklin, 1967.

Woolf, Rosemary, *The English Religious Lyric in the Middle Ages*, Oxford: Clarendon Press, 1968.

Wordsworth, William, *Wordsworth: Poetical Works*, ed. Thomas Hutchinson and Ernest de Selincourt, Oxford: Oxford University Press, 1936.

Wright, Sylvia, "The Author Portraits in the Bedford Psalter-Hours: Gower, Chaucer, and Hoccleve," *British Library Journal* 18 (1992), 190–201.

"The *Gesta Henrici Quinti* and the Bedford Psalter-Hours," in *The Court and Cultural Diversity*, ed. Mullally and Thompson, pp. 267–85.

Wyatt, Sir Thomas, *Collected Poems of Sir Thomas Wyatt*, ed. Kenneth Muir and Patricia Thomson, Liverpool: Liverpool University Press, 1969.

Yeager, Robert F., "Death is a Lady: *The Regement of Princes* as Gendered Political Commentary," *Studies in the Age of Chaucer* 26 (2004), 147–93.

Yeats, W. B., *Essays*, New York: Macmillan, 1924.

Zagorin, Perez, "Sir Thomas Wyatt and the Court of Henry VIII: The Courtier's Ambivalence," *Journal of Medieval and Renaissance Studies* 23 (1993), 113–41.

Index

Cambridge Studies in Medieval Literature